THE NEW LIFE INSURANCE INVESTMENT ADVISOR

SECOND EDITION

BEN G. BALDWIN

McGraw-Hill

New York   Chicago   San Francisco   Lisbon   London
Madrid   Mexico City   Milan   New Delhi
San Juan   Seoul   Singapore
Sydney   Toronto

Library of Congress Cataloging-in-Publication Data

Baldwin, Ben G.
    The new life insurance investment advisor/by Ben G. Baldwin.—2nd ed.
      p. cm.
    ISBN 0-07-136364-5
    1. Insurance, Life—United States. 2. Annuities—United States. 3. Variable
annuities—United States. 4. Investments—United States. I. Title.

HG8951 .B35 2001
368.32'00973—dc21

00-051526

McGraw-Hill

*A Division of The **McGraw·Hill** Companies*

    4 5 6 7 8 9 0 AGM/AGM 0 9 8 7 6 5 4 3

ISBN 0-07-136364-5

This book was set in Palatino by Binghamton Valley Composition.

Printed and bound by Quebecor/Martinsburg.

This publication is designed to provide accurate and authoritative information in regard to the subject matter covered. It is sold with the understanding that the publisher is not engaged in rendering legal, accounting, or other professional service. If legal advice or other expert assistance is required, the services of a competent professional person should be sought.
> *—From a declaration of principles jointly adopted by a committee of the American Bar Association and a committee of publishers.*

 This book is printed on recycled, acid-free paper containing a minimum of 50% recycled, de-inked fiber.

McGraw-Hill books are available at special quantity discounts to use as premiums and sales promotions, or for use in corporate training programs. For more information, please write to the Director of Special Sales, Professional Publishing, McGraw-Hill, Two Penn Plaza, New York, NY 10121-2298. Or contact your local bookstore.

To my family: My wife, Maureen Margaret McGuigan Baldwin, the glue that holds us all together. Her folks, Leonard Michael (Pete) McGuigan, MD, and Isabelle McGuigan. My dad and mom, Benjamin George Baldwin, Sr., and Dorothy Bell Orr Baldwin. Our oldest son, Benjamin George Baldwin III, and his wife, Rosemary Martin Baldwin, and their daughters, Hannah Rachel Baldwin and Madeleine Claire Baldwin. Our second son, Peter Michael Baldwin, his wife, Susan Gough Baldwin, and their daughters, Margaret McGuigan Baldwin and Eleanor Stahley Baldwin. Our oldest daughter, Kathleen Marie Baldwin Leipprandt, her husband, Douglas John Leipprandt, and their children, Douglas Scott Leipprandt and Lauren Baldwin Leipprandt. Our third son, Michael Patrick Baldwin, his wife, Mary Karen Barg Baldwin, and their children, Mary Emma Baldwin and Owen Michael Baldwin. And to yet unborn grandchildren— with love. To our very special friends, Loren and Marta Dunton.

CONTENTS

This book is about insurance company products: life insurance and annuities. Not just how to understand and manage them, but more importantly, how to understand and effectively manage the investment aspects involved.

No one likes to talk or think about life insurance, but most of us have it. We say we don't understand it, but we buy it anyway. Some say they don't believe in it, and that is fine. It is not a religion—it's a financial tool. We are about to treat life insurance as a most versatile financial tool and as an investment vehicle, contrary to the conventional wisdom that for years had cautioned against mixing life insurance with investments.

That's what Ellen's father told her: "Don't mix your investments with your life insurance!" He was right in his day . . . but he is not right today.

Have you looked lately at how much money you have tied up in life insurance policies? How about your parents' old policies? Look at those that your company owns on your life or on the lives of other key people in your firm. You may be among those who believe that the return on that capital isn't worthy of much attention, won't impact the bottom line, or that tax or death benefits will make up for low returns.

The truth is that these investment returns matter a great deal. A very substantial amount of individual and company assets are retained in the form of cash surrender values. Moreover, a large proportion of those assets may not be performing as well as they could be.

In the past, some people made a practice of financing their life insurance payments through a "minimum deposit" strategy. They borrowed against the asset values within their policies as they grew to pay premiums. The fact that the loan interest was a deductible item from income tax made this worthwhile. But those were the good old days, and the world has changed. Insurance companies have moved away from fixed-cost loan interest. The Internal Revenue Code of 1986 has deemed policy-loan interest as consumer interest and is therefore nondeductible. In most cases, loans on contracts under previous law aren't even "grandfathered" or exempted. Most importantly, insurance companies now are offering investment alternatives worthy of consideration because they provide profitable tax-sheltered returns within the policy.

We at Baldwin Financial Systems have heard all kinds of advisors, financial planners, accountants, attorneys, trust officers, and other money managers say that they don't want to manage life insurance policy assets, that they don't understand life insurance, and that they don't believe in it as an investment tool. To them and to you we say, *read this book!* We will give you the tools you need to manage life insurance products both profitably and efficiently so that they provide the financial security you and your family need, or the families of your clients. There is a great new world of life insurance out there that can be very profitable to you and yours. Do not let the old clichés keep you from understanding and using this financial tool. The late Loren Dunton, the father of the financial planning movement in this country, said to me in 1986 that the life insurance industry had improved its products for the consumer more than any other industry. Those of you who knew Loren know that the next thing he said was, "Of course they had more room for improvement than any other industry." The products have continued to improve since that time. It is time for you to evaluate if they can serve you and yours profitably, and this is a great place to start.

ACKNOWLEDGMENTS

A debt of gratitude is owed to many who have been and continue to be instrumental in the ongoing success of this book. The original *Life Insurance Investment Advisor* (1988) never would have been written without the encouragement of coauthor William G. Droms, Ph.D., CFA, Professor of Finance at the Georgetown University School of Business and a past director of Baldwin Financial Systems, Inc. He had the courage to shepherd me through the authoring process, and I am forever in his debt.

I also want to thank all of my associates in the life insurance industry, especially Marvin R. Rotter, President of the Central Region of AXA Advisors, who has encouraged me and used the books to help new advisors become more comfortable with the new life insurance products.

And then there are the consumer advocates who take it upon themselves to help the public cope with today's financial world. Financial analyst and author Terry Savage and the late Loren Dunton, founder and president of the National Center for Financial Education, have been particularly encouraging and helpful in their efforts to let the public know that judicious use of today's improved insurance products can be beneficial to their economic health.

The folks at McGraw-Hill, Stephen Isaacs and Pattie Amoroso, have not only been helpful, but patient with me and my late manuscripts, beyond what I have any right to expect. In this edition of this book the McGraw-Hill editors have worked above and beyond the call of duty to improve the way the book reads and the way the exhibits communicate.

There is also a very special group of people out there who work very hard and travel a great deal to educate as many financial advisors as they can as to how important it is for them to understand the new insurance products so that they can help you use these financial tools properly and profitably. Representative of that group are Jim Johnson, Paul Widzowski, Kevin M. Hogan, David Smith, Madalin Keeble, Larry Langemo, Tom Holt, Kevin

McLain, Matt Coben, Patty Abram, Steve Lundquist, Curly Morrison, Mark Madden, and Clark Lee.

Then too there are the clients of three generations of Baldwins. You have taught us in your offices, living rooms, and at your kitchen tables what you need to know to use life insurance profitably. We thank you and have made you an integral part of this book as the audience motivating our every endeavor. We want you to know all there is to know about the products you own so they can work profitably for you.

Finally there is my wife, Maureen. She is more than an editor; in truth, she could be considered my ghostwriter. At times she got angry and tired but never let one detail escape her careful scrutiny. Without the many hours she willingly gave, this book would never have taken form. Thank you, Moses.

BEN G. BALDWIN, JR.

The Insurance Industry Today

"Life" As We Know It

In the original 1988 edition of *The Life Insurance Investment Advisor*, Chapter 1 began, stating "The financial services businesses have been revolutionized . . ." Little did I know then that it was just the tip of the iceberg, that "You ain't seen nothing yet" better described the situation.

Since then, the insurance industry has been in turmoil. Insurance commissioners of various states had to take over 47 failing companies in 1989, 41 in 1990, 69 in 1991 (the year such industry giants as Executive Life, Mutual Benefit Life, First Capital, and Monarch Life failed), 32 in 1992, 22 in 1993, 12 in 1994, 8 in 1995, 7 in 1996, and 11 in 1997. It is not over. On August 10, 1999, St. Louis-based General American Life Insurance Company asked for and received regulatory protection from a virtual run on the bank by its institutional investors as a result of the fact that its ratings had been downgraded by the rating services. At the time, the company had $1.3 billion in capital to meet its obligations but was out of cash to meet liquidation demands. By the end of August, Met Life had committed to buy General American for $1.2 billion and assure the healthy continuation of the company. Today you cannot be sure that the insurance company that you buy from will be the insurance company that you die with.

Insurance commissioners take over when they question an insurance company's ability to fulfill its obligations to its policy

1

owners. Their first action usually is to stop or reduce payments to all creditors, including policy owners with general account products. Anyone who has suffered the consequences of this action realizes that investments within insurance contracts *are* important and deserve attention. In many cases, these people regretfully learned that chasing the highest interest rate led them to the weakest insurance company. Salespeople also finally realized that those companies offering the highest commissions and interest rates were often the most vulnerable. None of us—consumers, insurance agents, insurance companies, or insurance regulators—will ever be the same, and yet many still fall prey to making the same mistakes today.

This does not mean that the 1988 version of *The Life Insurance Investment Advisor* is in error or no longer of value. In fact, it is valuable for its historic perspective and as a balanced, even academic, study of the industry and its products at that time. It contained statements like "We hope Executive Life can pay." It couldn't! In retrospect, it turned out to be one of the most traumatic of the insurance company failures.

This book, *The New Life Insurance Investment Advisor*, the first edition of which was published in 1994, does not treat life insurance academically. It is a consumer's handbook. The objective is to show the consumer what life insurance policies are available, how to choose among them, and, most importantly, how to manage the policies once they own them. It is a book "with an attitude" that does not treat kindly those products that this author considers unacceptable for the new generation of life insurance buyers.

THE INSURANCE INDUSTRY YESTERDAY AND TODAY

To understand life insurance, it is important to appreciate the economic and sociological forces impacting the industry, causing changes in its structure and products. The objective is to select appropriate products to provide long-term satisfaction. Risk and return are very much a part of the picture, and one must understand the risks to realize the potential returns.

In John Watt's prophetic 1987 book addressed to the insurance industry, *The Financial Services Shockwave*, he discusses "Six diverse, largely unrelated forces (shockwaves) at work to alter your lifestyle forever."

- The economy
- Deregulation
- Legislation
- Demographics
- Technology
- Consumer knowledge, attitudes, and habits

We will examine some of these briefly.

The Economy

The general account life insurance products of whole life and universal life are interest rate–driven products. The managers of the general account try to manage that account to obtain the best return possible using interest-bearing investments. The life insurance industry existed for almost 150 years within a very stable economy. For example, the prime rate from 1930 to 1969 ranged between 1.5 and 8.5 percent, averaging 3.62 percent in a relatively predictable economic environment. The life insurance industry had an easy time investing the assets in those general accounts for this extended period of time.

In the period from 1970 to 1979, the average prime rate was 9.63 percent, with a range of 5 to 15.5 percent. In a 60-day period in May and June 1980, the prime rate went from a low of 12 to a high of 19, a movement of 7 percent. Between 1980 and 1982, the rate not only averaged 17.6 percent, but also experienced unprecedented volatility, ranging from 11 percent to an all-time high of 21.5 in December 1980. Then came the tumble throughout the 1990s, with long-term interest rates approaching 5.5 percent in the fall of 2000.

Exhibit 1.1 presents a graph illustrating that interest rate trends have been of long duration. Long-term bond rates were in a downtrend for 135 years, from 1799 to 1935. Those rates then moved sideways over 20 years and were in the 2 to 3 percent ranges from 1935 through 1956. Interest rates then started an

EXHIBIT 1.1

Where Are Interest Rates Going?

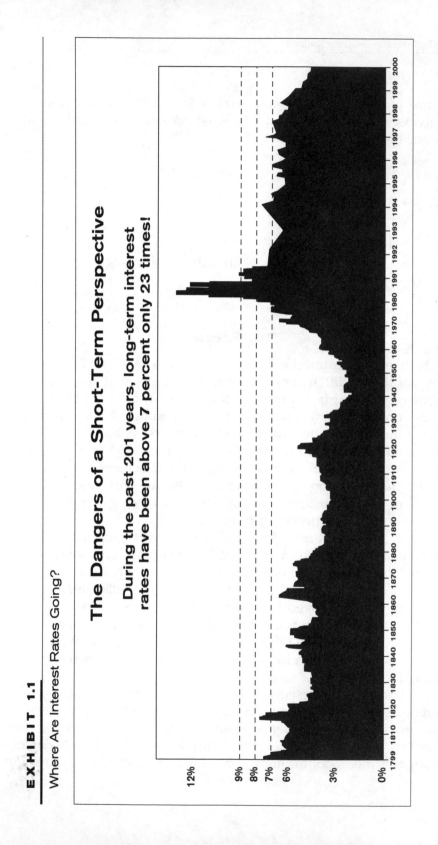

The Dangers of a Short-Term Perspective

During the past 201 years, long-term interest rates have been above 7 percent only 23 times!

uptrend that ended 35 years later with the yield on the 30-year Treasury bond at about 15 percent. Since 1981, the cyclical trend of interest rates has been down.

We have no idea whether interest rates will go up, will tend to go back to their 200-year average of 5.5 percent, or will go below that average for an extended period of time. The point is that extended periods of low interest rates have happened, and some economists and analysts are predicting that they will happen again. If this long term, low-interest-rate environment should occur, the rate of return passed through to policy owners holding general account products also will be low.

While interest rates were volatile and hitting unprecedented highs in the 1980s, the stock market was also making dramatic changes. The Dow Jones Industrial Average (DJIA) first rose to 200 in 1928. It then rose to 400 just prior to the crash of 1929 and did not get back to 200 until 1950. It finally hit 400 again in 1954. For 26 years the DJIA volatility was 200 points. The 1000-point level was not breached until November 1972. It took 77 years to get to the first 1000 points on the Dow. But in May 1999, it took only 24 trading days to go from 10,000 to 11,000.

We all have seen that these dramatic economic changes have had an equally dramatic impact on the way the consumer saves and invests. Saving for retirement is not the same for a person born in 1950 as it was for a person born in 1900. Today's retirees cannot manage retirement the same way that their parents did. As the consumer has changed, insurance companies have had to change their products and their approach to the consumer.

Deregulation

You used to buy life insurance from a salesperson who specialized in life insurance. Now the properly licensed individual may be a ".com" on Internet, a banker, a CPA, a lawyer, a stockbroker, a CFP, or any other financial advisor. Consumers today are demanding that they be able to buy their life insurance from an advisor they trust. And they expect that advisor to have, or to obtain, the life insurance expertise their situation demands. The elimination of the regulatory barriers has vastly increased competition for the consumer's life insurance business. Today's well-educated and very demanding consumer is drawing more consumer-orientated products into the marketplace. Of course, deregulation leads to reregulation and legislation.

Legislation

Because the industry was built in a climate of legislation, regulation, and business plans designed for a stable economy with a 3.62 percent average prime rate, its performance was less than satisfactory in the volatile 1970s and 1980s. In fact, in the early 1980s, the Federal Trade Commission's report on life insurance cost disclosure stated that effective price competition did not exist in the life insurance business and that rates of return were not what they could be. The government was complaining about *low* rates of return! In a turnabout, after the blizzard of failures in the 1990s, the government forced through legislation that requires the general accounts of insurance companies to be invested in safe portfolios that *will* have low rates of return.

The government-mandated portfolios of long-term bonds and mortgages, which insurance companies accumulated during the long period of relatively low interest rates, did look bad in the period from 1979 through 1983. The rates of return looked especially low when compared with the money-market rates that were available in the early 1980s, for example, 12.78 percent in 1980, 16.82 percent in 1981, and 12.23 percent in 1982. But, then, all long-term, interest-sensitive investment vehicles, such as whole life insurance policies, look bad in an economy in which the interest rate is increasing.

The Tax Reform Act of 1984 created a niche market for single-premium life that would pay the high current interest rates of the day. Then legislation in 1988 limited the amount of money that could be put into this type of policy to earn the high interest rates and consequently snuffed out the product. The insurance industry in those days went for higher interest rates as consumers cried, "Higher than the rest . . . why take less?" Aggressive companies like Executive Life pushed the junk bond mania beyond the limits and failed. Consumers learned from these failures, and the pendulum swung back. The next cry, heard in the 1990s, was "Rated best . . . I won't take less."

Insurance company rating services sprang into prominence. Standard & Poor's (standardandpoors.com), Moody's (moodys.com), Duff and Phelps (which joined with Fitch Financial) (dcrco.com), Weiss (weissratings.com), and A. M. Best (ambest.com) all blessed or damned insurance companies with their ABCs and created the public demand for "AAA." Meanwhile the supply of AAA-rated companies decreased to a handful.

Of course, we all criticized the government and state insurance commissioners for not correcting the problems sooner and preventing insurance company failures. Now the insurance commissioners of the various states are responding through their central organization, the National Association of Insurance Commissioners (naic.org). They tell the insurance companies how much surplus (assets in *excess* of liabilities) the companies need to be considered financially sound. They call this measure the *risk-based capital ratio.*

Thus if an insurance company has assets the commissioners define as risky, the company needs to have more surplus than if it has assets the commissioners deem to be safe, such as short-term government bonds. So what do you think the insurance companies are doing? They are managing their general account investments to get high grades from the commissioners because they know that you, the public, want *that* now. You and the regulators are getting what you have asked for, squeaky clean general accounts that are earning what you would expect from a low-risk, low-return type of investment. The returns in the general account type of product are often so low that they are close to the minimum contract guarantee. It is entirely possible that the day will come when your company skips its dividend in your whole life policy, or says it will pay only the minimum interest guaranteed in your universal life contract.

Technology

The fifth wave impacting the insurance industry is technology. Without modern technology, we could not manage, manufacture, monitor, and service the products offered today. The technological requirements of today's products have had a unique impact of their own. While tremendous capital investment is required to implement change, the expenditures for hardware, software, and education don't guarantee success. Proper identification of the problem, together with the right technology, software, and people, often appears to be a matter of luck. The unlucky find that they have spent substantial sums of money developing systems to handle yesterday's problems. The large, well-capitalized company has an advantage over the smaller one in coping in a world in which a system tends to be obsolete by the time it is operational. Substantial capital is required to stay current.

These tremendous costs are being incurred in a cost-conscious world that demands instant communication and total disclosure. This results in pressure on companies to reduce expenses and to increase their competitive positions and efficiency. Companies and salespeople are now required to master the technology necessary to manage the information that supports all their products and to provide you with "usable-on-demand" information. The Internet is here. The capability to provide you with information on your life insurance policy and the capability to make changes to your policy over the Internet exists. Some companies already provide this service, and your demands will drive the rest to do the same.

Consumer Knowledge, Attitudes, and Habits

The very existence of financial planning is an example of consumerism in action. The consumer demands an understanding of how and where his or her money is to be invested. The regulators demand that the consumer receive complete disclosure. Heretofore, placing money in a whole life insurance policy was like putting it in a black box. The money went in, mysteriously did whatever it did, and neither the policy owner nor the salesperson had usable information regarding return and expenses. Black-box money management is unsatisfactory to today's consumer.

It is important to have a picture of what has been going on behind the scenes in the last few years to understand why many insurance companies are stumbling as they try to cope with change. They are being asked to both increase returns and reduce expenses. They are being asked to become more flexible to provide more consumer information and new products, and to do this all in an environment of economic and regulatory instability. Furthermore, the companies are managed by people who perceive the need to change at different times and in different ways from one another. We have seen major companies start to adapt and then suddenly pull back as political forces within the company change and as new people with new views take over the decision-making positions. The good news today is that market forces have taken over. More and more companies are stressing the fact to their agents, brokers, salespeople, or advisors that the first loyalty must be to you, the consumer. All sales must be "suitable," and the salesperson must be able to prove that suitability to company-trained compliance officers. Indeed many salespeople have signed documents acknowledging that they have a "fiduciary" relationship with you, the client. This means that the salespeople must put your interests ahead of their own, must disclose to you all their business relationships, must disclose any conflicts of interest they might have, and must respect the confidentiality of your records and financial information. Clients who have reason to doubt that they have been treated in accordance with these very strict standards have a great deal of assistance and support in pressing their complaints. It is wise for today's consumer to seek out intermediaries who recognize this fiduciary relationship with their clients.

YOUR ALLY IN THE INSURANCE BUYING AND SERVICING PROCESS

People selling insurance products also face their own unique set of problems. Looking to their companies for leadership can be a disappointing and frustrating experience as the companies vacillate in their commitment to adapt to a consumer-oriented economy and culture. Time and time again companies that agreed to throw money into client financial-planning services neglected to also throw in the necessary talent. Instead, the money went to attractive offices and greater overhead, failing to provide a profit center because of the lack of ability and support of those occupying the offices. The typical company then terminated another "pilot" and a vice president someplace said, "See, I told you financial-planning services would be unprofitable." A step backward was taken from the idea of providing the customer base with usable, understandable information on which to base financial decisions. And the company went back to machine-gunning the public with "new and improved" products.*

You have been inundated with information. The Internet is your best friend and your worst enemy. Most of us as consumers are road kill on the information highway because the information is so voluminous, disjointed, and contradictory. We all need a traffic cop to direct us to the usable and credible information and to help us adapt that information to our personal situation. The life insurance industry has discovered that what you, the consumer, want and need is a trusted financial advisor to work with toward your financial security. Yes, you're right. The buzzwords of the day are *financial planner* and *financial advisor*, but do not let that turn you into a skeptic. In my 36 years as a participant, educator, and observer in this business, more than 90 percent of the people that you perceive as trying to sell you something are trying to do the best job they can *for you*. After all, your financial success is their financial success. What is wonderful is that in the year 2000, the major companies are helping and encouraging these people to become better qualified to help you. The companies are training them in financial planning, and they are not only telling them, but mandating, that their first loyalty and obligation is to you, the client. That does not mean that you can become complacent. You still must interview your intermediary extensively. But it does mean that the corporate mantra has changed. It used to be "Get out and sell something!" It is now "Was what you sold *suitable* for this particular client's personal situation?" This is a sea change for the companies. Most of you have been working with caring, professional salespeople for years. The people with whom you have worked were compensated by commissions but understood that your best interests were in their best interest. The sea change in attitude is not with the people with whom you deal. It is with their employers. In the past, the employers turned a blind eye to the shyster, the rogue salesperson who took advantage of people. Indeed, very often these unscrupulous salespeople were showered with accolades as long as they sold huge quantities of life insur-

---

* *The New Life Insurance Investment Advisor*, 1994 edition.

ance. Employers today know that this is no longer an acceptable practice. They know that the class-action suits brought against companies as a result of unethical sales practices are far too expensive to fight. Today every effort is made to support only ethical sales practices. Salespeople must prove to the compliance officers of their company that they have done their best for you. Rogue salespeople are eliminated as soon as the company identifies them. Does this mean that you, the consumer, can be less vigilant? No, you still need to continue to deal with your trusted professionals, to keep those long-term relationships, and to work by referrals when new advisors are needed. It does mean that if you are ever mistreated, you have far greater support and assistance in addressing your complaint. It is a better world for you than it was in the past.

Professional salespeople also have changed. They have found that insurance companies they considered bastions of stability were not immune to financial problems. They have had to deal with client panic as the press launched a media blitz on any company that was downgraded by the rating services. Those were difficult times for you and for the agents. And yet it was just those difficult times that caused a profound change in thought about how to deal with life insurance company products. As you read this book, you will find that my opinions are far more polarized today than they were in the past. More than ever before, I believe quality in an insurance product is related to policy owner *control*. The greater your control over your insurance product, the happier you will be.

It is important to identify those companies and salespeople who will survive and prosper within the environment just described. Will it be the bigger companies because of their capital base and diversity? If one product is legislated out of existence, larger firms normally switch emphasis to another line or to the latest product legislated into existence. The smaller companies, many of which come into being because they recognize a niche market opened by legislative change, are exposed to a higher degree of risk. Either the successful niche company will leverage its success into a more diverse product line, allowing it to grow, prosper, and handle the change, or it will face acquisition at best, and bankruptcy at worst. The consumer must face the fact that dealing with a niche company carries with it the potential for company failure.

Many of the new life insurance products are securities, and this has changed the life insurance selection process. We now are looking for the company that, in its capacity as a provider of security products, has the best due diligence (thorough product examination and screening) and the best investment and product management people within its organization. Once found, the consumer then can seek out a professional, registered company representative.

Professional salespeople constantly make demands on insurance companies. They demand quality products, superior due diligence, and sponsors that will stand behind the products and services they offer. Salespeople seek companies that will come to their defense when, as a result of a product failure, they become subject to lawsuits. In turn, the companies require that salespeople not sell products of competing companies and not be "dually licensed," so to speak. Companies demand loyalty. As a result, the consumer may find fewer salespeople willing to search the marketplace and act as brokers for more than one company's products. This frequently limits the consumer to the offerings of the chosen company.

How do you deal with this world? The proactive consumer first will select a quality company by asking, "Will the company be there keeping its promises year in and year out for the rest of my life?" "Does the company have the products I need, and will it service them in the way I want them serviced?"

The next choice involves the intermediary—the agent, broker, or financial planner. Never before have you needed an up-to-date, well-educated professional intermediary more than you do today to deal with the life insurance products of today. If that person has not read this book, you will probably know more about the new variable products than he or she does after you complete the book.

CHAPTER 2

Understanding Life Insurance

What "Life" Has to Offer

Ellen's father said, "Don't invest in life insurance. I did and it didn't work for me and it won't work for you." So she didn't.

Ellen's father was wrong. He made a judgment based on obsolete information.

Have you ever heard anyone say, "I just can't understand life insurance?" What is disturbing is that this attitude is prevalent not only among the public but also among many professionals in the financial services industry. They say it as a matter of fact, as if the situation couldn't be changed. Their eyes say, "... and you can't make me understand it." We have to eliminate this attitude in our advisors and ourselves if we are to be intelligent consumers of life insurance company products.

Doing so might be easier if we understand the origin of insurance. Term insurance is not the problem. We all can understand that if we pay a premium and die, our beneficiary receives a death benefit. The problem occurs when we put more money into a policy than what is needed to cover the cost of the death benefit. For the first 150 years that insurance was in existence, the whole life policy was the only type of policy that could accept more than the amount required for term insurance. The insurance company would tell a prospective client how much was required each year for a specified death benefit. What happened to that money? What were the costs? What was the investment or the return on that investment? None of that was disclosed—it remained a mystery. In fact, the favorite response to the question regarding the money in a whole life policy was that the money *was not an investment.* "Life insurance is not an investment" are words that flow easily off the tongue, and certainly the statement is true when you consider term life insurance. Term insurance is *not* an investment. It is a commodity that you pay for like auto insurance; it provides protection for a specified period of time. However, can we say the same thing about the money in a whole life policy? The policy owner's capital is voluntarily left in the policy "in order to gain profit or interest," which is the definition of the word *invest* according to the *American Heritage Dictionary, Second College Edition.* To sum up the problem, the financial world and the consumer are having difficulty trying to figure out the investment and the investment return on the cash value in a whole life insurance policy. At the same time, the insurance industry denies whole life is an investment while many salespeople are trying to prove that buying cash-value life insurance is better than buying term life insurance and investing the difference. It's no wonder many people throw up their hands in despair and cry, "I can't understand life insurance . . . and don't intend to try!"

The new market-driven life insurance products, consumerism, technology, the economy, and regulatory authorities have destroyed the "not-an-investment" myth forever by mandating transparency in products. As a result of the development of universal life and the SEC rules that regulate variable and variable universal life, products can be divided into their component parts. One part is the amount of the insurance company's money that is *at risk* in a life insurance policy. That part we will call *life insurance,* or *term life insurance.* The second part is policy owner money, called variously *cash value, surrender value,* or *account value.* What this means to you, the consumer, is that now, in the newer products, you will be able to identify and quantify the expenses, the cost of the life insurance (amount at risk or term life insurance), and the investment capital and the return on that capital in a life insurance policy. It allows you and your advisor(s) to determine the acceptability of each of the parts of the product to determine if it will serve your purposes. This makes understanding life insurance much easier.

And now a word about your advisor. Yes, your chosen life insurance intermediary who helps you buy and manage your life insurance products over a lifetime may have a conflict of interest. A fee-based intermediary needs to keep you paying, and a commission-based intermediary wants to keep you buying and owning your life insurance product. Choose an advisor who has a good reputation, who has experience, and who expects and appreciates a *long-term* relationship with you. Well-informed advisors with integrity are motivated to give you advice that stands the test of time and products that serve your needs efficiently. They know that this is how they will keep your business no matter how they are compensated.

As you try and learn how to deal with today's complex world of finance, remember that financial reporters have conflicts of interest in their dealings with the consumer also. The reporters must cater to the needs of editors, who in turn need to generate sales of their publications. Many a publication has been responsible for causing confusion and fear in the public and has made people feel stupid if they bought other than *no-load* products on their own, using only the help of one publication or another. In too many cases, the result has been inaction on the part of the public. People tend to do nothing because they don't know what to do. Money these people should invest may languish in money-market funds and certificates of deposit, earning returns that will not accomplish their objectives. Worse yet, that money may hop around among the latest hot tips in the press and generate a great deal in the way of expenses and taxes, but little in the way of return. This is the real cost of the conflict of interest in the media—this and attracting people to investments that are inordinately high in price and panicking them out when those investments are inordinately low in price. Buying high and selling low causes some people to never invest again. The real cost of the "by self" method of investing and financial planning can be far more than will ever be incurred by paying an empathetic, caring, competent intermediary who is trying to earn your business for life.

People often underestimate the importance of understanding life insurance products. Just the word "premium" can be confusing when dealing with investment types of life insurance. To most people, "premium" as related to insurance means "cost." However, as you will learn, the premium you pay and the cost of the life insurance can be very different in investment types of life insurance. The amount of the premium and the amount of that premium that gets to their investment account may look small relative to the death benefit in the early years and thus not important. However, over the years your capital builds up in the contract, and one day you will consider it "important money." You will be very disappointed and chagrined if you did not take the time to invest it wisely. The bottom line is that too much money is tied up in the life insurance products of today to ignore their investment performance.

DEFINING LIFE INSURANCE

Section 7702 of the Deficit Reduction Act of 1984 (DEFRA) defines life insurance for income tax purposes in terms of requiring an "amount at risk." In other words, if the insured dies, the law stipulates that to enjoy all the income tax benefits of a life insurance policy, a significant amount of *insurance company* money must be paid out to the beneficiary. If the policy fails this test—of adequate *amount at risk*—then it is not considered a life insurance policy and all income tax benefits are eliminated. As you review the following tests that are required by the tax laws to determine whether a contract qualifies as life insurance or not, keep in mind why Uncle Sam is so concerned. Uncle Sam knows and appreciates the income tax benefits of life insurance and creates these rules to limit how much money you can put into a policy.

The inside buildup, meaning the compounding that goes on inside the policy on your capital, occurs without taxation, giving you tax-free compounding. Life insurance proceeds are paid at death without being subject to income tax, meaning your lifetime of compounding and the *amount at risk* escape income taxation entirely at death. In variable policies, you can choose among the investment alternatives offered within your policy and then change your mind and choose to use others without incurring income taxation or additional expenses. You can use investment strategies such as dollar cost averaging, asset allocation, and rebalancing, all without income taxation or additional expenses. You also can access the money in your policy by policy loan, and sometimes withdrawal, if you treat the policy properly, again without income taxes. It is not surprising that the federal government wants to limit how much you can put into such a contract.

The definition in the law is expressed in terms of *net amount at risk*: "only the excess of the amount paid by reason of the insured's death over the contract's net surrender value should be deemed to be . . . life insurance. . . ."

Section 7702 of the Internal Revenue Code lays out the requirements that *"net amount at risk"* exist and be in sufficient amount for the contract containing such net amount at risk for it to be considered "life insurance." Section 7702 also lays out two alternative tests that a policy must pass for it to be considered "life insurance." They are the cash-value accumulation test and the guideline premium/corridor test.

The basic tests of sufficiency of net amount at risk are:

1. *Cash-value accumulation test (CVAT)*. The net cash surrender value (the policy owner's current equity in the contract) cannot exceed the discounted value of the net single premium that could compound to the face amount of the policy at age 95. The discount factor is 4 percent, or the minimum rate guaranteed in the contract.

2. *Guideline premium test (GPT)*. The guideline premium is based upon the guideline single premium or the sum of the guideline level premiums to date.

   The *guideline-single-premium* portion of the test limits the amount a policy owner may invest in a policy. You cannot pay more into a life insurance policy than the net present value of the future benefits to be paid at age 95 (the full face amount of the policy), discounted at 6 percent, assuming the contract's stated mortality and expenses.

   The *guideline level premium* refers to the level annual amount that will fund the future benefits (the face amount at age 95) payable to age 95, assuming the contract's stated mortality and expense charges and 4 percent interest.

   The *cash-value corridor requirement* refers to the percentage relationship of the policy's death benefit to the policy owner's equity. These percentage limitations are contained in Section 7702(d)(2) of the code and are shown in Exhibit 2.1.

In some cases you may be given the opportunity to choose the test to use for your policy, the GPT or the CVAT. Note that the cash-value accumulation test governs the cash value, not the premium or what you pay into the policy, which means that this test would be preferable if you wanted to maximum-fund your flexible-premium policy. The following situations, which will make more sense to you as you get deeper into this book, would call for the use of the CVAT rather than the GPT:

1. When you want to pay the full 7-pay modified endowment premium into the policy over the first 7 years
2. When you want the lowest amount of death benefit for a given premium
3. If you plan to reduce the death benefit during the life of the policy to avoid paying taxes, which could happen with a GPT policy but is not required with a CVAT policy

Section 7702 of the Internal Revenue Code is a historic and important document because it represents the first time life insurance has been defined for income tax purposes. In dealing with today's life insurance and these regulations, it becomes pragmatic to define *life insurance* as "insurance company money to be received by a beneficiary upon the death of the insured," which is referred to in the code as "amount at risk." The distinction here is that only the money that is *not* the property of the policy owner prior to the insured's death qualifies as life insurance.

It helps us understand and evaluate today's life insurance products if we use the term *life insurance* only to refer to the amount that is paid over and above that policy owner money in the event of the insured's death (insurance company money). We buy life insurance because, in the event of our death, the life insurance company will pay our beneficiary more than what we have deposited with the company. These life insurance–company dollars are desirable, have value, and must be paid for. If a policy should ever fail to meet the Section 7702 requirements, then it

EXHIBIT 2.1

Death Benefit Corridor

"The death benefit may not be less than the following percentage of the cash surrender value."

Age of Insured	Amount at Risk (Life Insurance) as a % of Surrender Value	Age of Insured	Amount at Risk (Life Insurance) as a % of Surrender Value
40	250	68	117
41	243	69	116
42	236	70	115
43	229	71	113
44	222	72	111
45	215	73	109
46	209	74	107
47	203	75	105
48	197	76	105
49	191	77	105
50	185	78	105
51	178	79	105
52	171	80	105
53	164	81	105
54	157	82	105
55	150	83	105
56	146	84	105
57	142	85	105
58	138	86	105
59	134	07	105
60	130	88	105
61	128	89	105
62	126	90	105
63	124	91	104
64	122	92	103
65	120	93	102
66	119	94	101
67	118	95	100

would not qualify as a contract of life insurance. Therefore, the primary tax advantages of life insurance would be lost and a current income tax liability would be created.

The tax benefits of a life insurance policy are threefold:

1. *The total death benefit* of a life insurance contract received by the beneficiary is excluded from the beneficiary's taxable income under Internal Revenue Code Section 101. Of course, this benefit would be lost if the contract, under Internal Revenue Code Section 7702, was deemed not to be life insurance. The account value of the policy would be subject to ordinary income tax to the extent that it exceeded the policy owner's cost basis. Cost basis is what the policy owner has paid into the contract.

2. *The annual inside buildup* increases in cash value (account value), is tax-deferred during a policy owner's lifetime, and is tax-free if received as a result of the insured's death. If the contract was deemed not to be not a life insurance contract, these annual increases would be subject to current ordinary income tax.

3. *The total accumulated income*, exceeding the policy owner's cost basis in the contract compounds income tax free in a qualifying life insurance policy. It would be immediately subject to ordinary income tax the product failed to meet the tests of Internal Revenue Code Section 7702.

It is obvious that Uncle Sam makes a great distinction between the *living account values* of a life insurance contract and the *net amount at risk*. It will help you to understand life insurance if you do the same. As we continue to study this situation, it becomes obvious that life insurance companies do not provide this net amount at risk without a charge. There is no free life insurance just as there is no free lunch. Every policy, new or old, that has a net amount at risk must charge for it. These mortality charges for the life insurance are taken from a policy each year either by extracting payment directly from the policy owner or by using a part of the account value or the return earned on the account cash value to pay those expenses.

You have come a long way in understanding if you have

accepted our pragmatic definition of life insurance as being syn-onymous with net amount at risk, and have determined that you actually are paying the increasing cost for that at-risk portion each year as you age. You can equate this *mortality charge* with the cost of your term life insurance. Most people are familiar with term insurance. They pay a specific amount of money for a specific amount at risk (i.e., life insurance) for a period of 1 year. At the end of the year, no excess premium is left over. To continue the policy, they must pay an additional premium for the next year. This is commonly referred to as *yearly renewable term insurance.* Knowing what this cost is for you is another step toward understanding.

Life insurance, or net amount at risk, is paid for each year by increasing mortality costs per $1000 of life insurance. All life insurance, including term life insurance, works exactly the same way. We can conclude, then, that *all life insurance* (net amount at risk, net coverage, excess over a contract's surrender value) is *term insurance.* All life insurance includes the cost of term insurance. The question is not, "What kind of life insurance is available and what should I purchase?" but rather, "I need life insurance. What is the best way for me to pay for it?"

HOW TO PAY FOR LIFE INSURANCE

You may pay for life insurance in two ways. You may purchase off-the-shelf, retail, yearly renewable term life insurance and pay for it with your after-tax income, or you may place investment funds with the insurance company, funds in excess of what is required for the yearly renewable term insurance. The insurance company will invest those extra funds on your behalf and earn a return that will *not* be subject to income tax. The insurance company will then use a portion, or all, of this return to pay the annual mortality and expense charges required by your life insurance contract. You can choose to pay for life insurance with the pretax earnings on your investments within the insurance policy.

Under the first method, retail term life insurance, you would be paying for these same benefits with dollars that had been sub-ject to taxation. This is better described in the "President's Tax Proposals to the Congress for Fairness, Growth and Simplicity" of

May 1985.* It explains what went on in congressional committee meetings on the proposal to impose current taxation on the *inside buildup* of insurance—a proposal that was not successful! Following are two quotes taken from the committee minutes.

> Thus, a policy-owner who pays a premium in excess of the cost of insurance and loading charges for the year in which the premium is paid is, in effect, making a deposit into a savings account that earns income for the benefit of the policy-owner.

> Current law permits life insurance policy-owners to earn this income on amounts invested in the policy free of current tax. This untaxed investment income is commonly referred to as inside build-up.

The document goes on to explain that if a policy owner holds a life insurance policy until death, the investment income within the policy, which was not taxed during the insured's lifetime, escapes tax permanently as it passes to the beneficiary without income tax. If a policyholder can avoid estate taxes as well as income taxes on the proceeds of the life insurance policy, the policy serves as a very efficient tool for the accumulation and transmittal of family wealth.

The proposal to tax the inside buildup went on to explain that even if the policy owner did surrender the policy during his or her lifetime and therefore incurred ordinary income tax on the amount of policy value received in excess of the policy owner's investment, that policy owner still has reaped a substantial income tax benefit. This is because the tax basis in the policy "includes the portion of his premium that had been used to pay the cost of life insurance for past periods." Consequently, the income to be taxed is reduced by the cost of the life insurance, even though this cost is a personal expense and would not be deductible if paid directly. The cost of life insurance has become equivalent to a tax-deductible expense in these policies.

The proposal argued in favor of taxation of the inside buildup of life insurance for a number of other reasons.

1. The deregulation of financial institutions, along with various economic factors, has resulted in an increase in

---

* In *Pension and Profit Sharing Bulletin 8 Extra*, Prentice-Hall, June 3, 1985.

the rate of interest and investment return paid on investments within insurance policies.

2. The investment orientation of cash-value life insurance products is increasing.

3. The favorable tax treatment of the inside buildup in an insurance policy can be obtained through a contract that provides relatively small amounts of *pure insurance coverage*. *Note*: The proposal refers to *pure insurance*, which also is often referred to as *net amount at risk*, which we are defining as *life insurance*.

4. Comparable investment products generally are not tax-free or tax-deferred.

5. Life insurance is not subject to significant limitations on the timing and amount of contributions. (Contributions were subsequently subject to greater limitations under the tax law passed in 1988. See "Modified Endowment Insurance" in Chapter 8.)

6. The tax-favored treatment of the buildup within an insurance policy goes in distorted fashion more to the wealthy than to the not so wealthy.

When this issue comes up again in Congress, you can expect these same arguments to be presented. It is interesting to note that our politicians are able to present the benefits of life insurance so forcefully, whereas the life insurance industry itself still seems unable to convey these same benefits without confusion.

There are many arguments against losing the tax-favored treatment of the inside buildup available within life insurance policies. Many purchasers of life insurance find the increasing after-tax cost of retail yearly renewable and convertible term insurance intolerable. Statistics from the Life Insurance Marketing Research Association (LIMRA) indicate that death benefits are paid out for only 1 percent of retail term insurance policies. The other 99 percent are dropped without value. How many families have been saved from economic ruin and from dependence on the welfare system as a result of life insurance contracts that contained the tax-favored inside buildup that stayed in force until death? How many companies and jobs have been saved by death benefits provided by this same source? Life insurance exists in its present form because it works. People buy it and keep it! It assists all of us by relieving us as taxpayers from the burden of picking up the economic cost of the deaths of others. It enhances economic independence. It rewards the thrifty and encourages self-reliance. The new theme of all legislation should be reduced reliance on government (and thus reduced taxes) and more reliance on the individual, thus encouraging individual enterprise.

Life insurance is an economic tool that not only provides security to families in the event of a death but also serves as an efficient accumulation vehicle. It is available to almost all of us to enable us to save reasonable amounts of money so that we can pay for *our own* children's college educations, *our own* family emergencies, and *our own* retirement. At this time, government and employers cannot and will not provide for these things. Continued need for the tax-favored nature of life insurance has never been greater.

SUMMARY

The old concepts of life insurance no longer work. The idea that we cannot divide the protection components from the accumulation components of a permanent life insurance policy is no longer valid. We must replace it with a new theory that says all life insurance is term insurance. You pay for life insurance each year whether you make the payment directly or have the payment taken from the earnings on your investment account. In the following chapters we will review the various methods of payment, using six generic names to cover all the life insurance products available today.

CHAPTER 3

Term Life Insurance

Just for Now

Joe said, "I have investment capital, but I want it invested in my business." Joe bought after-tax term life insurance. Dan said, "I have a wife and a child and I need lots of life insurance but I can't be an investor just yet." Dan bought after-tax term life insurance.

The menu of life insurance products is a matrix that was developed for the executive financial services coordinators (financial planners) of Price Waterhouse in 1985 (see Exhibit 3.1). The objective of the menu is to take all the generic forms of life insurance contracts and describe them based on their major characteristics and applications. The menu is presented here as an aid to understanding the life insurance marketplace. It will help you to evaluate the advantages and disadvantages of the various policies and select the one(s) appropriate for you.

While the objective here is to evaluate the merits of investing in various life insurance contracts, in doing so it is essential to recognize that the investment results of any contract are uniquely diminished by charges for mortality (life insurance cost) and expenses. Therefore, you must understand the alternatives.

AFTER-TAX TERM OR PRETAX TERM

You may purchase retail term life insurance by using sufficient after-tax dollars to pay yearly mortality and expense charges, or you may pay for life insurance with the pretax earnings on investment capital you choose to deposit within an insurance contract. Exhibit 3.1 refers to two types of term coverage with

EXHIBIT 3.1

Life Insurance Products

	Term Only = Mortality and Expenses Only				
	General Description	Investment	Investment Flexibility	Premium Flexibility	Face Amount Flexibility
Nonguaranteed term	Low cost, low control	None	N/A	None	None
Yearly Renewable and convertible term	Higher cost, more control	None	N/A	None	None
	Term Plus = Mortality, Expenses, and Investment				
Whole life	Dividends provide investment return	Insurance company long-term bonds and mortgages	None	None	None
Variable life	You direct the investment	Common stock, money market, etc.	Maximum	None	None
Universal life	Current interest rates	Short-term interest investments	None	Maximum	Maximum
Variable universal life	Control disclosure	Common stock, money market, etc.	Maximum	Maximum	Maximum

Source: Ben G. Baldwin, 1985.

accompanying charges for mortality and expenses: *nonguaranteed term* and *yearly renewable and convertible term*. Exhibit 3.2 illustrates the cost of each for a $250,000 policy for a nonsmoking male.

The premiums for the limited 3-year term insurance in Exhibit 3.2 are for nonguaranteed term, insurance that cannot be renewed beyond the third year and cannot be converted by the policy owner. The insurance company can charge low rates be-

EXHIBIT 3.2

Nonguaranteed Term and Yearly Renewable and
Convertible Term
Unisex/Male Standard
Rates per $1000 per Year

Age	Limited 1-year Term Insurance*	Yearly Renewable and Convertible Term†	Age	Limited 1-Year Term Insurance*	Yearly Renewable and Convertible Term†
30	0.50	0.42	50	1.08	1.02
35	0.50	0.43	51	1.10	1.08
36	0.52	0.44	52	1.15	1.16
37	0.53	0.47	53	1.22	1.24
38	0.56	0.50	54	1.29	1.34
39	0.58	0.53	55	1.36	1.46
40	0.62	0.57	56	1.44	1.60
41	0.67	0.61	57	1.52	1.77
42	0.73	0.65	58	1.58	1.96
43	0.81	0.70	59	1.64	2.19
44	0.89	0.74	60	1.69	2.46
45	1.00	0.78	61	1.95	2.78
46	1.01	0.82	62	2.25	3.14
47	1.03	0.87	63	2.60	3.56
48	1.06	0.91	64	2.98	4.04
49	1.06	0.97	65	3.43	4.59

*Nonconvertible; nonrenewable; nonparticipating; add $75-per-year policy fee.
†Add $75-per-year policy fee.

cause it *retains control*. It examines you prior to issuing the insurance, and if, based on this examination, the underwriters determine that you have at least a 3-year life expectancy, the insurance company issues the policy, collects its 3 years of premium, terminates the contract at the end of the stated period, and eliminates the risk. No wonder it is cheap! Because there is very little risk, the company can charge very little for it. If it serves your objectives and those objectives don't change, the policy may be a perfect solution. The risk you take is that your personal objectives might change or your health might deteriorate. When the policy expires, you may have no way of obtaining a replacement.

POLICY OWNER CONTROL

The spectrum of *control* ranging from insurance company to policy owner varies greatly in different policies. An experience I had with a client and an insurance company may help to explain why I have become a control freak.

In the early 1980s when interest rates were at their peak, I was asked by a client to find him the best deal on a term life insurance policy with a large face amount. He specified that he needed it for only 5 years. I searched the marketplace and prepared a spreadsheet comparing 17 different policies. All had different costs for the same face amount, and all gave different amounts of control to the policy owner. The insurance companies were competing fiercely for premium income at that time because they could invest those incoming dollars at the high interest rates available then.

The least expensive choice was a *reentry* term policy that required reentry in 5 years. Given 20/20 hindsight, it isn't surprising that it was offered by Executive Life. Reentry means the insured has to reapply for the policy and qualify for another 5 years by passing a new physical exam and financial inspection. If he passed, he would get the lower reentry rates. If he did not pass, the insurance company would charge the much higher guaranteed rates listed in the contract. This was the policy that was put in force.

Five years passed quickly, and the client's dynamic life had not slowed down. He wished to continue the policy, so we applied for reentry. I breathed a sigh of relief when he passed the physical with flying colors, and we fully expected the lower rates to be continued. But Executive Life said no! It did not matter that the insured had done all that was required; Executive Life would not offer the lower rates because "its reinsurers would not provide the coverage at the lower rates." Interest rates had tumbled. Executive Life was not that interested in that type of business any longer. Just imagine the situation that both the client and I would have been in if his health had deteriorated to the point where he was no longer an acceptable risk to another company. We ceased doing business with Executive Life in 1985 and moved his term insurance coverage to a company that gave the policy owner more control. It provided a renewability feature without an age limit, and a convertibility feature that would allow the policy owner to change that policy into any of the investment policies offered by the issuing company. We learned two lessons: (1) It costs more to maintain policy owner control, but it is worth it, and (2) it's amazing how needs for life insurance change over time but do not necessarily go away.

In Exhibit 3.2, note the representative rates for yearly renewable and convertible term insurance. These rates are higher because the insurance company now must continue to renew the policy at the policy owner's option. The convertibility feature gives the policy owner the added option of changing the policy without charge, so a higher premium is charged for a policy that is renewable and convertible. This is referred to as *quality* term insurance because it gives the policy owner greater control, as opposed to nonguaranteed term which gives the insurance company more control.

AFTER-TAX TERM

A nonsmoking policy owner, age 50, who needs $200,000 of insurance, could buy the nonguaranteed term insurance for $500 per year. How much will he have to earn to pay for it? The policy owner will have to allocate earnings to pay both the insurance company and Uncle Sam.

Earnings required netting $500:
$500/(1 − 30\%) = \$714.29$

Income tax liability:
$(\$714.29 \times 30\%) = \$214.29$

Earnings minus income tax paid:
Net premium payment $= \$714.29 − \$214.29 = \$500.00$

The policy owner actually must earn $714.29 to pay a $500 term premium. If you are in the 30 percent tax bracket, you have to earn $1.43 to spend $1.00 on life insurance.

TERM INSURANCE DESIGNS

There are, of course, other forms of term insurance that add features to the two basic types just described. For example, you will find policies referred to as 5-, 10-, 20-, or even 30-year term policies. These designs attempt to avoid the objection people have to the annual increase in the cost of term insurance. The insurance company adds up the number of term premiums that will be required on the policy in total, divides by the number of years for which a level premium is guaranteed, discounts for the time value of the money using the interest rates available at the time, and charges the resulting level premiums rather than the actual yearly renewable term rate. In this, you can see the evolution toward level premium life insurance. In effect, the insurance companies charge more in the beginning so that they don't have to charge such a high amount at the end.

Yearly renewable term insurance normally is the most efficient way to provide for life insurance needs when maximum protection is desired with the minimum current outlay of cash. We can level the cost of term insurance through the use of *mortgage term insurance*. With mortgage insurance, coverage is taken away (i.e., the amount of life insurance is reduced) and the same amount is charged each year for a smaller amount of life insurance, as the policy owner gets older. Thus, the cost per $1000 of coverage does increase with age, but the premium stays the same because there is less coverage.

Watch out for the various level term premium policies. They may be what are called *brick wall* policies. At the end of the level premium period, the substantial increase in cost to continue the policy may put you up against a brick wall of cost. You will have lost control. The policy will terminate before you do, and everything you paid into it becomes past history.

TERM "PLUS"

In our redefinition of life insurance, we determined that the payment made to a beneficiary as the result of the death of an insured consisted of two parts. One was the account investment, or *plus*, that the policy owner had built up during the time the policy was in force prior to the insured's death. This is commonly referred to as the *account value* (also *policy owner equity* or *cash value*—it is the amount the policy owner could have withdrawn during the insured's life). This part of the death benefit is the policy owner's money. It is not the life insurance element that the policy owner wished to purchase on the insured's life. The policy owner's purpose was to have the insurance company pay "its money" to the beneficiary in the event of the insured's death. This money makes up the second part of life insurance. It is these death benefit proceeds that are considered as life insurance (also called *net amount at risk* or *pure insurance*). The amount of the proceeds may vary each year as the investment results of the policy owner's account vary, or it may remain fixed. But the element of death benefit proceeds must *exist* in every contract that is to be accepted as life insurance under Internal Revenue Code Section 7702. And it *must exist* in amounts at least sufficient to meet the cash-value and corridor tests of the code to qualify as life insurance, as explained in Chapter 1. In every policy, there is a charge for each $1000 of life insurance (amount at risk) that increases as the insured gets older. Now, why would a person choose to pay mortality and expenses for life insurance and, in addition, pay extra dollars into a contract

EXHIBIT 3.3

Term—Mortality and Expenses *Only*

	General Description	Investment Vehicle	Investment Flexibility	Premium Flexibility	Face Amount Flexibility	Appropriate for
Non-guaranteed term	Lowest cost, *no control*	None	N/A	None, increases	None	Very limited situations
Yearly renewable and convertible term	Policy owner control	None	N/A	None, increases	None	Limited cashflow; temporary; needs protection *now*

Source: Ben G. Balwin, 1985.

to build up an investment account? This question will be explored in the coming chapters. But, meanwhile, you must answer the following questions before investing. Exhibit 3.3 will help you sort out your answers.

- Where will these extra funds be invested?
- What return can you expect to receive from these funds?
- What risks do you take?
- How much can or should you invest?
- What control will you have over the investments within the policy?
- Can you change your investment selection in the future?

Keep these questions in mind as you read on.

CHAPTER 4

Whole Life Insurance

'Til Death Do Us Part

Whole life insurance evolved out of what were considered the negative aspects of yearly renewable term life insurance: increasing premiums and no living values. The premium, which is the annual cost for yearly renewable term life insurance, increases each year, as shown in Exhibit 4.1.

Because the premiums for the young are very low, term insurance is popular with those in the younger age groups. However, as age increases, the cost per $1000 of insurance escalates to unacceptable levels. Whole life insurance is one of the insurance industry's solutions to this escalation.

Whole life is a policy in which the premium remains level for the *whole* of the insured's life. It is relatively easy for the actuaries to design. The whole life premium is the result of calculating the increasing annual insurance costs per $1000 of amount at risk, spreading them over the life of the insured, and at the same time accumulating a portion of the policy owner's payments in the policy each year. This reduces the amount at risk and eventually results in zero amount at risk at age 95 or 100, at which time the death benefit is entirely policy owner money. This policy type is illustrated in Exhibit 4.2.

The level premiums shown in Exhibit 4.2 are more than sufficient in the early years of the contract, during which time the insurance company has a significant amount at risk because the

EXHIBIT 4.1

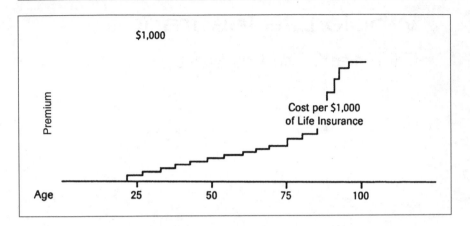

policy owner's cash-value account has not built up very significantly, and the premiums are less than adequate in the later years.
You will note that in the latter years of the policy, the most significant part of the death benefit is provided by the policy owner's
cash value. The insufficiency of the annual premium in the later
years is offset by the overpayment of premium in the early years,
along with the earnings on those overpayments, that compounds

EXHIBIT 4.2

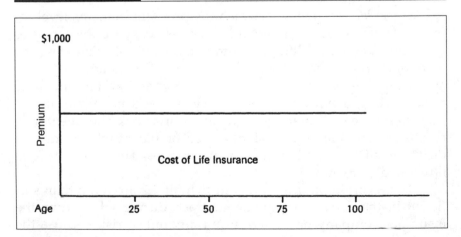

income tax–free and creates a cash reserve that reduces the insurance company's amount at risk. Exhibit 4.3 represents typical whole life policies.

You will note that the portion of the contract that is "life insurance" (insurance company money, net amount at risk) decreases with age. The result is that even though the cost per $1000 increases each year as you get older, you have to buy fewer units, eliminating both cost and life insurance by age 100. At age 100, the death benefit is entirely policy owner money, plus the income tax–free earnings on that money. The amount you could take out while living is equal to your death benefit. That does not mean that if you reach the age of 100, you would want to cash in your policy and take the money, because then you would have to pay income taxes on all the gain in the policy. But if the proceeds are eventually paid out as a death benefit, no income taxes have to be paid. Most life insurance policies in the United States that were issued prior to 1977 and that involve savings or investment are whole life–type policies. However, they may have different labels: *family plan, 20-pay life plan, life paid up at age 65* (Exhibit 4.4), *endowment plan,* or some other name referring to a particular policy feature. The name may be related to the fact that the

EXHIBIT 4.3

Conventional Whole Life Insurance Face Amount

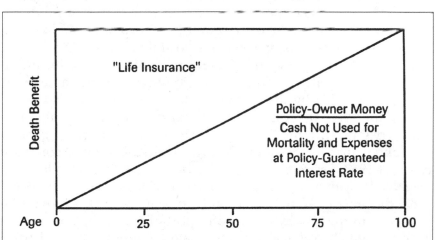

EXHIBIT 4.4

Life Paid Up at Age 65

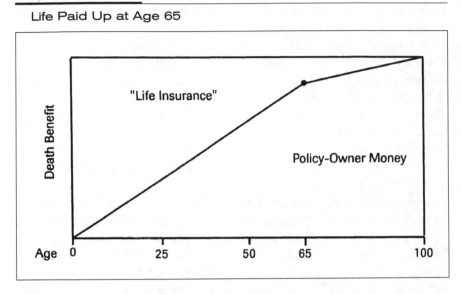

premium-payment period has been adjusted to something less than the whole of the insured's life. The shortened premium-payment period is achieved by increasing the level premium so that the required amount of money is collected over a shorter period of time—by the time the insured is age 65 rather than for the "whole of life," which is when the insured is age 100. The dollars entering these whole life policies that are in excess of funds required for the current year's mortality and expenses are invested in the insurance company's general portfolio.

It is safe to say that the general portfolio of a life insurance company primarily is composed of long-term bonds and mortgages, as dictated by the various state insurance laws. However, during the 1980s it became evident that there could be rather different risk-reward relationships in insurance company general portfolio management. In the Baldwin United Insurance company fiasco of 1983, for example, it was found that Baldwin United was illegally investing in the stock of its own subsidiaries. In 1986–1987, the state of New York found problems with Executive Life in regard to the quality of its bond portfolio and the reinsurance arrangements it was using to eliminate liabilities from its books.

In June 1987, New York mandated that insurance companies licensed to do business in that state must not include more than 20 percent of "less than investment grade" bonds (junk bonds) in their general portfolios. At that time, it was reported that Executive Life of New York's portfolio contained some 57 percent of this type bond. The rest is history. Executive Life failed and was taken over by the state insurance commissioner. Those people who shopped for life insurance and made their decision based upon which company illustrated the highest return learned about *risk*. They found out why they should have settled for a more realistic but possibly lower value on the illustration—and should have opted for a better-run insurance company.

In April 1991 when Executive Life failed, the insurance commissioner of the state of California, John Garamendi, was named conservator of the company. The case was still winding through the legal system in 1994 while 337,000 policy owners were waiting to find out what value their policies might eventually have. There are no guarantees; there are only guarantors. The guarantees are only as good as the company behind them!

The fact is that there are variations in the quality of insurance company general account portfolios. The risk of the investments and the return on the investments also will vary from company to company. Company selection is very important. The ratings provided by the various rating services and the risk-based capital ratings stipulated by the regulators are important, but they are not everything! You will want to look at the quality and the integrity of the company, the availability of useful products, and the quality of management.

The insurance company's general portfolio is the investment vehicle for whole life insurance. The combined general account of all life insurance companies is composed of about $2 trillion, as shown in Exhibit 4.5.

You can expect investment results within this portfolio to parallel those of a portfolio that is approximately 95 percent long-term bonds and mortgages and 5 percent stock. Based upon the performance history for the past 74 years, such a portfolio would produce a gross return of between 5 and 6 percent. Because of the regulatory pressures of the 1990s that came about as a result of so many company failures, these general account portfolios have

EXHIBIT 4.5

1999 Life Insurance Company Asset General Account Distribution

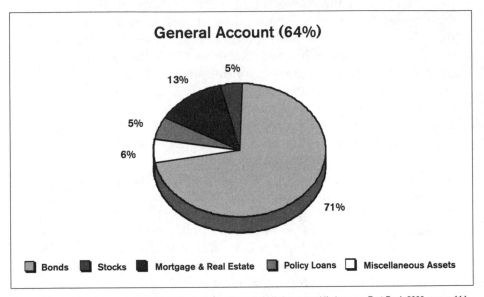

Source: Data for this graph was obtained from the American Council of Life Insurance Life Insurace Fact Book 2000, pages 114–115 and 124, www.acli.com

bonds of shorter maturities, fewer mortgages, and lower returns than they had in the early years before the failures. You need to evaluate the results that can be expected from these shorter-term, higher-quality investments and decide whether you are willing to accept the risk and limitations inherent in investing in these products. Also, you need to decide if you want part of these investment results expended on your behalf to pay for your life insurance. If, after you have examined all these facts, your answer is yes—you do want bonds and mortgages in your portfolio—and yes—you do want to have part of your return buy life insurance—then your next step is to zero in on the *company*. How does the company you are considering manage its general portfolio? What have its investment results been in the past, and what can you expect in the future? You can check the company's annual reports, Best's *Insurance Reports*, Joseph Belth's *Insurance Forum*, and the numerous rating agencies such as S&P, Moody's, Fitch, and Weiss.

Best's *Insurance Reports—Life/Health* offers annual, comprehensive statistical information on the financial position, history, and operating results of life insurance companies in the United States and Canada. *The Insurance Forum* is a monthly publication distributed by Joseph M. Belth, who is a professor emeritus of insurance in the School of Business at Indiana University in Bloomington. He is the Ralph Nader of the life insurance industry and is admired for his tenacity in penetrating the world of insurance industry finances. From these sources you should be able to obtain a company's track record of portfolio rates of return, ascertain the general makeup of its portfolio, and garner an opinion from Belth on risk-reward relationships as a result of how the company is being managed.

NONPARTICIPATING WHOLE LIFE INSURANCE

A part of the return earned on the company portfolio is paid to the policy owner. The policy owner receives a return in only *one way* if the policy is a *nonparticipating* whole life policy. Nonparticipating policies do not provide dividends, but rather only a guaranteed cash value. The amount is stipulated within the contract at issue, and if the policy owner pays the stipulated premium, the guaranteed cash value is the only return earned. If the policy happens to be profitable to the insurance company, the profits will be paid to shareholders of the stock in the life insurance company and not to the policy owners.

PARTICIPATING WHOLE LIFE INSURANCE

Whole life insurance policies that provide portfolio returns to policy owners are called *participating* policies. These policies provide contractually guaranteed cash values as well as *dividends*, allowing flow-through of investment results to the policy owner. Life insurance dividends are not like corporate dividends that are received for ownership of stock. They are not taxable until the amount of the dividend received exceeds the premium paid. Life insurance dividends are considered a return of excess premium. If the premiums paid turn out to be more than the company needs because fewer insureds died than was expected, the company's expenses were lower than expected, or the company's portfolio investment returns were larger than assumed, the company will return some of this excess premium to the policyholders. It is not that difficult to predict with relative accuracy how many insureds will die each year, and expenses are not declining for most insurance companies, so you can safely figure that a substantial part of the dividends paid by participating companies come as a result of better investment returns than assumed in the guarantees.

Where whole life insurance is concerned (insurance with its reserve or cash-value investment that is held within the company's general portfolio), dividends are the only way a variability of returns can be passed on to the policy owner. Because nonparticipating whole life policies have not been able to pass on favorable returns, the competitive position of these policies has diminished to almost nothing.

DIVIDEND CREDITING—PORTFOLIO METHOD

Insurance companies have complicated the lives of policy owners by changing the way they credit dividends on participating whole life insurance policies. Traditionally, the companies used the *portfolio* method, which meant that they would determine the total investment return on the portfolio held by the company and then credit each policy owner with his or her share of the divisible surplus, i.e., the rate of return that exceeded what had been guaranteed in the contract. No attempt was made to distinguish the rate of return earned on monies invested with the company in previous years from the rate of return earned on those funds deposited recently. This portfolio method homogenized rates of return and made them more stable over time. It favored new policy owners in periods of decreasing interest rates since they were able to invest in a portfolio that held securities with rates higher than generally would be available at the time they entered. The portfolio method was a disadvantage to new policy owners during periods of increasing rates because they picked up investments in the older, low-interest bonds.

Long-term policy owners were disadvantaged under this portfolio method during periods of decreasing interest rates because they had to share their higher returns with the new policy owners. But it assisted old policy owners during periods of increasing interest rates when new policy owners were entering with new money that could be invested at higher rates of return, thus improving overall portfolio return.

DIVIDEND CREDITING–CURRENT MONEY METHOD

Some insurance companies decided it would be more equitable to move from the portfolio method of crediting dividends to a *current money method* or *new money method*. With this method, the return earned on the money invested in the insurance policy depends on *when* the investment is made. The rate of return is determined by the rate the company is able to secure at the time the policy owner invests. It has been referred to as the *segmented* or *investment-block method* since certain blocks of business receive different dividend amounts.

It is very difficult to determine which method of crediting dividends is the best for any one policy or policy owner. It depends upon the market interest rates combined with the policy owner's cashflow into and out of the policy, both of which are difficult to predict. This type of investment return is unique to whole life insurance policies that utilize the company's general portfolio. If you stay in a policy long enough, it is not likely to matter which method is used since time has a way of equalizing them.

LIFE INSURANCE ILLUSTRATIONS

Insurance companies typically provide *illustrations* showing how a policy might perform under various conditions. It is easy to believe that there is some connection between these illustrations and reality. However, it is more likely that neither you nor your professional salesperson knows the underlying assumptions. You can be confident of several things—that the assumptions used in illustrations vary from company to company, and that the illustrations are *not* comparable. When you focus on policy values 10 or 20 or more years into the future, you are focusing on the results of compounded errors, and any resemblance between these numbers and reality is purely coincidental.

The Society of Financial Services Professionals came out with an Illustration Questionnaire (IQ) in 1993 to help you and the professional salesperson understand the different assumptions used in illustrations. It asks the insurance company to provide answers to questions such as the following:

- Does what you are showing in this illustration differ from what is going on now in your company?
- Do you treat new policy owners and existing policy owners consistently?
- Is the number of deaths assumed in your illustration the same as the number your company currently is experiencing?
- Does the illustration assume that the number of people dying in the future will increase, decrease, or stay the same as your current experience?
- Do the mortality costs generated by your assumptions about the number of people dying include some expenses or margin of profit?
- Do these changes vary by product?
- What is the basis for the interest rate used in the illustration?
- Is that interest rate net or gross?
- Does the interest rate illustrated exceed what you are currently earning?
- Do the expense assumptions in the illustration reflect your actual expense experience?
- If more people keep your policies than your illustrations assume, would that result in all the policy owners getting less? (This is referred to as *lapse supporting pricing*. The forfeitures paid by people terminating their policies go to support the returns earned by people who keep their policies. The catch is that if too many people keep their policies, the returns for all will be less.)
- Do the illustrations include nonguaranteed bonuses after the policy has been held for a specific number of years?

These are not all the questions. Understand that the further into the future you compound the difference in illustrations, and the higher the return as assumed the larger the deviation from the truth. The bottom line is that you cannot depend upon illustrations to compare policies. In a forecasting situation, the illustration game of "Look at how much money you will have!" is a game in which the biggest liar wins. The most valuable function of illustrations is to help you identify and quantify expenses. You must determine if these expenses in the relatively early years of the policy are acceptable to you based upon your personal situation. Since dividends can and will change depending upon what happens in the future, it is *not* possible that your policy will perform as illustrated.

At this point you might ask, "So what can I depend on?" My advice is to depend on your common sense and what may be referred to as *economic gravity*. Economic gravity presumes that investments will tend to do in the future what they have done over the period of recorded history. Keep in mind that past performance does not necessarily predict future results. We have little else to go on. For historic returns, it is a good idea to consult *Ibbotson Associates' Yearbook on Stocks, Bonds, Bills and Inflation*. This book shows that bonds have tended to provide an average annual return between 5 and 6 percent, or 2 to 2.5 percent more than inflation (which has averaged 3.1 percent). To expect bonds to do differently over the long term is to expect history to change. The economic gravity theory assumes that investment returns will vary, but tend to return to their historic norms. On the basis of common sense, you could assume that the investments within your whole life policy will not defy economic gravity, and if they attempt to do so, the company could end up failing. Whole life insurance will retain its viability as a way of paying for life insurance protection because of the relative stability of returns and the fact that it is an old, familiar product. Furthermore, some insurance companies are using various strategies to enhance the rate of return. For example, some companies are offering dividend addition riders. The company constructs a paid-up additional life insurance policy that offers maximum cash value and the lowest possible amount at risk. The objective is to provide a greater return on that supplemental additional investment. This can be accomplished because less of the rate of return on the cash value of this small additional policy must be used to cover mortality and expense charges, so the rate of return within the policy as a whole is enhanced. Companies can also enter into special compensation contracts with sales representatives to defer the receipt of commissions in order to enhance front-end investment returns in policies.

DEMUTUALIZATION

Demutualization offers another opportunity to earn a return in a whole life policy. On November 6, 1986, Union Mutual, a mutual life insurance company, became UNUM Corp., a publicly traded Delaware corporation with a public offering of 22 million shares of common stock at an initial offering price of $25.50 per share.

On July 22, 1992, Equitable Life Assurance Society went public with stock selling at $9 per share. The stock doubled in price in 6 months and tripled in little more than 1 year. In December 2000 it was bought out by AXA, a French International insurance company, at the equivalent of over $110 per share. By virtue of their ownership rights in the mutual company, policy owners were entitled to receive cash or stock from the new company. The demutualization process is a difficult one. It is almost impossible to predict what success a company will have, or what value the policy owners will receive in exchange for their ownership rights when a company demutualizes.

THE WHOLE LIFE INVESTMENT

Once you know the nature of the investment within the whole life contract and the risk-reward relationships involved, you will want to know how much of an investment you will be required to make in the policy in addition to what is required to pay the mortality and expense charges. In other words, how much will you have to pay into that whole life policy over and above what you would pay for an equivalent amount of term life insurance?

Whole life insurance is a *fixed-premium* product. You give the insurance company your age, sex, and risk information, and the company gives you a stated level premium for the premium-paying period selected. The stated premium is billed to you each year (or for the period selected). The company cannot increase the premiums, and the only way you can reduce the cashflow into the contract is to take some of the investment results out either through the use of dividend credits, if this is a participating insurance policy, or through policy loans. This inflexible premium requirement is an important consideration in the financial planning process. Obligatory premium payments can be a problem during periods of unemployment or of high expenses. A second important element is the fact that the policy owner does not control the investment vehicle in a whole life contract. The insurance company selects the long-term bonds and mortgages and continues to invest and reinvest in the assets selected by its portfolio managers. If you decide that you don't like that particular investment, you have few alternatives. You may borrow on the policy, or drop the policy and thus lose whatever life insurance has been provided. If you surrender the contract, you can expect to pay ordinary income tax on any accumulated gain, that is, any amount you receive back over what you have paid in. The net after-tax results are then available for you to reinvest elsewhere.

1035 TAX-FREE EXCHANGE

A *1035 tax-free exchange* is another alternative, provided you are still insurable at acceptable rates. You may make an absolute assignment of the current contract to the same or another company and trade the policy in on a new contract without incurring current tax liability. Once the absolute assignment is complete, the new insurance company directs the old one to drop the old policy and send a check for the proceeds directly to the new company. The new company then manages the investment as provided in accordance with the replacement contract. This provides a tax-free transfer of your cost basis from the old contract into the new one. This might retain the large cost basis of an old, unprofitable policy, or it might protect a gain in the policy that otherwise would be taxable.

The unique advantage of whole life insurance is that if you pay the level premium, you have the coverage and do not have to worry about personal management of the investment vehicle. The company's long-term bond and mortgage portfolio is supposed to provide stable and historically consistent results. These results have been used to establish life insurance purchasing strategies.

Short-pay, quick-pay, four-pay life, and seven-pay life are premium-paying strategies frequently presented as possible with a whole life contract that normally requires premiums payable for life. These limited pay periods are made possible by using part of the investment return, dividends from the long-term bonds and mortgages, to pay the mortality and expense charges for the rest of the insured's life. Whether such proposals actually work or not depends upon whether the actual investment results are at least as good as or better than the predicted results in the illustration presented. In the distant past, these strategies worked well to minimize cashflow into a policy while maintaining life insurance protection. They have not worked well in the present. Decreasing interest rates and increasing regulation have reduced dividends for all life insurance companies and have caused dividend disappointments for all. Actual investment results of quality companies have exceeded the illustrations in periods of increasing interest rates and been below those illustrated in periods of decreasing interest rates. You can count on it—that is economic gravity.

The intense competition within the life insurance industry to provide high-interest-rate returns in the 1980s gave way to the demand for higher-rated companies in the 1990s as consumers reacted to the tragic failures of too many insurance companies. Also, during the 1990s interest rates decreased, and the actual dividends paid on whole life policies tended to be less than what was illustrated in the 1980s. Policy owners who had been sold policies based upon the promise that premiums would "vanish" in a certain number of years because the dividends would pay the premiums found out that the premiums did not vanish. Contrary to what was shown in the illustrations, the dividends were insufficient to cover the premiums. Not surprisingly, this led to a great deal of legal action and brought about a number of class-action suits in which many companies have been required to pay large sums to settle the claims of disgruntled policy owners.

Many policy owners used a minimum deposit strategy with whole life. Within a participating whole life policy, as soon as the combination of the cash-value increase (guaranteed within the contract) and the dividend was more than the whole life premium, they would use the dividend and also borrow against the cash value to cover the current premium due. *Minimum deposit* was the term used to describe the strategy of paying as little as possible into a policy.

You could access the asset base in the policy through loans offered at somewhere between 5 and 8 percent interest. Therefore, if you wanted to use the minimum deposit strategy, you would instruct the company to reduce the annual premium requirement by the amount of the current dividend and pay the balance of the premium due with a loan against the policy cash value. Implicit in all these methods of limiting the amount of money going into whole life policies was the idea that investment results from whole life policies were inferior, so it made sense to invest as little as possible.

As the policy loans on minimum deposit life insurance contracts increased in amount, so did the interest costs. In the past, there was little reason to be concerned about a 5 percent policy loan that was deductible. Additionally, the loan didn't affect the investment results of the contract. Policy owners received the same dividend regardless of whether they had borrowed on their policies or not. This strategy was particularly advantageous when interest rates were increasing in the 1970s and early 1980s. However, it was inevitable that insurance companies would have to do something about the disintermediation (people borrowing at the low 5 percent guaranteed rate to invest at higher rates of return elsewhere). The flow of funds being lent out at 5 percent when money-market mutual funds were paying rates in the high teens was devastating to insurance company portfolios. As a result, companies took the following actions:

1. They either increased the guaranteed loan interest rate on whole life policies being issued at the time to 8 percent or made the interest rate adjustable.
2. They made *upgrade* and *enhancement* offers to existing policy owners. The basics of these offers were that if the policy owner agreed to pay current market rates of interest for any loans, the company would provide higher future dividends.

3. They began issuing *conduit*-type policies, such as variable and variable universal life (VUL). These are policies in which the policy owner accepts the return provided by market conditions. Variable policies provide separate accounts, often in addition to the company's general portfolio and, after charging a management fee, pass *all* investment returns (good and bad) on to the policy owner.

The cost of using policy loans has increased. You receive the increased dividend of the upgrade offer only if you also accept higher interest rates on any loan you may take. If you don't accept the upgrade offer (to retain low interest charges on policy loans), you then accept dividends on a lower scale. Trying to quantify the actual increases in policy loan costs (increased interest costs and/or decreased dividends) as a result of these changes has added to the complexity of managing whole life policies.

On top of the increased costs coming from insurance companies, the Tax Reform Act of 1986 (TRA-86) ruled out deductibility of these policy loan interest charges for both the personal and the corporate borrower, in most cases. For the personal borrower, TRA-86 generally regards interest paid on policy loans as consumer interest, thereby eliminating its deductibility. Loans to finance investments continue to be deductible to the extent of net investment income. Also, loans on policies held for trade or business purposes on the lives of officers, owners, or employees generate deductible loan interest for businesses on loans aggregating no more than $50,000 per officer, employee, or owner. TRA-86 grandfathered policies owned for business purposes issued prior to June 21, 1986, and allow businesses to continue to deduct all policy loan interest as they did in the past. For business policies issued after June 20, 1986, only interest on loans up to $50,000 is deductible. The impact of (1) higher insurance company interest rates on policy loans, (2) lower dividends on policies with outstanding loans, and (3) reduction or elimination of policy loan interest deductibility has served to destroy the economic viability of the minimum deposit strategy for paying whole life insurance premiums.

CAPITAL IN WHOLE LIFE POLICIES

One of the premises of this book is that there is too much capital residing inside life insurance contracts to ignore it. At policy inception, you may not be too concerned about investment return because the premium is small relative to the face amount and the cash value has not had a chance to accumulate to any great sum. However, over the years, as you can see if you look back at Exhibit 4.3, the guaranteed cash value of these contracts will accumulate to equal the face amount of the policy at age 95 or 100, depending upon the contract. As policy owners approach this significant level of capital, they are more and more likely to become concerned about what is happening with their money. For example, my mother is a healthy, active, involved individual at 94 years of age. The whole life policy my father bought for her many years ago now has virtually *no amount at risk* left in the policy, no life insurance. The death benefit is equal to the policy cash value, which, because she is the policy owner, is her money. The current return on that money is the current dividend paid by the insurance company, which represents a 4.7 percent return on her capital. Since she elected to take the dividends in cash over the years, she now has received more in dividends than was paid into the policy in premiums. Therefore, the dividends are now subject to income taxes. Is she happy with that return? Are her beneficiaries happy with that return? To put the answer to that question in context, you need to know that my mom and dad retired in 1969, so mom has been economically retired for over 30 years and we are hoping for another 10 to 15 years. As a result she has experienced the corrosive effects of inflation on her cost of living. Fortunately, her investment capital outside of her Life Insurance Policy was diversified in stocks and bonds, and in spite of the difficult years in the stock market between 1969 and 1982, her asset allocation of about 30 percent bonds and cash and 70 percent equities (stocks) was maintained. As a result, her retirement portfolio has provided for her needs in spite of the cost of living increasing almost fourfold during these years. Diversification, especially investing in equities, is something that she understands is a necessity for retirees to meet retirement needs, and she is frustrated that she cannot diversify the capital in her whole life policy in a similar manner.

BUT IS IT A GOOD INVESTMENT?

A question that follows naturally is whether, in general, the capital held in a whole life policy provides an acceptable investment alternative for today's insurance buyer. Before we get to the answer, please remember that each person's situation is different, so you need to filter the general suggestions through your personal situation. You need to examine the assumptions upon which the answer is based. If you are in agreement with the "whys" of the conclusion, then maybe you are in agreement with the conclusion.

Now, to the answer: *No, whole life is not an acceptable alternative* for most people today. The reasons and assumptions underlying this conclusion are as follows (also see Exhibit 4.6).

1. The bond mortgage general account investment of any life insurance company cannot be expected to provide in excess of a 5 to 6 percent return over an insured's lifetime.
2. Inflation causes the policy values to decrease over a lifetime.
3. A bond mortgage account provides insufficient diversification for the long-term investor.

EXHIBIT 4.6

Term "Plus"—Mortality and Expenses "Plus" Additional Dollars for Investments

	General Description	Investment Vehicle	Investment Flexibility	Premium Flexibility	Face Amount Flexibility	Appropriate for
Whole life	Fixed life; dividends provide investment return	Primarily, long-term bonds and mortgages, selected by the insurance company	None; to change investments, it is necessary to borrow and reinvest	None; dividends can reduce or eliminate fixed, billed premium	None; if you want more, you need to buy new, *if* you can pass a physical	Conservative policyholders and substandard insureds

4. The general account creditor risk, the fact that the general account assets are subject to the creditors of the company and the company can fail, such as happened with Executive Life, Mutual Benefit Life, Confederation Life, etc., is unacceptable and unnecessary.

5. The policy provides the policy owner with insufficient control over the investment. It requires an irrevocable decision at policy inception to remain in the general account investment for the insured's lifetime.

6. The policy is a single-pocket policy. It offers only the bond mortgage account and provides no method of changing that investment if investment needs or desires change.

7. The policy is inflexible with regard to premium payment and face amount.

8. You are insurable and you have no trouble obtaining insurance at acceptable rates.

9. If you do not intend to commit suicide, or commit fraud on any of the papers you complete to obtain a policy, then you can exchange your existing whole life for a more flexible contract (underwriting requirements).

When is a whole life policy a good choice?

1. When it is doing what *you* want it to do

2. When it is providing an acceptable tax-free rate of return

3. When you already own a whole life policy and your health insurability has deteriorated for some reason

4. When there is not an acceptable alternative

5. When the *guaranteed* cash value and guaranteed premium are a comfort to you.

6. When you do not want to take the responsibility or time to manage a policy that relegates policy control to the policy owner

7. When the money in the policy does not represent a significant investment to you and you do not care to be concerned with the return on it

Caution: Do not act on any of this until you have thoroughly discussed it with your beneficiaries, your doctor, your tax and legal advisors, and your personal insurance and financial advisors. Actions taken will have an impact on you and your family's economic security and should only be taken in the context of an overall financial plan carefully discussed with your trusted financial advisors. Never terminate a life insurance contract until a replacement contract has been underwritten and issued, and you and your advisors find it acceptable and preferable in every way.

CHAPTER 5

Universal Life Insurance

Short-Term Investments for Long-Term Plans?

John bought one of the first universal life policies from E. F. Hutton Life in 1981. The interest rate that first year was 14 percent. Policies like this are renewing at 5 percent. When E. F. Hutton Life changed to First Capital Life, the policy no longer offered all John wanted. The economics of First Capital Life worried him. John decided to trade (1035 tax-free exchange) his First Capital policy in on a policy that gave him investment control and separate accounts. John's investment objectives change over time. The investments within his policy now change to accommodate his changing needs. John was lucky—or wise—in wanting to be in control. First Capital Life eventually failed and was taken over by the state insurance commissioner. John made it out in time.

As interest rates skyrocketed in the late 1970s and early 1980s, money-market mutual funds were born. The public demanded an opportunity to participate in the higher yields of the day, and the mutual fund industry responded. As interest rates went up, the return on old, low-interest-rate, long-term bond and mortgage portfolios of whole life insurance contracts looked worse and worse. Money moved out of insurance policies and into money-market accounts. In 1979 the Federal Trade Commission released its report that was critical of the investment merits of life insurance. People in life insurance and people in long-term bond mutual funds all learned that no one likes investments in long-term bonds when interest rates are rapidly increasing—the market value of those bonds deteriorates.

The life insurance market demanded a response, and the appropriate vehicle, a money-market mutual fund, was there to provide the investment du jour. The market-driven insurance industry was ready to offer short-term money-market investments within their insurance policies instead of the long-term bonds and mortgages of whole life.

It is interesting to note that it took a life insurance company executive, John Watts, working with a brokerage industry firm, E. F. Hutton, to get universal life into the marketplace. Watts was able to help brokers understand universal life as an investment alternative for people who were paying income taxes on their interest earnings. Universal life could provide tax-deferred interest earnings since those earnings occurred within the insurance contract, and under the proper circumstances, policy owners could even use those earnings without paying income taxes. Income tax–free earnings and the possibility of income tax–free spending rapidly caught on.

E. F. Hutton's success with universal life brought in small niche companies born in the days of very high interest rates. The baggage of portfolios of old, low-interest-rate, long-term bonds and mortgages did not burden the new companies. These new companies were able to get a fast and effective start. The old-line life insurance companies looked fearfully at universal life as a vehicle that would create more rather than less disintermediation problems. According to a 1981 Life Insurance Marketing Research Association study, 78 percent of the annualized premiums went into traditional cash-value life insurance, 19 percent paid for term insurance, and only 3 percent of new premium was allocated to the newer products, such as universal life. By 1985, these figures changed dramatically (see Exhibit 5.1). Only 47 percent of the new annualized premium was going to traditional whole life insurance, while universal life's market share had risen to 38 percent. Of the rest, 11 percent went to term insurance; 3 percent to fixed-premium variable life, which became available in 1976; and 1 percent to variable universal life, which first became available in 1985. The shift in market share has continued. By the first quarter of the year 2000, among the 89 companies tracked by LIMRA—which

EXHIBIT 5.1

Percentage of Annualized New Premiums

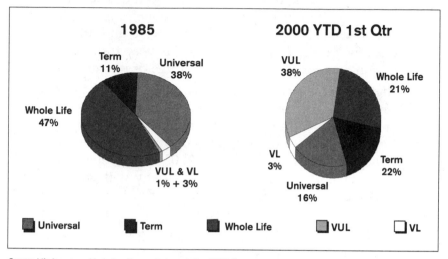

1985

- Term 11%
- Universal 38%
- Whole Life 47%
- VUL & VL 1% + 3%

2000 YTD 1st Qtr

- VUL 38%
- Whole Life 21%
- VL 3%
- Term 22%
- Universal 16%

Legend: ▮ Universal   ▮ Term   ▮ Whole Life   ▮ VUL   ☐ VL

Source: Life Insurance Marketing Research Association (LIMRA)

make up 75 percent of the total industry—variable universal life had become the dominant product with a 38 percent market share. Term insurance was second with a 22 percent market share, whole life third with 21 percent, then universal with 16 percent, and fixed-premium variable with 3 percent.

As you can see by these numbers, universal life's market share has gone down as interest rates have decreased. However, universal life brought a brand-new chassis to the life insurance industry that has changed life insurance forever. The unique features that universal life brought are:

- *Complete transparency*. You, the policy owner, are shown the specific expense charges, the costs deducted for the amount at risk (the life insurance), the specific account value, and the amount of interest that is being paid on that account value. This was a revolutionary change in the makeup of life insurance that did not exist in the other investment-oriented life insurance available at the time, whole life and fixed-premium variable life. Up until that time we all knew that the ingredients necessary for creating an investment-oriented life insurance were (1) cost of life insurance, (2) expenses, and (3) investment capital, but none of these has ever been quantified. The fixed-premium, fixed-face-amount policies of the day did not specifically identify each. They were and are, in effect, black-box types of policies. It is this very transparency that allows for the following features of universal life.

- *Ability to vary and skip premiums.* Since the policy owner can see the expenses, it is easy to identify the minimum amount that can be paid into the policy in order to keep it in force. The maximum amount that can be put into a policy is stipulated by Section 7702 of the Internal Revenue Code. The insurance company will provide the policy owner with the actual amount of the maximum that can be put into the policy.

- *Flexibility of death benefit.* If the policy owner wants the insurance company to increase the amount at risk (life insurance), all that is needed is evidence of insurability (medical, personal, and financial) of the insured, and the payment of the increased costs of insurance (COIs). A decrease in the amount of life insurance, or amount at risk, merely requires a request, and the COIs will decrease with the decrease in coverage.

- *Death benefit options.* A policy owner may have the death benefit option that was described in Chapter 4 for whole life, in which the total death benefit is a set amount. At the insured's death, the beneficiary is paid that contracted amount, and the death benefit is made up of the amount at risk at the time and the cash value or account value. This is most commonly referred to as *option A or 1*. Alternatively, the policy owner may stipulate that the amount at risk is not to decrease as the cash or account value increases. At the insured's death, the death benefit is to be the entire, originally contracted for, amount at risk plus the account value at the time of death. This is most commonly referred to as *option B or 2*.

- *Right to withdraw account value.* Prior to the existence of universal life, the only way for a policy owner to get money out of an ongoing policy was to borrow it. That is, the policy owner would ask the insurance company for a loan using the policy as collateral. The insurance company would lend the money, usually at 5 to 8 percent interest, and put a lien against the policy until the loan was paid off. If death or policy termination occurred prior to the loan being paid off, the insurance company would subtract the amount of the loan, plus any interest owed, and pay out the balance. In policies that have dividends—participating policies—the dividend credits always can be taken out in cash. Universal life, on the other hand, allows a policy owner to borrow or withdraw account value at the policy owner's option.

Universal life has all these unique characteristics, but the most notable is that when it entered the life insurance marketplace in the late 1970s, its basic investment vehicle was current interest rate investments. The interest rate to be earned on the account value of this type of policy usually is guaranteed for 1 year. At the end of that year, the policy owner is informed of the rate for the next 12-month period.

Universal life brought total disclosure to the life insurance industry. The specific charges, expenses, and credits are itemized and available to the policy owner. The policies were referred to as *transparent* because of the fact that detailed information regarding expenses, cost of insurance, account value, and interest earnings was provided for the first time in universal life. Each item now is disclosed, allowing you to shop for policies with the lowest expenses, the lowest costs of life insurance (amount at risk), and competitive interest rates.

When you are considering putting premium into a universal life policy, ask to see the expenses and credits on a monthly basis. Those for the most current years will provide the most valid information because the insurance company has the right to change expenses, COIs, and interest crediting rates in the future. Their right to change expenses and COIs is limited by contractually stated limits.

You will want to ask the following questions of whomever is assisting you in putting the policy in force:

1. What deposit do you recommend for this policy?

2. How often should I make these deposits?

3. How long should I expect to make these deposits using *conservative* interest rate assumptions?

4. How much is taken out for state premium tax?

5. What amounts are deducted for insurance company expenses initially, and then per month?

6. What is the maximum expense charge that could be made?

7. What is the amount at risk, meaning how much life insurance is being offered by this policy? Does the death benefit include my account value (option A or 1), or is it paid in addition to my account value (option B or 2)?

8. What are the current monthly cost and the annual cost for this amount at risk? You will find that this is referred to as the mortality charge or costs of insurance. You will recognize it as the cost of the term insurance within the contract.

9. What is the contractual maximum mortality charge that could be made?

10. Are there any other additional charges being made against the policy account for other policy benefits?

11. What earnings currently are being credited to the policy account on a monthly and annual basis? Historically, how much has that interest dropped in the second policy year? Show me the history of the interest rates credited to this policy's account value.

12. Are any minimum earnings guaranteed?

13. How much remains in the policy owner's account at the end of the first month and at the end of the first year?

14. If I choose to surrender the policy at the end of the first month, how much will I receive? At the end of the first year?

15. For how long is the cash surrender value less than the account value; i.e., how long does the back-end load

(expense charged if you cancel the contract before the insurance company recoups its expenses) stay in existence?

Keep in mind that the insurance company retains the right to change the charges it makes for mortality and expenses. It is important to know what the company is charging presently and the range within which it can charge. You often will find that charges for mortality are based on the company's current experience. Therefore, the long-term results of a universal life policy depend upon how well the company selects new insureds. Since this an element over which you have no control, you can do only two things: (1) Choose a quality company with careful underwriting standards, and (2) determine whether or not the maximum potential charges for mortality guaranteed within the contract are acceptable. The maximums by statute are contained in the *1980 Commissioners Standard Ordinary Mortality Table.*

Since universal life policies are transparent, you can know the charges being made for mortality at various ages. Because those charges are an important point of comparison, you also will want to check them against the various tables, benchmarks, and existing market rates for term insurance. Exhibit 5.2 provides a summary of four standard mortality tables that can be used for such comparisons. It shows how many people per 1000 are expected to die within 1 year in any particular age category. The first table, the "American Experience," shows how many deaths per 1000 occurred from 1843 to 1858. (It appears that this period was a hazardous time in which to live!) Mortality rates improve as you read to the right. The 1941 table was constructed from statistics for 1930 to 1940; the 1958 table, from statistics for 1950 to 1954; and the most current 1980 table, from statistics for 1970 to 1975. As a result of the continuing improvements in life expectancy, a new mortality table is expected to be adopted in 2001.

FLEXIBILITY OF FACE AMOUNT AND PREMIUM

The flexibility of the face amount and the premium features of universal life allows you to adjust the face amount and what is paid into the policy so that it fits you, rather than having a

EXHIBIT 5.2

Deaths per 1000 in Four Statutory Mortality Tables

Age	American Experience Table	Commissioners 1941 Table	Commissioners 1958 Table	Commissioners 1980 Table
20	7.80	2.43	1.79	1.90
21	7.86	2.51	1.83	1.91
22	7.91	2.59	1.86	1.89
23	7.96	2.68	1.89	1.86
24	8.01	2.77	1.91	1.82
25	8.06	2.88	1.93	1.77
26	8.13	2.99	1.96	1.73
27	8.20	3.11	1.99	1.71
28	8.26	3.25	2.03	1.70
29	8.34	2.40	2.08	1.71
30	8.43	2.56	2.13	1.73
31	8.51	3.73	2.19	1.78
32	8.61	3.92	2.25	1.83
33	8.72	4.12	2.32	1.91
34	8.83	4.35	2.40	2.00
35	8.95	4.59	2.51	2.11
36	9.09	4.86	2.64	2.24
37	9.23	5.15	2.80	2.40
38	9.41	5.46	3.01	2.58
39	9.59	5.81	3.25	2.79
40	9.79	6.18	3.53	3.02
41	10.01	6.59	3.84	3.29
42	10.25	7.03	4.17	3.56
43	10.52	7.51	4.53	3.87
44	10.83	8.04	4.92	4.19
45	11.16	8.61	5.35	4.55
46	11.56	9.23	5.83	4.92
47	12.00	9.91	6.36	5.32
48	12.51	10.64	6.95	5.74
49	13.11	11.45	7.60	6.21
50	13.78	12.32	8.32	6.71
51	14.54	13.27	9.11	7.30
52	15.39	14.30	9.96	7.96
53	16.33	15.43	10.89	8.71
54	17.40	16.65	11.90	9.56
55	18.57	17.98	13.00	10.47
56	19.89	19.43	14.21	11.46
57	21.34	21.00	15.24	12.49
58	22.94	22.71	17.00	13.59
59	24.72	24.57	18.59	14.77
60	26.69	26.59	20.34	16.08

contractually stipulated face amount and payment of premium, as in whole life. You are able to change the face amount or premium level to suit your own particular needs. Once all the policy data are in the computer, it's not difficult to raise or lessen the amount at risk (life insurance). If you buy a policy and shortly thereafter elect to reduce the amount at risk, you likely will forfeit a portion of your account value in the form of a back-end load. The amount of that forfeiture will be disclosed in the contract. On the other hand, if you direct the company to increase the amount at risk, the insurance company probably will ask you to provide evidence that you are still in good health. Be sure to ask what expenses you will incur at the time of increase. With some contracts, this is the most efficient (least costly) method of increasing your life insurance coverage. It is important that the universal life is flexible and can adapt to your lifestyle.

You'll like universal life if you prefer an investment that pays current, competitive market rates of interest as opposed to the long-term bond and mortgage account returns of whole life. It also has appeal if you think that you may want to use its adjustable features. The market share of this product has decreased dramatically since 1986 because of the decreasing interest rates and competition from variable life. In fact, it has dropped from 38 percent in 1985 to 16 percent in 2000.

The transparency of universal life can be seen in the annual report page shown in Exhibit 5.3. The policy surrender value is $1,199,528.25. There is no longer any surrender charge that the policy owner would be exposed to if they chose to terminate this policy and take the cash surrender value. Surrender charges may also be referred to as Contingent Deferred Sales Charges (CDSC) or back-end loads.

You can see that the amounts required to keep the policy in force are the charges for expenses ($72) and mortality charges for the $127,600.24 of life insurance for a male, age 77. A premium payment of $156,416 went into the policy on January 21, 2000, from which $782.08 was deducted for Illinois State Premium Tax (½ of 1 percent). The insurance costs were deducted from the investment account and totaled $127,600.24 for the year for an approximate amount at risk of $4,000,000 ($5.2 million death benefit minus $1.2 million Account Value). Alternatively, you could use

EXHIBIT 5.3

Summary of Policy Values

Policy Values as of:	01/12/00	01/11/01
Face Amount	$5,200,000.00	$5,200,000.00
Death Benefit	$5,200,000.00	$5,200,000.00
Death Benefit Option	A	A
Policy Amount	$1,112,020.27	$1,199,528.25
Less: Surrender Charge		
Outstanding Loans	$0.00	$0.00
Net Cash Surrender Value	$0.00	$0.00
	$1,112,020.27	$1,199,526.25

Transactions for Guaranteed Interest Account-Unloaned

	Premium Payments			Other Transactions		Monthly Deductions			Policy Values	
Effective Date	Total	Charges	Net Premium	Type	Amount	Month/ Day	Insurance Costs	Admin Charge	Interest Credited 5.00%	Policy Account
01/21/00	$158,418.00	$782.08	$155,633.92							
						Jan 12	$10,948.77	$6.00	$0.00	$1,101,065.50
						Feb 12	$10,547.84	$6.00	$5,016.67	$1,251,162.25
						Mar 12	$10,563.13	$6.00	$4,846.21	$1,245,439.33
						Apr 12	$10,577.62	$6.00	$5,157.43	$1,240,013.14
						May 12	$10,592.66	$6.00	$4,968.98	$1,234,383.46
						Jun 12	$10,607.36	$6.00	$5,111.64	$1,228,881.74

EXHIBIT 5.3 Continued

	Jul 12	$10,622.59	$6.00	$4,924.38	$1,223,177.63
	Aug 12	$10,637.49	$6.00	$5,085.24	$1,217,599.28
	Sep 12	$10,652.50	$6.00	$5,042.14	$1,211,982.92
	Oct 12	$10,668.04	$6.00	$4,856.66	$1,206,165.54
	Nov 12	$10,683.25	$6.00	$4,994.79	$1,200,471.08
	Dec 12	$10,698.99	$6.00	$4,810.53	$1,194,576.62
	Jan 11			$4,951.63	$1,199,528.25
Total	$156,416.00	$782.06	$155,633.92	$0.00	$127,600.24	$72.00	$59,746.30

the investment feature of the policy and ask the insurance company for the amount of the maximum that could be put in. You might wish to specify that you want to have access to this extra deposit without taxation or penalties through withdrawal or policy loan. This requires that you stay below what is called the *seven-pay-maximum*, which is covered in Chapter 8, Modified Endowment Contract.

MINIMUM FUNDING LEVEL

The minimum funding level requires that there be enough money in the policy account to recover the insurance and expense charges for the year. Under a minimum funding arrangement, the policy account could dwindle to zero or to the amount of the remaining back-end load, at which time the insurance company would call on you for more money. Unless you made a premium deposit sufficient to cover the insurance and expenses, the policy could terminate. In some cases, the company will not require payment to cover the full year, but rather a shorter period, such as one quarter. Remember that if you decide *not* to make an additional premium payment, the policy will terminate, and you will pay the back-end load within the policy. When you use a minimum funding strategy, you really are purchasing yearly renewable term insurance. Generally, it is not economical to use a universal life policy as a term policy. The expenses of such a policy typically are more than a regular term policy, and you also have to contend with the back-end load. Furthermore, there usually is a *target* premium on these flexible-premium products. This is the premium the company considers adequate to maintain the policy on a long-term basis.

EFFICIENT/TAX-FREE/PARITY FUNDING

Efficient funding, tax-free funding, and *parity funding* are all terms used to describe that point in the life of the policy when you have an amount on deposit large enough so that *tax-free* interest earnings are sufficient to pay for the mortality and expenses of the contract in the current year. At this point, you are buying term life insurance protection entirely with interest earnings that have not been diminished by income taxes. This type of funding allows you to pay the minimum amount possible for the protection you desire. For example, if you are in the 30 percent tax bracket, you have to earn $1.43 ($1.00 divided by the quantity 1 minus your income tax bracket) in order to pay an after-tax dollar for a term premium. But if you earn interest inside a policy, you use that whole dollar, undiminished by taxes, to pay the term premium within the policy. You save 43 cents on taxes for every dollar of premium paid in this fashion.

OVERFUNDING

What would happen if you decided to *overfund* your universal life policy by putting in an extra $10,000 for investment purposes? Before making this decision, you need to look at whether or not the policy is a good investment alternative. What does it cost to get the money into the policy? Does the deposit increase any back-end loads? How would you get the money out if you needed it?

You know what interest your policy account is earning, and so you can calculate or ask what interest you may expect from the extra investment for the year. The interest earned on the money within the contract is considered inside buildup and is not subject to current income taxation. Make your decision based upon the alternative investments available at the time. Where else could you put those funds to provide higher net after-tax earnings with comparable liquidity and safety? Keep in mind that the company uses some of the return you earn to pay for your life insurance, so unless you need the insurance coverage, unwarranted expenses are reducing your returns.

Universal life is not without downside risk. It now has been used throughout an entire business cycle. It came into existence at a time when interest rates were at an all-time high. At first, even some of the agents selling it did not understand it, and in some cases, it was improperly sold. Some policy owners who purchased contracts in 1979 have insurance company illustrations for periods of 20 to 50 years based on 12 percent or more interest rate assumptions for the entire period. Often those who bought these contracts did not even realize that part of that return would be used up by expense and mortality charges. They bought universal life because of its high-gross interest rate predictions and the bad publicity surrounding whole life as interest rates rose to those high levels in 1980. What was most damaging was that policy-holders determined the amount of money that they would put into the universal life policy based on those assumptions about high interest rates. As a result, they minimized their annual deposits and underfunded their contracts. As interest rates have decreased and the policy earnings on their accounts have diminished, many of these policy owners are finding that the earnings on their accounts are not sufficient to cover mortality and expense charges. A portion of the principal in the policy account is being utilized to cover these costs, and so their policy accounts are being systematically eliminated. Also, some policy owners treat universal life as they did whole life—they put the policies away and forget them. They may be totally unaware of decreases in the principal amount of their account values. Unfortunately, they will be shocked when they are notified by the insurance company that their policy account has diminished to a level that cannot sustain the policy and that more money will be required if the policy is to stay in force. These policy owners will receive a *call* on their policies similar to a *call* on margin accounts from stockbrokers. This is why you need to make a conscious decision about the funding level in your universal life policy and then watch it to make sure it is doing what you want it to do.

Most people fail to appreciate the interest rate sensitivity of these policies. Let's use an example to try to increase our understanding. In 1980 a 45-year-old nonsmoking male in good health purchased a $1 million universal life insurance policy on option A. Remember, option A is the one in which the $1 million will be made up of part policy owner money (the account value) and part amount at risk (life insurance company money). He asked the agent how much he should put into the policy each year so that at age 100, should he be so fortunate to live that long, the $1 million death benefit would be made up entirely of his money, the account value. At that point, there would no longer be any amount at risk and consequently no more COIs to be paid. The illustration system calculated, using the 12 percent level interest rate available in 1980, that the amount he needed to pay into the policy each year was $7160. Exhibit 5.4 diagrams the illustration

EXHIBIT 5.4

Healthy Age 45 Male 12 Percent Illustration Endowment at Age 100

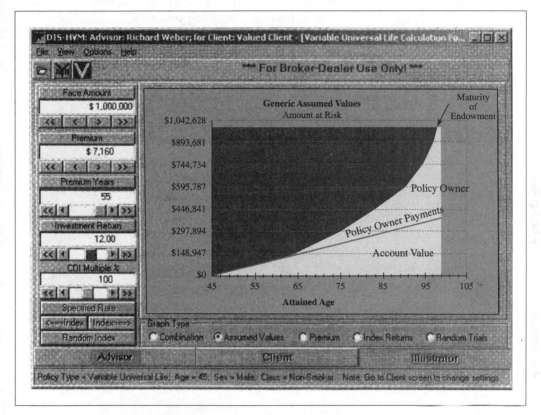

showing the account growing in value until it equals the policy death benefit at age 100. The arrival of a policy at this point is referred to as *policy maturity* or *endowment*.

Neither the policy owner nor the agent had the tools in those days to show what we can now show using a newly developed software program currently going through the regulatory approval process. This software is called Dynamic Insurance Solutions, Historic Variability Module and is being brought to market by Financial Profiles of Carlsbad, California. Using this software you can reduce the assumed interest rate. If we reduce the interest rate by just ½₀ of 1 percent, from 12 percent to 11.95 percent, what impact do you think it would have on our ending account value at age 100?

Instead of that account being worth $1 million, how much do you think it might be worth? When we execute this change with the software, we instantly see the result, as shown in Exhibit 5.5.

The value of the policy owner's account at age 99 as a result of reducing the interest rate by only ½₀ of 1 percent is $0 instead of $1 million. It is entirely possible that the policy terminated without value before the insured terminated. Of course, the policy owner would have the right to pay an amount to keep the policy in force for one more year. The software informs us that we could expect a bill for $400,000 to do that rather than the $7160 that we had been paying. Of course, that bill alone might be enough of a shock to kill the insured.

EXHIBIT 5.5

Healthy Age 45 Male 11.95 Percent Illustration at Age 100

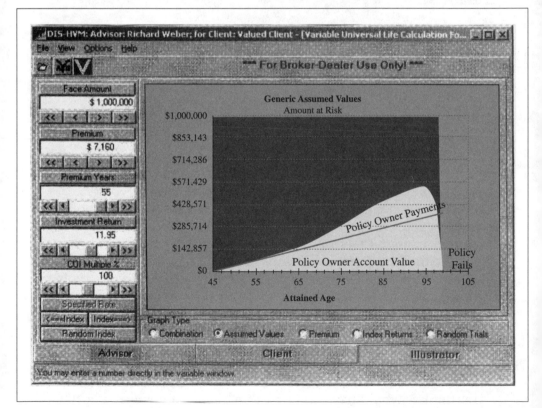

In the year 2001, twenty years after this policy was put in force, it is not renewing at 11.9 percent but at 6 percent or less. Our insured is now age 65, has paid $7160 into this policy for each of those twenty years, and observes the account value to be approximately $100,000 but decreasing in value each year. When we put that information into the software, it shows us that we should expect the policy to terminate without value in about ten years, the insured's age 75, well before our insured's life expectancy. We then ask the software to show us how we can get back on track for an endowment of $1 million at age 100, assuming the current 6 percent interest. The software suggests that we should now pay $30,000 per year into the policy.

If, at policy inception in 1980, our advisor had suggested that the funding level of the policy be determined based upon a more conservative interest rate assumption of 6 percent, this software would have suggested that we pay about $15,000 per year into the policy instead of $7160. Had that been done at inception, this policy at the insured's age 65 would have a value of over $300,000. If funding of the policy is continued at $15,000 per year and interest rates continue at 6 percent, the account value of the policy should pass through an account value of $1 million by age 95, and be about $1.3 million by age 100. This demonstrates that the most important thing we can do to assure a successful policy is to fund it adequately. The more we put in, the more successful it will be.

However, suppose this policy owner arrived at age 65 with the underfunded original policy and could not afford to pay $30,000 per year to salvage it. What alternative does he have to keep the policy from disappearing without value at age 75? The software suggests that if he reduces the death benefit of the policy from $1 million to about $400,000, if he continues the premium payment of $7160, and if interest rates remain at 6 percent, the policy should mature when the insured reaches age 100 for $400,000. The two alternatives for turning an unhealthy policy into a healthy policy are to increase funding or reduce the amount of life insurance.

When you consider the fact that many universal life policies are not properly funded because the illustration assumed such high long-term interest rate earnings, and add to that the following factors, you can understand the problems that policy owners may encounter if they do not actively manage their policies.

1. The insurance company can, at its discretion, increase the mortality charges up to the maximum guaranteed within the contract, e.g., from the lower current rates to 1980 Commissioners Standard Ordinary mortality rates.

2. The insurance company can increase expense charges up to the maximum guaranteed within the contract, e.g., from $6 to $8.

3. Mortality charges will inevitably continue to rise as a result of the policy owner's advancing age.

All factors occurring together can result in the rapid decline of an account value to zero. If, as this point approaches, your health has deteriorated to such an extent that you can no longer obtain life insurance, you have no alternative but to meet the call for more money. In a worst-case scenario, if your resources also have decreased, you might find it difficult or impossible to meet the call and could lose your insurance coverage altogether.

Life insurance companies, insurance agents, and financial planners will have a great deal of difficulty explaining this situation to these policy owners. Policy owners should be encouraged to maintain at least adequate funding levels, and to overfund their contracts during good times when they have excess resources and the policy is a reasonable investment alternative.

The risks in universal life are as follows:

1. The interest earnings on the policy account will move up and down as market rates fluctuate.

2. The insurance companies can and will change mortality rates.

3. The insurance companies can and will change expense charges.

4. The policy requires policy owner management and continued vigilance.

5. Interest rates have moved from a cyclical high in December 1980 and have been moving lower ever since. You probably won't like your policy very much if it is paying no more than the minimum guaranteed interest

rate, which may be 3 or 4 percent. If the insurance company is maintaining a high interest rate, but paying out more than it is earning to do so, you won't like the policy for long either because that could cause company failure.

If you aren't aware of the risks in universal life or don't intend to deal with them, you probably would be better off with retail term life insurance.

If you look at the risks associated with universal life, you might conclude that this type of policy requires an inordinate amount of confidence in a company. The account from which you earn your interest is a part of the general account of the insurance company and could be frozen by the state insurance commissioner if the company has problems. This points out the importance of dealing with an investment-grade insurance company that is rated well by the various services. Criteria for company selection are covered more extensively in Chapter 15.

MANAGEMENT

To manage your policy, you need complete, accurate, and prompt reports on what is going on within the policy. Insurance companies have the technology to track and provide this data, so ask for a current report from your agent or company. It is your money.

INTEREST RATE ADVANTAGE

Insurance companies may be able to pay slightly higher than current market interest rates on the policy accounts within their universal life policies. They guarantee those rates for a 12-month period and can be fairly sure that most of the money on which they are paying interest will remain with the company for more than 1 year. If experience bears this out, the company will be able to lend out reserves of these policies for periods somewhat longer than 12 months and, as a result, earn a higher rate of return for you. You can expect universal life interest rates to track the interest rate you see in your newspaper for 3- to 5-year U.S. Treasury bonds.

Universal life is a *single-pocket* policy providing no investment flexibility. You may want to look at a *multiple-pocket* policy similar to your multiple-pocket 401(k) plan, so you can diversify for greater safety and a higher return.

MAXIMUM FUNDING LEVEL

If your universal life policy has proved to be a good place to store cash, if it has provided a competitive after-tax rate of return, you might maximum-fund it and run up against the maximum funding level. Your policy can accept only a limited amount of money if it is to retain the tax advantages of a life insurance policy. Contact your company to find out just how much is allowed. If you want to put more money in than code permits, you can ask the insurance company to increase your death benefit. This entails expenses, additional mortality costs, and proof of insurability. The increased death benefit will provide an increased maximum-funding level.

EXPENSES

Universal life is relatively new compared with whole life. But insurance companies and their personnel are learning how to manage this type of policy while being assisted by the improvements in technology. There is a possibility that the expenses associated with its management could go down. This will benefit us all—policy owners, companies, and intermediaries. The good news is that you can watch your expenses, and you should. Complain if they are no longer competitive, and if that doesn't work, consider moving to a better contract. Do it carefully with the help of your advisors if you are attempting to do a 1035 tax-free exchange.

MORTALITY COSTS

What about mortality? Will it continue to improve as shown in Exhibit 5.2, or will some new illness cause rates to go up to the maximum guaranteed by the contract? The AIDS threat, for example, has made insurance companies fear the latter. The risk of reduced returns as a result of increasing mortality costs is not unique to universal life. Higher death rates affect all insurance. Term rates can go up, and whole life dividends can be diminished.

The fact is that mortality rates have been coming down. We are expecting the industry to come out with a new mortality table soon. People are living longer, healthier lives. Think about how many centenarians you are aware of and understand that you could be in their ranks one day. The maturity value of your policy, its face amount or more, could be very important to you or your beneficiaries.

MANAGING THE DEATH BENEFIT

We have been talking about the premium associated with a universal life policy. You also have the ability to manage the amount at risk—the life insurance. You will be asked whether you want death benefit option A (sometimes referred to as option 1) or option B (or option 2) (see Exhibit 5.6). Option A is the conventional, whole life design, whereby the death benefit stays equal to the face amount you select when you purchase the policy (say, $100,000), in spite of the fact that the account within the policy grows. Therefore, if you die and the insurance company pays off the $100,000 required, that $100,000 would be partially your own account value money and partially insurance company money, i.e., life insurance. In effect, in an option A policy, every time you put money into the policy, or the account value grows as a result of interest earnings, the amount of life insurance is decreased. Alternatively, you could request option B (option 2), making the amount at risk a constant. That is, the insurance company promises to pay your beneficiary $100,000 of insurance company money (life insurance), in addition to the amount of money in your policy owner account. In most cases, when applying for one of these policies, you will want to keep the life insurance company at risk for the maximum amount, so that you will want to choose option B (option 2). In the future, when you are more concerned about expenses in the policy than in the death benefit, it would be logical to switch from option B (2) to option A (1). This would result in the total death benefit being leveled to the benefit in force at the time of the change. Thereafter, further increases in the account value would diminish the insurance company's amount at risk and thereby reduce mortality charges within the policy.

EXHIBIT 5.6

Death Benefit Options

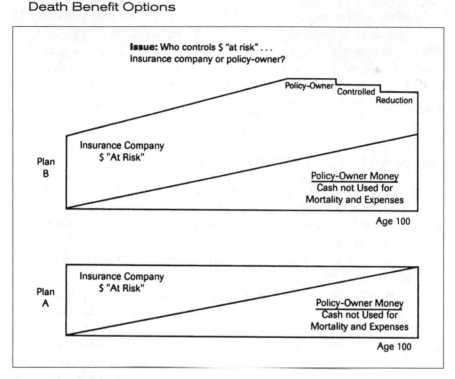

Source: Ben G. Baldwin, 1991.

You may come to a point where you want to decrease the mortality charges even more. In that case, you may request that the insurance company reduce the death benefit on your policy to the minimum amount possible. Do this with caution if you request such a reduction in the early years, because you may have to pay a partial surrender charge, or it might cause a force-out of money from within the policy which is likely to create an income tax liability. The insurance company will limit any death benefit reductions that would disqualify the policy as a life insurance policy under Internal Revenue Code Section 7702. With the minimum face amount, the minimum amount of investment return from the account value will be used to pay mortality charges, but the policy will remain a life insurance policy. Earnings will remain sheltered from income taxes, and the policy will serve primarily as an investment vehicle.

Very often we find the reverse scenario when working with young policy owners. A young couple gets married; both parties are working and are relatively independent of each other economically. They buy a universal life policy with a minimum face amount and adjust their premium payments to reach the desired funding level. At some future date, children come along, and one spouse becomes more economically dependent upon the other. In this case, the young marrieds may ask that the policy death benefit be increased. In many cases, this is far less expensive than applying for and starting a new insurance policy to increase coverage. In fact, if they had maximized the premium payment while both were working, they might now decrease their cashflow into the contract while increasing the amount at risk.

CONCLUSION

The key to a proper analysis of universal life insurance is having a breakdown of state premium taxes, expenses, amounts at risk, mortality charges, account values, interest earnings, and potential surrender charges. The insurance company providing the policy earns a profit (if it plans to stay in business) in a number of ways. It can profit on the expense charges by charging you more than it costs to administer the policy. There also has to be some sort of profit margin built into the mortality charges, so that the charge may be for more than the mortality being experienced at the current time. In addition, the company is paying you less interest than it is earning on the policy account and/or is charging investment management fees against your account. It is very important for you to have your policy with a profitable company so that the company continues to exist and service your policy for your lifetime.

BUT IS IT A GOOD INVESTMENT?

Generally speaking, does the account value within universal life policies provide an acceptable investment alternative to today's insurance buyer? Generally speaking, *no*, universal life is not an acceptable alternative for today's insurance buyer. The reasons and assumptions behind this generalization are as follows (also see Exhibit 5.7):

1. There are better contracts available as long as you are insurable and will have no trouble obtaining new insurance at acceptable rates.
2. You do not intend to commit suicide or commit fraud by giving false answers to any of the questions on any of the papers you complete to obtain a different policy.
3. On the basis of historical averages, you cannot expect the interest rates provided by the insurance companies to be more than 2 to 3 percent over the inflation rate.
4. An interest-only investment account provides insufficient investment diversification for large amounts of capital within a life insurance policy that is likely to be the longest-term investment capital that a policy owner will possess—lasting for the lifetime of the insured.
5. The insurance company creditor risk assumed when investing in the general account of an insurance company is unacceptable and unnecessary. Too many insurance companies have failed to survive as long as their insureds.
6. You do not have control over the investments in a universal life policy.
7. The policy is a single-pocket policy. It offers only the guaranteed interest account and provides no method of changing that investment if investment needs or desires change.

When is a universal life policy a good investment?

1. When it is doing what *you* want it to do
2. When it is providing an acceptable tax-free rate of return
3. When you already own it and your insurability status has deteriorated for *any* reason
4. When there is not an acceptable alternative

EXHIBIT 5.7

Term "Plus"–Mortality and Expenses "Plus" Additional Dollars for Investment

	General Description	Investment Vehicle	Investment Flexibility	Premium Flexibility	Face Amount Flexibility	Appropriate for
Universal life	Current interest rate; flexibility; transparency	Insurance company general account short-term interest investments	None; borrow or withdraw	Maximum; enough for mortality and expenses, or as much as the law allows	Maximum; increase or decrease— stay healthy for major increases	Variable needs, like short-term interest rate investments

Source: Ben G. Baldwin, 1990.

5. When the *guaranteed* minimum interest rate is a comfort to you

6. When it does not represent a significant investment to you

Caution: Do not act on any of this advice until you have thoroughly discussed it with your beneficiaries, your doctor, your tax and legal advisors, and your personal insurance and financial advisors.

CHAPTER 6

Variable Life Insurance

The Beginning—Life Insurance Meets Wall Street

*Kay purchased a variable life policy in
September 1981 for diversification, since she
already owned a number of whole life
policies. It outperformed all, even the best, of
her whole life policies.*

Variable life insurance was first brought to the marketplace in
the United States by the Equitable Life Assurance Society in 1976.
It took 4 years of development, negotiations with the Securities
and Exchange Commission (SEC), and the approval of the various
state insurance commissioners to bring this revolutionary product
to market. It was not until 4 years later that another company,
John Hancock, did the same, followed shortly thereafter by Monarch Life. Variable life insurance was slow to develop for a number
of reasons. First, the policy had to be registered under the Securities Act of 1933 as a security. Second, the agent selling it had to
be registered under the Securities and Exchange Act of 1934 and
had to pass the National Association of Security Dealers (NASD)
Series 6 Exam to obtain a license to sell it, and so early on, there
were very few agents properly licensed to sell it. Third, life insurance agents at the time were uncomfortable with securities.
They were used to guarantees, perceived that whole life offered
those guarantees, and therefore did not readily take to or feel comfortable with variable life.

It was in December 1976 that the SEC came out with Rule
6E-2, providing the limited exception from sections of the Investment Company Act of 1940, which gave this product life. This
rule (1) requires that insurance companies provide an accounting
to contract holders, (2) imposes *limitations on sales charges* (there

are no such SEC limitations on whole life or universal life), and (3) requires that the insurers offer refunds or exchanges to variable life purchasers under certain circumstances. Policy owners also must be offered the option of returning to a whole life–type policy.

Rule 6E-2 defines variable life insurance as a policy in which *the insurance element is predominant*, and the cash values are funded by the separate account of the life insurance company. The "separate account" is an account separate from the general account of the insurance company and *not* subject to the claims of the creditors of the insurance company. The separate account contains subaccounts that are similar to mutual funds. Death benefits and cash values vary to reflect investment experience of the policy owner-chosen subaccounts. The policy also must provide a minimum death benefit guarantee, and mortality and expense risks must be borne by the insurance company. The basic policy structure is similar to whole life insurance in that the stated face amount at a stated age requires a specific, level, fixed-premium payment. Once the policy is issued, the cash value of the contract increases or decreases daily depending on the investment results of the underlying investment funds. There is no guaranteed minimum below which that fund cannot fall. Fixed-premium variable life contracts do guarantee that the face amount will not go below the originally issued face amount, regardless of investment experience, and that only the guaranteed level premium will be required to keep the policy in force. If investment experience is positive, on the anniversary date of the policy, the face amount of the contract is adjusted upward, reflecting that investment experience. If negative, the death benefit will be adjusted downward, *but never below* the face amount of the original contract. The original variable life policies had only a money-market account and a common stock account available for investment.

POLICY LOANS IMPACT VARIABLE LIFE RETURNS

You affect the investment results of a variable policy by borrowing from it. By taking a policy loan, you collateralize the equity from the underlying investment accounts. When this happens, the insurance company moves an amount equal to what you have borrowed to a loan guarantee account not subject to market risk, where it will earn 1 or 2 percent less interest than you are paying for the loan. The collateralized equity will stay in that account, securing the loan, until such time as the loan is paid off. Therefore, if you borrow on the policy during a period of time when your chosen investment accounts are decreasing in value, you have avoided those potential losses. However, if you have borrowed on your policies during a period of time when your chosen accounts were appreciating, your policy loan has cost you not only the non-deductible loan interest on the loan but also the opportunity cost of what you would have gained on those accounts had you not borrowed.

20-PLUS YEARS OF INVESTMENT IN VARIABLE LIFE

The principal difference between whole life and variable life is that whole life offers but one investment opportunity, the general account—which is controlled by the insurance company. Variable life offers both a general account and a separate account alternative to be used at the ongoing discretion of the policy owner. In 1976 the concept of a separate account was a new legal entity to life insurance. Separate from what, you might ask. The answer to that is that it is separate from the general creditors of the life insurance company. The general account assets within an insurance company are subject to the general creditors of that company. If the insurance company gets into financial difficulties that require the state insurance commissioner to take over the company with the objective of trying to save the company, the first thing that the regulators do is to stop all payments except for death benefits. Neither creditors nor policy owners can have access to the general account assets until the state is satisfied that an adequate restoration plan is in place. Then funds may be paid out. This could mean that general account assets could be frozen for many years and the earnings during those years could be significantly reduced. Such a company shutdown can cost policy owners both peace of mind and money. The separate account is still owned by the insurance company; however, it is "separate" from the general account and specifically not subject to the claims of general creditors. Therefore, if an insurance company has financial difficulties, policy owners with assets in the separate accounts still can manage those assets among the subaccount investment alternatives, which are similar to mutual funds, and have access to the assets in the separate account via policy loan.

You will prefer the variable contract over the whole life contract if you want the capital in your policy invested in an assortment of subaccounts similar to mutual funds, rather than in a long-term bond and mortgage general account portfolio typical of a whole life policy. Fixed-premium variable life provides downside protection basically by guaranteeing that the face amount of the policy will never be less than the originally issued face amount no matter what the investment results are, as long as the scheduled premiums are paid. For a policy owner to have the insurance company guarantee the death benefit, the policy owner must guarantee the insurance company the payment of the required premiums.

When variable life was first introduced, critics questioned the competency of insurance companies to manage equity accounts. This criticism has been dealt with in two ways. One way has been to hire the best outside money managers available from the mutual fund world to manage similar subaccounts within life insurance policies. Insurance companies give the policy owner a number of choices among management firms with which they are familiar and which are well regarded. Policy owners find that they have two managers working for them in these policies. First, the insurance company searches the world for the best managers to manage the assets in the subaccounts and then performs the ongoing task of monitoring their performance and replacing the ones they find lacking. Then, for example, if the insurance company hires a Fidelity manager, Fidelity also is monitoring that manager and will work hard to make sure its best talent is managing the account. This gives the policy owner the opportunity to move money among the subaccounts of a policy without having to pay income taxes or expenses, and across fund families as provided within the contract by the manager of managers. This is almost impossible to do within taxable mutual fund accounts without exorbitant expense and taxation.

In addition to hiring outside money managers, the life insurance industry itself has been proved to have some of the best. Exhibit 6.1 presents the record of the first common stock fund placed in a variable policy. Tyler Smith of Equitable Life Assurance Society created this common stock fund on January 13, 1976, and managed it through the year 2000, a period of 24 years during which he provided Life Insurance investors in his fund an average annual compound rate of return of 14.62 percent.

Variable life provides the potential for future growth of the death benefit if the investment experience proves to be favorable. A LIMRA study entitled *The Performance of Variable Life* reported that only three companies sold equity-based variable life insurance before 1981. Variable life sales from 1976 to 1980 represented only about 1 percent of the life insurance market. By 1981 approximately 10 companies were selling the product, and market share increased to 2.5 percent of the ordinary life premium. LIMRA reported that variable life sales remained fairly flat at 3 percent in 1986. This seems a rather inauspicious beginning for the product born in 1976. Its growth was inhibited by the cost to the companies of the development of the product, the licensing requirements for agents, and the agents' discomfort with mutual fund products.

The key advantage of variable life is that you have the *ability to direct your account value* to the investment of choice from among those offered. Furthermore, a variety of new accounts constantly are being added to existing policies, giving policy owners more choice and opportunity for diversification. Even though higher expenses have been associated with first-generation variable life insurance policies, these policies have offered the highest net return available from a life insurance policy from 1976 to the present when the assets are invested in the common stock account.

These variable policies must be sold with a prospectus that divulges more information regarding the workings of a life insurance policy than ever before. The data have to be extracted from the prospectus to be useful, but you will find that the prospectus is a great source of readily available, quality information.

When these policies work efficiently, your investment in the contract provides you with life insurance protection, multiple subaccounts for your investment capital, professional management, and the ability to redirect your investments. All this can be

EXHIBIT 6.1

Annual Rates of Return for a Variable Life Insurance
Common Stock Account

Year Ending December 31	Common Stock
1976	9.2%*
1977	−9.2
1978	8.2
1979	29.8
1980	50.1
1981	−5.8
1982	17.6
1983	26.1
1984	−2.0
1985	33.4
1986	17.3
1987	7.5
1988	22.4
1989	25.6
1990	−8.1
1991	37.9
1992	3.2
1993	23.7
1994	−3.02
1995	31.26
1996	23.15
1997	28.06
1998	28.22
1999	24.07
2000	−14.03

*Unannualized from the inception date of January 13, 1976.

accomplished without incurring income tax liability as you move
your assets within the contract. The income tax shelter of the contract protects interest, dividends, and capital gains from current
income taxation. The sale of one fund and purchase of another
within the contract is *not a taxable event*. As a result, investment
strategies such as dollar cost averaging, asset allocation, and

rebalancing can be carried on without the expense, burden, and complication of income taxes that these same strategies would produce in taxable portfolios.

A distinctive feature of the fixed-premium variable life policy is that once you have purchased it, you cannot increase or decrease the contractual amount to be paid into it. It is designed to be a fixed-premium contract that may require anything from a single premium to a lifetime of level payments. The lifetime-of-payments feature can be considered an advantage since policy owners are required to keep up their premium payments, and thus their investments into the contract, which may be just the incentive many people need to continue investing. Too many people have interpreted the *flexibility-of-investment* feature in universal policies as *an excuse not to invest*. Instead, they choose to spend, which is often detrimental to their economic well-being.

The amount of life insurance in fixed-premium variable life is fixed at its minimum level upon the date of purchase. The face amount varies thereafter only as a result of positive and negative investment account results above the initial face amount. This policy offers a unique advantage in that even if investment results are disastrously poor, you will never be called upon to pay a larger premium than contracted for originally, nor can the face amount of your policy decrease below that at which you originally purchased it. This is unique to fixed-premium variable life.

While variable life policies have had positive investment results right from the start, the product, until recently, has been slow to catch on with the insurance companies, the public, the life insurance sales force, attorneys, accountants, bankers, and the financial planning and investment communities. Of the more than 1000 life insurance companies actively selling life insurance in the United States, only about 70 can be considered to be in the business of selling variable life insurance. Life insurance agents have been known to drag their feet when considering variable life because of their relatively conservative backgrounds and training, as well as the additional licensing and education required for selling this product. Investment advisors have been reluctant to recommend it, in spite of its long history of credible results, because many planners have their minds so set against *mixing insurance and investments* that they have not stopped to study it.

Surprisingly, lawyers, accountants, and bankers have resisted the use of variable life in helping their clients plan their estates. It is surprising because a tenet of their profession, the Prudent Investor Act, requires diversification, and no other type of life insurance contract allows diversification. The planning community will have to become more aware as more clients ask about it. You personally may have to encourage the planners to do so.

Variable life does require a level premium that is substantially higher than that required by a yearly renewable and convertible term insurance policy, and so the decision to invest that additional capital is an important one. Just as you inquire about expenses, management fees, and other factors when you decide to make an investment within a mutual fund, you will need to make similar inquiries when you are about to invest in variable life.

FIXED-PREMIUM VARIABLE LIFE— SPECIAL APPLICATIONS

Jack bought his $100,000 fixed-premium variable life policy in 1980 at the age of 42. His required monthly premium is $185, which he has maintained over the last 20 years. The policy has provided life insurance protection for his family, which increased over time to the current level of $219,910. He has borrowed on his policy at times to buy cars, to pay for college education for his children, etc., so its living values have served him well in times of need. The policy now has an asset value of $106,000. His investment of $185 per month has provided not only the benefits of a life insurance death benefit and cash without taxation in times of need, but also a compound net cash-on-cash rate of return of over 8 percent. Jack has said to me that if his bill of $185 per month had been optional (as in variable universal life) rather than fixed (as in variable life), he just might not have made the same effort to make the payment and thus might not be in the happy situation that he is in now. A required premium has served him well.

Single-premium variable life is one form of variable life that is very useful for what we might call *earmarked* money. That means the money is being set aside for a special person or reason, and that it is not to be delivered to that person until the insured's death. For example, Aunt Sue has $10,000 that she wants her niece to receive at her death. Where can she invest the $10,000 and have it compound for her lifetime without creating income taxes for someone, all the while having it private and knowing that it will go to her niece when the time comes? Investing the $10,000 in a single-premium variable life policy on her life with her niece named as the beneficiary will accomplish her purpose quietly and conveniently without legal documents or expense. The slippage, or expense, caused by the life insurance benefit cost may be no more than the income tax cost might have been if the money had been invested in taxable mutual funds.

Fixed-premium variable life lacks flexibility of premium and face amount. Variable universal life, introduced in 1985, brought both flexibility of premium and death benefits to the variable life policy.

As we discuss variable universal life insurance in the following chapters, keep in mind that when you move from a fixed-premium variable life contract to a variable universal life contract, you are exposing yourself to an additional downside risk. You may have to pay a higher premium to keep the variable universal life contract in force than the guaranteed level premium in a variable life policy if expenses and mortality costs increase to the maximum contractually allowable level and investment results are negative.

BUT IS IT A GOOD INVESTMENT?

Generally speaking, do variable life policies provide an acceptable investment alternative for today's insurance buyer? The rule of thumb is yes, variable whole life is an acceptable alternative for today's insurance buyer. Implicit in the assumption that it could be good for you are the following considerations (see also Exhibit 6.2):

1. You are insurable. You will have no trouble obtaining a new variable life insurance policy at acceptable rates.
2. You do not intend to commit suicide or perjure yourself by giving fraudulent information on any of the papers you complete to obtain a policy.

EXHIBIT 6.2

Term "Plus"—Mortality and Expenses "Plus" Additional Dollars for Investment

	General Description	Investment Vehicle	Investment Flexibility	Premium Flexibility	Face Amount Flexibility	Appropriate for
Variable life	You direct the investment	Common stock, bond funds, guaranteed interest rates, zero coupons, money markets, etc.	Maximum. Your decision; split it, move it, etc.	None. Fixed premium; single or remains level; loans available	None. Want more? Buy new, *if* you can pass a physical	Long-term investors; an alternative to buying term and investing the difference

3. The creditor risk of the insurance company as it relates to the death benefit and to any general account investment alternatives is not a concern for you.
4. The policy provides you with sufficient control over the investment.
5. The policy is a multiple-pocket policy (provides a variety of investment alternatives).
6. The policy is inflexible with regard to premium payment and face amount, and this limitation is considered desirable or acceptable to you.

When is a variable life policy a good investment?

1. When it is doing what *you* want it to do
2. When it is providing an acceptable tax-free rate of return
3. When you already own it and your insurability status has deteriorated for any reason
4. When there is not an acceptable alternative

Caution: Do not act on any of this advice until you have thoroughly discussed it with your beneficiaries, your doctor, your tax and legal advisors, and your personal insurance and financial advisors.

CHAPTER 7

Variable Universal Life Expenses

Much Ado about Nothing

Not everything that can be counted counts, and not everything that counts can be counted.

ALBERT EINSTEIN

Mark called from Germany. He said his friend, who is a pilot, says that he senses VUL is not a good deal because he has read and heard that it is expensive.

We suggested to Mark that he ask his pilot friend if the engines on his airplane were expensive, and why, and if he wanted the company to use cheaper engines. As you might expect, he responded that the expensive engines were more reliable and that, while engine expense is important, keeping the plane in the air is more important.

We suggested that Mark explain to his pilot friend, "It's the engine, dummy!" The extra administrative expense in VUL is for the engine; and while engine expense is a consideration, getting the policy to a profitable destination is more important.

PROLOGUE

Variable universal life is the reason this book exists. In the spirit of total disclosure, this author considers variable universal life to be *the financial product of the century*, a veritable financial Swiss Army knife of financial products, a product that is capable of helping almost everyone. In over 36 years of helping people attain financial independence, no financial product has been able to do so much, so efficiently, for so many. Like a Swiss Army knife, it is a very versatile tool; however, also like a Swiss Army knife, if you use it improperly, or for something it was not designed to do, it can injure your financial health instead of improving it.

It is the most efficient life insurance and investment product for the consumer if used correctly and for those specific purposes for which it is meant. It is efficient in that, generally speaking, costs are competitive and investments are tax-sheltered, diversified, and productive. That is a pretty big statement and one that certainly has been contradicted in the popular press. What follows here are the reasons for this conclusion and the tools that will allow you to determine if this product can help you.

QUESTIONS AND ANSWERS: IS VUL FOR YOU?

You have a very short list of questions to answer to determine if a variable universal life insurance product is efficient for *you*.

1. Are the term life insurance costs (mortality costs) of the product competitive and acceptable to you? This depends upon your insurability. Get a no-cost offer for you after an insurance company physical.

2. Are the expenses associated with the contract acceptable? Do you expect them to be offset by the income tax savings on your investment capital and the income tax and transaction cost savings as you move money among the various subaccounts (similar to mutual funds, but they are inside a life insurance policy) within the contract?

3. Is this a profitable product to the issuing company? If it is not, the company will not support that product for long, so you want a well-run insurance company that makes a profit on what it sells to you so that your product continues to be well supported.

4. Is the subaccount family within your contract broad enough and performing well enough that it is likely to provide good investment opportunities for the rest of your life?

5. Do you expect to maximum-fund the policy as soon and as often as practical and possible for you? Remember,

the cost-benefit ratio of this product works best when you maximum-fund your policy.

Those are the questions, and it is not difficult to come up with the answers. Do not accept inaccurate generalizations such as those published in *The Wall Street Journal* of August 12, 1993, such as "It's the most expensive form of insurance you can buy." Such statements from your standpoint, that of the consumer, focus on costs and ignore value. Or "Annual costs may exceed four percent of your investment in some policies." Now how can that make sense when the writer has no idea how much money you intend to invest in your contract? If you invest very little, the expenses could be four times the amount of your investment rather than 4 percent of your investment. If you choose to invest a great deal, your expenses may amount to only ½ half of 1 percent of your investment. It is up to you, isn't it? Let's talk the basics of the policy, and then let's deal with the relative value of investment-oriented life insurance.

THE BASICS

Variable universal life insurance is created from a combination of universal and variable life. Universal life provides the policy chassis that we discussed in Chapter 5, and variable life provides the chassis that brings with it investment flexibility, described in Chapter 6. The combination of these two policy designs has created a life insurance policy that is absolutely unique in what it is able to do for you over a lifetime. The features of a variable universal life policy are:

- *Complete transparency.* You are shown the specific expense charges, the costs deducted for the amount at risk, the life insurance, the specific account value, the charges against that account, and the amount of gain or loss on the account value.
- *Ability to vary and skip premiums.* It is easy to identify the minimum amount that can be paid into the policy in order to keep it in force. All you have to do is determine the expenses that the policy will incur for the year, and make sure they are covered either by paying in enough to

cover them or by using capital or the earnings from the policy asset value. The insurance company will provide you with the maximum amount that can be put into a policy—that amount is stipulated in Section 7702 of the Internal Revenue Code.

- *Flexibility of death benefit.* If the policy owner wants to increase the amount at risk (life insurance), the insurance company will ask the policy owner to provide evidence of insurability (medical, personal, and financial) of the insured. The policy owner then must be willing to pay the increased cost of insurance for the increased amount at risk. A decrease in the amount of life insurance, or amount at risk, merely requires a request, and the COIs will decrease with the decrease in coverage.

- *Death benefit options A and B.* A policy owner may choose death benefit option A (1) or B (2) and, in most cases, may change from one option to the other by making a written request to the insurance company. Under option A at the insured's death, the beneficiary receives the contracted amount, the face amount of the contract. The option A death benefit is the sum of the amount at risk at the time of death and the cash value or account value. Alternatively, using option B, the policy owner stipulates that the amount at risk is not to decrease as the cash or account value increases. At the insured's death, the death benefit will be the entire, originally contracted for, amount at risk (face amount) plus the account value at the time of death. In some policies you will find options C and D. Option C will pay the beneficiary the contracted amount at risk plus the return of all that has been paid in premium, rather than account value. Option D is a specific increase in the amount at risk over a period of years until the amount at risk is double the original amount. There probably will be other alternatives, so watch for them.

- *Right to withdraw account value.* Prior to the introduction of universal life, the only way for a policy owner to get money out of an ongoing policy was to borrow from the policy. That is, the policy owner would ask the insurance company for a loan using the policy as collateral. The insurance company would lend the money, typically at an interest rate between 5 and 8 percent, and put a lien against the policy until the loan was paid off. If death or policy termination occurred prior to the loan being paid off, the insurance company would subtract the amount owed and pay out the balance. In policies that have dividends (participating policies), the dividend credits always can be taken in cash. However, that is not the same as the contractual right to withdraw. The universal life policy design is the only design that allows a policy owner to withdraw account value at the policy owner's option.

- *General and separate account investment choices.* The variable portion of the chassis provides the availability of the insurance company separate account with its subaccount investment alternatives. This makes ongoing diversification and adaptability available as a contractual feature of the contract. General account–only policies require the policy owner to make an irrevocable decision at policy inception to use the general account, and *only the general account*, for the lifetime of the insured, or the policy.

In short, VUL provides flexibility of face amount, premium payments or *amount to be invested*, and investment choice. This combined flexibility makes it a unique life insurance policy with capabilities to adapt that do not exist in other forms of investment-oriented life insurance.

Whole life insurance dictates the investment vehicle, premium amount, and face amount. It leaves little room for change. In 1976 variable life came along and allowed the policy owner to dictate the investment vehicle but continued to insist upon a level face amount and a level premium payment throughout the policy lifetime. In 1979 universal life came along and gave the public the investment vehicle it seemed to want at that time—a money-market type of account. Universal life allowed the policy owner to decide on the amount of the premium, within certain parameters, and permitted the policy owner to change the level of the policy face amount and the amount of premium to suit personal objectives over time. Since 1981, the consumer has seen the rate of return diminish on interest rate–sensitive accounts and has become increasingly disenchanted with interest-only contracts.

Variable universal life generates new enthusiasm because it is not only a fifth-generation variable life policy, but also a fifth-generation universal life policy. You can go into a variable universal policy and have its performance emulate that of the old universal life—just use the guaranteed-interest account available within the contract as your only investment. In fact, in spite of the fact that it costs the insurance company more to administrate a VUL policy than it does a UL policy, you may find that the expenses and back-end loads are lower in some variable universal policies than they are in universal life. A variable universal policy may make a more cost-effective universal life policy (using just the guaranteed-interest account) than a regular universal life policy. At the same time, the VUL policy allows the policy owner to change how the capital in the policy is invested in the future without having to qualify for a new policy or incur additional expenses.

TRANSFERRING THE REINS TO THE POLICYHOLDER

The three strings of insurance company control—investment vehicle, face amount, and premium payment—are transferred to the policy owner in a variable universal policy. The policy owner controls the face amount, premium allocation, and investment. You may direct the insurance company to bill you a certain amount at specific times, to increase or decrease your face amount, to change the allocation of incoming deposits in the various investment accounts, and to move existing investment from one policy subaccount to another. You may make withdrawals and/or borrow, using your policy as collateral. In some policies, you may be able to specify the account that is to be charged for the expense and mortality costs.

Pruco Life, a subsidiary of Prudential Life, was the first to market a variable universal life product in 1985, closely followed by Equitable Life in 1986. By 2000, the product has reached critical mass. There are many more products available to the consumer, and more respected companies are offering them. VUL has proved that it can be a profitable product for the policy owner and the company offering it. And you want the VUL product you purchase to be a profitable product for the company from which you purchase it, because for the product to serve you well for the rest of your life, it is essential that the company stand behind it. Unprofitable products are not supported and eventually will be eliminated from the company menu of products.

There are now information services—such as Morningstar of Chicago; *VARDS Reports* from Financial Planning Resources of Marietta, Georgia; and CDA Weisenberg—that provide up-to-date information on both the companies providing these products and the performance of the underlying investment accounts.

FINANCIAL EVALUATION OF VARIABLE UNIVERSAL LIFE

Financial evaluation of a variable universal life policy is very similar to the process followed for universal life. It requires an illustration using an agreed-upon premium and a specified assumed rate of return to produce a year-by-year illustration to age 95. The illustration will show the point in time when back-end loads are no longer a factor, and the possible failure of the policy if the chosen premium results in a policy that is underfunded. The "guaranteed" illustration shows the downside risk if the insurance company increases its expense-loading or mortality costs to the maximum allowable under the contract. The rate of return illustrated on the account values within the contract should be the rate *you* consider conservatively sustainable in the future.

Exhibit 7.1 is an actual annual report on the inner workings of a VUL policy. You want to be able to identify charges for state premium taxes, expenses and administrative charges, and mortality charges. When ordering illustrations from the insurance company, take advantage of breakpoints (face amount levels at which mortality or expense charges decline). Life insurance can be like doughnuts by the dozen, cheaper per $1000 when you buy larger face amounts.

EXHIBIT 7.1

Specimen Variable Universal Annual Report

SUMMARY OF POLICY VALUES

	09/19/99	02/18/00
Policy Values as of:		
Face Amount	$500,000.00	$500,000.00
Death Benefit	$921,181,38	$1,125,188.60
Death Benefit Option	B	B
Policy Account Value	$421,181.36	$625,188.50
Less:		
Surrender Charge	$0.00	$0.00
Outstanding Loan	$0.00	$0.00
Net Cash Surrender Value	$421,181.35	$625,188.50

SUMMARY OF POLICY ACCOUNT ACTIVITY

Opening Policy Account Value as of 09/19/99	$421,181.36
Premiums	$130,000.00
Withdrawals	$0.00
Insurance Costs	($5,273.52)
Other Charges	($722.00)
Investment Gain/(Loss)	$80,002.66
Ending Policy Account Value as of 09/18/00	$625,188.50

EXHIBIT 7.1 Continued

SUMMARY OF POLICY ACCOUNT VALUES BY INVESTMENT FUND AS OF 09/18/00

	Amount	Units	Unit Price	Rate of Return	Allocations for	
					Premiums	Deductions
Guaranteed Interest Account—Unloaned <<	$47,915.26	N/A	N/A	N/A	0%	100%
Alliance Common Stock	$69,219.61	74,185	933,065	10.03%	0%	0%
Alliance Equity Index	$11,402.59	34,889	326,829	7.94%	0%	0%
Alliance Global	$82,037.68	177,659	461,770	13.57%	0%	0%
Alliance Growth & Income	$41,101.60	145,383	282,712	17.96%	0%	0%
EQ/Alliance Premier Growth	$140,638.84	1,164,458	120,776	17.30%	0%	0%
Alliance Small Cap Growth	$52,646.28	268,583	196,015	64.32%	34%	0%
MFS Emerging Growth Companies	$123,877,31	455,438	271,996	41.08%	33%	0%
MFS Research	$12,912.04	88,839	187,568	23.91%	0%	0%
FI Small/Mid Cap Value	$43,437.29	421,987	102,935	3.55%	33%	0%
Policy Account Value	$625,188.50				100%	100%

<<Guaranteed Interest Account transfers are subject to the limitations outlined in the product prospectus.

EXHIBIT 7.1 Continued

SUMMARY OF TRANSACTIONS FOR YEAR ENDING 09/18/00

Effective Date	Premium Payments			Other Transactions		Month/Day	Monthly Deductions		Policy Values	
	Total	Charges	Net Premium	Type	Amount		Insurance Costs	Admin Charge	Investment Gain/(Loss)	Policy Account
						Sep 19	$439.46	$6.00	$0.00	$420,735.90
						Oct 19	$439.46	$6.00	($17,603.39)	$402,687.05
						Nov 19	$439.46	$6.00	$57,153.02	$459,394.61
						Dec 19	$439.46	$6.00	$8,558.09	$467,507.24
						Jan 19	$439.46	$6.00	$23,157.12	$490,218.90
02/07/00	$120,000.00	$600.00	$119,400.00			Feb 19	$439.46	$6.00	($7,589.45)	$501,583.99
02/25/00	$10,000.00	$50.00	$9,950.00			Mar 19	$439.46	$6.00	$41,581.92	$652,670.45
						Apr 19	$439.46	$6.00	($38,415.39)	$613,809.60
						May 19	$439.46	$6.00	($21,336.58)	$592,027.56
						Jun 19	$439.46	$6.00	$52,132.86	$643,714.96
						Jul 19	$439.46	$6.00	$5,513.61	$648,783.11
						Aug 19	$439.46	$6.00	($2,081.72)	$646,255.93
						Sep 18			($21,067.43)	$626,188.50
Total	$130,000.00	$650.00	$129,350.00		$0.00		$5,273.52	$72.00	$80,002.66	

For policy year beginning 09/19/00, the estimated monthly cost of insurance charge is $481.82 and the estimated monthly expense charge is $8.00

The primary function of the illustration when you are buying a policy is to identify and quantify costs so that you can determine if they are acceptable to you and are competitive in the marketplace. Insurance companies can adjust costs on existing policies within certain limits, and so it is inevitable that the costs presented in the "current" portion of the illustration (which means that they represent what the insurance company is currently charging) will change during your lifetime. The assumptions in the illustration will not happen as presented. The illustrations are allowed by the regulators to compound those errors at interest rates up to 12 percent. The 12 percent maximum allowable interest rate may be used in an illustration being presented to you to appeal to your greed factor. You like to look at the part of the illustration that shows how much money you might have in your policy in the future. Just understand that the only way that illustration could represent the actual performance of the policy would be for all the assumptions to be absolutely accurate. Who has a crystal ball? It will not happen! Glenn S. Daily, a fee-only insurance consultant specializing in life insurance and annuities, was asked by a client to help obtain the best policy at the lowest cost. Daily responded, "The future hasn't happened yet, so no one knows which policy will be the best."

Now, you want to look at the part of the illustration marked "Guaranteed." The illustration identifies the maximum costs that can be charged in the "Guaranteed" section of the illustration. Compare the generous number you were so enthusiatic about under the 12 percent current costs, column with the zero percent guaranteed column for that same year. It would not be unusual if that zero percent guaranteed column showed a zero value. The illustration is telling you accurately that you may have a big number or that you may have no number. Let's determine how you can make sure that your policy is as successful as it can possibly be.

The illustration has done its job if it has identified costs in the early years of the policy (when the assumed costs are most likely to be accurate) with the assumptions that you asked be used in the illustration. Your first job is to determine if those charges are acceptable to you and are competitive in the marketplace.

After-Tax Term or Pretax Term

Exhibit 7.2 provides a list of the various costs of term insurance for a male, age 50. You will note that the term rate within the variable universal policy for a 50-year-old nonsmoking male is $4.68 per $1000 per year, which is $3.66 per $1000 per year more than the $1.02 cost of retail yearly renewable and convertible term insurance for a nonsmoking male. Column B makes the assumption that this purchaser is in the 30 percent marginal income tax bracket. The numbers given in column B indicate how much money the individual *must earn* to pay the amount required in column A. This points out that the mortality charge within the variable universal life policy is being paid with the pretax earnings on the investment within the contract. It also points out that insurance companies expect to pay death claims under variable universal life policies, whereas they do no expect to pay death claims under term insurance. Insureds terminate term insurance during life. Less than 1 percent of term policies stay in force long enough to pay death claims.

Using this procedure and applying it to your personal situ-

EXHIBIT 7.2

Cost of Term Insurance
Male, Age 50

Scale	Column A Annual Cost per $1000	Column B Col. A ÷ 1(1−0.30)= Pretax Earnings Necessary to Service Premium (30% Tax Bracket)
American Experience Table	$13.78	
Commissioners 1958 Table	12.32	
Commissioners 1958 Table	8.32	
Commissioners 1980 Table	6.71	
Variable Universal	4.68	4.68
Cheap term, smoker	2.97	4.24
Cheap term, nonsmoker	1.02	1.46
One-year term (cheapest)	0.83	1.19

ation, you can decide which is the most efficient and practical way to pay for and maintain your desired insurance protection. If you decide to use VUL—buying term insurance using untaxed investment earnings is an efficient method—then you can evaluate the investment alternatives and flexibility available within the various policies and choose one appropriate to your needs. Check the track records of the subaccounts available within the policies you are considering.

You also will want to identify and match your investment objectives with the proper investment alternatives and investment managers in your policy.

EXPENSES IN VARIABLE UNIVERSAL LIFE

"Ben, why should I read all this? I just saw in the *Wall Street Journal* that variable life is the most expensive form of insurance you can buy!"

It is appropriate that we address the fact that the media emphasize the expenses when they have anything to say about VUL. What is true in what they say, and how does what they say mislead the consumer?

What can be said with great accuracy is that there are more expenses itemized in VUL than in any other policy. Remember, however, that having more listed expenses does not mean that the policy costs more. It is also fair to say that it costs more for an insurance company to administer a variable universal life policy than a whole life, universal life, or even a fixed-premium variable life. But that does not prove that VUL costs more than the other forms of investment-oriented life insurance. You, the consumer, consider insurance company margin (profit) and the expenses of the overall management of the company as an expense to you. You do not get what the company keeps. The insurance company's board of directors meets each year and decides how much of the general account surplus can be distributed in dividends to policy owners of whole life contracts, and how much excess interest may be paid to policy owners of universal life policies. The more they give back, the lower your cost. Determining if the "give-back" will make the expenses in these contracts less than the itemized and disclosed costs of VUL is very difficult, since it depends upon future, unknown events. Exhibit 7.3 presents a procedure that you might use to determine the relative cost to you of the various investment-oriented types of life insurance. The exhibit has been filled in with generic information, which you would replace with information specifically applicable to you.

We may conclude from this exhibit that, for the policies compared, expenses during this period from the consumers' standpoint are highest in whole life and lowest in universal life, and the expenses in variable universal life are in between the two. A policy owner will want to consider what the approximately $20,000 of capital in any one of these policies in the tenth year is likely to do in the future. In whole life and universal life, the board of directors of the insurance company will allocate dividends and excess interest as dictated by company circumstances and the economic and regulatory environment. The investment results to be shared are from a general account portfolio, which is allocated 95 percent to bonds and mortgages and 5 percent to stock. The policy

EXHIBIT 7.3

Cost to the Consumer of Investment-Oriented Life Insurance

Assumes the amount of premium paid into each policy is equal to the required premium of the whole life policy for a 45-year-old, nonsmoking male, which is $2000. Uses current nonguaranteed projections from illustrations with differing underlying assumptions.* The interest rate assumption used in the universal life policies was 6.7%.

	Whole Life	Universal Life	Variable Life	Variable Universal Life
End of year 2 cash surrender value as a percent of premium paid	0%	33%	57%	55%
End of year 5 cash surrender value as a percent of premium paid	53%	78%	72%	77%
End of year 10 cash surrender value as a percent of premium paid	87%	114%	81%	97%

*This exhibit is not carried beyond 10 years because the credibility of all illustrations deteriorates beyond year 1 and gets less and less credible as the time frame is extended.

owner must accept the decisions made by the board of directors every year for the lifetime of the insured. In variable life products, the policy owner selects the general or subaccounts to be used, and the investment results of those decisions are passed directly to the policy owner, net of the insurance company's expenses. These expenses, which are identified in the prospectus for the product, averaged 1.55 percent in the over 5162 subaccounts inside VUL policies tracked by Morningstar on December 31, 2000.

Another way to look at the costs in investment types of life insurance policies is shown in Exhibit 7.4. Exhibit 7.5 is a summary of all the VUL charges that we will discuss in detail.

The three elements of investment-type life insurance—expense, mortality, and investment—vary in degree of importance. As Exhibit 7.6 shows, the investment element is the part of the policy that has the greatest impact on your economic well-being. It can make a relatively expensive policy, such as the first

EXHIBIT 7.4

Relative Cost to the Consumer

	Whole Life	Universal Life	Variable Life	Variable Universal Life
Expenses and fees to administer	Lowest	Higher than whole life	Higher than universal life	Highest
Cost of insurance	Not disclosed	Disclosed/ compare	Not disclosed	Disclosed/ compare
Margin/ company profit	Not disclosed	In disclosed costs and spread on interest rate	Not disclosed	In disclosed costs and spread on interest rate
Less positive returns from investment engine	Typical allocation—a long-term bond account. Typically, 95% long-term bond, 5% stock	Returns typically track 3- to 5- year Treasury notes	Portfolio dictated and diversified portfolio by policy owner	Portfolio dictated and diversified portfolio by policy owner
Expected average return	Discuss with your advisor	Discuss with your advisor	Discuss with your advisor	Discuss with your advisor

EXHIBIT 7.5

Variable Universal Expense Summary

From What You Pay into the Policy

	Low	Average	High
Sales charges	0%	8%	10%
State premium taxes	0.75%	2%	5%
DAC tax	0%	1.5%	2%
First-year expense	$200	$300–$400	$700

From Your Policy Account (Itemized Charges)

	Low	Average	High
Ongoing administration fees	$4 per month	$5–$7 per month	$15 per month
Fees for services Cost per Move	$0	Limited number free	$25 per move
Moves per year	4 per year	4 to 12	Unlimited
Policy loans	75% CSV,* 4% spread	90% CSV, 1–2% spread	100% CSV, 0% spread
Withdrawals	Cannot withdraw	90% CSV, $25 per charge	75% CSV, 4% spread
Surrender charges	None	10- to 15-year/ disappearing	% of account value

Asset Charges against Subaccounts (Gross Return Less Asset Charges Equals Net Return)

	Low	Average	High
Mortality and expense charge	0.4%	0.72%	1.3%
Investment management	0.4%	0.80%	2.8%
Contract administration charge	0%	0%	0.3%
Overall expense ratio	1%	1.55%	4.4%

*Cash surrender value.

EXHIBIT 7.6

The Life Policy Recipe

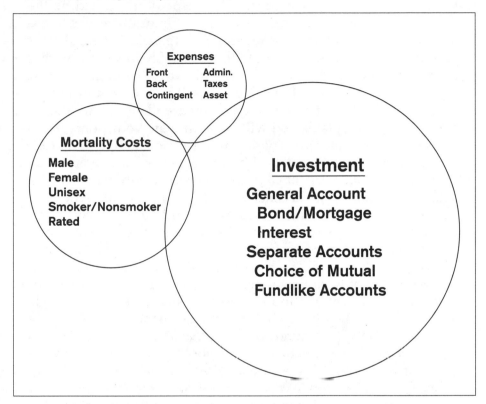

Expenses

Front	Admin.
Back	Taxes
Contingent	Asset

Mortality Costs

Male
Female
Unisex
Smoker/Nonsmoker
Rated

Investment

General Account
Bond/Mortgage
Interest
Separate Accounts
Choice of Mutual
Fundlike Accounts

generation of variable life in 1976, outperform its less expensive competitors by a substantial margin. Those first 1976 variable life policies did just that by investing in the stock subaccounts. Those first-generation variable life policies, even though they would be considered high-expense policies, have done more for their policy owners than all the whole life and universal life policies issued at that time. The death benefits and asset values of these policies have more than doubled, while the competing whole life and universal life have lagged behind. Profitable insurance companies (the only kind you want to do business with) exercise long-term control over the expenses and the mortality charges (COIs) in their VUL policies to make sure that the companies remain profitable and that their VUL policies remain competitive. The mortality cost, which is the cost of the life insurance, while controlled by the insurance company, is accepted or rejected by the policy owner by either maximizing the amount of life insurance or minimizing it, or even terminating or replacing the policy. If you are in good health and able to qualify for insurance with a carrier of your choice, you can and will leave the company that chooses not to be competitive. However, if you are not insurable, if your health has deteriorated, then you are likely to find the increased costs acceptable and will not terminate your policy. Consequently, the company whose costs are not competitive suddenly will find that all the healthy insureds are leaving and only those in ill health are staying. This causes death claims to increase, profitability to decline, and new business to cease. The company that chooses the high-expense-and-mortality-cost strategy will end up destroying profitability rather than enhancing it.

Expenses are important, but the media put so much emphasis on them that many people become paralyzed or wallow around in a potpourri of what they perceive as low-load or no-load products improperly applied to their situations. This is where people lose the most—they think they are saving money by not paying for any help. Keep in mind that even *the best* often hire coaches to help them do even better. Many people, who are perfectly capable of exercising on their own, hire personal trainers to help them do it better. Money coaches or personal money trainers can do as much for your finances as a personal trainer can do for your body. Don't be afraid to hire someone who is paid by commissions but who understands VUL. That way if he or she is not able to help you, you don't pay. But meanwhile it's important to obtain the necessary information to determine the competitiveness of a VUL policy.

TARGET PREMIUM

Target premium is a premium dollar amount, and you will find references to it over and over again as you examine sales loads, surrender charges, and commissions. It is also an amount that is considered to be the average minimum level amount you should pay into a VUL policy to have it funded well enough to work beneficially for you. In whole life or fixed-premium variable life, the insurance company mandates a specific premium. However, in universal life and variable universal life, since you have the right to put into the policy what you wish, the insurance company sets a "target premium." You can expect the target premium to be approximately 75 percent of the fixed premium requirement for the same insured and policy face amount in a fixed premium policy. When you are considering the feasibility of a VUL policy, it's a good idea to make sure that the target premium, rounded up to the nearest $100 or $1000, is an amount with which you can live comfortably. The basic target premium for insurance companies licensed in New York State is the premium level on which commissions are calculated on flexible premium contracts as determined by the Commissioner of the State of New York. Normally, in New York State the commission allowed on this type of policy is about 50 percent of the target premium, plus 4 percent of payments in excess of the target premium. Insurance companies not under the jurisdiction of the New York State Insurance Department may pay commissions up to 100 percent of target premium. Renewal commissions based upon your continued investment into your policy for years 2 through 10 average approximately 4 percent of premium paid, and for the eleventh year and thereafter, 2 percent. The 2 percent is a transferable service fee payable to the agent that provides the policy owner with service and currently is applicable only to new money being paid into the contract. These commissions are paid out of the expenses you pay to the insurance company. You will note that what the insurance company deducts from what you pay into your policy in the first year may be insufficient to cover the commission paid to the agent. The insurance company advances the commissions to the agent and then amortizes those expenses out of what the company earns in future years on your policy. Commissions also are paid to the agent when you request an increase in the face amount of the policy.

There has been, and continues to be, a movement toward reducing sales loads and redesigning commissions. There are those who think that a movement away from high first-year and low renewal commissions would create a healthier environment for the insurance industry. The movement toward more level commissions and commissions based upon the asset value of your policy (a percentage of the capital in your policy each year) may be better in the long run for salespeople, the insurance company, and you. With these policies, the help of a knowledgeable agent in managing your policy profitably can be invaluable, and you want that help to continue. But if an agent's commissions are based upon the money being put into the policy, and you choose not to put any more into the contract or if the policy cannot accept any more money, the agent won't earn commissions and thus will not be able to afford to service your policy. In the long run, agents cannot spend time doing what they are not paid to do. Another possibility is that one day there will be sufficient choice among low-load products so that VUL policies will be sold by agents but serviced by your financial planner, who would incorporate the contract into your overall financial plan and to whom you would pay a fee for service.

The target premium on your policy is determined when your policy is issued. It is based upon your age, sex, smoker (non-smoker) status, and policy face amount. The insurance company will give you this all-important number. You will want to read your contract and prospectus to find the limitations on various expenses based upon target premium so that you can calculate the dollar amount of those costs and determine how they will affect the performance of your policy. If you were about to buy a $100,000 VUL policy, the premiums in Exhibit 7.7 are the approximate target premiums, the amount per $100,000 with which you should feel comfortable and be confident you will be able to invest each year (with the understanding that more and sooner is better for you). The columns under "Seven-Pay Premiums" show the maximum amount you would want to invest each year in your VUL policy. Ask the insurance company to give you its unique target and seven-pay premiums specifically for your situation. Exceeding the seven-pay maximums would cause you to lose some of the income tax benefits of your policy that you will not want to lose—but more on that later. (See Chapter 8 under "Modified Endowment Insurance" for a complete explanation of the seven-pay limitations.)

EXHIBIT 7.7

Approximate Target Premium and Seven-Pay Premium
Examples $100,000

Issue Age	Target Premium, Preferred Nonsmoker		Seven-Pay Premium, Preferred Nonsmoker	
	Male	Female	Male	Female
15	$500	$400	$2,000	$1,700
20	$600	$500	$2,300	$2,000
25	$700	$600	$2,700	$2,400
30	$800	$700	$3,200	$2,800
35	$1,000	$800	$3,800	$3,400
40	$1,200	$1,000	$4,500	$4,000
45	$1,500	$1,200	$5,300	$4,700
50	$2,000	$1,500	$6,300	$5,500
55	$2,500	$1,900	$7,400	$6,500
60	$3,300	$2,500	$8,700	$7,600
65	$4,400	$3,200	$10,000	$9,000
70	$5,200	$4,100	$12,000	$10,000
75	$5,700	$5,300	$14,000	$12,000
80	$6,300	$6,000	$17,000	$15,000

EXPENSES CHARGED AGAINST YOUR MONEY AS IT COMES IN

Expenses in variable universal exist at both the policy and investment account levels. This section deals with the expenses you incur before your money gets to the policy investment choices. These are insurance company charges that cover its costs, commissions to intermediaries, company profit provisions, etc.

Front Sales Load

This is an expense charged against money being deposited into the policy (see Exhibit 7.8). You can expect to pay 8 percent, and with luck you may find a policy that drops the charge after some stipulated sum has been paid. At the low end, some policies

EXHIBIT 7.8

Front Sales Load

Low	Average	High
0%	8%	10%

charge no front-end sales load, whereas some charge front-end loads of up to 10 percent.

State Premium Taxes

You will not be the first to be surprised (and annoyed) to find that taxes will get you even when you pay premiums into your life insurance. These taxes are state and other area premium taxes, and they are deducted from every dollar you pay into a policy. Exhibit 7.9 shows the premium taxes for every state and for Washington, D.C., Guam, Puerto Rico, and the U.S. Virgin Islands.

Some variable universal life policies don't specifically identify this tax. It may just be included as part of the front-end sales charge, e.g., 6 percent for the company and 2 percent for the state, for a total of 8 percent of your investment. Insurance companies used to specify the state (or area) premium tax and charge the state-specific amount against your incoming money. For example, if you lived in Illinois it would charge you 0.5 percent; if you lived in Nevada, it would charge you 3.5 percent. Things changed when the financial press complained about all the expenses in VUL by referring to the number of expenses itemized in VUL in comparison to other life insurance policies, which do not happen to set out each one of their expenses. The insurance companies reacted by trying to slim down the number of expenses that they identify, so that now, very frequently, they just lump the premium tax in with the front-end load charge. Many companies also have moved toward a flat amount for the tax in every area, such as 2½ percent. This disadvantages those consumers who live in places where the premium tax is low, such as Illinois, but is an advantage to those who live in places that have

EXHIBIT 7.9

Premium Taxes as of 2000—States and Other Areas

State/Area	Curr. Tax	State/Area	Curr. Tax	State/Area	Curr. Tax
AL	2.30	KY	1.90	OH	2.09
AK	2.70	LA	2.25	OK	2.25
AZ	2.00	ME	2.00	OR	0
AR	2.50	MD	2.00	PA	2.00
CA	2.35	MA	2.00	PR	4.00
CO	2.05	MI	1.3	RI	2.00
CT	1.75	MN	2.00	SC	0.75
DE	2.00	MS	3.00	SD	2.50
DC	1.70	MO	2.00	TN	1.75
FL	1.75	MT	2.75	TX	1.79
GA	2.25	NE	1.00	UT	2.25
GU	0.00	NV	3.50	VT	2.00
HI	2.75	NH	2.00	VI	5.00
ID	2.75	NJ	2.10	VA	2.25
IL	0.50	NM	3.00	WA	2.00
IN	2.00	NY	0.70	WV	3.00
IA	2.00	NC	1.90	WI	2.00
KS	2.00	ND	2.00	WY	0.75

a high premium tax, such as Nevada at 3.5 percent or the U.S. Virgin Islands at 5 percent.

Deferred Acquisition Cost Taxes

The so-called deferred acquisition cost (DAC) tax is a corporate federal income tax that is imposed on insurance companies. Insurance companies used to expense all of their business acquisition costs in the first year of the policy, thus reducing taxable income. Now companies must defer the expenses of acquiring business over a longer period of time, creating income in the early policy years and thus income taxes. The additional federal tax burden is passed on to you, the consumer. In some policies it is set out as a separate charge, such as 1.5 percent of your premium.

EXHIBIT 7.10

First-year Administration Fees

Low	Average	High
$200	$300 to $400	$700

In other policies, it is taken from the front-load you are paying without the company specifically identifying it.

Initial Administration Fees

First-year administration fees typically are higher than ongoing administration fees. The higher first-year fee covers the costs of setting up the policy and the costs incurred in determining if you are healthy, wealthy, and cautious enough to buy a policy. The average first-year cost is usually between $300 and $400, with a high of around $600 or $700, as shown in Exhibit 7.10. Initial administration fees have been increasing and extending beyond the first year, so you will want to examine them carefully.

EXPENSES CHARGED AGAINST YOUR POLICY ACCOUNT EACH MONTH

Ongoing Monthly Administration Fee

This fee enables the insurance company to provide continuing services such as mailing your confirmation notices, giving you periodic reports, and providing telephone reports, the prospectus, and annual reports. As you can see in Exhibit 7.11, it can run from $4 to $15 a month, with $5 to $7 being typical. The company will tell you what it currently is charging and the maximum it can charge by contract.

More and more companies are adding an asset-based administrative charge to their policies. Asset-based charges are deducted from your subaccounts based upon the amount of the assets in the account and can become the most significant cost you pay for the ongoing services provided with your policy.

EXHIBIT 7.11

Continuing Administration Fees

Low	Average	High
Low	**Average**	**High**
$4 per month	$5–$7 per month	$15 per month

Monthly Expenses/Cost of Insurance

This is the cost of the life insurance provided by your policy. Good questions in evaluating these costs are:

1. Do I need/want the life insurance?   Yes/No
   (a) If I die, will someone experience an economic loss?   Yes/No
   (b) Do I care?   Yes/No

(Three no answers and you're out of here. You don't need to pay mortality costs that will reduce your investment returns. You don't *need* life insurance.)

If you made it through, your next question is:

2. Are the mortality charges fair and competitive?

As you go about answering this question, you will be amazed at how expensive those mortality costs appear at the older ages. The younger and healthier you are, enjoying that immortal phase of life during which death occurs to others but not to you, the more outrageous these future costs look! But how minor these costs become as life chooses ways (heart attack, death of a contemporary, using your reserve chute on a parachute jump) to suggest that your time here also is temporary. The bottom line is that mortality costs are always too high for the young and healthy and always a bargain when you are no longer insurable. Insureds experience both periods.

Your monthly cost for life insurance will vary initially based upon your age, sex, health, use or nonuse of any nicotine products (smoker/nonsmoker), and occupation and avocations. Once your initial status is determined, through a process the insurance companies call *underwriting*, your status should be set for the life of the policy. A future change in health, smoking habits, avocations, etc., cannot increase your rates. However, should your situation change for the better, do ask the company to consider reducing your rates. If, for example, you have given up all nicotine products for a period in excess of 12 months, get that smoker's rate removed!

Your cost of insurance will increase, nevertheless, as you age. Understand that this is true with every insurance policy. In spite of the fact that this inevitably increasing cost may be masked and unseen in fixed-premium, fixed-face-amount offerings, it exists!

The question we all ask is "Are my costs for life insurance competitive?" We all want to be treated fairly by the insurance companies. How much would it cost you to buy term life insurance today? If the company you are considering just issued you term insurance without the possibility of investing, how much would it charge? Is the cost you are looking at a *low bid* or a cost determined after you have been underwritten to determine *your real status?* That is important. Fictional, unobtainable rates by low bidders do not count!

Once you have determined that the costs for insurance are fair, does that mean you can quit looking at them? Will they always be fair? The insurance company will increase your cost of life insurance as you get older. It also can change the cost based upon the company's actual experience. You should watch the cost of life insurance within your policy over the years to make sure it doesn't get out of line with the competition. There will be services to help you with this in the future, and there are people working to keep these costs in line right now.

1. Salespeople want the costs within the products they sell to remain competitive because they know you won't buy them and keep them in force otherwise. Salespeople are your allies. Your voice coupled with theirs will be heard by companies that charge unjustifiably high mortality costs. Your salesperson and you together vote with your money and your feet. You both can go to other companies that make reasonable charges, fair for you

and fair for company purposes. You don't want a company issuing policies that are not profitable for the company either. In spite of the fact that the separate account is not attachable by the creditors of the company, you do not need a disappearing company!

2. Your life insurance contract will contain a page that lists the guaranteed maximum cost of insurance rates based on state insurance regulations. The maximum rates will be based on the *Commissioners 1980 Standard Ordinary Male and Female Smoker and Non-Smoker Mortality Tables.* For the maximums applicable to you, see the appropriate page in a policy issued for you.

Mortality Charge/Cost of Life Insurance Management Tip

Show me a life insurance policy that has no cost of life insurance and I'll show you a policy with no net amount at risk, no life insurance.

A diagram of a typical fixed-premium, fixed-face-amount whole life policy would look like the one shown in Exhibit 7.12. A diagram of a typical fixed-premium, fixed-face-amount *variable*

EXHIBIT 7.12

Conventional Whole Life Insurance Face Amount

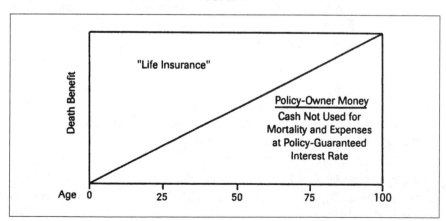

whole life policy would look similar to this, but with more ups and downs in the diagonal line, depending upon investment performance.

Death Benefit Option A Level (Option 1)

You can ask your insurance company to make your variable universal life insurance policy look just like the variable whole life as long as it complies with the definition of life insurance in Internal Revenue Code Section 7702. You need to understand the implications of your decision if you select what is commonly referred to as the death benefit option A or (option 1).

If selecting option A (option 1), keep in mind that:

1. The amount of life insurance will go down as your account value goes up. The insurance company will have less net amount at risk since it will be providing you with less life insurance as your policy account value increases, and more and more of the total death benefit becomes *your* money. The bigger the account value grows, the smaller the net amount at risk will be. Each month the company calculates the net amount at risk and multiplies that number by the cost per $1000 of life insurance to determine the total monthly amount to be charged against your policy account that month. Less life insurance results in less cost for life insurance.

2. The insurance company gets to eliminate the amount it has at risk (see Exhibit 7.13). Do you want this to happen, or do you want the life insurance (insurance company money) in the event of your death?

If you would prefer to maintain the amount of insurance company money at a constant level, rather than reducing its amount at risk with each dollar you pay in and each time your investment accounts show positive results, then ask for the increasing death benefit option, option B (or option 2).

Death Benefit Option B Level (Option 2)

With option B (option 2), at your death the policy would pay as a death benefit the original face amount *plus* your policy account

EXHIBIT 7.13

Death Benefit Options

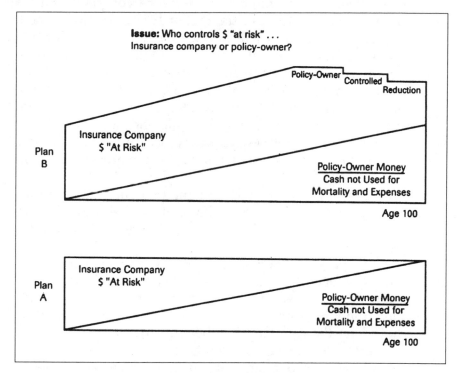

Issue: Who controls $ "at risk" . . .
Insurance company or policy-owner?

value. Generally, it is a good strategy to start off using option B during your account-building days. Then, when you see that you have enough, or are no longer adding capital to your policy, you can consider a change to option A if you wish. It is unlikely that you would want to switch to option A if your health has deteriorated. However, you can ask the company to reduce your face amount (being careful to avoid partial surrender charges or income taxes) to eliminate unneeded life insurance and mortality charges.

Guaranteed Interest Account Expenses

The expenses charged against a guaranteed interest account, should you have one within your policy, are taken prior to the company's quote on your guaranteed interest rate for the period. The company quotes you the "net" interest rate. This account is a part of the general account of the insurance company and, as such, is not subject to the Securities Act of 1933 or the Investment Company Act of 1940. You will not see the expenses considered as the company determines its gross expected rate of return on your money within the guaranteed interest division, nor will you see how the company arrived at the net interest it is willing to pay you. The difference between what the company earns and what it pays you is called the *spread*, and the process is called *spread-based pricing*. Sometimes you may hear it referred to as a *haircut*, as in the statement, "The haircut off the gross return was 2 percent."

You will want to know whether the guaranteed interest account is guaranteed for both principal and interest, how the current interest is credited, and for how long a period that interest is guaranteed (see Exhibit 7.14).

For the separate accounts, you will see charges listed in the prospectus. You should investigate whether the account management team of the subaccounts has been consistent in meeting the stated fund investment objectives. You also will want to know how long the company has been in the business of managing variable life separate accounts and how well those accounts have performed over that time. In some VUL policies you will find more than one guaranteed interest account. One may have the standard one-year guarantee, while others will have different use requirements and will guarantee a rate for a longer period of time.

EXHIBIT 7.14

Guarantee Periods

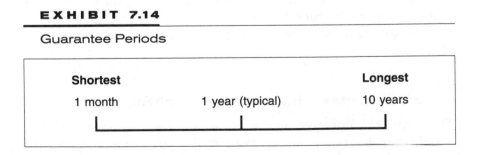

Shortest		**Longest**
1 month	1 year (typical)	10 years

EXPENSES AT THE SEPARATE ACCOUNT AND SUBACCOUNT LEVELS

The distinction between the expenses at the investment account level and those itemized in your policy reports is that the former are charged against and reduce the return of your investment accounts. Your subaccount investment return is reported net of these charges.

Since your investment accounts are reported to you net of these charges, they are not readily seen, but you will find them reported in detail within your policy prospectus and annual reports. Morningstar, an independent rating service, also reports these costs.

There is a tendency in each of us to look at the net rate of return, whether it is from the guaranteed interest account or from the various subaccounts offered. If we find it competitive, we don't worry about what the insurance company deducts for itself and for management of the account. The problem is that over the long term, high expenses at the investment account level will affect your return and can be the most significant charge in your policy. You want to make sure that what you are paying is *competitive* with the other variable universal life policies available.

Mortality and Expense Charges

Your insurance company provides you with a number of guarantees within your policy, and it charges you for these guarantees by deducting some of the return from your subaccount investment results, prior to reporting the net return to you. The average mortality and expense (M&E) risk charge in the 4012 VUL subaccounts that were tracked by Morningstar's Principia in 2000 was 0.73 percent. This charge is to pay for such things as the following services if the insurance company did not estimate its actual costs properly in the policy. If it did estimate the costs properly, and these funds are not called upon, the excess ends up as insurance company profit. Keep in mind you want the company to be profitable and interested in the continuing success of your policy.

- Continuing lifetime service
- Maximum monthly administrative charges

EXHIBIT 7.15

Mortality and Expense Charges

Lowest	Average	Highest
0.20%	0.73%	1.25%

- Maximum monthly cost of life insurance charges
- Guaranteed annuity factors within the contract

The ranges of charges are shown in Exhibit 7.15. These charges are made against your account prior to the reporting of your rate of return. Can they be important? You bet. Remember our friend Jack from Chapter 6 whose policy started out 20 years ago with a $100,000 death benefit and a $185 monthly premium going into it? That policy now has a death benefit of over $200,000 and has over $100,000 of capital in it. His asset-based charge using the low range of 0.2 percent would be $200, mid-range $230, and high range $1,250 per year. When the assets in your policy get to be significant, this charge will be significant. Look for companies that reduce this fee at some time in the future. For example, the policy may start out charging 0.90 percent but guarantee that, after you have had your policy 10 years, it will drop down to 0.40 percent. The savings can be substantial after you have built up significant investment in your contract.

Fund Expense or Investment Management Fee

This is the fee charged for the overall management of the underlying subaccounts. It is what you pay for the professional management of your money. It is taken daily from the underlying daily net assets of the subaccounts, and may go down as the size of the funds under management grows (e.g., 0.50 percent on the first $350 million down to 0.45 percent on amounts over that). It also will vary with the different subaccounts in the family of funds within your policy based upon the amount of management required (.20 percent) for a money-market fund. For example, from

EXHIBIT 7.16

Investment Management / Advisory Fee

Low	Average	High
0.00%	0.79%	5.16%

a low of zero in an index fund to as high as 5.16 percent for a real estate fund. The average fund expense charge in the 4012 VUL subaccounts tracked by Morningstar's Principia in 2000 was 0.79 percent, as shown in Exhibit 7.16.

Overall Expense Ratio

The overall expense ratio combines all the asset-based charges we have just discussed. It gives you a number that you can use to compare the cost of managing your money within and outside of life insurance. You could have your money managed within mutual funds, through a brokerage account, by a personal money manager, or by a bank or an annuity, rather than within life insurance. How much can you expect to have to pay under these arrangements? Generally speaking, you will find that it costs you at least 1.00 percent to have any help at all managing your first $1 million. Above that it might get cheaper.

In 2000 Morningstar's Principia put the average total expense charge, for the 4012 VUL subaccounts it tracked, at 1.55 percent. To put this into a comparative context, the average expense ratio in the 12,081 mutual funds Morningstar tracked was 1.37 percent, or 0.18 percent less than the variable life average. The average expense ratio inside the 9822 annuity subaccounts Morningstar tracked was 2.14 percent, or 0.59 percent more than the variable life average, and 0.77 percent more than the average mutual fund. The question becomes, "What value do you receive in these various ways of managing money?"

Mutual funds give you professional management but no income tax shelter unless the mutual fund is inside some sort of a retirement plan or IRA. Taxable mutual funds accounts are taxed whether or not you take money out, first when the money manager realizes earnings and gains on your behalf, and then again when you take money out to the extent that your shares have appreciated. Distributions might be at the lower capital gains rate of taxation or at the higher income tax rates.

The annuity gives you the same professional management you get in mutual funds, shelter from current income taxes, and often a manager of managers. That is, if you see multiple managers within the annuity contract such as Janus, Fidelity, AIM, Vanguard, and Alliance, someone is in charge of going out and getting you the best managers possible and making them available to you within the annuity contract. They then will monitor those managers, terminate the ones that do not seem to be doing the job for you, and replace them with better managers. When you take money out of an annuity, you will be taxed at ordinary income tax rates to the extent of the gain in your contract. You also may be subject to IRS penalties of 10 percent of the amount added to your income if you make withdrawals prior to age 59½.

The capital inside a life insurance policy has the same features of the annuity contract. In addition, you can get money out of your policy any time without taxation and penalties (before age 59½) as long as you have adhered to the seven-pay limitations (discussed in Chapter 8) on how much you invest into the life insurance policy. You can withdraw from your policy up to its cost basis (what you put in) without income taxation, and also borrow against it without income taxation.

BACK-END LOADS

Back loads, contingent deferred sales charges (CDSC), and surrender charges are all names for back-end loads, that is, the amount of the policy account value you forfeit if you surrender (terminate) your policy within the surrender period. The back-end charge reimburses the insurance company for expenses that have not yet been recovered at the time you choose to terminate your contract. If the existence of this charge is a concern to you, do not start a VUL. Be very careful of a rolling surrender charge that measures the length of time the charge will apply from the time the money is placed in the policy. This could cause the surrender charge to be a concern for an unacceptably long period of time.

It is important to note how this surrender charge or contingent deferred sales charge is limited and when it is no longer a threat. If you plan to invest substantially above the basic premium, be careful to determine if and how such contributions will affect surrender charges. Also, if you decide that you want to reduce your face amount while the surrender charge still is applicable, you will need to determine how much of the surrender charge will be applied as a result. Normally, no more than a pro rata share would be deducted, proportional to the amount of policy reduction.

As with universal life, variable universal policies make inefficient term insurance contracts. Underfunded policies are not economical. The additional expenses incurred in setting up these contracts are higher than setup costs for a term policy. Don't purchase a VUL if you don't intend to be an investor and to keep the policy beyond the back-end load period. To the extent that the contract has been successful and the policy account values exceed your total premium contributions, the amount of gain will be subject to ordinary income tax in the year of policy surrender. If you intend to hold the policy at least beyond the period in which a back-end load is charged, the back load will be preferable to a front-end load in most circumstances. Front loads reduce your investment, while back-end loads make those funds available to earn an investment return.

The back-end load is an expense that you pay when you terminate your contract. It could go on forever, meaning there could always be a surrender charge no matter how long you own your policy, although that would be unusual. More typically, you will find a contingent deferred sales charge. It's *contingent* upon how long you have owned your contract.

Surrender charges, or contingent deferred sales charges, frequently are defined as a percent of *target premium* but stated in dollar amounts in your policy (see Exhibit 7.17). You will want to know the amount of the charge at any time because your ability to withdraw or borrow from the policy will be limited by its existence.

EXHIBIT 7.17

Surrender Charges

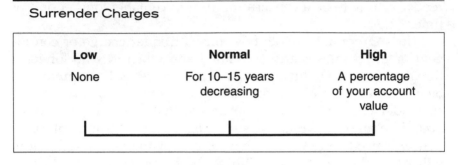

Low	Normal	High
None	For 10–15 years decreasing	A percentage of your account value

FEES FOR SERVICES

Moving Your Investments within Your Policy

Your variable universal policy will give you the right to move your existing investments among the subaccounts within you policy but may limit the number of moves you may make per year and/or charge for the moves. Your objective is to have freedom to move as often as possible at the least amount of cost. Most companies make no charge for 12 moves per year and thereafter reserve the right to charge up to $25 per move (see Exhibits 7.18 and 7.19).

EXHIBIT 7.18

Moves per Year

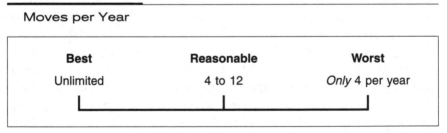

Best	Reasonable	Worst
Unlimited	4 to 12	*Only* 4 per year

Policy Loans and Withdrawals

The provisions relating to policy loans and withdrawals are important to examine. They tell you what it takes to get your money out of the policy without terminating it. They determine the liquidity of your variable universal life investment. When you ask

EXHIBIT 7.19

Cost per Move
Exceeding the Free Move Limit

Best	Worst
$0	$25 per move

for information about loans and withdrawals, the insurance company will give it to you in terms of *cash surrender value*. Let's define terms so that you don't get confused.

Policy account value (gross value of money in policy)
− surrender charge = cash surrender value (CSV)

Typically you will be able to borrow 90 percent of the cash surrender value without a charge other than interest. You can expect to be charged $25 to process a withdrawal (see Exhibit 7.20), but usually there is no charge to process a loan.

EXHIBIT 7.20

Withdrawals

Best	Average	Worst
100% CSV, no charge	90% CSV, $25 charge	Cannot withdraw

What Is *Spread*?

People do get confused about policy loans. They think they are taking money out of their policies, but they aren't. What they are doing is borrowing from the insurance company, using their policy as perfect collateral.

If you don't pay off your loan, some day the insurance

EXHIBIT 7.21

Policy Loans

Best	Typical	Worst
100% CSV	90% CSV	75% CSV

company will take the money from your policy. If you terminate your policy, the company will deduct the amount of the loan plus any loan interest due prior to giving you the cash surrender value, or the company will do the same from the death benefit prior to paying the net amount to your beneficiary.

When you borrow from your policy, the insurance company takes an amount in your policy equal to what you have borrowed and moves it into the loan guarantee fund. This fund then earns interest for you. You pay interest to the company for money you borrow, and the company pays you interest on the amount in the loan guarantee fund. The difference between the two is called the *spread*. Typically you will find the company crediting you 1 to 2 percent less than you are paying it. The spread at best could be zero, whereby you would be paying each other the same interest, or at worst, up to 4 percent in excess of what the company is paying you, as shown in Exhibit 7.22.

EXHIBIT 7.22

Loan Interest Spread

Best	Average	High
0%	2%	4%

LOAN OR WITHDRAWAL?

Management Tip

Mike and Karen call. They need some money from their policy for a down payment on a home. They like their policy, need the insurance, and have determined that the expenses and insurance costs are fair. They like the investment results within their policy, so their intention is to "fill the policy back up" as soon as their finances allow. Should they borrow on the policy or simply make a withdrawal?

The answer depends upon the loan interest spread. What is the difference between the interest they pay for the loan and the interest the insurance company pays them on the collateralized portion of the policy? They find that the spread is 1 percent. The company credits the collateral portion of their policy account with 1 percent less than it charges them for the loan.

How about new money coming into the policy? What does it cost to get new money in? They find that there is a 2 percent state premium tax and a 4 percent front sales load. The cost to get new money in is 6 percent, 5 percent more than the 1 percent spread.

Answer: Borrow the money! The cost is 1 percent, and they can pay back that loan without paying the 2 percent state premium tax or the 4 percent front load. They can fill their policy back up faster, and with less cost (1 percent versus 6 percent), than if they withdrew the money and put it back in as new money.

If they decide to make a partial withdrawal, it should be contractually available from the company. However, the Tax Reform Act of 1986, Section 7702, may have made such policy withdrawals impractical from an income tax standpoint. Withdrawals can create ordinary income tax liabilities if taken within the first 15 years of the policy's life. It is important to know your rights under the partial withdrawal provision. In some cases, there may be a minimum withdrawal, such as $500, and fees may be assessed for making such withdrawals, such as $25 each time. There also may be a limit on the amount that may be withdrawn, and from a practical standpoint, it would not be wise to so diminish the account that the policy could fail (lapse) for lack of sufficient cash to continue. Failed policies create income tax consequences.

FUNDING TO PAY EXPENSES

An important policy investment objective should be to earn sufficient return each year on the capital invested to pay for the expenses and term insurance costs for that particular year. If this is accomplished, you will have paid for your life insurance costs with the pretax earnings on your investments. This is the least expensive way to cover these costs.

This means that a specific amount of capital within your policy is used to meet an important near-term objective, i.e., to pay the costs charged against your policy each month. In some VUL policies it is possible to specify which account should be charged with the monthly expenses that will be deducted from your policy each month. If you have purchased a policy with that valuable feature, you will want an amount of capital sufficient to generate the monthly earnings to cover these costs in a relatively conservative account that has a high likelihood of generating the required income. The accounts most certain to accomplish this objective may be those accounts that guarantee both principal and interest, or those that can be depended upon to generate income. One strategy, although it may be more conservative than you can stand, would be to put enough into that account to generate the income required to cover all mortality and expense charges. For example, if policy expenses were $100 per month and the guaranteed interest account was earning 5 percent, you would want $24,000 ($1200 ÷ 5 percent) in that account. Another way would be to just make sure the account always held enough to cover the expenses. If you do not do this, the typical VUL policy will deduct the policy costs proportionately from all your other accounts in the policy. This could mean that assets in your equity accounts are being sold to cover expenses. If this occurs when the equity funds are down, more units have to be sold to cover the costs and you are selling *low* that which you may have bought *high*. Beside the fact that it is better to buy low and sell high, if the unit value goes up, the next month, you do not own as much as you used to. You lost the opportunity for gain because of the way your policy was structured.

FUNDING FOR OTHER OBJECTIVES

Additional capital placed in the variable universal contract would be used to accomplish your other investment objectives. In so doing, you have these advantages:

1. *No* current income taxes are being assessed against your investment earnings.
2. Changes of investment allocation within the subaccounts offered under the insurance contract are made without creating income tax liabilities or transaction costs. This allows you to execute investment strategies such as dollar cost averaging, asset allocation, and rebalancing easily, conveniently, and normally with zero expenses. These strategies can be very expensive in taxable accounts.
3. You have access to your capital and earnings without current taxation from properly structured policies. (Look back at "Policy Loans and Withdrawals.")

WHAT ELSE CAN YOU BUY WITH YOUR ACCOUNT EARNINGS?

There often are additional purchases you can make with the income tax–free earnings within your life insurance policy. To be able to earn income tax–free and spend income tax–free is a significant advantage of a life insurance policy. You can also buy riders such as disability premium waivers, accidental death benefits, children's term insurance, term insurance for spouses and others, guaranteed insurability on yourself or others, cost-of-living increase options, automatic increase options, and survivor insurability provisions.

Long-term care benefits that include living benefits riders have been available in most states since 1994. There normally is no charge for these riders. The riders allow you to use a portion of the *death benefit* if the insured is medically diagnosed with a condition limiting life expectancy to 6 months. If you live in Oklahoma or Vermont, the insurance companies use a 12-month life expectancy, as required by those states. Since the rider provides for the payment of some portion (25 to 75 percent) of the death benefit, it is applicable to all life insurance contracts, including term life insurance. Policy owners can always access the asset value of investment types of policies for any purpose by means of policy loans or withdrawals.

If a policy owner is in a situation in which he or she has a choice of calling on the living benefits or taking a policy loan or withdrawal, the living benefits alternative probably would be best. It would be less expensive, and the loan or withdrawal option would still be available if needed.

Recently VUL applicants have been given the opportunity to add a tax-qualified long-term care acceleration rider to their VUL policy. This rider would make benefits available on a much more liberal basis. Instead of requiring a terminal situation to access benefits, they would be available if the insured needed assistance with at least two activities of daily living or if the person suffered cognitive impairment. They pay whether in a nursing home or at home, and offer most of the services of a stand-alone long-term care policy, such as a 100-day elimination period, 21-day bed reservation benefit, provider discounts, and long-term-care advisory services. Applicants can apply for monthly benefits of a percentage of the policy face amount, from 1 to 4 percent, which will continue to pay out until the entire face amount of the policy has been paid out. John Hancock gives an example of a 45-year-old preferred healthy male buying a $250,000 face amount VUL. He would pay in $18,000 for the policy and an extra 5 percent, or $900, for the long-term care rider.

The desirability of any of these is unique to each policy owner. An advantage of purchasing these riders within the policy could be the ability to pay for the rider with pretax dollars earned on the investment capital in the VUL contract, although the regulators could veto this tax treatment. This assumes that the full $18,900 premium required by John Hancock will be considered a part of this person's cost basis in the VUL contract. You will want to know exactly what will be deducted from the investment account(s) each month to pay for the long-term care benefits and if the amount deducted can change in the future. The cost-benefit relationship of obtaining long-term care benefits by buying a long-term care rider within a life insurance policy is based upon your personal situation, insurability, other resources, and the final income tax determination, etc.

EXCHANGE PRIVILEGE

The exchange privilege allows you to change insureds on an existing life insurance policy. You can take a policy on your life that you no longer need and have it insure the life of another individual who might need it. In family situations and those involving key-employee life insurance, this privilege can be very valuable because you can make one policy provide for a succession of insureds. Policy charges are adjusted based upon the new insured's age, sex, and insurability status, but start-up charges are eliminated. Look for this important feature in your policy. Since first-generation variable universal policies often were more favorable to the consumer than the "new improved models," when you no longer want your policy, find someone who does! When a policy is exchanged any investment gain in the contract is subject to ordinary income tax to the exchanging policy owner.

CONCLUSION

You have the ability to manage flexible-premium variable life insurance and adapt it to your changing needs and economic situations. This is its advantage. Its disadvantage is the same. You have to actively manage it. In 15 years of working with VUL policies, no one yet who has funded the policy between the target premium rounded up and the MEC limits has gotten in trouble with a VUL policy. The way to deal with VUL is to maintain a healthy funding level, ensure asset allocation, and review the policy and adjust it to your needs. The help you get from advisors who understand VUL can be invaluable. Keep in touch with them, making sure they know what you are trying to accomplish. They work with these policies every day, and they have learned from policy owners and through continuing education how to make them perform best for you. It is good for their business to have you *very* happy with your policy.

> It's unwise to pay too much, but it's worse to pay too little.
> When you pay too much, you lose a little money, that's all.
> When you pay too little, you sometimes lose everything, because the thing you bought was incapable of doing the thing it was bought to do.

The common law of business balance prohibits paying a little and
getting a lot—it cant' be done.
If you deal with the lowest bidder, it is well to add something for
the risk you run and if you do that you will have enough to pay
for something better.

JOHN RUSKIN

You now know enough about the various forms of life insurance to take the following "Suitability" test designed to help
you check which type of policy is best suited to your needs and
wants. (See Exhibit 7.23.)

EXHIBIT 7.23

The "Menu" of Life Insurance Products

Term only = Mortality & Expense ONLY

	General Description	Cash Value	Investment Flexibility	Premium Flexibility	Face Amount Flexibility
Non-Guaranteed Term	Low Cost Low Control	None	N/A	None	None
Renewable & Convertible Term	Higher Cost More Control	None	N/A	None	None

Term PLUS = Mortality, Expenses AND Investment

	General Description	Cash Value	Investment Flexibility	Premium Flexibility	Face Amount Flexibility
Whole Life	Guaranteed Cash Value	Bonds and Mortgages	None	None	None
Variable Life	Select Investments	Stocks and Bond Funds	MAX	None	None
Universal Life	Current Interest Rate	Shorter Term Investment	None	MAX	MAX
Variable Universal Life	Control Disclosure	Stocks and Bond Funds	MAX	MAX	MAX

Life Insurance Policy Suitability & Selection Questionnaire
Suit Yourself!

1. Put a check mark under the word that best describes your initial reaction to the type of policy named.

Policy Type	Highly Prefer	Prefer	Satisfactory	Acceptable	Unsatisfactory
Non-Guaranteed Term					
Renewable & Convertible Term					
Whole Life					
Variable Life					
Universal Life					
Variable Universal Life					

E X H I B I T 7.23 Continued

Term Life Insurance

---

2. I wish to put enough money into a life insurance policy to buy   ❑Yes   ❑No
   the life insurance protection only—no investment.

3. At this time, I am NOT able to consider investing with an   ❑Yes   ❑No
   insurance company.

4. The term policy need not be renewable or convertible as long   ❑Yes   ❑No
   as it provides uninterrupted life insurance for at least ___
   years.

5. I want the term policy to be renewable and convertible.   ❑Yes   ❑No

6. I would prefer NOT to have the charges for expenses and   ❑Yes   ❑No
   term insurance (mortality costs) deducted, pre-tax, from my
   policy investment account earnings.

Whole Life Insurance

---

7. I prefer the *whole life* arrangement of paying for life insurance for all of the
   following reasons:
   ❑ Not applicable

   ❑ I like the long-term bond and mortgage, general account, investments of
   whole life insurance.

   ❑ I understand that I can only use this general account for the life of my policy.

   ❑ I desire low volatility.

   ❑ I prefer a fixed, contractually guaranteed premium that I must pay or risk
   losing my policy.

   ❑ I desire a policy with an insurance company guaranteed cash value.

   ❑ I am not concerned by possible reductions in dividends.

   ❑ I prefer a low management type of policy.

   ❑ I do not want premium, face amount or investment flexibility.

Universal Life Insurance

---

8. I prefer the *universal life* arrangement of paying for life insurance for all of the
   following reasons:

   ❑ I prefer having the insurance company specify the interest I will earn each
   year on the capital invested within my policy.

   ❑ The guaranteed interest account is sufficient for my life insurance investment
   purposes. I do not and will not want or need any other investment
   alternatives in the future.

   ❑ I like being able to see exactly what my investment is earning and the exact
   charges being made against my policy.

   ❑ I like the flexibility of being able to adjust the face amount of the policy.

   ❑ I like the flexibility of being able to vary my premium payments.

   ❑ I want face amount and premium flexibility but not investment flexibility.

   ❑ I like the fact that I can get at my money within this policy by either policy
   loans or withdrawals.

EXHIBIT 7.23 Continued

Variable Whole Life
Fixed Premium Variable Life

9. I prefer the *variable whole life* arrangement of paying for life insurance for all the following reasons:

   ❑ I like the security of knowing that I only need to pay a fixed premium to maintain my policy regardless of what happens to my policy investments, mortality costs or expenses.

   ❑ I like the fixed premium arrangement.

   ❑ I like having the ability to invest in a variety of investment accounts and being able to reposition these investments.

   ❑ I do not want premium or face amount flexibility, just investment flexibility.

   ❑ I like the guarantee that my death benefit will never go below the original face amount of the policy as long as I pay the required premium.

   ❑ It does not concern me that I cannot withdraw money from this type of policy but can only access my money via policy loans.

Variable Universal Life

10. I prefer the *variable universal life* arrangement of paying for life insurance for all the following reasons:

    ❑ I prefer to retain premium, face amount and investment flexibility.

    ❑ I welcome the opportunity to exercise management control over premium, face amount and investments in this policy and to enjoy the living benefits that it offers to enhance my family's / company's security.

    ❑ I am aware of the responsibility that is inherent in such flexibility.

    ❑ I understand that it is up to me to guarantee that my policy stays in force by making sure it always has enough money in it to cover the expenses in the policy each year.

    ❑ I want to have the opportunity to use the family of alternative investment options within a policy to accumulate for family investment objectives without creating income tax liabilities.

    ❑ I understand that the more money I put into this type of policy the more opportunity I have to earn investment returns not subject to current taxation and that the best way to take advantage of this opportunity is to maximize what I put into it whereas with other policy designs I often minimized what I put into them.

CHAPTER 8

VUL Funding Levels

The Key Is the Money

What is a funding level? Using the word *premium* in connection with life insurance implies cost to many people, whereas the money put into a flexible-premium life insurance policy may be applied partially to expenses (cost) and partially to investment. The funding levels described in this chapter are to help you understand the advantages and disadvantages of choosing to fund a flexible-premium variable universal life insurance policy at the highest to the lowest levels. Keep in mind that, after all of our discussion about the costs inside a VUL policy in Chapter 7, it is the engine inside the VUL policy that is important. The separate account within the policy is the engine, the subaccounts within the separate account are the cylinders, and the investment within the subaccounts is the fuel. You may own the Rolls Royce of VUL policies—one with 30 to 40 investment choices—but if you do not put any gas (money) in the engine, it cannot do you any good. You might as well own a single-cylinder policy like whole life or universal life. If you do not put any money into the policy, it will not run at all. If you are able to and choose to put a lot of money (gas) into a VUL policy, it will run very well indeed.

WHY PUT MONEY IN A VUL

We are concerned here with economic uncertainty—the "Will I have enough?" question. Look at the economic lifeline shown in Exhibit 8.1.

We all come into this world as an economic negative, dependent upon others. As our feet get larger and the cost of education increases, we become greater economic negatives to our parents. At some time, we cross the line. We become economic positives, and our parents, in most cases, breathe an economic sigh of relief.

Some day our ability to earn a living by our personal efforts, or our desire to do so, will deteriorate or cease, and we will again become economic negatives. The hope is that we will have chopped off a large enough part of those earnings and set them aside for the future during our productive years to build ourselves an income generator, an accumulation of capital that can provide income. We need a pool of capital that, properly invested, will generate *enough* ever-replaceable income to provide for our lifetime economic needs. We need to transfer purchasing power from our productive years to provide for us in our less productive years. Aren't you thankful your folks did that and are not de-

E X H I B I T   8.1

The Economic Life Cycle

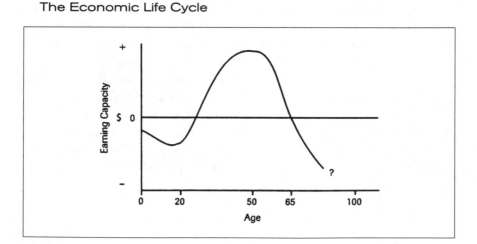

pendent upon you, or if they didn't, don't you wish they had? You can bet that your children, if you have them, or other potential caregivers are hoping that you have provided for yourself economically so that they can provide the care you need without suffering economically themselves.

BUILDING CAPITAL WHEELS

Someday we are all going to need a "capital wheel." (See Exhibit 8.2.) We will, during our working and productive lives, generate income to sustain our families and ourselves by our personal efforts, our ability to go to work and earn income. Many things can take that ability away from us, and so our financial advisor will encourage us to build a capital wheel that will provide income if we are unable to work. We need a capital wheel that will provide continuing income in the event of our disability or our death. We would like to have it filled as soon as possible so that we can be working for the fun of it rather than being an economic slave to

EXHIBIT 8.2

The Income Generators

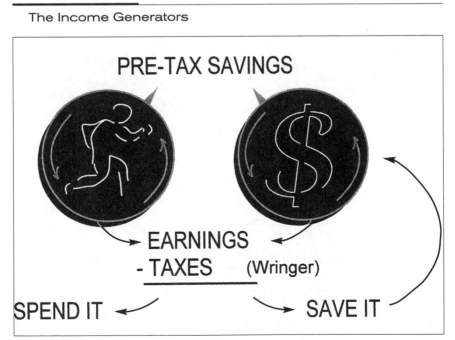

a job. The task is to use all the financial tools at our disposal to fill the capital wheel as quickly and efficiently as possible while minimizing those things that are counterproductive to accomplishing this goal, such as unnecessary expenses and unnecessary taxation.

In building your capital wheel, expenses that do not provide valuable benefits certainly should be avoided, but, by far, taxation is the biggest enemy of accumulating capital. In his book *Stocks for the Long Run*,* Jeremy Siegel presents a chart showing what $1 invested in gold, bonds, and stocks would have grown to from the year 1802 to 1997. (See Exhibit 8.3.) In addition to pointing out that gold, in comparison to the consumer price index, has seldom been an effective inflation hedge, the chart dramatically shows how income taxes have reduced the capital in your capital wheel. Take, for example, the difference between the after-tax bonds of

EXHIBIT 8.3

Total Nominal Return Indices
Before and After Federal Tax 1802–1997

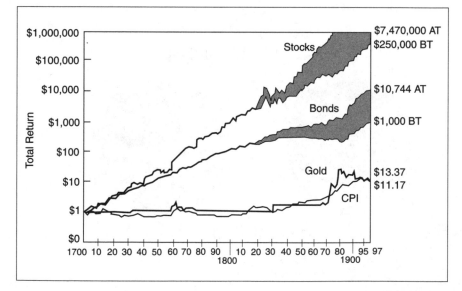

Stocks for the Long Run, McGraw-Hill, New York, 1998.

$1000 or the pretax bonds of $10,744, or between the after-tax stocks of $250,000 or the pretax stocks of $7,470,000.

In the introduction to the proposed rule on disclosure of mutual fund after-tax returns (7-3-2000), the Securities and Exchange Commission on its web site www.sec.gov states the following:

- Taxes are one of the most significant costs of investing in subaccounts through taxable accounts.
- Shareholders investing in stock and bond funds paid an estimated 34 billion in taxes in 1997 on distributions by their funds.
- Recent estimates suggest that more than 2½% of the average stock fund's total return is lost to taxes each year.
- In the last five years it is estimated that investors in diversified U.S. stock funds surrendered an average of 15% of their annual gains to taxes.

The point of all this is that it is important that you take advantage of the opportunity to compound investment earning without current income taxation within your VUL life insurance policy. Knowing how to do it and where you can put money within your policy is important.

WHERE TO PUT MONEY IN A VUL

Once you have decided to transfer purchasing power from the present to the future, the next question is where should that purchasing power be stored?

Exhibit 8.4 tells you what various investments have done over the past 75 years. You could assume that these investments will tend to track these norms in the future, or you could say that because history has changed, these investment results likewise will change. Which takes greater courage or arrogance? We will assume that the various investment classes will do as they have done in the past.

Asset allocation studies and the effects of *economic gravity* as shown in Exhibit 8.4 suggest that you should not invest in only one asset class or *anything that inflexibly dictates and provides only one class for long-term investment*. The conclusion is that investment

EXHIBIT 8.4

Economic Gravity

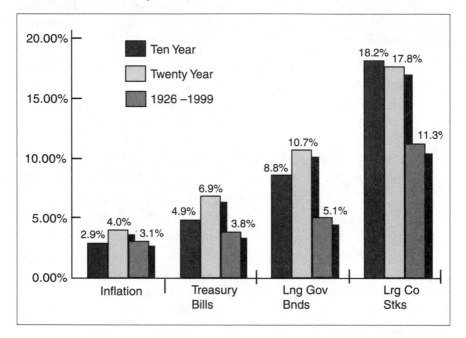

Source: *Stocks, Bonds, Bills, and Inflation,* Ibbotson Associates 2000 Yearbook.

in single-pocket insurance contracts (providing only one investment alternative) is hazardous to your economic health. On the
other hand, multiple-pocket contracts, providing a degree of control to the contract owner, can be very beneficial to your economic
health. The opportunity that a variable universal life insurance
contract gives you makes it an absolutely unique financial tool, in
that you can invest among asset classes, move your investments
without significant transaction costs, and not incur current income
tax liabilities while you are building your asset base.

The only investment advice this book can offer as a rule of
thumb to people buying whole life or universal life as an investment today is *don't*! If economic history repeats itself, these vehicles cannot provide an inflation-adjusted rate of return. Life insurance policies are rate-of-return–driven. Expenses and mortality
charges are most significant in policies that can't generate invest-

ment returns significant enough to pay those costs and help you get ahead.

GUARANTEES?

But I'm still afraid of stocks. Won't the
guarantees like the guaranteed cash value and
the guaranteed minimum interest rate in
universal life be enough so that I don't have to
worry about diversifying my investments
within a policy?

In spite of (and maybe because of) the fact that life is uncertain, we look to guarantees. What we often fail to do is to examine the *guarantor,* the strength behind the guarantee and what is being guaranteed. It has been wisely stated that (and as noted earlier) there are no guarantees, only guarantors.

If you are going to depend on guarantees, you may be tempted to shop for the company with the best guarantee, the highest guaranteed cash value, and the highest guaranteed interest rate. Acting on that, you may well find yourself buying from a company doomed to disappear. If general interest rates drop below the company's guaranteed rate and the company's general account becomes unable to earn what its guarantee promises to pay, the company's surplus will be diminished as it delivers its promise to you and continues to pay you more than it is earning. Today's regulatory environment requires companies to own higher-quality and lower-yielding investments in their general accounts. It also dictates that state insurance commissioners take over companies whose surpluses fall below certain levels. In this environment, companies that could have survived economic aberrations in the past will find it more difficult to do so in the future. *Conclusion*: When minimum guarantees become important to you, your guarantor is heading for trouble. The security you seek within the guarantee is weakening. Flexibility, asset allocations, and maximum investing are *more important* than *guarantees.*

How do you buy guarantees in life insurance policies?

You purchase a guarantee by promising to pay a contractually fixed premium! Guaranteed cash value occurs only when the policy owner provides the fixed-premium payments required by the contract. If you violate the pay-in provisions, you lose your guarantee!

Guaranteed death benefits are purchased the same way. You must agree to invest some minimum amount, and if you don't, you lose your guarantee. But so-and-so (the latest financial guru who spouts platitudes rather than useful information) wrote that in variable universal there is no guaranteed cash value, and often no guaranteed death benefit, and if you invest unwisely in your policy, it could self-destruct!

Like the persistent lawyer interrogating the expert witness, the witness must acknowledge that a variable universal policy could fail. You, the jury, go away concluding that this makes it riskier than a policy with guarantees. This is in spite of the fact that the risk of failure also exists within the policy with the guarantees and in a variable universal policy if *you* mismanage it. You can control the risk in a variable universal policy; you cannot control the risks in those policies perceived to have guarantees. To address your concern, the life insurance marketplace has responded by constructing universal design policies that do guarantee a death benefit. You retain that guarantee by agreeing to pay a certain minimum amount.

How can I mismanage a life insurance policy?

There are two primary ways in which you can mismanage a variable universal policy: (1) by investing too little in your policy and (2) by not using common sense and diversification in investing your capital within the policy. If you fund a variable universal policy with the same level of investment required with a comparable fixed-premium whole life policy, and use reasonable care and diversification within your policy investments, the chances of the policy self-destructing are between slim and none.

The way to get rich with variable universal is to invest as much in your policy as you can and as the law allows while still retaining *all* the income tax benefits unique to the life insurance policy investment. The old concepts of whole life—*paid up* at age?, *short pay, vanishing premium,* or whatever other label that implies that you no longer have to pay in—are obsolete. They became obsolete the day the investment returns available within the contract were able to compete favorably with your taxable investment portfolio, the day variable universal life became available to you.

To enjoy maximum investment results within your variable universal policy, you will want to maximize your investment. To enjoy maximum income tax benefits in your policy, maximize your investment. Your question is no longer "How little can I put into this policy?" but "How much?"

However, the advantage of this policy is that it is flexible. You will be, at times, a maximum funder of your life insurance policy, and at other times a minimum funder. Let's address the subject of variable universal funding levels.

FUNDING LEVELS IN VARIABLE UNIVERSAL LIFE

Once you have made the decision to buy life insurance with pretax dollars earned on an investment account, you still have to decide *how much* to invest and *where* to invest (see Exhibit 8.5). If you have decided on conventional whole life and its long-term bonds and mortgages, or the interest-sensitive variety and its short-term

EXHIBIT 8.5

Funding Worksheet for Variable Universal Life

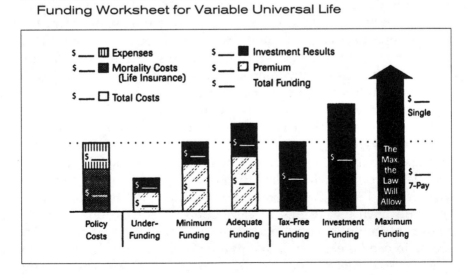

Source: Ben G. Baldwin, 1991.

money-market types of investments, decisions about *how much* and *where to invest* have been made for you. The company tells you how much to pay based upon the face amount and the type of policy in which you invest. There is little flexibility of premium payment after that. Similarly, with variable whole life, you agree, at contract inception, to a set premium and face amount, but retain management control and flexibility over where the money is to be invested in the contract. On the other hand, if you have purchased a variable universal life contract, your level of funding is important not only on the day you decide on a specific face amount of life insurance and put the policy in force but also throughout the life of the contract. The ability to vary payments gives you important investment opportunities. To take advantage of these opportunities, it may help you to think of your funding strategy as one of the following: underfunding, minimum funding, adequate funding, tax-free funding, investment funding, or maximum funding.

Underfunding

If the mortality and expense charges exceed the combined total of the investment earnings in the policy and the current year's payment into the policy (see Exhibit 8.6), your variable universal policy is underfunded—and in trouble! For example, you look at the annual report on your variable universal life policy and find that your expenses for the year were $500. Upon further examination, you find that your policy interest earnings amounted to only $100 and that you have paid only $100 into the policy during the year. Your contribution and the interest earnings totaled $200, whereas expenses totaled $500. To cover the $500 due in expenses, a $300 bite was taken out of principal (capital) that had previously accumulated within the policy. At the end of the year, you will find $300 less capital in the policy than you had when you began the year. If you ignore this process, you will find in the coming year that you have less capital to earn interest. If you don't increase your contributions, you'll find at the end of that year another decrease in capital exceeding that of the previous year. The situation gets worse as the mortality charges in the policy increase as you get older. The expense charges also may be increased to some

EXHIBIT 8.6

Underfunding

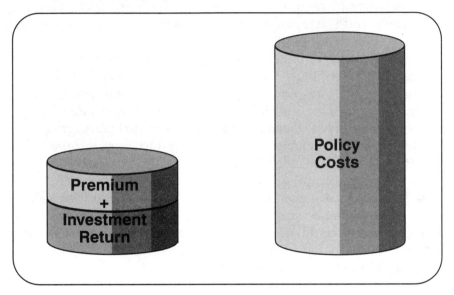

contractual maximum, and the interest earnings in the policy could be decreased because of changes in the prevailing level of interest rates. If all four events occur simultaneously (capital down, interest rates down, expenses up, mortality costs up), your policy costs will consume your policy principal at a rapid pace. As the capital base in your policy approaches depletion, the insurance company will warn you that the contract will terminate unless you start making substantial payments into that contract. Underfunded policies eat up principal at an ever-increasing rate. Don't let this happen to you!

Let me give you an example of the problem underfunding can cause. A 45-year-old male assumed, or was led to believe, that his policy was adequately funded with about $7000 per year because he assumed the capital in it would earn a level 12 percent interest. If all went as the illustration indicated, his policy would accumulate capital equal to the face amount of the policy of $1 million at age 100. Age 100 was a possibility in his family because of his good health and ancestors who had lived to that age. If, as has happened, the earnings drop from 12 percent to 11.95 percent, a 5-basis-point decrease, the policy will have zero cash in it at age 99, and to continue his life insurance one more year, the insurance company would require a payment of about $400,000. This has happened, and is happening, to people who choose to ignore their policies.

When universal life policies first appeared in 1979 and 1980, interest rates were high. Funding levels were chosen based on the assumption that those inordinately high rates were going to stay there. Many of these policies are underfunded, and indeed many of them actually have been involuntarily terminated. Angry policy owners don't understand why the policy has been terminated, a situation that has resulted in numerous consumer complaints to state insurance commissioners.

In many cases, even insurance salespeople who were selling did not understand what they were selling. In competitive situations, an agent could sell you the same amount of coverage at a cheaper rate. This smaller premium represented a lower investment and lower investment returns.

Lower investment returns meant lower tax-free interest and thus a less efficient policy. Underfunding is the poorest of strategies with a universal or variable universal life policy. It is wiser to buy a yearly renewable and convertible term policy with after-tax dollars. Minimum funding should be the lowest funding level considered in universal policies.

Minimum Funding

The minimum funding level for universal types of policies should be the level at which the policy interest earnings and your contributions to the policy are no less than the amount of the mortality and expense charges in that particular year (see Exhibit 8.7). This will assure that the capital accumulated within your contract stays at a constant level for the year and is not depleted by policy costs. You can, in effect, adjust what you put into it back to that of a straight term policy during times when you have no extra money to invest. This feature can be a great benefit and comfort if you suddenly find yourself out of work. Your life insurance continues uninterrupted at minimal outlay.

EXHIBIT 8.7

Minimum Funding

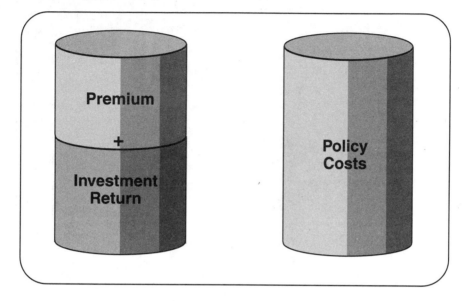

Adequate Funding

Tax-free funding is a strategy whereby investment proceeds in the policy generate enough investment return to pay all mortality and expense charges incurred in the policy in the year in question. Adequate funding is a strategy for you to use to reach the tax-free funding level over time (see Exhibit 8.8). The more you choose to put in, the more rapidly you will get to the tax-free funding level. We have talked about target premium, which is the insurance company's suggested target amount to put into your policy to make it build capital at a respectable rate. This book recommends that you not even start a VUL policy until you can comfortably commit to an ongoing level of at least the target premium rounded up to the nearest $100 of $1000. Periodically—at least yearly—check your policy to see how it is progressing and adjust the funding level to your current situation and investment objectives.

EXHIBIT 8.8

Adequate Funding

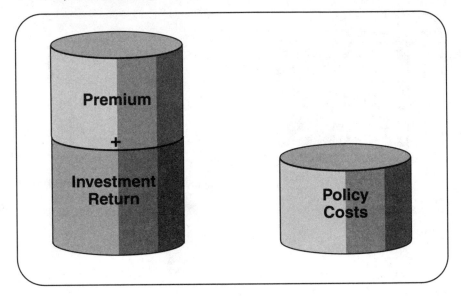

Tax-Free Funding

The primary objective of the life insurance policy is to provide life insurance protection in the amount you consider necessary. You may want to pay for this insurance with income tax–free earnings on an investment account. The tax-free funding point is reached when the amount of capital invested inside the policy will earn enough nontaxable return in the year in question to pay all the mortality and expense charges within the policy in that year (Exhibit 8.9). Such a strategy assures that you will be paying for your life insurance with the pretax earnings on the after-tax capital you have invested. As long as the mortality and expense charges are fair and competitive, you will have accomplished your objective.

To determine the tax-free funding level, you need to know the amount of the expenses and mortality charges within your policy for the year. This information is readily available for universal and variable universal policies. These funding levels are determined by dividing the amount of the expenses and mortality

EXHIBIT 8.9

Tax-Free Funding

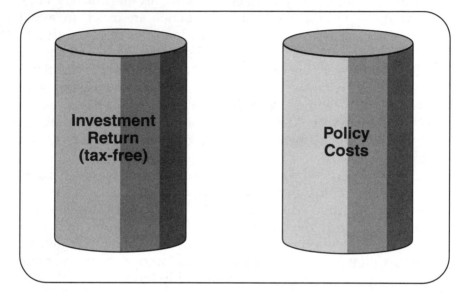

charges for the year by the return expected or guaranteed for that year. If your mortality and expenses are to be $400 this year and your expected return is 5 percent, then you will need $8000 in your policy to reach the optimum funding level. Your $8000 earning 5 percent will generate $400 of pretax interest, which is sufficient to cover $400 in expenses and mortality charges.

Suppose that you are a 50-year-old buying a $250,000 straight term insurance policy with an annual premium of $800 in the first year. To generate the $800 after taxes, you would have to earn $1143 [$800 ÷ (1 − marginal tax bracket), or $800/0.70]. Alternatively, you could have elected to pay $1170 inside a variable universal policy. You have the option of investing enough after-tax capital in the policy so that the untaxed earnings are sufficient to pay the $1170. You would about match the YRT cost in the year in question if the tax-free return on $23,400 of capital ($1170 ÷ 5 percent) in the policy is competitive with alternative investment opportunities.

The returns offered within variable universal policy subaccounts typically are very competitive with taxable mutual funds and provide for diversification, asset allocation, rebalancing, and dollar cost averaging, all without income taxation. It is not unusual to find young 50-year-olds allocating an inordinately large part of their portfolio to municipal bonds in order to avoid income taxes in spite of the fact that doing so restricts growth in the portfolio. Building a capital engine inside a VUL policy budgets for the payment of future term costs so that life insurance may continue, whereas trying to pay the ever-increasing term costs in a policy without a capital engine fails 99 percent of the time. Life Insurance Marketing Research Association statistics indicate that only 1 percent of term-only policies results in a death claim.

The next decision you have to make concerns where to invest the capital, given the choices offered within the policy. The first investment objective will be to service the policy's expense and mortality charges. The need is for monthly income to cover monthly costs, so you'll want to look at the guaranteed interest account, a money-market account, a bond account, or some other account that generates dependable monthly income.

Investment Funding

If you have reached the tax-free funding level and policy earnings are sufficient to cover all policy expenses, why would you choose to invest even more capital? Let's assume that you have purchased a variable universal life policy and have started out with a strategy of adequate funding. This strategy, though interspersed (in times of stress) with years of minimum funding, has helped you attain income tax–free funding, the point at which expenses and mortality charges are entirely covered by policy earnings. You have been utilizing the guaranteed principal, guaranteed interest account to hold the monies that represent the tax-free funding level, and you still have the family of subaccounts available for your use. These funds differ from commercially available funds because the capital gains, dividends, and interest earnings within them create no current income tax liability. You have enjoyed tax-free compounding in your IRAs and qualified retirement plans, and now this is available to you within your life insurance policy as well! (see Exhibit 8.10).

EXHIBIT 8.10

Investment Funding

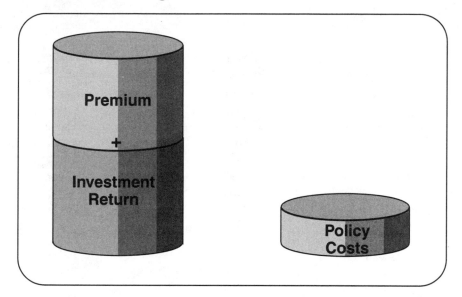

Many of you participate in successful mutual funds and use them to build family wealth. But if they are not part of a life insurance policy, an annuity, or a qualified retirement plan, you have to pay income taxes on those holdings each year. Ordinary income taxation is incurred on any earnings when individual stocks in the portfolio pay dividends into the fund, which the manager must pass through to you. Capital gains taxation is passed through to you when individual securities in the mutual fund portfolio are sold at a profit or loss. Just look at last year's income tax return to see the investment results on which you paid taxes even though all you did was hold your position in the fund all year.

Since the owner of shares in a mutual fund cannot control distribution from these funds that result in taxation, there has been a great deal of attention being paid to what are presumed to be "tax-efficient" mutual funds, mutual funds that minimize income taxation. Exhibit 8.11 is a snapshot of the tax efficiency of index funds based on information taken from a column by Aaron Lucchetti in *The Wall Street Journal*.

The column described the huge amount of taxes that Harold

EXHIBIT 8.11

Index Funds Aren't Always Tax Efficient

Fund	Year Distributed	20% Capital Gains Tax Paid	Tax Paid as a % of NAV*
Galaxy II Small Co. Index	1997	18,851,200	6.86%
MainStay Instl. EAFE Index	1997	3,911,600	5.08%
Dreyfus MidCap Index	1998	17,286,000	4.30%
Calif Invt. S&P MidCap Index	1999	2,653,200	4.02%
Dreyfus MidCap Index	1999	14,311,200	3.56%
iShares MSCI Belglum Index	1998	456,400	3.26%
STI Classic Intl. Equity Index	1998	162,000	3.24%
DFA U.S. Large Cap Value	1999		2.00%
Vanguard's Standard Index	1999		1.57%
Average Stock Index Fund	1999		0.53%
U.S. Stock Funds	1999		1.23%
Large Blend Funds	1999		1.05%
Large Cap Funds	1999		1.23%
Mid-Cap Funds	1999		1.53%
Small Cap Funds	1999		1.31%

*As a percent of fund's net asset value.
Source: Prepared by Ben G. Baldwin, August 5, 2000, from the Fund Track Column by Aaron Lucchetti, The Wall Street Journal. Friday, July 28, 2000, pp. C1, C19.

Evensky, chairman of Evensky, Brown & Katz had to deal with. Lucchetti went on to say: "Mr. Evensky, who oversees about $100 million in index-fund assets for clients, now takes steps to try to mitigate the tax problems. For one, he is putting some index-fund money that once would have resided in taxable accounts into tax-sheltered vehicles. This way, the tax issue is moot until the assets are withdrawn." Mr. Evensky and other financial planners will be looking toward properly funded VUL policies as a partial solution to this income tax problem when they realize that the insurance costs and ongoing expenses can be less than the income tax cost of their taxable investment portfolio.

If you decide to sell one of your mutual funds and reinvest the money in a different mutual fund, the transaction will result in current taxation on the capital gains realized. Yes, even if you sell your investment in one of the family funds and reposition those assets in another of that family's funds, you still are subject to taxation on any capital gains realized from the sale.

The subaccounts in your variable universal policy treat you more generously, because you don't have to share your gains with Uncle Sam. The gains may be reinvested intact within the accounts in your policy, and taxation will be either deferred until some future time or eliminated entirely if the policy pays off as a death benefit. If you own a variable universal policy, taxable mutual funds are a poor investment for you until that policy has reached its maximum funding level.

Maximum Funding

The maximum funding level (Exhibit 8.12) is based upon the policy death benefit for your age and sex. The death benefit dictates the point at which no additional funds can be added to the policy based upon the controlling income tax provisions in Internal Revenue Code Section 7702. According to the tax code, a policy funded above this level ceases to be a life insurance policy, resulting in immediate taxation of all deferred earnings. Your insurance company should not, and in all likelihood will not, accept money that would cause your policy to go above maximum funding. To determine if a maximum funding strategy would be advantageous, you have to determine exactly what additional expenses, if any, will be incurred when you send in additional investment dollars. For one thing, these dollars will be diminished by state premium taxes. The taxes are charged by your state of residence on every premium paid into a life insurance policy and typically run about 2 percent. You also may have to pay a front-end sales load, which averages about 4 percent.

Exhibit 7.9 lists the premium taxes charged by the individual states and areas. If you live in New York, you will find that only about $7/10$ of 1 percent of your investment goes to state premium tax, and in Illinois only ½ of 1 percent. A $100 premium would incur only a 50 cent tax in Illinois. If the insurance company makes no additional charges against your investment, $99.50 would go to work for you in your accumulation account. In this case, this charge will probably be lower than most low-load mutual funds.

EXHIBIT 8.12

Maximum Funding

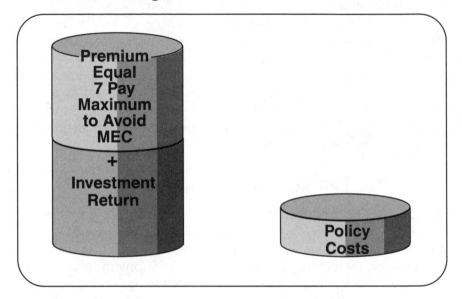

On the other hand, if you live in the Virgin Islands, which has a premium tax of 5 percent, a $100 deposit going into a variable universal policy would be diminished by $5—only $95 would be invested. In either case, you probably can find investments within your policy advantageous to you because the income tax savings involved and the tax-free compounding you can enjoy far outweigh these one-time charges. Determine these costs before you buy a policy.

THE INCOME TAX BENEFITS OF LIFE INSURANCE

The income tax benefits of life insurance are summed up in Exhibit 8.13. Here we will examine them in detail.

Death Benefits—Tax-Free

The primary advantage of life insurance is that if you contribute a small sum when the life insurance hat is passed, the whole

EXHIBIT 8.13

Income Tax Benefits of Life Insurance

1. The total death benefit received by the beneficiary from a life insurance contract is excluded from the beneficiary's income. This total death benefit includes not only the net amount at risk but also the total amount of the policy owner's equity accumulated within the contract and the earnings on that equity over the years.

2. The annual increases in value (inside buildup) and the accumulated increases in value, be they interest or investment appreciation, are not subject to current taxation and will escape taxation entirely if they are eventually delivered as a death benefit. Money moved among the subaccounts within the policy is not subject to current taxation.

3. Policy "cost basis," the amount you can withdraw income tax–free, includes funds spent on the expenses and mortality cost within a policy, making such expenditures *tax-free* whether a policy terminates as a death benefit or is otherwise terminated.

4. Policies issued after June 20, 1988, whose premium payments exceed the seven-pay threshold are modified endowment contracts (MEC). Withdrawals and loans from a MEC create immediate income taxation to the extent of the gain in the policy and, if the policy owner is under age 59½, also 10 percent IRS income tax penalties on the amount included in income. However, policy values generally can be accessed via policy loans, collateralizations, or withdrawals without the imposition of current taxation or 10 percent penalties if the policy owner puts no more money into the policy than the MEC limit.

hat will be given to your beneficiary when you subsequently die (see Exhibit 8.13). This is good not only for you and your beneficiaries, but for all of us too. Your beneficiaries do not become economically dependent upon us. This is the reason that the death benefits of life insurance policies have been exempted from income taxation. It doesn't matter whether the death benefit comes from net amount at risk, the policy owner's investment in the contract, or positive investment results. It is *all* tax-free income under Section 101 of the Internal Revenue Code. This, the first income tax benefit of life insurance, is enjoyed by all life insurance policyholders. However, there are ways that you may mismanage your policy (such as selling it to another for valuable consideration) that might result in a taxable death benefit. Don't make any such changes without considering them carefully with your tax advisor.

Current Earnings and Gains Not Currently Taxed

The second advantage of life insurance is that during your lifetime and while the policy is still in force, all interest earned, dividends earned, and capital gains realized on the policy investments are not subject to current income tax. You can even take your gains from a very profitable policy subaccount and move them to another subaccount within the contract without being subject to current taxation, capital gains taxes, and often, transaction costs. The taxation is deferred until you take gains from the policy. All investment life insurance policies provide for tax deferral on this inside buildup and the possibility of total tax exemption on investment returns when the proceeds are disbursed as death benefits.

The Basis Includes Payments
for Life Insurance Expenses

The third income tax benefit of life insurance containing investment capital is the amount of money you recover tax-free when you surrender your policy and have a gain. Your tax basis includes all the life insurance costs that the policy has incurred during the time the policy has been in force. In this situation, the costs *increase your basis* and thus are recovered tax-free. The life insurance that you paid for while you owned the policy was paid for with money that has never and will never be subject to income taxes. Your life insurance has been purchased with income tax-free dollars.

Tax-Free Use of Untaxed Earnings and Gains

The fourth income tax benefit is that you can use the values accumulated within the life insurance policy while it is still in force, and still (1) withdraw, (2) borrow against them, or (3) pledge the policy as collateral for a loan (e.g., borrow from a bank). If you withdraw an amount exceeding your investment in the contract, the amount withdrawn above your cost basis is subject to ordinary income tax. As a result, you normally would withdraw no more than what you put into a policy. If you want additional funds, you could borrow against the policy or collateralize the policy to get at those funds without being currently taxed on them. Prior to June 21, 1988, this could be done on almost any policy without paying income tax on any accumulated gain within the contract. However, as of that date, the tax laws were changed to limit the amount you can invest in a policy and still access the money without income taxation and a 10 percent, pre–age 59½ penalty. If you exceed that limit you have what is called a modified endowment contract (MEC) and withdrawals will be subject to income taxes to the extent of gain. If you are under age 59½ you will also have a 10 percent IRS penalty on the amount you have to pay income tax on.

MODIFIED ENDOWMENT INSURANCE– TAMRA 88

Single-premium life policies are the most investment-oriented of life insurance policies. In effect, they are maximum-funded policies with the first and only premium. Prior to June 21, 1988, they combined:

1. High returns (because of the relatively high interest rates available at that time)
2. Deferral (no tax on those returns)
3. The ability to access those returns without current taxation of penalties.

In 1988, Congress decided this was too much of a good thing. The result was that in November 1988, the Technical and Miscellaneous Revenue Act of 1988 (TAMRA) was signed into law. This new law defined modified endowment contracts (MEC), a new class of life insurance policies that Uncle Sam considered too investment-oriented. It removed the tax-free accessibility to the cash in them. Any policy that was issued after June 20, 1988, and that is classified as a modified endowment contract, cannot provide the policy owner with the privilege of withdrawing from, borrowing from, or collateralizing the values accrued within the policy without incurring immediate taxation on policy gains. Indeed, if you're under age 59½, not only do income taxes become due on the amount of gain accessed in the contract, but you also are subject to a 10 percent penalty on the amount included in gross income as a result of the withdrawal, borrowing, or collateralization. The only exceptions to this penalty are if the funds are withdrawn as a result of disability or over a period related to the policy owner's lifetime (i.e., annuitized).

How to Avoid Modified Endowment Status

We'll assume that you, the policy owner, want all four income tax benefits. In particular, you want the ability to make withdrawals up to your basis, or loans on your policy, without being exposed to ordinary income tax or penalties. To accomplish this with a policy issued after June 20, 1988, you may invest no more during the first seven policy years than an amount determined by the government-mandated test called the *seven-pay test*. The seven-pay test has nothing to do with your paying seven premiums; it only limits the amount that you can pay into your policy within the first seven years of its existence. For example, if the insurance company offering you a policy informs you (and it *should*) that the seven-pay test allows no more than $1000 per policy year, you could put up to, but no more than, $1000 into the policy in the first year. You could pay up to, but not more than, a total of $2000 by the end of the second year. For the first seven policy years, the cumulative maximum you could contribute would be $7000. At that point, your policy would have completed the testing period, it would not be a modified endowment contract, and your accessibility to policy values by way of loans and withdrawals up to basis should not incur taxation or penalties. Other provisions of Internal Revenue Code Section 7702 also control the amount of your contributions to your policy. Indeed, often you will find these more restrictive in the fifth through seventh policy years than the seven-pay test restrictions, and you will not be able to contribute even as much as the seven-pay test indicates. Your insurance company should inform you if your contributions have exceeded both those allowed by the provisions of Section 7702 and the seven-pay test limits, and your company should refund any excess to you. Most insurance companies do offer tracking assistance. Find out how your company does it.

Material Change to a Pre-TAMRA Policy

The TAMRA 1988 provisions also put restrictions on any policy issued prior to June 21, 1988, if it is subject to a *material change*. Almost any change in a policy is likely to be deemed a material change, other than death benefit and future policy value increases resulting naturally from the payment of premiums that comply with the seven-pay test in the first seven contract years and benefit increases resulting from investment and/or interest earnings on those premiums. A material change will result in the policy being considered a *new* contract entered into after June 20, 1988, and subject to the seven-pay test as of the date the material change takes effect. The policy then must be tested under the 1988 rules. If it fails the test at any time in the following seven years, it becomes a modified endowment contract. Policies that can pass the seven-pay test are *not* modified endowments and retain *all* the tax benefits of life insurance. Be careful in making changes to any existing policy, particularly your currently grandfathered policies, those taken out prior to June 21, 1988.

When to Ignore Seven-Pay Test Limits

If you wish, you can still buy a single-premium investment-oriented policy, the policy referred to by Uncle Sam as a modified endowment contract. These policies still pay the tax-free death benefit of the total proceeds and the tax deferral on the inside buildup or earnings within the policy as a result of interest, dividends, and capital gains. Just be aware these policies that if you borrow against, withdraw from, or collateralize this policy, you will have to pay income taxes to the extent that you have gain in your policy. You also will have to pay a 10 percent penalty on any amount included in income as a result of withdrawing, borrowing, or collateralizing if you're under age 59½ (the exceptions being disability or annuity payouts). If the inability to access the money within your policy without current taxation is *not* important to you, then the 1988 change in the law is irrelevant and you may continue to use these policies to accomplish your objectives. In the past, less than 10 percent of purchasers of single-premium policies have borrowed from them. If you don't intend to use this money during your lifetime, the MEC rules will have no impact, and these policies are very efficient at holding earmarked money and moving it to specific beneficiaries at your death. For example, you may have $10,000 that you want to get to that beneficiary in an efficient manner at your death without going through probate. You want the money to be invested in a diversified portfolio that includes many different investment managers, and you want to use asset allocation and rebalancing until your death, but neither you nor the beneficiaries want to pay income taxes on the investment earnings. A single-premium variable life policy might just be the correct tool to accomplish your objectives.

If you are not sure whether or not it will be necessary to access the money in the future, it is probably best to comply with the seven-pay test regulations, so that you may keep the fourth advantage of life insurance available to you—tax-free and penalty-free access to your cash.

In short, the rule of thumb in determining how much to invest in variable universal is *as much as you can* while still retaining *all* the income tax benefits. The next consideration is how and where to put your investment.

CHAPTER 9

Investment Choice in VUL

The More You Invest, the Better It Works!

When you assess the available investment options within your variable universal policy, you must make what investment professionals refer to as the *asset allocation decision*. That is, you must select the kinds of investment accounts to be used and determine the percentage of money to be allocated to each. A simple asset allocation model called the *portfolio allocation scoring system* (PASS), developed by Professor William G. Droms of Georgetown University, serves as a tool to assist you.*

PASS has been extensively tested and implemented by major insurance companies and used successfully to plan investment portfolios for literally thousands of clients. The system also has been used by a number of banks and CPA firms, has been published in the *Journal of Accountancy*,† and is included in the American Institute of Certified Public Accountants' *Personal Financial Planning Practice Management Handbook*.

The system is easy to use and is based on your unique risk-reward preferences. Successfully implementing it requires that

---

*The author expresses his particular thanks to Dr. William G. Droms, CFA, Powers Professor of Finance and International Business at Georgetown University, for the use of his portfolio allocation scoring system and for his careful review of this chapter and many beneficial suggestions.
†William G. Droms, "Investment Asset Allocation for PFP Clients." *Journal of Accountancy*, April 1987, pp. 114–118.

you understand the asset allocation process, the risk constraints you should impose on your portfolio, and the return opportunities available from the various investment alternatives offered to you. PASS brings all these factors together in an easy-to-understand system that you can use to guide your investment selections.

ASSET ALLOCATION AS A STRATEGIC DECISION

Asset allocation is a process of distributing portfolio investments among the various available categories of investment assets, such as money-market instruments, bonds, and stocks. *Selection of the asset mix is the single most important determinant of long-term investment performance.* In a widely diversified portfolio, for example, the selection of specific stocks to hold within the equity portion of the portfolio normally has much less impact on total portfolio performance than does the percentage of the total portfolio that will be allocated to equity investments, such as common stocks (see Exhibit 9.1).

EXHIBIT 9.1

Determinants of Portfolio Performance

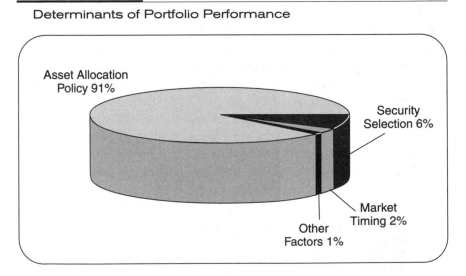

Source: Data for this graph was obtained from Brinson, Singer, and Beebower, "Determinants of Portfolio Performance," *Financial Analysts Journal*, May–June 1991.

Exhibit 9.1 is taken from a study by Brinson, Singer, and Bee-bower. Its message is that the determination of how much of your portfolio is to be invested in equities is by far the most important decision you make (91 percent impact). Over the longterm, your portfolio performance is affected relatively little by how well you do in picking stocks (security selection 6 percent impact) or how great a market timer you think you can be (market timing 2 percent impact).

Asset allocation is the key strategic decision to be made in planning your investment portfolio. Once the strategic decision of how much of each asset category to hold is made, tactical decisions can be made to implement the overall investment strategy. Tactical decisions involve selections made from the subaccounts available within your policy.

Making strategic asset allocation decisions requires consideration of your return objectives as well as the constraints on these objectives. Constraints would include such factors as the degree and types of risk to which you submit your portfolio along with your liquidity requirements, income needs, long-term growth expectations, tax situation, and investment time horizon. For most of us, return objectives and planning constraints tend to be extremely broad and highly qualitative in nature, making the asset allocation problem more difficult for individuals than it is for institutions.

Exhibit 9.2 shows the effect of your asset allocation decision on your expected return and risk. As you examine the exhibit, you will note that downside losses were less in the past when people owned at 30 percent stock (−3.5 percent) and greater when they owned 100 percent bonds (−4.0 percent). The point is that diversifying a portfolio away from 100 percent bonds and going to 30 percent stock and 70 percent bonds creates a *less* risky portfolio than a 100 percent bond portfolio over long time periods.

ASSET CATEGORIES FOR INDIVIDUALS

From the virtually unlimited array of possible investments, the asset allocation framework (PASS) proposed here focuses on three generic investment classes: money-market funds, bond funds, and equity investments in common stock subaccounts. This classifi-

EXHIBIT 9.2

Asset Allocation Strategies (And What You Can Expect from Them)

Global Balanced Portfolio	1973–1999 Average	Best Year	Worst Year
100% stock/0% bonds	14.0%	43.8%	(23.3%)
90% stock/10% bonds	13.5%	41.6%	(20.7%)
70% stock/30% bonds	12.6%	37.2%	(15.1%)
50% stock/50% bonds	11.5%	32.9%	(9.4%)
30% stock/70% bonds	10.4%	28.7%	(3.5%)
10% stock/90% bonds	9.3%	28.4%	(3.2%)
0% stock/100% bonds	8.6%	29.9%	(4.0%)

Source: Morgan Stanley Capital International, Standard & Poor's State Street Securities, Compustat and Bernstein. Intermediate Bonds are State Street Securities and Bernstein. Equities are 70 percent S&P 500, 30 percent EAFE GDP weighted, unhedged asset allocation rebalanced monthly. Past performance is not an indication of a future result.

cation scheme is adopted because these investment options are now commonly available in insurance policies, and reliable long-term risk and return data are available on the investment performance of these asset categories. This approach does not imply that other types of investments, such as real estate, precious metals, commodity options, or venture capital, may not be appropriate for some other portions of your portfolio. It merely is adopted as a means of simplifying the conceptual process and as a method that reflects the asset allocation choices made by most individuals and available within variable universal policies. The three generic categories are characterized by different types of investment risk-return trade-off patterns and meet different investor needs and objectives.

Money-market instruments, such as Treasury bills, short-term bank certificates of deposit, banker's acceptances, and bond repurchase agreements, generally are purchased by individuals in the form of money-market mutual funds or through bank money-market deposit accounts. Such investments offer a high degree of safety of principal, immediate liquidity, and a rate of return commensurate with inflation.

Fixed-income mutual funds, such as corporate or government bond funds and mortgage-backed funds generally, offer a high

EXHIBIT 9.3

What Is Interest Rate Risk?

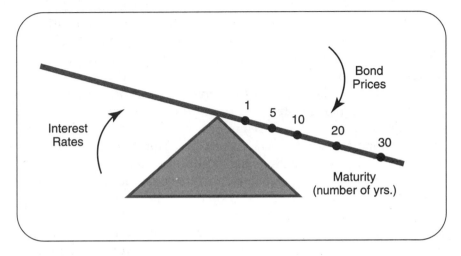

degree of current yield, moderate liquidity (from virtually instantaneous marketability for bonds to lesser degrees of liquidity for mortgages), and, if of high quality, excellent protection of principal. In times of falling prices and interest rates, *bonds are king* because they increase in principal value as interest rates fall. In increasing-interest-rate environments, the opposite is true. Bond values typically decrease as interest rates go up. See Exhibit 9.3.

Equity investments, such as common stock mutual funds, offer the best opportunity for long-term capital appreciation, but do have the potential for loss and fluctuation in principal values. Common stock equity investments are the classic hedges against inflation in that they generally increase in value over long periods of time as the economy expands.

INVESTMENT RISKS AND RETURN

It is not too much of an exaggeration to note that in planning our individual investment portfolios many of us know exactly what we want in an investment—something that will double in 6 months with no risk. It is critical that we assess our attitudes toward risk before designating objectives for return.

It is important to understand that there is no such thing as a risk-free investment. We cannot avoid risk with our investment capital. The choice of *doing nothing* or *leaving it in the bank* is extremely important in terms of the impact on our wealth. Risk is commonly measured quantitatively in terms of standard deviation about the mean total annual return. This measure of total risk can be applied to virtually any investment. Standard deviation measures dispersion about the mean of the distribution of total annual returns; the higher the standard deviation of return relative to the mean level of return, the greater the risk. Exhibit 9.4 shows the long-term historical returns and risks for a number of asset classes. The standard deviation essentially tells you the range about the mean return within which security returns can be expected to fall most (approximately 70 percent) of the time. The standard deviation for large-company stock is 20.1 percent (the difference between the mean and the high and the mean and the low 70 percent of the time). Thus, for example, large-company stock returns, which average 11 percent over this 74-year period in any single year, have a 70 percent probability of falling between −9.2 percent and +31.2 percent. Treasury bills, by comparison, average a 3.8 percent return. Their standard deviation of return is much lower, 3.2 percent compared with 20.1 percent for common stocks.

In short, you pick Treasury bills, an investment with a rela-

EXHIBIT 9.4

Total Annual Returns, 1926–2000

Investment	Average Mean Annual Compound Return	Standard Deviation of Return
Consumer prices	3.1%	4.5%
United States Treasury bills	3.8%	3.2%
Long-term government bonds	5.3%	9.4%
Long-term corporate bonds	5.7%	8.7%
Large-company stocks	11.0%	20.2%
Small stocks	12.4%	33.4%

Source: *Stocks, Bonds, Bills and Inflation 2001 Yearbook.* Published by Ibbotson Associates, Capital Market Research Center, Chicago, Illinois.

tively low average return of 3.8 percent, and 70 percent of the time the return ends up within ±3.2 percent of the 3.7 percent average. Whereas when you pick an investment with a higher average rate of return, like common stocks at 11.3 percent, 70 percent of the time your return will end up within 20.1 percent of that average. You can see why risk is sometimes equated with standard deviation and standard deviation with volatility. More risk is more deviation from the average or mean return—more volatility. It is just that we hate volatility down and love volatility up. Now take that to your next cocktail party!

Individual investors also are concerned with other aspects of risk that may not be captured by the standard deviation of total return. Liquidity risk (the inability to liquidate promptly without the loss of principal) and the risk of incurring a loss within a particular investment holding period are chief among these risk factors. The latter risk is especially important to investors in the stock market, because while historical experience shows that stocks provide higher returns in the long run than do fixed-income instruments, they do so at the price of incurring losses during some years. The PASS asset allocation model attempts to capture all these risk concerns and balance them against return objectives.

A PORTFOLIO ALLOCATION SCORING SYSTEM

Modern portfolio theory provides the formal theoretical framework for most quantitatively based asset allocation models used by institutional portfolios, such as pension funds and endowment funds. Portfolio theory assumes that investors base their portfolio decision on only two considerations: (1) the expected return from an investment and (2) its level of risk as measured by the standard deviation of expected return. Investors are assumed to attempt investment in *efficient portfolios*, defined as those portfolios that provide the greatest return at a given level of risk—or, alternatively and equivalently, the least risk for a given return objective.

For individual investors, risk is a more complex and subtle concept than the simple standard deviation of expected future return. However, we should not abandon the lessons of modern portfolio theory altogether. In particular, two central lessons should guide any asset allocation system. First, the risk-return trade-off hypothesized by portfolio theory does in fact exist, and we must recognize that attempts to earn higher rates of return necessitate accepting greater volatility in our annual returns. Second, portfolio theory concludes that portfolio diversification reduces risk (volatility of return). Rational investment management dictates that portfolios must be diversified among asset classes as well as among individual securities within asset classes. Developing an appropriate asset allocation strategy requires that you make a realistic assessment of the type and magnitude of the risk you are willing to accept, commensurate with the rate of return you desire to earn. Exhibit 9.5 presents the portfolio allocation scoring system for determining an appropriate portfolio allocation scheme. PASS is designed to provide a rough outline of an action strategy for an individual investor.

PASS requires that you score yourself on a 1-to-5 scale of important return and risk objectives. The more points you score, the more your portfolio should be oriented toward equity investments. Conversely, a low score would indicate that your portfolio

EXHIBIT 9.5

Portfolio Allocation Scoring System

		Strongly Agree	Agree	Neutral	Disagree	Strongly Disagree
1.	Earning a high long-term return that will allow my capital to grow faster than the inflation rate is one of my most important investment objectives.	5	4	3	2	1
2.	I would like an investment that allows me to defer taxation of capital gains and/or interest to future years.	5	4	3	2	1
3.	I do not require a high level of current income from my investments.	5	4	3	2	1
4.	My major investment goals are relatively long-term.	5	4	3	2	1
5.	I am willing to tolerate sharp up and down swings in the return on my investments in order to seek a higher return than would normally be expected from more stable investments.	5	4	3	2	1
6.	I am willing to risk short-term losses in return for a potentially higher long-run rate of return.	5	4	3	2	1
7.	I am financially able to accept a low level of liquidity in my investment portfolio.	5	4	3	2	1

Portfolio Allocation Models

Total Score	Money Market Instruments	Fixed-Income Securities	Equity Investments
30–35	10%	10%	80%
22–29	20	20	60
14–21	30	30	40
7–13	40	40	20

Source: William G. Droms, "Investment Asset Allocation for PEP Clients," *Journal of Accountancy* (April 1987).

should be oriented more toward fixed-income investments. As a result, PASS demonstrates that in order to earn higher returns you would have to accept greater risks, and one way to mitigate these risks is to diversify.

To use PASS, simply circle the number under the column that best describes the importance of each investment objective to you. After responding to each statement, add up the total value of all the numbers you circled and use this score to determine your diversification guidelines, given in the lower section. The PASS statements are structured to award 5 points for a response of "strongly agree" and 1 point for a response of "strongly disagree." A "neutral" response scores 3 points.

The first three statements measure return objectives. Strong agreement with the first statement—that you need to earn a high long-term goal return so your capital will grow faster than the inflation rate—results in a score of 5. If this objective is not at all important to you, you would strongly disagree with the statement and score 1 point. Remember that this is *not* an exam. A high score is best only if it most closely matches your attitude toward risk and return. It is important that you answer these questions carefully and thoughtfully.

The second statement deals with the importance of deferring taxation on capital gains and interest; opportunities to defer taxes generally are associated with equity investments. The third statement assesses the extent to which you need the portfolio to generate current income. A lower current income requirement allows you to orient the portfolio toward more aggressive long-term capital gains.

The last four statements on the PASS survey deal with your time horizon, fluctuations in total return, the probability of realizing losses in some years, and liquidity needs. These statements measure four different aspects of your risk tolerance. More willingness to tolerate these kinds of risk is reflected in a higher PASS score, suggesting a stronger orientation toward equities in the portfolio.

The highest possible score that you can achieve in the PASS system is 35 and would mean that you strongly agreed with all the statements on the form. This indicates a set of risk and return objectives best met by allocating nearly all your capital to equity investments, such as common stocks or common stock subaccounts. Even with a PASS score of 35, your overall portfolio should combine 10 percent of money-market instruments and 10 percent of fixed-income securities with the high—80 percent—proportion of common stock.

The lowest possible PASS score of 7 would result if you strongly disagreed with all the statements about your investment risk and return objectives. With this score, PASS suggests that you invest only 20 percent of your assets in equity investments, allocating 40 percent of your remaining capital to money-market instruments and 40 percent to fixed-income securities. A PASS score between the extremes suggests that you allocate your portfolio among the three asset classes in some intermediate proportion.

Obviously, PASS provides only a rough guideline for portfolio allocation. It is not meant to be a fail-safe, mechanical system to meet all your planning needs. The PASS score does, however, provide an approximation of your optimal portfolio, which you can use to turn your personal risk and return objectives into a portfolio action strategy. The system also forces you to recognize the trade-off between risk and return and come to grips with your own *risk-return preferences* and income needs.

APPLYING YOUR PASS RESULTS TO A VARIABLE UNIVERSAL POLICY

Risk-return preference: The amount of volatility an investor is willing to accept in pursuit of increasing investment returns.

Suppose your PASS results suggest that 60 percent equity–40 percent debt (20 percent fixed income, 20 percent money market) asset allocation would be appropriate for you. Your next question may be, "Which subaccounts do I want to use?"

First you have to define how much you intend to invest and how often? If your answer is not much and not often, then you probably should *not use variable universal* life insurance. If you are not or will not be an investor, variable universal life is not for you. Just buy term insurance until you learn to be an investor. It makes no sense to buy a VUL with a 30- or 40-cylinder engine (subaccounts) and then not put any gas (money) in the tank.

On the other hand, suppose you are going to:

1. Invest a significant amount, defined as target premium, rounded up or more
2. Utilize a 1035 tax-free exchange to move money from an old life insurance policy into a VUL policy
3. Plan on maximum-funding your policy up to its modified endowment limits as soon as possible

If any of these describes your situation, then you need to select the separate account investments with care, knowing the nature of each investment alternative.

The reason variable universal has been referred to as the "Swiss Army knife of financial products" and the "financial product of this century" is because it gives a vast majority of people a flexible, low-hassle, convenient and economical way to invest. For example, look at Exhibit 9.6, which shows the allocation of a $100

EXHIBIT 9.6

Allocation Percentages and Investment Division Activity

Allocation Percentages

Investment Division	Allocation
Guaranteed interest/money market	10%
Common stock	30%
Aggressive stock	20%
Balanced	20%
High yield	20%

Investment Division Activity (Effective Date: June 15, 1987)

Transaction Investment Divisions	No. of Units	Unit Value	Amount
Gross premium			$100.00
State premium taxes			(2.00)
Guaranteed interest			9.80
Common stock	0.195	$150.396	29.40
Aggressive stock	0.111	$175.850	19.60
Balanced	0.128	$152.068	19.60
High yield	0.193	$202.114	19.60

EXHIBIT 9.7

Review of Unit Values

	Unit Value		1987–1993 % Increases	Unit Value	1993–2000 % Increases
	1987	1993		2000	
Common stock	150.396	289.33	92%	963.75	333%
Aggressive stock	175.850	462.89	163%	921.74	199%
Balanced	152.068	265.72	75%	524.80	198%
High yield	101.117	191.25	89%		

deposit in Katie's variable universal life insurance policy on June 15, 1987. Where else could a 25-year-old newlywed carve up a $100 bill and take advantage of so many and varied investments, knowing it would have no impact on her tax return?

This got her started on a lifetime of investing. A more recent review of the unit values is shown in Exhibit 9.7. You will note that this asset allocation is 60 percent equity (common stock, aggressive stock, and one-half of the balanced fund) and 40 percent fixed-income (guaranteed interest, high yield, and one-half of the balanced fund). She concluded that she should invest in this way because she strongly agreed on PASS questions 1 and 2, generating 10 points, and was neutral on questions 3 through 7 because some investment account income was needed to pay her monthly policy expenses and life insurance costs. At that point in her life she really wasn't sure what her answers were. Her PASS score of 22 led her to the 60 percent equity, 40 percent fixed-income split she used when choosing among funds available within her policy. She might otherwise easily have chosen to try shotgun investing, firing $100 per month into multiple accounts just to see what would happen. Would that have been thoughtless? No. It would have been investing in her investment education with a relatively small amount of money, and that education could pay a lifetime of investment benefits.

HOW TO CHOOSE AMONG SEPARATE ACCOUNTS

It is the nature of the beast. Go to the basic makeup of the investment, know what that type of investment has done in the past. Do not ask your investments to do something other than what they have done in the past. No! They cannot leap tall buildings in a single bound! The past does not predict the future . . . but it is the best indicator.

At this point it is helpful to look at an economic gravity chart. Katie's conclusion, after reviewing the economic gravity chart shown in Exhibit 9.8, was that stocks have tended to provide a better inflation-adjusted rate of return than bonds or fixed-income investments. However, bonds and fixed income investments do better than stocks in providing the monthly income necessary to cover her monthly policy costs.

Exhibit 9.9 shows what the investment alternatives available within a typical policy might do. Exhibit 9.10 shows investment objectives and the accounts to use to achieve those objectives.

Katie feared the loss of her principal, just as you probably do. But if you look at the generic categories in which you can invest, that risk of loss of principal can really be viewed as a risk

EXHIBIT 9.8

Economic Gravity

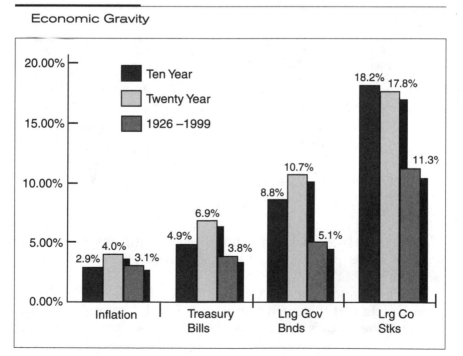

EXHIBIT 9.9

Variable Universal Separate Accounts—What to Expect

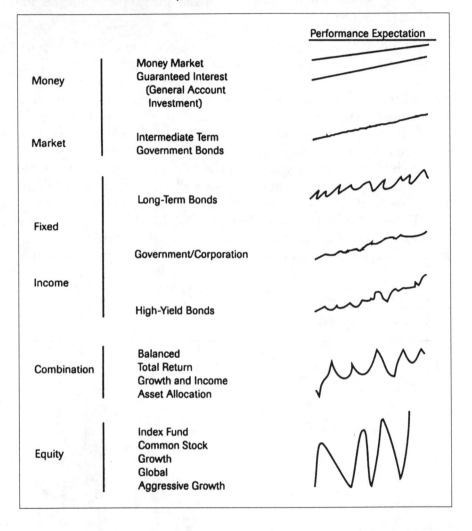

of volatility. Historically, although these investments periodically were in a loss position, all eventually provided positive returns (see Exhibit 9.11).

Will common stocks do it again? Nobody knows! Should Katie conclude that they won't do it again? It did seem presumptuous to Katie to defy history. She decided that economic gravity

EXHIBIT 9.10

Achieving Investment Objectives

Investment Objective	Accounts to Use
Pay policy costs	Guaranteed interest
	Intermediate-term bonds (when interest rates are inordinately low)
	Longer-term high-yield bonds (when interest rates are inordinately high)
	Any of the above if interest rates are staying constant (but who can tell?)
Funds that are *important* for a purpose within 5 years	Same as above
Funds that are for growth and purposes beyond 5 years based upon how much volatility Katie thinks she can stand	Balanced, growth and income Common stock Global Aggressive
Dollar cost averaging: From account to account Within the contract	Source account: nonvolatile accounts Target account: the most volatile ones!
Monthly, quarterly investments for dollar cost averaging	Most volatile Most growth-oriented accounts Diversity

was not going to change. Katie is betting on history repeating itself.

DOLLAR COST AVERAGING

Why the most volatile account for dollar cost averaging—and by the way, what does dollar cost-averaging mean?

As you can see in Exhibit 9.12, if you just got on the Treasury bill line, you would have a relatively smooth ride, but you would not get very far ahead relative to inflation. It is a smooth ride but

EXHIBIT 9.11

The Power of Time Can Reduce Risk

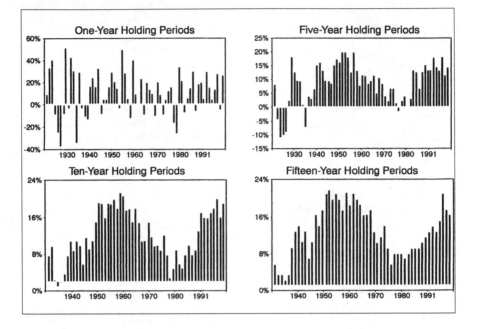

with very little progress. The common stock line, on the other hand, shows significant growth of wealth but a bumpy ride along the way. So the questions are, how do you get into the fast lane? And how do you handle the bumps in the road?

One answer to this question is to use the dollar-cost-averaging strategy. Exhibit 9.13 shows what would happen if you started out with an investment of $100 per period in a diversified stock subaccount, and it swooned just after you started. Look where this investor made the most money—by buying while everyone else was panicking and selling. The investor who was using a dollar-cost-averaging strategy was able to hold on until the market recovered and made a friend out of downside volatility. There are always those who will panic and predict that the market is going to hell in a hand basket. Bad news sells! But the truth is that we probably will muddle through. We've done it before—best bet on it again. When the market sees we have survived another crisis, it will get euphoric and stock prices will attain new

EXHIBIT 9.12

Wealth Indices of Investments in the U.S. Capital Markets,
1925–2000

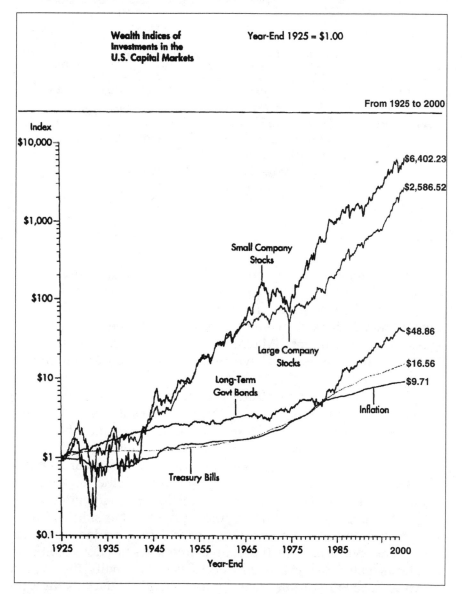

Source: *Stocks, Bonds, Bills, and Inflation 2001 Year Book.* © Ibbotsow Associates, Chicago, Illinois. All Rights
Reserved.

EXHIBIT 9.13

Dollar Cost Averaging
Invest Constant-Dollar Amounts at Equal Intervals over Long
Periods of Time

	Period 1	Period 2	Period 3	Period 4	Period 5	Totals
Investment	$100	$100	$100	$100	$100	= $500
Unit market value	$100	$50	$25	$50	$100	
Units purchased	1	2	4	2	1	= 10 units

Period 5 unit market value	=	$100
Number of accumulated units	=	× 10
Total market value	=	$1000
Total investment all periods	=	$500
Gain	=	$500

Source: Ben G. Baldwin, 1990.

highs. That may be when you want to get out of the most volatile of accounts and step down to a milder ride with your now larger base of *important* capital so that you can rest more easily. But don't give up that dollar cost averaging into your volatile common stock subaccount investments. Maybe now you can also use the earnings on your accumulated investment to dollar-cost-average into equity accounts.

This is an excellent strategy to help you cope with uncertainty and volatility in investing, and it makes it easy to become a successful investor for a lifetime. One of the most harmful things that a financial advisor can do is to put too much of a person's investments into volatile accounts, causing that investor to panic and sell out at the bottom, vowing never to touch the stock market again. That too-hot-to-handle reaction is likely to engender a lifelong aversion, making it almost impossible for that skittish investor to overcome the eroding effect of inflation on long-term investments. But aren't all those investment transactions going to create income taxes and transaction costs? Normally this would be true, but here you are inside your variable universal life policy—no income tax hassle and probably no transaction costs. These savings are likely to far exceed the costs in your policy.

The well-constructed variable universal life policy is second only to your income tax–deductible IRA, 401(k), or other qualified retirement plans as a wealth accumulator. Use them all! You will, however, learn that VUL is your best "weath *retainer*."

SUMMARY

Everyone who is insurable or owns a life insurance policy today can do this type of investing. If you already are insured, you are paying part of the costs associated with a variable universal policy, but into your existing contract. The possibility of a 1035 tax-free exchange is certainly one to be explored with your advisors.

If you are paying for a term life insurance policy, you are paying for a tax-shelter *sack* (the expenses and cost of life insurance), but are not putting anything into it—not investing. When the original *Life Insurance Investment Advisor* was published in early 1988, there were very few variable universal life policies on the market and very few people who understood what they could do. Today the variable universal market is exploding, and there is no reason not to explore how this very important family wealth builder would work for you. Variable universal life insurance

EXHIBIT 9.14

The Cost of Taxes in Taxable Mutual Funds
10-Year Period Ending 1997

	Average Pre-Tax	Average After-Tax	Average Annual Tax Cost
Large Cap Growth Funds	13.4%	11.0%	2.4%
Large Cap Blend Funds	13.1%	10.4%	2.5%
Large Cap Value Funds	12.2%	9.6%	2.6%
Small-Cap Funds	15.1%	12.7%	2.4%
Foreign Stock Funds	7.6%	5.8%	1.8%
Balanced Funds	12.9%	10.2%	2.7%
High Yield Funds	9.9%	5.6%	4.3%
Inter Term Government Bond Funds	7.9%	5.0%	2.9%

Source: Morningstar, 1838 Investment Advisors, L.P. Adapted by Ben G. Baldwin, 1999

competes for your aftertax investment dollars that may currently be residing in taxable mutual funds. Exhibit 9.14 shows the pre- and posttax returns for various classes of mutual funds and the average annual tax cost of owning them. It is very possible with a well-funded VUL policy that you could find your life insurance costs and expenses to be lower than what you would be paying in income taxes if you held the same capital in taxable mutual funds rather than comparable investments within your VUL policy.

CHAPTER 10

Financial Analysis of Life Insurance

Calculating ROR in Life Insurance

Jim came in because he was disturbed that the policy values in his universal life policy were going down. We showed him that the policy would terminate without value in a very few years if he did not put some money into the contract. Jim said the agent told him back in 1985 that the policy would go for life without premium payment. Jim pulled an illustration out of his file that showed this result. Jim's illustration assumed a 10 percent steady interest rate. It did not happen. Jim had purchased an illustration, not a life insurance contract. Unfortunately the illustration was worthless.

In 1975 the Institute of Life Insurance and the Life Insurance Marketing Research Association (LIMRA) prepared a joint study of life insurance consumers. The results showed that of those surveyed 54 percent erroneously equated a policy's premium with policy cost, 61 percent indicated that they had experienced difficulty in determining whether their policies were cost-efficient, and 73 percent said they had trouble understanding their policies. In March and May 1998, LIMRA did another consumer study using focus groups in the United States and Canada. Group participants had either bought life insurance within the past 10 years or seriously considered buying life insurance during the past 2 years. The 1998 findings confirmed the findings of the 1975 study.

- Consumers have a hard time distinguishing whole life from term insurance.

- Consumers have a hard time explaining how a whole life insurance policy works.
- Consumers have rarely heard of variable life, universal life, or variable universal life—let alone knowing how they differ.
- The process of buying life insurance intimidates consumers.
- Consumers find it hard to trust an agent who has a vested interest in what they buy.
- Consumers are interested in learning more.

The variations and alternatives available in life insurance have increased significantly, but the industry still is unable to communicate clearly the costs and benefits of life insurance policies to the public. The study did find that most consumers approach the subject of buying investment-oriented life insurance on a rate-of-return basis. Consumers want to know what the capital in their life insurance is doing, to what costs it is exposed, and what return may be accruing for their own benefit or that of their family.

Over the years, a number of systems have been developed to assist the consumer in the financial analysis of a life insurance policy. In general, they can be divided into two types: those that attempt to be predictive using numbers from illustrations provided by insurance companies and those that try to evaluate existing policies using current policy data. Predictive illustration-based methods are doomed to failure because the numbers used in the illustrations are filled with assumptions that are not comparable company to company and that are more and more flawed, and less and less reliable, as they project further into the future. The illustration-based predictive systems, which this author considers totally unreliable but which are discussed in detail in this chapter, are the traditional net-cost method, the net present value method, the retention method, the regulator-mandated interest-adjusted indices methods, the Linton yield method, and the Barnes system.

The other methods described, the Joseph M. Belth method and the rate of return (ROR) method, do not try to be predictive. Rather, they seek to calculate the rate of return in existing policies based upon what is going on in the present. They do not use illustrations, but instead use what is actually going on at present. The information going into them are current actual results. You will want to examine the methodology and the results to see if either has value to you.

Here is a brief summary of the methods just mentioned. We will then examine the methods in detail.

1. *Traditional net-cost method.* This probably is the easiest method. What goes in, minus what comes out, is cost, or gain. But this method engenders much criticism. Its biggest problem is that people use it with an inordinate degree of confidence in its predictive ability. They look at an illustration generated by an insurance company, compare it with another illustration generated by another insurance company, and think that they can rely on the illustrations to see which policy will actually produce the biggest payout in the distant future. They buy the policy whose illustration predicted the bigger number, ignoring the fact that illustrations are notoriously unreliable. The policy with the most aggressive illustration is likely to be the worst performer. Don't fall under the spell of those who are wont to say to you, "Golly, gee whiz, look how much money you will have 30 or 40 years from now." Make sure you buy a policy, not an illustration.

2. *Net present value method.* The net present value method also seeks to be predictive of future results. And it also uses illustration numbers, but it adds the time value of money into the equation. Using a chosen interest rate, this method calculates the present value of the money going into the policy over some specific period of years. It then uses the illustration-predicted values for that same year and discounts that amount back to the present using the same interest rate. The difference between the present value of what goes into the policy and the present value of the future benefits is cost, or gain. This method is just as reliable as an insurance policy illustration—not very!

3. *Retention method.* The retention method is a predictive method that reverses the present value method. It solves for future value at some chosen interest rate and term of years. The future value of the illustration-given number is subtracted from the future value of the premium payments, and the result is assumed to be what the insurance company has retained (retention).

4. *Interest-adjusted indices.* The interest-adjusted indices are also illustration-based. They are unique because they are endorsed by regulators and are a mandatory part of every general account policy illustration. The regulators have mandated that calculations be determined for 10 and 20 years at 5 percent interest and that two indices be used as if the policy had been surrendered on the specified date. Therefore, the entire cash value and termination dividends are part of the calculation. The calculation for a continuing policy uses only the dividends to reduce cost. Shortly after this method was mandated, insurance companies began to incorporate bigger termination dividends in the tenth and twentieth years, thus lowering their perceived cost indices. This method is no more valuable than net cost, present value, or retention and is probably more harmful to the consumer. The fact that the regulators have sanctioned this method gives it more credibility in the eyes of the consumer than it deserves.

5. *Linton yield method.* The Linton yield method is an academic study of life insurance done in 1919 by an actuary, M. Albert Linton. It was notable because it was the first time that anyone defined whole life insurance as a combination of term insurance and a savings account, and then tried to determine the rate of return on the savings element. The life insurance industry suppressed this view of whole life insurance for the next 70 years.

6. *Barnes Standard disclosure system.* This system is a throwback to using illustration data or demanding information from insurance companies that they cannot predict. It seems to be more a tirade against the

insurance company than a method that has any practical value in helping the consumer make decisions. Many methods have been built upon previous methods, seeking to eliminate perceived inaccuracies. Understanding the tools that have been used to evaluate life insurance will provide a basis for a system of financial evaluation that has validity not only with whole life but also with universal life, variable life, and variable universal life products.

7. *Joseph M. Belth method*. The Belth method, developed by Joseph M. Belth, Ph.D., Professor of Insurance Emeritus at Indiana University, does not seek to be predictive. The Belth method uses reliable numbers from the current year and previous year. The objective of this method is to help the consumer determine if the existing policy is performing adequately or if it should be replaced, if feasible. Professor Belth is the consumer's friend in his never-ending battle to demand integrity within the insurance industry.

8. *Rate-of-return method*. The ROR method springs from the Belth method. It does not use illustration data but uses actual policy performance from the current year and the previous year. It then calculates the rate of return on policy owner average equity during the year. Its refinements on the Belth method include using client-specific data, such as the actual cost of term life insurance for the client, and factoring in the client's tax bracket, because people in higher tax brackets benefit more from the tax shelter of life insurance than people in lower brackets. It is intended to be a useful tool for individual decision making.

NET-COST METHOD

The first of the six predictive methods is the traditional net-cost method. It adds up the total premiums as of a particular date. The total cash available to the policy owner as of that date (also referred to as *cash value plus dividends*, if available, *account value*, or *policy owner equity*) is subtracted from the sum of premiums paid to that date to determine the policy owner's net position. This is defined as *net cost*. In short, what you have paid, minus what you could realize, equals what it costs. The advantage of this traditional net-cost system is that it is simple, quick, and easy to understand.

Problems associated with it arise from its practical application. It includes inaccurate assumptions and does not take the time value of money into consideration. For example, if you put $20,000 in total premium payments into a policy, terminated the policy after 20 years, and got back $20,000, you could inaccurately conclude that the insurance cost you nothing. An amount equal to the premiums paid was returned to you. The error is that you have not accounted for interest earnings. You have forfeited the use of the $20,000 for the 20-year period. The insurance company retained the interest that it earned on the money to pay for the life insurance, expenses, and profits.

You might also conclude erroneously that two policies that have the same bottom line—$20,000 in and $20,000 out—cost the same. This would not be true if one of the policies required payment of the full $20,000 immediately and the other required that the $20,000 be paid in equal annual installments of $1000 each. The former obviously would be far more expensive when considering the time value of money.

You look to the policy illustration provided by the life insurance company as the source of information for the traditional net-cost method. The numbers that can be relied upon as accurate in a whole life illustration are the guaranteed face amount, premium, and guaranteed cash-value amounts.

Face amount, premium, and guaranteed cash value are *guaranteed* in the whole life insurance contract as of the date of issue. The columns referring to dividends are not guaranteed and become less credible each year that the policy is in force. This is because the insurance company figures are less likely to be accurate as they attempt to project farther into the future.

You might be inclined to use these policy illustrations as if they were accurate predictions. You would lay the illustrations side by side in a decision-making situation and make your purchase decision based upon which statement looked the best. The most optimistic prognostication wins! The facts are that actual dividends will differ from projected dividends, that insurance companies may change the ways they credit dividends for different policies, and that companies do not make such changes on a consistent or predictable basis. The only thing that you can be sure of when it comes to dividend projections is that what is presented in the policy illustration will not occur. Future dividends will be either more or less than what was predicted.

Dividends are paid from (1) excess investment earnings over and above what is expected on the insurance company's invested capital, (2) mortality savings (fewer people die than were expected to die), and (3) increased savings and lower-than-projected expenses. Until about 1975, the dividend projections provided by insurance companies had a higher degree of credibility than they do today. The business environment was relatively stable. The investment portfolios of all companies were relatively similar as a result of both regulation and the business practices of the day. Earnings on those investments and taxation on those earnings were fairly predictable. The expenses of operating an insurance company also were predictable and consistent. Old conservative mortality tables were being used during a period of improving mortality. In addition, there was not the intense competition that has resulted from the many new companies that have sprung up.

Today, these new companies, all seeking market share, have underlying portfolios with varying degrees of risk and reward, are charging very low current charges for mortality, but also have to deal with the challenges accompanying the threat of HIV/AIDS. Company expenses are increasing rapidly due to the requirements for sophisticated technology and the cost of distributing the product. Consequently, the companies are aggressively seeking alternative means of distribution and ways to cut expenses. These backfire, in some instances, as short-run expense-cutting efforts call for even higher expenditures to correct the mistakes that are made. All these factors make the forecasting of dividends very difficult and, thus, less reliable than in the past.

Policy illustrations generated for universal life, variable life, and variable universal life are even more prone to error than the policy illustrations for whole life policies. In fact, in his *Insurance Forum* publication of January 1987, Joseph M. Belth states, "In my opinion, life insurance sales illustrations are out of control."

The lack of credibility involved in illustrations was recognized formally by insurance professionals with the introduction of the Illustration Questionnaire (IQ) distributed by the Society of Financial Service Professionals in 1992 (formerly the American Society of CLU & ChFC). The questionnaire invites companies to answer a set of 25 questions dealing with the assumptions used in developing their illustrations. It is intended to help educate intermediaries on the methodology used to generate life insurance proposals, sales illustrations, and/or policy illustrations, as they are variously called. As the IQ states, "It is safe to say that the sales illustrations will never accurately portray the policy's actual performance."

The IQ asks for answers in five different areas:

1. *General.* Do non-guaranteed factors illustrated differ from current experience? Do you treat new and existing policyholders consistently? If not, describe.

2. *Mortality.* Are mortality rates in the illustration consistent with current experience? Are mortality improvements assumed in the illustration? Do the mortality rates (cost of insurance) include some expense charge? Do the mortality charges vary by product? When are the mortality rates the same by attained age?

3. *Interest or crediting rates.* Describe the basis of the interest rate used—gross, net, etc. Does this interest rate or crediting-rate exceed what the company currently is earning? Is there a different rate for existing vs. new policies?

4. *Expenses.* Do expense charges reflect actual experience? Are they different in new vs. existing policies? Are they adequate to cover actual expenses? Increased mortality charges? If not, where/how are these expenses covered?

5. *Persistency.* If the actual experience is better than that assumed, would that negatively impact illustrated values? Does the illustration include non-guaranteed persistency bonuses?

The purpose of the IQ is disclosure of nonguaranteed risk elements. It is intended as an educational tool. You can order the Illustration Questionnaires directly from:

The Society of Financial Service Professionals
Attention: Customer Service
270 S. Bryn Mawr Avenue
Bryn Mawr, PA 19010–2195
Toll free: 1–800–392–6900   Fax: 1–610–527–1499
E-mail: custserv@financialpro.org

The ledger illustrations on *interest-sensitive* and *investment-sensitive* whole life, universal life, variable life, and variable universal life policies are less reliable than those of whole life policies, because in the former there is a rapid flow-through of investment results and mortality and expense charges. With the whole life products, a change is not felt by the policy owner until the insurance company changes its dividend scales. There is lag time that cushions the impact. With new contracts, expense and mortality charges may be charged immediately, and investment changes are recorded immediately. In short, they are contracts that respond rapidly to the current economic environment.

It is highly unlikely that the policy illustrations generated for these products will resemble reality in any way. The accounting profession might describe 40- or 50-year policy illustrations as "affirmatively misleading minutiae"; i.e., they report amounts with such detail that they give an unrealistic impression of accuracy.

There are two appropriate uses of long-term policy illustrations with the new products:

1. The identification of policy costs in the early years so that you can decide if they are acceptable.
2. The determination of the point at which the policy could fail (lapse without value), using worst-case assumptions such as maximum contractual mortality charges, maximum expense charges, and very conservative interest earnings assumptions and funding-level input into the illustration.

The illustrations for universal life types of policies show both current expenses and mortality charges for each year. These illustrations can be of great value for comparison purposes during the first few years of the policy's life.

The problem with each of the first six methods of policy valuation cited at the beginning of this chapter is that they use illustration numbers typically for year 20 in their calculations, which dooms them to failure. Annual reports on existing policies show actual expenses and life insurance charges and can be depended upon. In-force illustrations on your existing policies can be requested from your company for use in short-term planning, but long-term projections are not credible.

NET PRESENT VALUE METHODS

The net present value method of comparing policies improves on the traditional net cost method by applying the time value of money to the numbers provided in a policy illustration. This method requires that you take the policy illustration of a traditional whole life policy over some predetermined period of time, and discount that flow at an assumed interest rate, usually between 5 and 8 percent, to determine the present value of the premium flow required. You would thereby answer the question, "How much money would I need today to provide the required premium payments for 20 years?" For example, assuming a $1000-per-year premium for a policy with $100,000 face value, 5 percent interest, and a 20-year time period, the net present value of this cashflow would be $12,462.21 (see Exhibit 10.1). Thus, you would need $12,462.21 in today's dollars to fund the minimum payments for the next 20 years.

EXHIBIT 10.1

Net Present Value Method

	Net Cost Method	No. of Years	Discount Factor	Present Value
Premium flow:				
$1000	($20,000)	20	5%	($12,462.21)
Future value				
$25,000	$25,000	20	5%	$ 9,422.24
Net gain	$5,000	Net present value policy cost		($ 3,039.97)

The next question is, "What will be the policy's reported total asset value on that date 20 years in the future?" Using our example, suppose that the policy illustrations indicated a total value on the policy illustration for the twentieth year of $25,000. Traditional net-cost calculation would indicate that the policy owner had earned a profit of $5000 ($20,000 paid in, $25,000 to be paid out). However, when the $25,000 figure to be delivered 20 years hence is discounted at 5 percent to its present value, we find that it has a present value of $9,422.24. The present value of the benefits expected from the policy is $9,422.24. Subtracting this from the present value of the payments that must be made to receive these benefits ($12,462.21 − $9,422.24) shows that the cost of the policy is $3,039.97, at a 5 percent discount rate.

This method makes an adjustment for the time value of money and also allows you to compare policies with dissimilar premiums and values. However, it continues to rely on numbers provided by the policy illustration. If this method is used to compare life insurance contracts with the objective of choosing the most efficient, the following assumptions are made, all of which are *wrong*.

1. The numbers presented in the ledger are accurate and comparable.
2. The current dividend scale will continue unchanged for each of the competing companies for the 20-year period.
3. The companies use similar assumptions in developing their dividends and setting dividend policy.
4. If there are future changes in dividend scales, it will affect all companies under consideration in an equal manner.
5. The contracts will be terminated at the end of the chosen period of time.
6. Death benefits are equal.
7. All other policy provisions are identical.

The results of this method must be used with a great deal of caution. It is not recommended as a final selection technique.

RETENTION METHOD

An alternative to the present value method is the retention method, which asks how much of the future value of the premium stream, at an assumed interest rate, is retained by the insurance company upon termination of the contract.

To continue our example, suppose that you want to know the future value of this premium stream of $1000 per year, at 5 percent interest, at the beginning of each year for the next 20 years. You would find the future value of that premium stream to be $33,065.95. If the insurance company returned $25,000 to you in the twentieth year when you terminated your policy, you would determine that the insurance company had retained $8,065.95 to pay mortality charges and expenses and take profits on your policy. Using this method, you would find that the best policy to select would be the one with the lowest retention level. Since this method uses the same invalid assumptions as the present value method, and also utilizes projected numbers from policy illustrations, you can expect it to provide the same unusable results.

INTEREST-ADJUSTED INDICES

The regulators have responded to the difficulties involved in comparing life insurance policies and their cost-effectiveness by recommending the interest-adjusted indices. The Joint Special Committee on Life Insurance Costs met and in 1970 recommended an alternative cost-comparison method known as the *interest-adjusted method*, which considers the time value of money. In 1976 the National Association of Insurance Commissioners (NAIC) adopted a model regulation for life insurance solicitation. The NAIC has recommended the regulation to the various states for their adoption, and approximately 38 states have adopted it.

The regulation requires insurers to provide buyers with an interest-adjusted surrender cost index and an interest-adjusted net payment cost index for the tenth and twentieth policy years, using a 5 percent interest assumption. The data required for the interest-adjusted methods are:

1. The annual level premiums accumulated at 5 percent.
2. The face amount.
3. The time period over which the analysis is to be made. (The model regulation requires it for 10 and 20 years.)
4. The interest rate. The NAIC mandates 5 percent. They consider 5 percent net after tax as an acceptable long-term interest rate from personal investments of comparable security and stability as general account life insurance policies.
5. Dividends are to be accumulated at 5 percent interest, if dividends are available in the contract.
6. The cash surrender value.

The NAIC requires that we use two indices. The interest-adjusted *net payment* cost index assumes that the policy is continuing in force, and therefore only the dividend values plus 5 percent interest earnings (if the policy in question pays dividends) are available to the policy owner to reduce cost. The cash surrender value is not available and, therefore, not included in the interest-adjusted net payment cost index. The interest-adjusted *surrender* cost index assumes the policy is terminated; the cash value is available to reduce cost and is included in the calculation of the surrender cost index.

INTEREST-ADJUSTED NET PAYMENT COST INDEX

The interest-adjusted net payment cost index builds an index based upon the continuation of a policy. Since the policy is continuing in force, it assumes that the cash value of the policy is not available to the policy owner. Dividends, and 5 percent interest on those dividends, are assumed to be available to the policy owner in participating policies.

Accumulate the annual dividends, if available, plus the 5 percent interest earnings on those dividends for the period of time in question. In order to convert those dividend credits and their interest earnings to a level annual amount for the specified period of time, the dividend amounts are divided by the future value of $1 at 5 percent for the period. The payment of $1 per year, assuming a 5 percent interest and a 20-year time period, results in a future value of $34.72. That is, if you deposit $1 each year at the beginning of the year in a 5 percent account, you will accumulate $34.72 in 20 years. By dividing the future dividend value (determined by the insurance company) by this 20-year divisor, you will find the number of dollars that would have been required annually to arrive at this amount. The 10-year divisor is $13.21; that is, $1 per year deposited at the beginning of the year in an account earning 5 percent would accumulate to $13.21 in 10 years.

The adjusted premium is the level annual premium accumulated at 5 percent. For example, a $1000 annual premium accumulated at 5 percent for 20 years would total $34,719.30. If the twentieth-year accumulation of dividends was $12,000, you would calculate the 5 percent interest-adjusted dividend value by dividing the $12,000 by 20 years ($600) and then determine the future value of that average annual dividend of $600 compounded at 5 percent for 20 years, arriving at an adjusted dividend value of $20,831.60. The difference between the interest-adjusted premium ($34,719.30) and the interest-adjusted dividend ($20,831.60), which amounts to $13,887.70, is the interest-adjusted cost for this $100,000 policy. To calculate what this $13,887.70 total cost is as an equivalent to a 20-year interest-adjusted annual premium, you may use your calculator or the 20-year factor of 34.72 just described. The $13,887.70 divided by 34.72 is $400. Dividing this by 100 gives us the per-$1000 interest-adjusted net payment cost index of $4 per $1000 per year.

INTEREST-ADJUSTED SURRENDER COST INDEX

The interest-adjusted *surrender* cost index assumes that the cash surrender value of the policy *and* any termination dividend available at policy termination will be available, along with the dividends and their interest earnings.

If in the preceding example the total cash available upon surrender amounted to $10,000, you would subtract the $10,000 from the $13,887.70 and arrive at $3,887.70 for the $100,000 policy. Dividing that by the 20-year 5 percent factor of 34.72 results in the amount of $112, and dividing this by 100 gives you the per-$1000 interest-adjusted surrender cost index of $1.12. This, the companies say, can then be used to compare the policy with others of comparable size and type.

According to the Joint Special Committee on Life Insurance Costs,* the advantages of these two interest-adjusted methods are as follows:

1. They take the time value of money into account.
2. They are easy to understand.
3. They do not require recourse to advanced mathematics.
4. They do not suggest a degree of accuracy that is beyond that justified by the circumstances.
5. They are significantly similar to the traditional methods, so that transition could be accomplished with a minimum of confusion.

Although these indices do take the time value of money into consideration, not you, nor I, nor many insurance agents have found them easy to understand or to communicate. Unfortunately, these indices are regarded by the public as having a degree of accuracy beyond that which is justified.

The press and the regulators still attribute a great deal of credibility to the 10- and 20-year interest-adjusted indices, in spite of the fact that the numbers are developed from policy illustrations that, quite probably, are unreliable. The insurance company that designs its illustration most aggressively for 10- and 20-year values will be rewarded with low cost indices even though its figures are less likely to be met than the company that presents a policy illustration based on more conservative assumptions.

Although the interest-adjusted indices do take the time value of money into consideration, they fail because you cannot rely on assumed policy values 10 and 20 years hence. Strict reliance on the indices provides for potential misuse that may mislead rather than help the consumer.

The policy illustrations from which the indices are derived

*Report to American Life Convention, Institute of Life Insurance, and Life Insurance Association of America, Institute of Life Insurance, New York, May 4, 1970, p. 6.

are becoming less and less accurate as a result of today's volatile economy and the many changes in the industry. To the degree that illustrations do not reflect what is going to happen within the policies, the indices become an inappropriate tool for comparing insurance products. Overreliance on the indices should be avoided.

LINTON YIELD METHOD

As noted earlier, the Linton yield method is named after an actuary, M. Albert Linton, who, in 1919, demonstrated that a whole life or an endowment life insurance policy could be mathematically analyzed as equivalent to a combination of decreasing term insurance and a savings fund. The method consists of subtracting the *cost of protection* from each year's policy premium, net of dividends, and treating the remainder as a savings deposit.

Linton decided that life insurance was a product that could be divided into component parts of protection and savings and analyzed on the basis of the value provided by each. The *Linton yield* would be the average interest rate on the invested amount over the selected period. This may be the first time, and the last time for many years, that anyone, let alone one with the credential of an actuary, referred to the "invested amount" in a life insurance policy. For the next 70 years the insurance industry denied that whole life could be separated into its component parts of term insurance and savings, and criticized agents who talked about the investment capital in a life insurance policy.

The method operates in this manner. The policy's savings or cash-value portion is subtracted from the face amount, giving you the amount at risk or the amount considered to be term insurance. This term insurance can be given a value based on the age, sex, and health of the insured, that is, on what it would cost the insured to replace this net amount at risk by purchasing retail term insurance. This amount, the value of the protection, is then subtracted from the annual premium for the policy as a whole, along with whatever current dividend the policy is generating, resulting in a net amount that is going into a savings portion of the contract. Annual premium, minus dividend minus cost of protection, equals savings.

The amount going into the savings portion is the investment element. The Linton yield is that average rate of return on the savings over the selected time period.

The problems associated with various published Linton yields are:

1. The term life insurance costs that go into calculating the yields are composite numbers, not necessarily accurate in any individual case.
2. The assumption is made that a policy is terminated at the end of the chosen period for which the Linton yield is calculated.
3. The Linton yield implies that the yield calculated is constant over the period of time chosen.
4. The Linton yield takes its future value assumptions from the same illustrations we have found lacking in accuracy.

Published Linton yields, then, are homogenizations of assumptions. The numbers are of value for rough comparison purposes only. They are invalid on an individual policy basis and do not give you personal decision-making information.

THE BARNES STANDARD DISCLOSURE SYSTEM

This system began getting some publicity in 1998. Mr. A. R. Barnes, Jr., CLU, ChFC, starts the process with a review of the claims-paying ability and financial strength of the insurance company. Advisors and purchasers will certainly want to know about the financial strength of any company with which they choose to do business. However, we all have to remember that the fortunes of any company can change, and it can happen more rapidly than the various services providing information about the company can react. The insurance company from which you buy may not be the one with which you die. Another insurance company may eventually pay your death benefit. You are well aware that life insurance companies have failed, consolidated, and merged, and will continue to do so. Every time that happens, the policy owner will have to question and review the claims-paying ability and financial strength of the new entity. This is particularly important to the following policy owners:

- Those who have the asset values of their policies within the general account of the insurance company and those who own whole life or universal life
- Those who have selected the general account investment alternative within a variable or variable universal life contract

The assets within the general account of an insurance company are subject to the claims of the creditors of the company. If an insurance commissioner takes over the company, as happens when it is necessary to ensure the survival of that company, those general account assets will be frozen until the problems have been resolved. While one cannot argue with the prudence of evaluating the claims-paying ability of an insurance company, it also must be understood that this step has proved to have little predictive value. Consider the reputable life insurance companies that have failed, such as Executive Life, Monarch Life, Capital Life, the Baldwin-United Companies, Confederation Life, and General American. Policies were purchased from these companies because they were highly regarded. They are examples of why advisors and clients cannot be sure of the continued claims-paying ability and financial strength of an insurance company and can hope only that if their company fails, the regulators will take appropriate steps to rescue it.

The next step recommended in this method is to send the Barnes Standard disclosure questionnaire to the insurance company in question to collect the essential data required in order to evaluate the financial contract. This questionnaire seeks to discover the essential information for a particular prospective insured, as well as the company's ratings with five different rating services. The current ratings and those for five previous years are requested in the questionnaire. For the policy and insured in question, the Barnes Standard disclosure questionnaire asks for the following *guaranteed* pricing information:

- Net single premium
- Net level premium

- Cash-value calculation rate
- Present value of gross level premiums using guaranteed interest rate, mortality charges, and expenses
- Gross level premium

For *current* pricing value information, the Barnes Standard disclosure questionnaire asks for the present value of the spread between the gross level premium and the net level premium. For *interest-sensitive illustrations,* the Barnes Standard disclosure questionnaire asks for the following:

- Current interest rate used in the illustration for all years
- Current mortality rates used in the illustration for all years
- Present value of illustrated dividends

It also asks for some general hybrid and sales illustration information, much like the information asked for in the Society of Financial Service Professionals illustration questionnaire.

The first problem with the Barnes system is in obtaining all this information. At this point, many companies refuse to respond to the questionnaire because it is costly to respond and because many consider it a waste of time. The information, even if provided, would not be useful to consumers and advisors in making individual life insurance decisions.

For instance, the insurance company that does respond provides a series of minimum and maximum guarantees. If the insurance company actually performs at these numbers, it can probably be assumed either that the policy will not be very competitive or that the environment in which all insurance companies operate is so negative that policy owners are happy just to have the insurance company survive. The environment could be negative for a number of reasons, such as the number of people dying, the cost of doing business, and marketplace returns. People who are happy just to have the company survive may include those who own general account products issued by large Japanese life insurance companies and who have accumulated significant values in their contracts on which they were guaranteed a 4 percent return. The 20-year Japanese bond, as reported on the Bloomberg web site, www.bloomberg.com, on November 9, 1998, was yielding 1.4 percent, on August 28, 2000, it was 2.4, and on June 19, 2001, it was 1.85 percent. Certainly that is a difficult environment in which to pay policy owners their 4 percent guaranteed interest rate.

Insurance contract guarantees provide peace of mind to policy owners until the time that paying out those guaranteed rates jeopardizes the very survival of the insurance company. The individual policy owner who owns the policy with the "best" guarantees could see that company be the first one to fail.

Next, the current pricing values are projected for many years into the future. The values of marketplace returns, mortality charges, and the expenses of doing business may accurately reflect what is currently the case within the illustration, but it is within the authority and responsibility of each insurance company to change these values as required by the environment. In the future, if the insurance company makes decisions that disadvantage policy owners, the healthy insureds will move to competing companies and only the uninsurable will stay. On the other hand, failure may befall a life insurance company that provides too many advantages to policy owners, relying on the decisions that are driven by the considerations of the marketing department and letting those considerations override actuarial reality. This would leave all existing policy owners with unpleasant options.

It is impossible to predict where an insurance company will choose to, and be able to, operate, considering the spectrum of the contract guarantees and marketplace competitive pricing for the lifetime of an insured. You must focus on what you can do in order to evaluate the value of a particular life insurance purchase. It is bound to frustrate many who purchase life insurance that you cannot know at policy inception exactly what the insurance company will charge for mortality and expenses in the future except for within the contractual limits. However, this uncertainty really works to benefit the policy owner in this competitive world and age of information. If insurance companies had to guarantee these costs, the regulators would require that the companies set up adequate reserves from policy owner money, in case their guarantees proved insufficient to cover costs. That would drive up policy costs. Continuing competition among companies is far more efficient for all of us in keeping prices down than irrevocable lifetime guarantees from insurance companies.

Let's concentrate on that part of a life insurance contract that can be controlled—the amount of capital that you put into the policy and when, where, and how it is invested. Future expense and mortality charges will have to be monitored on an ongoing basis. If expenses and charges are found to be uncompetitive in the future, complaints and public disclosure will drive the companies committed to the business back to more competitive charges. The amount of the investment committed to the contract, as well as judicious investing, will enable you to have the life insurance (amount at risk) paid for by the untaxed earnings within the policy and to pass on as much as possible to your beneficiaries. When capital invested within the contract is sufficient so that less than 2 percent of total return is necessary to cover the life insurance costs, you will find it difficult to find a better net-after-taxes-and-expenses place to put capital.

Here are suggestions for what you can and should do:

- Check the past and current claims-paying ability and financial strength of the insurance company by consulting all available rating services and reviewing the company's risk-based capital ratios and trends.
- Check the company's product line, product evolution, and long-term commitment to the life insurance product in which you are interested, as well as any products you may wish to buy in the future. Companies without sufficient market share, or a reasonable strategy to gain sufficient market share, may abandon unprofitable products, leaving you with poorly performing contracts and few acceptable options.
- Read the company's annual report, particularly the letters describing the company's strategy for the future, to make sure that there is a commitment to the continued support of the contracts in which you are interested.
- Know the costs in the early years of the policy when the numbers retain credibility, including commissions to be paid and all other policy start-up and ongoing expenses.
- Make a decision regarding allocation of sufficient funds to the life insurance policy to pay mortality and expense

costs (term life insurance) and capital for long-term investment purposes.

- Make a fully informed decision among the basic investment options offered within the life insurance policy.

JOSEPH M. BELTH METHOD

As mentioned previously, Joseph M. Belth, Ph.D., Professor of Insurance Emeritus at Indiana University, is noted for his work in determining the costs of life insurance policies. His level price approach is based on the premise that the protection provided by a policy is not the full-face amount of the policy but rather the face amount minus its cash surrender value, what we have been calling *net amount at risk* and define as *life insurance*. Belth used the level cost method to attempt to measure the average cost of this amount at risk for policy owners. He developed a price per thousand for each age for this net amount of protection. He then converted these yearly prices into amounts that represented a level price per thousand per net amount of protection provided by the policy for a particular time period. He has referred to them as *benchmark life insurance costs* that represent a base value of the protection provided by a policy.

In the June and October 1982 issues of *The Insurance Forum*, Belth published a method of determining costs and rates of return within policies that was more easily adapted by an individual to determine the cost-efficiency of an individual policy (see Exhibit 10.2).

Belth's inputs for his calculations are these:

1. Death benefit (F)
2. Policy cash surrender value as of the previous anniversary date (CVP)
3. Policy cash surrender value as of the current anniversary date (CSV)
4. Most recent annual premium (P)
5. Most recent annual dividend (D)
6. Insured's insurance age

EXHIBIT 10.2

Joseph Belth's Benchmarks and Formula

Belth's Benchmarks

Age	Price
Under 30	$1.50
30–34	2.00
35–39	3.00
40–44	4.00
45–49	6.50
50–54	10.00
55–59	15.00
60–64	25.00
65–69	35.00
70–74	50.00
75–79	80.00
80–84	125.00

Belth's Formula

$$\frac{(P + CVP)\,(1 + I) - (CSV + D)}{(F - CSV)\,(0.001)}$$

where P = premium
CVP = cash surrender value previous year
I = alternate use of funds interest rate (net after taxes)
CSV = cash surrender value this year
D = dividend
F = death benefit

7. Assumed alternative use of funds interest rate (I)—the rate of interest that the policy owner feels could be earned in an investment with equivalent safety and liquidity as that within a life insurance policy

8. Benchmark rates per $1000 of life insurance (net amount at risk)

You will note that seven of the eight items are specific to the policy owner; that is, you have to enter your personal information into the calculation. The information is of value in making a personal decision rather than just generally. This is a vast improvement over all previous methods when you are attempting to make personal life insurance decisions.

The eighth item in Professor Belth's formula, the cost of term insurance for the policy owner, is derived as he describes this way:

> The benchmarks were derived from certain United States population death rates. The benchmark figure for each 5-year age bracket is slightly above the death rate per $1,000 at the highest age in that bracket. What we are saying is that, if the price of your life insurance protection per $1,000 is in the vicinity of the "raw material cost" (that is the amount needed just to pay death claims based on population death rates), your life insurance protection is reasonably priced.*

Belth's formula, shown in Exhibit 10.2, may be described in the following manner. The cash value for the previous year and this year's premium input are considered the investment in the contract. To determine the amount to which that investment should have appreciated on your behalf in the year in question, Belth multiplies that amount by 1 plus the after-tax yield obtainable on a comparable investment. This determines what you *should have received*. From this amount, he subtracts the total current cash surrender value plus the dividend credited to the policy in the current year. This determines what you *actually did receive*.

You could say, "This is what I should have had: contract investment multiplied by 1 plus after-tax yield," and then subtract what you actually did receive. The difference between what you should have received and what you did receive is the net cost for the year.

Once the current year's cost has been determined, you divide it by the net amount at risk in thousands of dollars provided by this particular policy. This divisor is calculated by taking the death benefit, subtracting the current cash surrender value, and then multiplying by 0.001 to reduce that down to the thousands of dollars of coverage of net amount at risk in the policy.

Compare this calculated life insurance cost per $1000 per year with Belth's benchmarks. His rules of thumb are that if the policy cost per thousand is less than the benchmark, no replacement would be appropriate; if the policy cost per $1000 is more than the benchmark but less than twice the benchmark, probably no

---

*The Insurance Forum, Vol. 9, No. 6, June 1982, p. 168.

change is indicated; but if the policy cost per $1000 is more than twice the benchmark, replacement should be considered.

Belth's system has the advantage of being more client-specific and fairly easy to understand. It has been the most credible system of evaluating the cost of life insurance to date.

However, some of the inputs to Belth's system need to be examined.

1. *The benchmarks.* Consider the term insurance costs. Do they reflect what an individual actually pays for life insurance? For example, Belth's benchmark for a 50-year-old is $10. We find that a 50-year-old male nonsmoker could buy term insurance for from as low as $2.25 per thousand to as high as $6.71 per thousand. Belth's benchmarks are generalizations that appear to be higher than today's costs. To make an informed decision, you need to know your actual retail cost of term insurance based on your age, sex, and risk category.

2. *Policy loans.* Belth's formula, like the preceding methods discussed, does not take policy loans into consideration. Policy loans do affect the amount of investment within the policy and therefore have a substantial effect on the rate of return.

3. *Policy loan interest rate.* The interest rate paid on the policy loans will be either more or less than the reinvestment rate for the funds outside the policy. If the rate charged is higher, the policy cannot be leveraged profitably; if lower, it may be. To determine the net result, the net after-tax cost of the interest paid must be subtracted from the net after-tax gain realized by reinvesting the loan proceeds outside the policy.

4. *Policy loans affect policy dividends.* Currently, insurance companies pay you higher dividends on your whole life policies if you do not borrow or if you accept higher loan or variable loan interest charges.

5. *Marginal tax bracket, state and federal.* Earnings within a life insurance policy are not subject to current income taxation. Interest charged on policy loans is not deductible. The rate of return within a life insurance

policy is more valuable to a high-bracket taxpayer. By inserting your marginal tax bracket into the formula, you will be able to indicate the equivalent net after-tax rate of return required outside the policy to match the rate of return inside.

6. *Benchmark term costs.* The benchmark term costs using the Belth formula assume a negative result; they assume a cost for the term life insurance. However, with variable life policies, the formula often comes up with the policy earnings exceeding the cost of term life insurance. You may end up with a profit per $1000, which is not accounted for in the benchmarks. Thus this system is not helpful in making personal decisions with many variable contracts.

THE RATE-OF-RETURN SYSTEM

The rate-of-return method is built on many of the principles of the previous methods. It attempts to improve on those methods by building a procedure that is of value in individual decision making. The procedure includes using client-specific data such as the actual cost of term insurance for the individual insured and the policy owner's actual income tax bracket. The object is to calculate the rate of return for a specific policy year based upon the policy owner's average equity in the policy during the policy year. This step-by-step method proceeds as follows:

Step 1 Determine how much life insurance is provided by the policy

Total death benefit _____
Less total current asset value _____
Equals life insurance _____

Total Death Benefit
The total death benefit is the policy face amount plus any policy provisions that increase the death benefit in the event of a natural death, e.g., term insurance riders or paid-up additional life insur-

ance as a result of dividends being left in your policy, or account value being added to the policy face amount, etc.

Total Current Asset Value

The total current asset value is the capital at work in the policy on which you are earning a return. The objective of this calculation is to determine how much of the total death benefit is your money and how much is insurance company money, or life insurance.

Step 2 Determine what you have paid to maintain the life insurance in force this year

Premium _____
Plus loan interest cost _____
Equals total current year's cost _____

Premium

The premium is what you have paid into the policy in the current year. It is the billed gross premium for a fixed-premium policy or what you have chosen to pay if the policy is a type of universal life without a stated premium.

Policy Loan Interest Costs

Most companies have offered enhancements to their participating whole life insurance policies. If policy owners will accept an arrangement whereby higher interest may be charged on policy loans, they are rewarded with higher dividends. Conversely, if policy owners refuse the enhancement in order to maintain a low policy loan interest rate, they receive lower dividends. This dividend credit differential between borrowers and nonborrowers is effectively an increase in the cost of the policy loans. The precise dividend differential and loan interest rate alternatives offered to an individual policy owner in an enhancement or upgrade can be used to determine the impact on a specific policy and must be obtained directly from the issuing company.

Leveraging life insurance by borrowing to the pay premium—a minimum deposit plan—is obsolete today. Loan interest has to be paid. Loans reduce dividends. As stated in *Forbes*, "If you own a minimum deposit life insurance policy, condolences are in order."* The strategy was based upon the fact that noncompetitive rates of return were paid on investments within life insurance policies in the past, and so it made no sense to leave the money in the policy. This is no longer a fact. Investments in variable policies are very competitive. Economic conditions have made it difficult to borrow from a policy, pay loan interest, and profitably reinvest the money. The increased costs for policy loan interest, along with reduced dividends for policies that retained their low interest rate on policy loans, combined with the lower interest rates available on alternative safe investments, altogether provided little opportunity for gain.

Step 3   Determine the cash you received as a result of maintaining the policy in force for the current year

Current year's increase in cash value, account value, or asset value _____
Plus current year's dividend if any _____
Equals total policy owner credit _____

Critics will find weaknesses and advocates will find strengths in this particular section of this system for the financial analysis of life insurance. The critics will say that you are looking at the policy for only one particular year. They will question whether the financial results for any particular year are an accurate report of what has happened in the past or a predictor of what will happen in the future. The criticism is valid because the policy under analysis could be a variable life insurance policy with its investment in a common stock account in a year when the common stock fund has taken a substantial beating. If you concluded that a negative return in one year meant that you should get rid of the policy, that would certainly be an erroneous conclusion. You should perform further evaluation by reentering your numbers in the formula, using the average annual increase in account value and average annual dividend received since the policy's inception, as the credits received as a result of maintaining the policy in force. For input into the policy, you could use average annual

_____
Forbes magazine, June 29, 1987.

premium, average policy loan costs, and average net after-tax costs for maintaining cash within the policy. This would give you an indication of average return from policy inception. From the standpoint of trying to make a decision of "Where do I go from here?" the current year's actual return compared with the average return provides information that will help in determining how you can expect the policy to perform in the future. If you are considering an upgrade or enhancement offer, you can use the formula by entering assumptions, such as the elimination of the policy loan and the acceptance of the higher dividend yields, to determine the impact of the offer.

Step 4 Determine your investment in the contract

Total asset value _____
Less loan outstanding _____
Equals investment remaining in contract _____

The investment capital in the contract is extremely important, as it is that upon which you are going to calculate your investment return. You may want to refine this figure, bringing it closer to your average investment in the contract during the year in question. That is, you could calculate your investment in the contract at the beginning and at the end of the year, add the two together, subtract any policy loan, and divide by two to come up with the average investment in the contract for that year. Computerized calculations (Lotus spreadsheet) show a rate of return based upon both equity at the beginning of the year and average equity during the year. Dr. William G. Droms,* professor of finance at Georgetown University and coauthor on the first *Life Insurance Investment Advisor*, refined this system. In his May 1989 article in the *Journal of Accountancy*, he developed a Lotus spreadsheet to account for positive and negative policy cashflows on a monthly basis to come up with a more refined internal rate of return. When entering the figure for the outstanding policy loan, the unpaid outstanding in-

---

*Droms, "Evaluating the Investment Merits of Life Insurance," *Journal of Accountancy*, May 1989, pp. 63–70.

terest on the loan at the time of the evaluation should be added to the policy loan amount.

Step 5 Determine the dollar amount of return you have earned in the current policy year

From step 3, take your increased value for the current policy year and subtract your current input into the contract for the current year, shown in step 2.

Policy owner credit (step 3) _____
Minus policy owner costs (step 2) _____
Equals policy owner net gain (loss) _____

Step 6 Determine your cash-on-cash return for the current year

To determine your cash-on-cash annual percentage rate of return for the current year, take the amount of the credit from step 5 and divide it by the investment remaining in the contract from step 4.

Amount of credit (step 5) _____
Divided by amount invested (step 4) _____
Equals % of cash-on-cash return _____

Step 7 Determine your equivalent taxable return

The cash-on-cash return varies in value for high-bracket and low-bracket taxpayers. This step helps to calculate how much taxable return you would have to earn in order to net the cash-on-cash rate of return. Take your tax-free rate of return as calculated in step 6 and divide it by 1 minus your tax bracket.

Policy owner's untaxed cash-on-cash rate of return (step 6) _____
Divide by 1 minus tax bracket _____
Equals equivalent taxable return _____

Critics of this system question this step because it assumes that your investments outside the policy would be taxed at ordinary income tax rates. To adjust for that, either ignore this step or enter the capital gains rate you expect on outside investments.

Step 8   Determine the value
of your life insurance

This is a very important point of departure. If you are not in need of protection and place no value on the life insurance protection provided by the contract, then you need to go no further. Step 7 focuses on the cash-on-cash return, being all that matters. The viability of the contract as an investment depends upon the competitiveness of this cash-on-cash return with other investment alternatives available. Cash-on-cash return is a return net of all costs, including life insurance costs.

Various individuals will place varying degrees of value on the protection provided by the contract. The young nonsmoker who has an opportunity to purchase term insurance at discounted rates through some association, an employer, or another advantageous source might enter the term insurance cost reflecting his or her preferred status. An individual who is older, who has a great personal need for life insurance, and who has just had a heart attack—making existing insurance irreplaceable—would put a higher value on the net amount at risk. In some cases the insurance protection will be of so much value to the policy owner that the cash-on-cash return or investment return of the policy is irrelevant. The death benefit represents the entire value of the contract to that person.

Life insurance does have value, and that value has to be individually determined. The most accurate cost per thousand to be entered in this section of the formula would be the figure you obtained as a result of applying for an equivalent amount of term life insurance, submitting to a medical examination, and receiving an offer at a contractually guaranteed rate. All other entries are estimates, and the financial analysis is only as good as the accuracy of the estimate.

Once the equivalent retail value of $1000 of term life insurance is determined, it is multiplied by the amount of life insurance protection provided by the contract (face amount minus asset value of the policy as determined in step 1) to calculate the value of the life insurance within the contract. You could argue that your retail cost of the term insurance divided by 1 minus your current marginal tax bracket is the figure that should be entered. This figure would represent the amount you would have to *earn* in total to service a retail term insurance policy. For example, if you are in the 30 percent marginal state and federal tax bracket, you would have to earn $142.86 for every $100 you paid for term insurance [100 divided by $(1 - 0.30) = \$142.857$].

This method of valuing the cost of retail term insurance would be accurate if the untaxed earnings on an investment within the life insurance policy were entirely sufficient to cover all mortality and expense charges within the policy. We have taken the more conservative approach using just the equivalent retail cost of term insurance for the policy owner.

Life insurance in thousands (step 1) _____
Multiplied by policy owner's cost per $1000 _____
Equals value of life insurance _____

Step 9 Determine the total value you receive as a result of continuing this life insurance contract

The total value you receive as a result of continuing the life insurance contract is the cash-on-cash return plus the value you put on the life insurance protection. Add the life insurance value determined in step 8 to the cash return of step 5 to come up with the total dollar amount of benefit you receive from the contract.

Policy owner net gain (loss) (step 5) _____
Plus life insurance value (step 8) _____
Equals total benefit received _____

Step 10 Determine the percentage return on the contract when the cash-on-cash return is added to the life insurance value

Value received (step 9) _____
Divided by amount invested (step 10) _____
Equals % rate of return _____

EXHIBIT 10.3

The ROR System of Determining Rate of Return on Cash Invested in a Life Insurance Policy

Step 1 Life insurance provided:
Total death benefit
− Total current value

Life insurance: _____

Step 2 What was paid in:
Annual premium
+ Loan interest (net of tax savings, if any)

Total current cost: _____

Step 3 What benefit was received:
Increase in cash value/account value
(this year's value − last year's value)
+ Current year's dividend

Total cash benefit received: _____

Step 4 Policy owner's investment in policy:
Total asset value
− Loan outstanding

Policy owner's investment: _____

Step 5 Determine dollar amount of this year's gain or (loss):
Policy owner's credits
− Policy owner's costs

(step 3)
(step 2)
Policy owner's net gain (loss): _____

Step 6 Cash-on-cash return:
Amount of gain
÷ Amount of investment

(step 5)
(step 4)
Cash-on-cash return: _____%

Step 7 Policy owner's equivalent taxable return:
Cash-on-cash Return
÷ (1 − marginal tax bracket)

(step 6)
Equivalent taxable return: _____

Step 8 Value of life insurance:
Life insurance in thousands
× Policy owner's cost per $1000 of term life insurance

(step 1)
Life insurance value: _____

Step 9 Determine total value of benefit received:
This year's gain (loss)
+ Life insurance value

(step 5)
(step 8)
Total benefit received: _____

Step 10 Determine cash-on-cash and life insurance rate of return:
Total benefit received
+ Policy owner's investment

(step 9)
(step 4)
Total return on policy: _____

Step 11 Determine equivalent taxable rate of return to match policy's total return:
Total return:
÷ (1 − marginal tax bracket)

(step 10)
Equivalent taxable return: _____

Step 11   Determine the equivalent taxable return that you must earn to match this tax-deferred or tax-free return from the life insurance contract

Percent rate of return (step 10) _____
Divided by (1 minus tax bracket) _____
Equals % _____

CONCLUSION

The rate of return system may be used with all types of life insurance: term, whole life, single-premium life, universal life, variable life, and variable universal life. In testing and evaluating the system, a computer program was developed. The program gives simultaneous results for Belth's system of evaluating the cost-effectiveness of life insurance policies, the cash-on-cash rate of return, and the cash and life insurance value rate of return. A summary of the step-by-step method is presented in Exhibit 10.3.

The rate of return system has proved to be valuable in making individual decisions regarding existing life insurance and potential purchases. Although it takes a bit of effort to understand, it is easily computerized and therefore accessible to all at reasonable cost. Since you can understand the data that are used to come up with the conclusions, you are in a good position to evaluate the results.

CHAPTER 11

Life Insurance Strategies

Using the Swiss Army Knife

Throughout this book, we refer to monies going into life insurance company products, over and above that spent for mortality and expense charges, as investment. People who put money into these products expect a return. Certainly the allocation of your cash to buy term life insurance protection for a year, and then have it terminate without value, is more like a retail purchase of a consumable than an investment. Should you die during the term, however, your family would consider that allocation of assets one of your finest investments.

Let us consider the different opportunities offered to you by insurance company products as they relate to your situation as you pass through the different stages of life—protection, accumulation, and distribution. Your needs, attitudes, and opportunities change as you pass through the life cycle, and as they change, your use of insurance company products and the competitive alternatives available to you also will change.

In the following pages, we will consider young adults, young singles, young married couples, the middle-aged, and the mature as those general stages of the life cycle. In considering each stage, we will look at the typical problems and opportunities that relate to life insurance and annuities, including some typical business situations. At each stage, we also will determine how to evaluate each situation. For example, a youth might ask, "Why do I want or need life insurance or annuities, or an IRA? It will be eons before I'll retire. Why now?" We will review the many opportunities that may be offered to you through your employment during middle age, such as bonus plans, key-employee life insurance, salary continuation, deferred compensation, corporate, split-dollar plans, and 1035 tax-free exchanges from one insurance product to another.

When we arrive at the mature stage, we will discuss various ways to enjoy the income you have managed to accumulate and how you can protect those assets, if you wish, for the next generation. As we do this, we will analyze how a married couple have elected to use their life-cycle policy to serve their various needs and how they adjust it to their needs. We also will run through the quantitative analysis that led them to their decisions.

YOUNG ADULTHOOD STRATEGIES
Young and Single (The "Wow" Years)

During the young and single phase of your life cycle, it is difficult to be concerned about anything but improving career opportunities and making yourself more valuable to society. Your long-term security objectives will be to build sufficient net worth so that one day you can work for fun rather than for money. Your best investment opportunity at this time is to invest in education. That probably will continue to be your very best investment throughout your life. Generally, what insurance products are appropriate for consideration by the young and single?

The primary function of life insurance is to provide protection, *life insurance* or *net amount at risk*, in return for which you accept the loss of relatively small sums (policy costs, the COIs and expenses in all insurance policies), so that in the event of your death relatively large sums can be provided to your beneficiary. The means to accomplish this is unique to life insurance.

During this phase of your life, there probably is not anyone economically dependent upon you and your ability to continue to earn a living. If this is the case, paying for term insurance is an unnecessary expenditure. Why then do so many people do it? Life insurance costs less if you are in good health. It is often wise to

purchase it while you are healthy, assuring availability at preferred health rates when it is needed in the future. In addition,
since investment-oriented life insurance ("investasurance") becomes more self-supporting as it accumulates more investment
capital, you can justify starting a policy at this stage of life. You
can accumulate some capital within the contract during these relatively low-expense years so that you can suspend payments during the years when you have more expenses, such as those years
of marriage and child rearing.

Investasurance

What about paying more into the life insurance policy than is
required simply to have the insurance protection? This is a viable
alternative if you decide that there is a personal need for life insurance. If there is no need, then the costs associated with the
insurance protection and the expenses of maintaining the policy
diminish the value of your investment return. However, if you
decide that the expenditure for the insurance protection is justified
because of present or future needs or wants, the question becomes,
"What is the best way to pay for this insurance protection, not
only presently, but also in the future?"

There are a number of things you should keep in mind when
you begin to invest in a life insurance policy:

1. If you put extra cash into a policy, can you access some
   of it? Some of the capital will be expended for life
   insurance and expenses, or held for surrender charges,
   and you will want to know exactly how much remains
   accessible. The money should be readily available either
   by borrowing or withdrawing it from the policy
   (assuming you wish to keep the policy in force) or by
   canceling the policy and recovering your equity (which
   can have income tax consequences).
2. Today you can choose to control where the company
   invests your money.
3. You do not have to pay income taxes or penalty taxes
   when you borrow on your policy as long as you do not
   invest in excess of the seven-pay limits.

4. You do not have to pay current taxes on interest, dividends, or capital gains earned within your policy.
5. It can offer a comfortable, convenient accumulation device with broad diversification.
6. You will be assisted in your search for the best money managers available. You may have as many as two levels of management of money managers. The insurance company will hire the best managers it can find. Insurance companies typically no longer use just their own money managers; they go to the best money-management companies they can find, such as Fidelity, Alliance Capital, Franklin Tempelton, AIM, Putnam, T. Rowe Price, Alger, and others, whose unique capabilities will entice you to invest. And if the hired money-management companies do not do a good job for you, the insurace companies fire them and hire others. Also, when they hire one of these money-management companies, the money-management company finds its best talent and oversees their work on your behalf. Both levels are attempting to offer you the best managers available. You end up with having access to talent in not just one mutual fund family but many different ones, without costs or income taxes for moving your investment capital among them.

Some people will choose a series of investments, putting their money into a family of taxable mutual funds that are not inside a life insurance policy. But by choosing taxable mutual funds, you lose the tax shelter and death benefit of the life insurance contract. You will pay taxes each year on interest, dividends, and capital gains that the manager incurs as investments are changed within the fund. These taxable distributions are not within your control, and you must pay income taxes on them. To give you a dramatic example of how expensive this can be, it was reported in the *Wall Street Journal** that Warburg Pincus Japan Small Company Fund made a capital gains distribution of 55 percent of the fund's assets to shareholders. If the share value had been $10, the distribution

---

*August 15, 2000.

would have been $5.50. With a 20 percent capital gains tax rate, the income tax cost would have been $1.10 per share, or 11 percent of the share value. You could buy and pay for a great deal of life insurance with the amount of money that, in that instance, would have been sent to the federal government. On the Securities and Exchange Commission web site, www.sec.gov, it is reported that the average growth mutual fund creates income taxes of about 2.5 percent of its value each year, which would be only $0.25 in taxes, rather than the $1.10 in our example above.

Taxes are imposed when you move from one fund to another fund within a family of taxable mutual funds. Another difference between taxable mutual funds and the subaccounts inside life insurance is that taxable mutual funds don't carry the costs associated with life insurance. With lower expenses come higher taxes. Look at your income tax return. Schedule B will show you if you paid taxes on the positive results of taxable mutual funds. If you are allocating a part of your investment return to income taxes, you have the opportunity of redirecting that allocation to pay for life insurance. It is your choice—do you want part of that investment return to pay for the welfare of your family or to go for public welfare? The life insurance policy provides you with the income tax–free death benefit as well as shelter from income taxes on the investment earnings within the policy.

YOUNG MARRIEDS

Are you a DINK—dual income—no kids? At this stage in life, you still are two relatively economically independent individuals, with neither yet dependent upon the continued income of the other. Your economic interdependence may increase as you take on a home mortgage and have children. As this economic interdependence increases, your need for life insurance will increase, and insurance company products will become more attractive.

Nonqualified annuities are as attractive to DINKs as they are to young singles, meaning not very. The expenses—tax penalties if you are younger than 59½ and ordinary income tax liability for taking money out of annuities—make them inappropriate in most cases. That is longer term than most people can deal with at this age.

On the other hand, the qualified annuity (one that is part of a qualified retirement plan) is more important to DINKs than to young singles. Both partners are advised to make maximum contributions to the deductible retirement plans. At this stage, you should avoid the tendency to become dependent upon the continuation of *both* incomes for your standard of living. This is the time in your life for maximum accumulation of net worth. The basic conclusion is that qualified plans certainly are an appropriate investment, in spite of the fact that the young are penalized should they wish to use the money in such plans prior to age 59½. The lack of liquidity is important and should be considered. However, every time you complete a financial statement in order to borrow money, your habits of the past will be an important consideration to the lender. The lender will be far more interested in lending to you if you have shown a pattern of accumulation in the past.

What life insurance products serve the needs of a young couple? As is always the case, available resources are the first consideration. You have needs for adequate medical insurance, disability income insurance, and life insurance. Once funds are available to cover these basic needs, the question of additional investments can be addressed.

Emergency Funds

For instance, where should the emergency fund (3 to 6 months of gross income) be invested? What you require here are (1) liquidity (ready access to your cash without loss) and (2) a reasonable rate of return.

Let's use an example. We have a male nonsmoker, age 30, and a female nonsmoker, age 28. They each have purchased retail term insurance policies in the amount of $200,000. Their purchase decisions were made on the basis of wants and needs, and the contracts will cost them a total of about $500 in the current year. They are in the 30 percent marginal income tax bracket, so it takes gross family earnings of about $714 ($500 ÷ 0.70) to service these two policies. They send $214 to Uncle Sam, which leaves $500 to send to the insurance company.

They have a good start on their emergency fund. They have

accumulated it in a certificate of deposit (CD). It is now up for its 6-month renewal at current interest rates. The question is, where should they put that $10,000? Should it go into a life insurance policy? Should they leave it in the CD (earning a *net after-tax* amount of about 70 percent of the interest quoted), or should they put it someplace that provides the features they require of an emergency fund (liquidity and a reasonable rate of return)? The only way to find the answer is to look at the facts. If left in the CD, the $10,000 would have to earn $714, or 7.14 percent, to cover the cost of the life insurance with the taxable earnings from the CD, providing $214 for income taxes and $500 for life insurance. Ask the insurance company exactly what would happen if the couple each deposited $5000 within a variable universal life insurance product providing $200,000 of protection.

If the expenses were comparable to the term insurance, then the policy would be acceptable from a cost standpoint. Let's look at the investment side. You have $4000 per policy because $1000 was eaten up in policy expenses in the first year. So that's $4000 at work in each of the policy accounts. Each $4000 would have to earn about 6.25 percent (6.25 percent × $8,000 = $500) to get you to the point at which the *tax-free* earnings on the insurance investments could pay for life insurance without Uncle Sam receiving anything, a savings of about $214 in taxes. When you pay extra money into your policy for investment, it will be subject to front-end costs to get it into the policy; but once inside, extra investment does *not* change the insurance costs.

Although it would not be surprising to find that the account values within your policies totaled about $4000 of the $5000 you put into each policy, you also might find that only $3000 per policy was liquid, or could be borrowed, because of contingent-deferred sales charges. This might seem expensive, but it looks great when compared with a whole life policy that has no value in the early years. In the second year, you would look at the total policy expenses to see if they were approximately equal to what you would pay for term insurance. If acceptable, then *maximum-fund* your policies. "Burp" them, as it is sometimes said. Put in as much as you can up to the seven-pay maximum. (The insurance company will often return or burp back what you send in excess of the limit.) After all, someday you could face . . .

Single Income with Kids (The "Oh My!" Years)

Additional cash accumulation needs will arise as you get older. Those college education expenses may be a major concern in the future. Let's take these policies and use them to fund two college educations, based on the premise that you decided to put the $10,000 into the two variable universal life insurance policies for your emergency fund, paying in each year what you had been paying for term life insurance. The policies have reasonable and competitive rates of return, acceptable mortality and expense charges for life insurance, and the advantage of deferral on taxation. You even have considered the disadvantage of having to pay $25 if you wish to make a withdrawal, or paying a market rate of interest that would, in all likelihood, not be deductible should you choose to borrow on your policies rather than withdrawing cash.

Borrowing against Life Insurance

You understand that when you borrow, you have not removed monies from your policy, but rather you have collateralized your policy's asset value that is still held by the insurance company. You pay interest on the money you borrowed. The insurance company pays you interest on the collateral value of your policy that will be moved to a loan guarantee fund to keep it away from market risk. The interest the insurance company pays you usually will be 1 to 2 percent less than you pay them for the loan. A spread of 1 or 2 percent is what it costs you to get at your policy monies via policy loans.

You have decided that you wish to accumulate college education funds at a rate of $400 a month, the maximum you feel you can allocate at the present time. Yes, push yourself—you won't be sorry. Should you establish separate accounts, one for each child? Should you put your money in accounts under the Uniform Gift to Minors Act or some other minor's trust fund rather than into your insurance policies? These strategies are not the best alternatives. TRA-86 requires that a child's investment earnings over $1200 per year be taxed at the parent's tax rate until the child attains the age of 14. In addition, under the Uniform Gift to Minors Act, gifts are passed to the child in an outright fashion. You may find that at age 18 your child chooses to use the funds for some purpose other than education. Consider what you might have done had you found yourself with a lot of cash at age 18.

What investment alternatives are available within your variable universal life policies? You can dollar-cost-average into the investment accounts. This offers a relatively conservative means of investing in the stock market. Let's assume that in the third year that the policies are in force, you start making monthly contributions of $400 (in addition to the term insurance premiums) and continue with those contributions for the next 15 years. We also will assume current expense charges, current mortality charges, and an 8 percent return. What will be available to your family when college educations start 15 years hence? We are now in the fantasyland of assumptions, compound returns, and policy illustrations. The most important function of such illustrations is to show you how *projected* expenses may impact investment return.

Let's evaluate whether it makes sense to put $400 per month into your life insurance policies to help you accumulate for the children's educations. If you contribute $400 per month for the next 15 years and earn a net 8 percent, you will have accumulated $120,000 or more at the end of that time.

If you conclude that the expenses being charged within the policies are fair and less than what you projected paying on the outside for just term life insurance, you would proceed. If you like the tax shelter and the idea of dollar-cost-averaging into some of the stock accounts for at least the first 10 years (hoping to do better than the 8 percent), you probably would decide to go ahead. The life insurance plan offers a strategy (equity investment), convenience (monthly deposits), performance (diversification), and freedom from current taxation that probably appeals to you.

The strategy during the college years would be to discontinue deposits and to withdraw (or borrow) $12,000 a year to cover expenses. Understanding that all numbers within the projections will have changed significantly, ask to see what the projections would look like using the $12,000 withdrawals. In reviewing the printout, you may find that the $12,000 withdrawals at the beginning of each of six education years will reduce your policy accounts less significantly than you expected. The continued earnings within the policies may be able to support them nicely.

THE 1035 TAX-FREE EXCHANGE

This section could be entitled "The Insurance Contract You Own Is Not the Insurance Contract You Want." Your situation may have changed, or the insurance contract may not be doing what you had hoped it would do. What do you do with your underachievers—those policies that are no longer paying acceptable dividends or excess interest? Let's say you computed the rate of return within your insurance product using the system described in this book and have decided that the performance of one of your old contracts is not what you want it to be and feel you can get better elsewhere. You run a new product offering through the same evaluation, balance the risks and rewards, and decide that you would rather acquire the new risks and rewards than retain the old. The most economical alternative is a 1035 tax-free exchange from your old contract into the new one.

Internal Revenue Code Section 1035 allows a policy owner to exchange one life insurance contract for another on a tax-free basis. It provides that no gain or loss shall be recognized on the exchange of:

1. A contract of life insurance for another contract of life insurance
2. A contract of endowment insurance for another contract of endowment insurance that provides for the regular payments beginning at a date not later than the date that payments would have begun under the contract exchanged, or for an annuity contract
3. An annuity contract for an annuity contract
4. A contract of life insurance for an annuity contract

Section 1031(b) provides that gains from exchanges not solely in kind can create tax liabilities. When a life insurance policy subject to an existing loan is exchanged for a new life insurance policy without a policy loan, the exchanger has received what is referred to as *net debt relief*. As far as Uncle Sam is concerned, if you are relieved of a debt, it is exactly the same as being paid, so that you may be taxed at ordinary income tax rates to the extent of your net debt relief and the gain in your contract. The only way to avoid this problem is to make sure that the new policy is issued with a policy loan exactly the same as the old policy.

The IRS stated in Revenue Ruling 72-353 that an exchange qualified as a tax-free exchange under 1035(a) because the new policy would be issued in exchange for the old policy. With no money received by the taxpayer, the basis in the new policy would be the same as the basis in the old policy. The underlying principle justifying the nonrecognition of gain in the tax-free exchange situation, according to the IRS, is that "the property received in the exchange is substantially a continuation of the old investment still unliquidated." Tax–free exchanges for both life insurance and annuity contracts offer you the income tax free opportunity to try and turn a policy that is not serving your purposes into a better-performing contract. To do it properly, the policy owner should execute binding exchange assignment agreements with the insurance companies. *All* the old policy proceeds should be rolled over into the new contract. And as noted above, if the old contract was subject to a policy loan, the replacement policy should be subject to an identical policy loan. The paper trail is important. If you are ever questioned on the transaction, the paper trail will enable you to show Uncle Sam exactly what was intended as you went about the exchange process.

You may exchange policies with your present insurance company if it has a new contract that you feel better suits your current needs. Your present company may charge less in expenses for the change, and in some cases, you may not have to pass a physical or go through any underwriting requirements to obtain the new contract.

Moving to a new company is not difficult. The process is simple even though it takes a bit of paperwork. First, you apply for and make sure you can get a satisfactory new policy from the new company. At the same time that you are filling out the new application, you indicate on it that this is to be a 1035 tax-free exchange from policies X, Y, and Z to the new contract, after the new policy has been issued on a basis acceptable to you. You will have to complete the replacement forms required by your state that emphatically point out that replacing an existing policy with a new one usually is not a good idea. You may be giving up policy rights that may not be in the new policy. You will have to go through a new 2-year period during which your policy is contestable by the insurance company. You may be subject to surrender charges in your old policy and now again in the new one, and, of course, you have to be healthy if you are going to pass the underwriting requirements of a new life insurance policy. In short, the authorities are trying to help you not make a mistake as you go about such an important change. Evaluate the consequences in your situation carefully. Finally, when you know you have an acceptable policy issued and it is entirely as you want it, turn in the original executed exchange forms assigning your old policies to the new. The new company now owns your old policies. You instruct the new company to send those old policies in for exchange, collect the proceeds, and deposit them into your new policy. That completes the process.

MIDDLE AGE STRATEGIES

The "It's Time to Get Serious about Us" Years

Middle age is a time to accumulate for financial independence day (or if you prefer, retirement). The college educations are behind you. What a great day! A major goal in life—that of rearing your children as well as possible—has been completed. It is now time for *you*. Often, people will say that life insurance needs diminish at this stage in life. In some cases, this may be true; however, in most cases it is not. You buy the second home in Florida or Arizona with a mortgage. You decide that the family homestead is not what you want now, so you go out and buy a smaller new home with an even bigger mortgage. You are concerned about the fact that your spouse won't receive your entire pension if you die. The only thing that may have changed about your requirements for insurance is your reason for needing it.

For purposes of example, we will assume that you as a couple decide to start accumulating for retirement by saving $1000 per month. You will do this by dollar-cost-averaging into the common stock accounts of your variable universal policies. You are now ages 53 and 51.

The effect on your policies if you add to them at this rate for

7 years, until the older of you attains age 60, can be dramatic. At that time, you might like to consider retirement, or at least be in an economic situation where continued work is for the love of it and not of necessity.

At the end of the thirtieth policy year, assuming an 8 percent return and current expenses, you could find that if you were to withdraw $12,000 per year from the policies to supplement your retirement income, it would take until age 70 to withdraw your nontaxable cost basis (what you had invested). Thereafter, if the tax laws are as they are today, you could make your withdrawals by way of policy loans so that the $12,000 per year would not be subject to income tax. You could also find that your policy accounts have grown to over $600,000 and that, assuming the 8 percent return, the policies still are providing about $800,000 of life insurance and still increasing in value. That being the case, you could even increase your rate of withdrawal, but be careful, you do not want your policy to run out of money and terminate before you die. If that were to happen, income taxes would be due on all the profit you have borrowed out of your policy and you could find yourself without enough money to pay the taxes or to keep the policy in force. This is referred to as the "dreaded squeeze."

However, lets look at the whole picture now that you are facing age 70½. At this point you are considered to be in the mature years of your life, and must begin minimum distributions from your retirement plan accumulations, which you may have been avoiding up to now. Suppose for all these years you had maximized your contributions into all employer-offered retirement plans and, indeed, all employer-offered accumulation plans. You had done this not only because they were employer-subsidized, low-cost, good plans, but also because the employer deducted the contributions from your paycheck. You found that the plan worked because the money did not come home and then go into the plan but went directly to the plan. Putting money into your policy was harder if it came home first because there was always a reason to use that money for something else.

The point is, now, at age 70½ you find yourself with the choice of subsidizing your retirement income from one of three piles of money that you have accumulated: your life insurance policy, your retirement plan accumulations, or the money that you and your spouse have accumulated in savings and investments outside of the other two. You may even total all these up and find that after the death of you and your spouse, there will be a substantial federal estate tax preventing a good part of what you have accumulated from getting to your children. Your parents still are living, and you have watched their cost of living quadruple during their retirement years. You have a concern with outliving your resources, but you also would like to leave something to the children.

In talking to your advisors, they say the easiest (least expensive taxwise) resource to get to your children is your life insurance policy. They promise you they will find ways to pass it to them without gift taxes, without income taxes, and without estate taxes. A lifetime of compounding will go to the children entirely tax-free if you do not need it. They also tell you that your retirement capital will be hit the hardest by both income and estate taxes prior to passing the balance to the children. Under the tax law in 2000, taxes could take as much as 70 percent of the value of your qualified retirement plan and IRA assets.

Now, let's examine your choices again. From which pile of money should you support your standard of living in retirement: (1) the family money pile (2) the life insurance, or (3) the tax collector's money—the retirement plan? You object. You will have to pay income taxes on the retirement plan distributions if distributed to you and your spouse. Your children will pay both income and estate taxes. You object. Your withdrawals from the retirement plan may cause it to run out of money before you and your spouse run out of life. Good point. Here's a hypothetical case to get around that problem. Suppose your retirement plans totaled $1 million. You and your advisors have concluded that if you and your spouse were to die, the children would end up with about $300,000. Insurance companies are in the business of financial protection—how could they deal with this problem? The insurance company says you give it your $1 million and it will issue an immediate annuity contract that promises to pay you and your spouse a level income of $80,000 per year for the rest of both your lives, as well as to the survivor for the rest of his or her life. However, if you both die, the insurance company will confiscate the annuity money not paid out as income. Alternatively if you die and have not annuitized, the tax collector will confiscate the money in estate and income taxes.

How long does it take for you to get out in income all that might have gone to the children?

$80,000 taxable income
−$24,000 income taxes each year assuming the 30 percent tax bracket
$56,000 net after tax

At $56,000 per year it will take about 5 years and 4 months to have received $300,000 from your retirement plans. From that time forward your checks are from what otherwise would have gone to taxes after both of your deaths. The point is that there is opportunity for you and yours in how you use these three types of capital: retirement plan money, life insurance cash value, and family personal assets. At this mature stage in life it is not the size of the pile of assets that you have managed to accumulate that makes you feel free and secure, but rather the amount of ever-replaceable income that arrives every month, and that will continue to do so throughout your lifetimes.

This is the stage in life during which career and work are for *fun* and not for economic necessity. If you want to retire, you do; if you don't want to retire, you do what you like to do. Your need for life insurance will be based upon how you want your estate handled for the next generation unless your assets are illiquid (for example, if you have invested in real estate or you have your own closely held business). You will have ensured that your spouse can afford to live in the manner to which the two of you have been accustomed. You currently are receiving mandatory distributions (because you are over age 70½) from your IRA accounts, pension plans, profit-sharing plans, 401(k) plans, thrift plans, SEP plans, Keogh plans, and deferred-compensation contracts. Alternatively, you may have chosen a payout option that will pay a life income for your life only, in which case you would want to have provided sufficient death benefits in life insurance to make sure that your spouse will have enough capital to provide for income for her life also, should she survive you.

Life Insurance to Pay Federal Estate Taxes

You may need life insurance at this time, not to build an asset base for your surviving spouse, but to provide cash for your offspring so that they can pay estate taxes from life insurance proceeds, rather than sell the real estate or closely held business in your estate. Everything *over* $675,000 that you and over $675,000 that your spouse pass to your children will create an estate tax liability until 2002 and 2003 when the exemption increases to $1,000,000 for a person bequeathing assets to someone other than a spouse, or when the tax law is changed. The tax rate at $675,000 to $750,000 is 37 percent, a $27,750 tax liability for the first $75,000 over the $675,000 breakpoint. The rate is 39 percent for the next $250,000, 41 percent for the next $250,000, and so on, up to a maximum rate of 55 percent on amounts for transfers over $3 million. In short, the two of you currently can pass $1,350,000 of assets to your children without an estate tax liability. This amount is scheduled to increase to $2 million in 2002, and will increase to $7,000,000 in 2009 under the Economic Growth and Tax Relief Reconciliation Act of 2001. Your estate should have ready cash to pay any estate tax liability you foresee from cash within the estate or proceeds from life insurance. If it does not, then assets of your estate will have to be sold to pay the bill, which is due 9 months after the death that created the liability.

The Uniform Transfer Tax System establishes a means of taxing everything that you or I own and pass to others (see Exhibit 11.1). There are limited nontaxable transfers of assets during lifetime and at death. The general rule regarding these gifts is that if you own it and transfer that ownership, the transfer is a taxable event. This holds true with these exceptions.

1. If the recipient is your spouse (spousal gifts and marital deduction)
2. If it is a present interest gift of $10,000 or less per year, per individual recipient (joint with spouse gifts, $20,000)
3. If the total of all gifts, not counting the $10,000-per-year gifts, was less than $675,000 as adjusted in your whole lifetime, including the total of all you passed by inheritance at your death

The way to alleviate high estate taxes is to reduce the size of your estate. Life insurance in your estate currently that is gifted out of your estate can result in a substantial estate reduction. Life insurance will be taxed in the estate of the policy owner. If the policy owner and the insured are one and the same individual, it will be the death benefit of the life insurance that will be included

EXHIBIT 11.1

Uniform Transfer Tax Rate Schedule
(For Estates and Gifts after 1983)

If the Tax Base Is—		The Tentative Tax Is—		
Over	But Not Over	Flat Amount	+%	Of Excess Over
$0	$10,000	$0	18%	$0
$10,000	$20,000	$1,800	20%	$10,000
$20,000	$40,000	$3,800	22%	$20,000
$40,000	$60,000	$8.200	24%	$40,000
$60,000	$80,000	$13,000	26%	$60,000
$80,000	$100,000	$18,200	28%	$80,000
$100,000	$150,000	$23,800	30%	$100,000
$150,000	$250,000	$38,800	32%	$150,000
$250,000	$500,000	$70,800	34%	$250,000
$500,000	$750,000	$155,800	37%	$500,000
$750,000	$1,000,000	$248,300	39%	$750,000
$1,000,000	$1,250,000	$345,800	41%	$1,000,000
$1,250,000	$1,500,000	$448,300	43%	$1,250,000
$1,500,000	$2,000,000	$555,800	45%*	$1,500,000
$2,000,000	$2,500,000	$780,800	49%*	$2,000,000
$2,500,000	$3,000,000	$1,025,800	53%*	$2,500,000
$3,000,000	. . . .	$1,290,800	55%*	$3,000,000

*The maximum rate is to be gradually reduced to 45 percent by 2007.

within that estate. If that is an unsatisfactory arrangement, the solution is to give it away. If you give it away to your spouse, you will accomplish nothing—the full face amount of the life insurance policy still will be included in the estate of the second to die, regardless of whether you or your spouse owns the policy. If your spouse dies first and you are the insured, the cash value of the policy is a part of the spouse's estate, not the face amount. If special provisions were made to ensure that the policy passes to a new owner other than you, that would prevent inclusion of the life insurance face amount in your estate.

The benefits of the graduated rates and the unified credit, which save estate taxes for smaller estates, are phased out for larger estates. The savings are recaptured from estates over $10 million by adding a 5 percent extra tax for those estates exceeding $10 million up until the 5 percent has been applied to $11,040,000, recapturing some $552,000 in graduated rate and unified credit tax savings. The effective tax for estates between $10,000,000 and $21,040,000 is 60 percent, and above that it drops back to 55 percent. Keep in mind that this tax is due in cash 9 months from the date of death. The maximum rate is to be reduced to 45 percent by 2007. People use life insurance to make sure that the cash is there when the bill is due. They prefer paying the tax by way of installments in life insurance premiums for their estates, rather than paying the estate tax from their estates.

A better way to get life insurance outside your estate so that the death benefit is not taxed within your estate is to have someone other than you or your spouse own it. That person can buy life insurance on either or both of your lives, and be the policy owner and beneficiary. In this case you, the insured, would have no ownership rights and no control rights over any part of the policy, and would never have had such rights; consequently, the policy would not be included in your estate. The objective is to have the policies serve their required purposes and also be excluded from the estate owner's gross estate for estate tax purposes. The irrevocable life insurance trust offers one solution.

LIFE INSURANCE: IRREVOCABLE LIVING TRUSTS

You will need a good estate attorney to draft the irrevocable trust. Community property states have unique planning problems and opportunities that you will want to discuss. Internal Revenue Code Sections 2035 and 2042 are pertinent to this area of planning. Section 2035 says that a decedent's estate includes life insurance transferred within 3 years of death. This means that you will need to be cautious of the transferal of the policy itself and future premium payments. Section 2042 says that a decedent's estate includes the proceeds of life insurance if the decedent had any incidence of policy ownership. You will need to make sure that the estate owner, from whose estate you are trying to eliminate the policy, does not retain any incidence of ownership or control over the particular policy. This requires special consideration in community property states to avoid having the policy treated as community property.

The assets that flow into an irrevocable trust, such as a family trust owned and controlled by the children, then can be used to buy illiquid assets from the decedent's estate. This accomplishes transferal of the liquid assets, the life insurance proceeds, from the irrevocable trust for the benefit of the family, and provides cash to the decedent's estate to pay estate taxes.

The concept of an irrevocable trust is frightening to some because *irrevocable* is a very long time. Most people are reluctant to give up the control, use, and enjoyment of substantial assets during their lifetime. However, if the irrevocable trust can be established as a family trust (assuming good family relationships), many of the objections to an irrevocable trust can be overcome. For example, the assets of the trust could be used prior to the insured's death to accomplish the objectives of the beneficiaries of the trust (such as advanced education), and the trust could be established so as to self-destruct in the event that it no longer served family needs. Funding such trusts with today's variable universal life insurance policies allows the trustees to raise and lower payments into the policy, increase and decrease face amounts, and maintain strategic control over the investment of the assets within the life insurance contract. The irrevocable trust used in this way does not have to be as inflexible as it sounds. If at any time the trust is deemed to no longer be serving family purposes, payments into the trust may be terminated, assets may be removed from the policy and distributed to beneficiaries, and the policy may be allowed to implode, that is, using itself up and terminating. Yes, this may result in the trust or its beneficiaries being subject to an ordinary income tax liability on the gain in the policy in excess of the trustee policy owner's basis; however, a policy that uses up all accrued gains in term insurance costs and expenses will not leave taxable gains.

MULTIPLE-LIFE LIFE INSURANCE CONTRACTS

Popular for the Wrong Reason

Survivorship life insurance, joint and last survivor life insurance, and second-to-die and first-to-die joint life all provide life insurance on more than one life, with the death benefit paid out at *one* of the deaths. With survivorship, joint and last survivor, and second-to-die insurance, the death benefit is paid at the death of the second insured, but the death benefit is paid at the death of the first insured in a first-to-die contract (tricky names—did they give you a clue?). These policies are receiving much publicity because they require less premium than standard life policies on a single insured. They are purported to be *cheaper*. The fact is that the COIs (costs of insurance,) in survivorship life are amazingly low because the company depends upon the payout being delayed until the second death. Properly used, this is an incredibly good accumulation product with life insurance features and benefits for very tailored needs. The myth that this is cheap insurance has led to it being used without careful thought about how well it provides for specific and long-term needs.

First-to-Die Policies

In the case of first-to-die joint life, the policies are perceived as inexpensive when compared with two separate single-life policies. They do cost less because the insurance company needs to pay off only at the death of the first, leaving the survivor uninsured. If lack of insurance is a problem and the survivor is now uninsurable, or if resources are not available to pay for what now will be a standard single-life policy, then using the first-to-die contract was not a bargain but rather improperly used and costing dearly. Make sure that your first-to-die policy guarantees the insurability of the survivor.

Second-to-Die Policies

Second-to-die policies, even more popular than first-to-die ones, are perceived as inexpensive because people feel they have a lot of insurance at a premium much less than what it would be to insure them under two individual life policies. But again, the insurance company needs to pay off only at one death, the last of the two insureds to die. This dramatically delays the time that the company will be called upon to pay a death benefit. Therefore, it follows that the mortality costs for life insurance within the policy are much lower than with a conventional single-life policy. The *other shoe* in these policies is what happens when the first of the two insureds dies. The survivor may not receive any death benefit payments from this contract and now may have to pay the premium on what essentially is a standard single-life policy. Does the survivor have the resources and the desire to use them to service the ongoing premium requirements of a policy that is not beneficial personally? Also, what is to be the disposition of the policy if one of the insureds should no longer *be* one of the insureds, such as in a divorce situation, the termination of a key employee, or the breakup of a business arrangement?

The bottom line is that these policies should not be thought of as bargains but rather as merely policies that meet the needs of a particular situation very efficiently. Keep in mind that the very efficiency with which they provide for the *particular* situation is likely to make them quite inefficient should the situation change.

Let's take a look at some of the situations to which these policies are particularly well suited and then give some reasons why the *cheaper* approach may backfire.

Situation: Husband and Wife

The federal estate taxes must be paid at the death of the last surviving spouse. This is the situation in which the second-to-die policy is used most commonly. It hits the nail on the head. A husband and wife first plan their estate with their attorney, accountant, and other appropriate professionals. This assures that the estate passes to whom they wish with a minimum of cost, delay, and complication. Having determined the most efficient method of passing their property and minimizing the costs involved, they make an informed decision *not* to pay any estate taxes until the second death. After estimating the inflation-adjusted amount of the taxes and expenses to be paid, they buy a second-to-die policy sufficient to pay the estimated costs. The cash from the policy death benefit will arrive as a result of the same event that causes the taxes and expenses to become due. What could be more perfect? What could possibly make this a less than perfect decision? After all, the premium is less expensive than two individual policies and may be all the couple can allocate to insurance. One of the two insureds may have trouble getting insurance because of poor health, but the insurance company will accept the risk in this situation because it is based on two lives. Also, the purchasers went to a number of agents and carefully bought a policy that required sufficient premium so as not to include much term insurance, which later might become more expensive than predicted.

What Went Wrong

Well, here is what really happened. The couple's marriage ended in a divorce. The policy was owned by an irrevocable trust. It took some effort (time and expense) for the attorney to find that the trustee had the right to distribute the policy to the trust beneficiaries. They then looked to see if the policy could be divided into two policies, each for one-half the original face amount and allowing each of the insureds to become the owner of his or her own policy. Unfortunately, when the policy was being purchased, they did not buy the rider that would have allowed for such a split, and so it could not be done. Now we have a policy on two people who do not like each other, and neither wants to pay any money into it to keep it going, and the children (beneficiaries) can't afford to make payments. The policy is eating up its account values with expenses and ongoing COIs, and it will one day terminate without value. It was an expensive, unpleasant, difficult process because the outcome was not anticipated or provided for in advance.

What Else Could Go Wrong?

Or let's try this. They did not get divorced, but he died before she did and the cost of the policy was a burden to her. The policy did not help her, and she began to wonder why she should pay for it. The kids weren't being that great either, so she quit making the gifts to the irrevocable trust that were necessary to pay the premiums on the policy. The mortality (life insurance) costs and expenses were taken from the policy values and the policy terminated, leaving the trust an empty shell. At her death, Uncle Sam took his 50 percent, and the estate was destroyed for lack of cash. The company that the children had worked for had to be sold at a substantial loss to pay the tax bill within 9 months. Now there is no company, no job, and no money. The kids finally realized that they should have taken care of mom—or figured out some way to keep the policy in force.

Another Scenario

Voluntarily Pay Estate Taxes at the First Death

Bob Hales, an attorney from California, tells a story of someone who did not buy second-to-die insurance but elected years ago to pay $90,000 of estate taxes at the first death. This allowed a piece of property to be put in a trust for the limited benefit of the spouse during her lifetime, with the eventual benefit to the children when she died. The trust will not be subject to estate taxes on the value of the property since her interest in the trust is limited, and the $90,000 in taxes was paid when he died using life insurance proceeds from a policy on his life. That piece of property is a sizable portion of the Napa Valley. The children were not aware of the careful planning their father had done 25 years earlier and came into Bob's office recently with their mother, who is now 90 years old. They were terribly concerned because they had just attended a seminar on estate taxes and wanted Bob's estimate of the federal estate taxes they thought would be due at their mother's eventual death. The piece of property is now worth $36 million. The seminar leader had told them they would owe Uncle Sam $18 million payable 9 months after their mom's death. Bob happily told them that the correct figure was *zero* because of the strategic long-term thinking of their father (and the attorney), resulting in the payment of a $90,000 tax with life insurance proceeds 25 years earlier. He enjoyed their pleased surprise immensely. He is now concerned that this might no longer be a wise strategy because of the 2001 estate tax law that predicts the elimination of FET in 2010.

Survivorship Policies

When these policies work, they work very, very well. For example, our young couple needs life insurance to provide for their children in the event of their death. One of them has had a health incident and is uninsurable, and so they are just going to get life insurance on the healthy spouse. Let's try survivorship life. Usually we can get a second-to-die policy even if one insured is uninsurable, and we can put a first-to-die rider on the policy to insure the healthy one. Certainly we all worry about the death of the unhealthy one, but how many of us have seen situations like this in which the healthy one is the first to die from an accident or a health situation that no one knew about, while the spouse who had been considered higher risk lives on. If this were to happen in this situation, the first-to-die rider provides insurance and financial security for the surviving spouse who had been considered unhealthy, or uninsurable. The second-to-die insurance policy is now a standard first-to-die policy, providing security for the children when it would not have been obtainable any other way. Furthermore, there are some grandparents who have an interest in this situation. If both parents were lost, the grandparents certainly would feel financially responsible for their grandchildren. This policy makes sure that this is not a problem. The hope is that the grandparents will live to see the their grandchildren graduate from college (along with two very proud parents), and any contributions that they have made to this policy that have helped to pay for those educations will only make them more proud. Each one of the grandparents might have picked a special subaccount within the policy and stored gifts for college purposes. If you have room for more money in your policy, would you please let your folks use it?

The use of these policies is limited only by your imagination. The question is what do you really care about getting done that will not get done in the event that you die too soon. That is a priority question that too few of us stop to think about in the rush of everyday life.

BUSINESS LIFE INSURANCE FOR PROTECTION AND WEALTH ACCUMULATION

In addition to what you are doing for yourself, at some time during your mature career years, your employer may well come up with some individually designed employee benefit opportunities using variable universal life insurance products as a means of accumulating assets and providing death and disability benefits. The 1986 Tax Reform Act pretty much did away with corporate-owned, nonqualified tax-deferred *annuities* as accumulation vehicles. The act requires current income taxation on the earnings of any annuities begun, or contributed to, after February 28, 1986. However, the use of variable universal life insurance allows you to avoid current taxation. As a result, it has become even more popular, particularly in an increasing income tax environment.

There are myriad reasons for business life insurance. Businesses often buy insurance for their employees as a part of their compensation package because the business gets a better tax break on it, or because the business can negotiate a better deal on it than the individual could do, such as group life insurance. It is purchased for providing special benefit and compensation packages for key employees and for making sure that the business remains healthy financially in the event of the death of one of these key employees. It is purchased to make sure that the financial interests in the business of the existing owners go to the most appropriate new owners while the families of the deceased owners are fully compensated for their share of the ownership of the business. When life insurance is used in these ways, contractual promises and/or liabilities may be created for the corporation by its promises to employees or shareholders. Then, the employer will use key-employee life insurance as the vehicle to ensure that the funds required by the promises are available when the liabilities must be paid.

The following are among the many forms of business life insurance.

Group Term Life Insurance

It is highly likely that you have some death benefits provided through an employer's group life insurance plan. The employer may purchase up to $50,000 of life insurance per employee, deduct the cost, and not report any of these expenditures as taxable income to you as an employee as long as the plan is not discriminatory. Amounts in excess of $50,000 are subject to income tax based upon the imputed income value of the benefit provided. The amount to be taxed is calculated by dividing by $1000 the amount of life insurance that you have in excess of $50,000, and then multiplying that by the premiums shown in Exhibit 11.2.

The cost of taxable life insurance is calculated on a month-by-month basis. For example:

1. Enter the uniform premium table (commonly referred to as the *Table 1 rate*) at the individual insured's attained age on the last day of the taxable year.
2. Multiply this *cost per $1000 Table 1 rate* by the number of

EXHIBIT 11.2

Uniform Premium per $1000 after June 30, 1999
Group Term Life Insurance Protection

Table 1	
5-Year Age Bracket	Cost per $1000 of Protection for 1-Month Period
Under 25	5 cents
25 to 29	6 cents
30 to 34	8 cents
35 to 39	9 cents
40 to 44	10 cents
45 to 49	15 cents
50 to 54	23 cents
55 to 59	43 cents
60 to 64	66 cents
65 to 69	$1.27
70 and over	$2.06

thousands of taxable life insurance benefit (amount in excess of $50,000).

3. Subtract monthly employee contributions, if any.

4. Add together each month's calculations to determine the total reportable as taxable income for the tax year, which is referred to as *imputed income.*

If you contribute to your life insurance through payroll deduction, your employer will deduct what you pay from the amount that is reported to you as taxable income. You have to pay tax only on that life insurance over $50,000 that you have received and have not paid for. There are exceptions to this for business owners, officers, and highly compensated and key employees, who may be taxed on the actual cost of the coverage or the *Table 1 rates*, whichever is greater.

Taxation and Business Life Insurance

The only ways, other than group life insurance, that an employer can purchase life insurance for an employee and deduct the premium are if the insurance is purchased within a qualified retirement plan or if the premium is deductible as a part of the reasonable compensation of the employee.

The reason that the premium is deductible in the qualified retirement plan is that it is part of the employer's deductible contribution to the qualified plan. The trustees of the qualified plan purchase the life insurance on the employee's behalf.

A Section 162 plan includes life insurance in which the premium is deductible as compensation. The employer pays the premium for the employee and deducts it as employee compensation, and the employee picks up the premium as a fully taxable bonus.

The employing firm also may purchase insurance on the life of an employee to indemnify itself for a loss. *Key-employee life insurance*, as it is called, may be purchased only with nondeductible dollars. Internal Revenue Code Section 264(a)(1) expressly prohibits the employer from deducting any premiums paid on life insurance if the employer is directly or indirectly the beneficiary of the policy. The offsetting benefit is that the death proceeds generally are received income tax–free by the corporate beneficiary under Code Section 101.

The Tax Reform Act of 1986 created the possibility of corporate beneficiaries being subject to tax on the death benefits of life insurance. This act differentiated between the company's book and taxable incomes, and subjected that difference of the book over taxable income to an alternative minimum tax (AMT). Don't let the name fool you; the tax is neither *alternative* (it is mandatory) nor *minimum* (you pay the maximum). For corporations, this brings insurance policy gains in excess of premium, and death benefits in excess of cash value, into the web of the corporate AMT (mandatory maximum tax) since these gains are added to a corporation's book income.

Key Employee Life Insurance

The primary function of key-employee life insurance, as of all life insurance, is to offset the economic loss associated with the death of an individual (Exhibit 11.3). It may be purchased on the life of an employee whose services constitute a substantial asset to the company. The loss of that employee's services could result in substantial costs to replace the talent, and additional costs to replace

EXHIBIT 11.3

Key-Employee Insurance

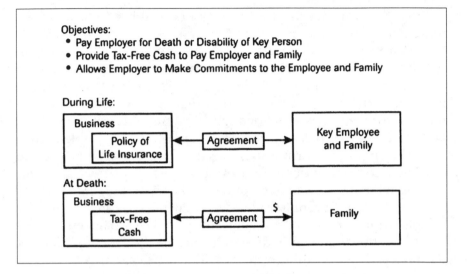

Objectives:
- Pay Employer for Death or Disability of Key Person
- Provide Tax-Free Cash to Pay Employer and Family
- Allows Employer to Make Commitments to the Employee and Family

During Life:

Business — Policy of Life Insurance ← Agreement → Key Employee and Family

At Death:

Business — Tax-Free Cash ← Agreement → $ → Family

business that the company may lose as a result of the employee's death. Key-employee life insurance also may enhance the credit standing of the business. It may serve as a source of collateral if it is the type of policy that accumulates asset value. It may also serve as a reserve-funding vehicle to pay promised death, disability, or supplemental retirement benefits. It can provide funds to the business through death benefits that can be used to assist the survivors.

Any business should be legally set up to survive; i.e., the business may use the funds to redeem a partial owner's interest so that the remaining owner-operators may continue the business knowing that they can purchase inherited stock for cash from inactive survivors. Such plans assist and maintain business continuity. If an owner-operator lives to retirement, the reserve built up in the key-employee life policy can be used to provide for a systematic buyout of the retiring shareholder's interest, conveniently coordinated with other retirement sources of income.

One basic common denominator in key-employee life insurance is that the business entity owns the policy. Under such circumstances, the business entity should also be the beneficiary of the policy. If the employee's spouse or some personal beneficiary is named on a corporate-owned policy, the IRS could claim that the policy is providing personal benefits. As a result, the premium could be construed as compensation subject to income taxes or, even worse, as a corporate dividend nondeductible to the corporation and as taxable income to the shareholder-employee. A more critical situation would arise in the event of a death of a shareholder-employee, when the death proceeds of the corporate-owned policy were paid directly to the spouse of that shareholder-employee. In this case, the total death benefit could be construed as a nondeductible dividend, fully taxable as ordinary income to the beneficiary.

In one recent case, a personally owned policy had a split beneficiary, with part going to the insured's corporation and part to the insured's spouse. Part was intended for buy-sell agreement purposes; however, no buy-sell agreement was ever put in force. In the event that the insured had died, the corporation and the spouse would have received money. The surviving, nonworking spouse would have become an equal shareholder with the surviving, working shareholder in a professional service company. Murphy's law implies that if it can be done wrong, it will be; and if it is done wrong, litigation and business failures are likely to follow. It is important to check ownership and beneficiary provisions.

Salary-Continuation or Deferred-Compensation Plans

The principal difference between a *salary-continuation* plan and a *deferred-compensation* plan is who initiates it. If an employee requests that the employer defer partial compensation until some future date, the plan is a true employee-motivated *deferred-compensation* plan. This request must be made before such compensation is earned. In this case, the two obligations of the corporation, should it agree to such a plan, would be to pay corporate income taxes on the compensation not paid and to pay the compensation deferred at the agreed-upon future date. To avoid current taxation to the employee, the employee's status would have to be that of a general creditor of the corporation. Assets could *not* be set aside by the corporation so as to prevent the allocated assets from being accessible by the corporation's general creditors. This does not mean that the employer is not free to *informally* fund such an arrangement (reserve for it) as long as any reserve so established is still available to satisfy the claims of the general creditors.

In these days of mergers and acquisitions, it is difficult for employees to accept the fact that their deferred compensation or salary continuation also could be subject to the whims of new management. Employees usually prefer to see informal funding rather than hope for "pay-as-you-go" deferred compensation. That assumes that the employer will pay your retirement benefits out of current earnings when you retire. With informal funding, at least there is a corporate asset available to fund a recognized liability of the employer. The more closely the asset is identified with the employee, the more secure the employee is likely to feel. Some employees have had employers establish what are referred to as *rabbi trusts*. Assets are placed in an irrevocable trust established by the employer to fulfill the liabilities stated within the trust agreement. The trust assets are accessible to the general creditors of the business but are not available to business management to do anything else but to pay the promised amounts. The existence of the trust makes it highly unlikely that either current or new management will touch the assets of the trust; however, the trust assets specifically are made available to the creditors of the corporation in the event of a corporate bankruptcy. Favorable IRS revenue rulings have been issued regarding these trusts.

It also is highly likely that the employee would like some return on that deferred compensation. In some instances, this may be done on a straight book basis, and, for example, some corporations make book entry of paying the current prime rate of interest on such funds. With smaller employers, reserve of the actual cash may be preferable, and if such is the case, the employer will strive to put the cash in a place that will not create income tax problems for the company. Any investments that generate taxable interest, taxable dividends, or capital gains create an extra asset to be tracked by the corporation, along with corporate income tax liabilities. Until February 28, 1986, the annuity contract was the investment vehicle of choice for many deferred-compensation plans. Prior to that date, the inside buildup of interest, dividends, or capital gains of an annuity was not subject to tax. Since then, contributions that result in inside buildup for corporate-owned annuity contracts are subject to income tax. With annuities owned by corporations losing the income tax shelter, variable universal life insurance has become the preferred investment vehicle. The life insurance contract has retained its tax shelter on the inside buildup, and the corporation can use the income tax–free (AMT excepted) death benefit to meet corporate obligations.

Employer-motivated salary-continuation plans usually use life insurance as an investment vehicle because employers promise employees not only a supplemental employee retirement plan (SERP) but also benefits in the event of the employee's premature death or disability. A SERP is used by employers to build special compensation packages to help hire and keep key people. In the event of the employee's death, the life insurance proceeds provide the corporate asset necessary to fulfill and pay corporate liability under the salary-continuation plan. In the event of employee disability, individual disability income contracts, the disability premium waiver on the life insurance contracts, and the assets built up in the insurance policy would be available to provide the cash necessary. Retirement benefits would be paid from the reserve built up in the asset value of the life insurance policy. Today's variable universal life policies make the design of such plans very easy, efficient, and flexible. VUL allows asset diversification appropriate for retirement plan assets.

Regardless of whether the nonqualified plan was a deferred-compensation or a salary-continuation plan, in most cases the life insurance policy would be established as a regular key-employee life insurance contract. The company would be the owner and beneficiary of the contract without reference to the legal agreement established between employer and employee that laid out the payment schedules in the event of the employee's death, disability, or retirement.

Buy-Sell Agreements and Cross-Purchase Agreements

Business owners who do not arrange for the continuation of their business in the event of death are likely to have their survivors realize little or nothing from that business interest.

Sole Proprietors

The sole proprietor has the problem of trying to identify the person or persons who would be interested in buying out the business and continuing it in the event of his or her death. The question comes down to transferability of the customer base. Can a new owner expect to retain that base? If so, the business has value, and a buy-sell agreement is feasible. The next question for the sole proprietor is who would both retain the business and want it? It could be a competitor, an employee, or another family member. The type of agreement will depend upon the relationship between the sole proprietor and the potential buyer. It is likely to be a one-way arrangement. In the event of the sole proprietor's death, the one chosen to be the new owner will buy the business; however, if the key employee or relative dies, there may be no necessity for the surviving sole proprietor to buy anything. Sole proprietor buyout agreements are between individuals and may be one-way buyout contracts or cross-purchase contracts between the two sole proprietors. In cross-purchase arrangements, the one who is obligated to purchase the business will want to own and be the beneficiary of insurance on the life of the sole proprietor he or she is obligated to buy out.

In key-employee and relative buyout situations, there is often the difficulty of finding money to pay premiums. If the key employee or relative does not have sufficient resources, assistance will be sought from the sole proprietor. It often is difficult for the sole proprietor to understand why he or she should pay to help someone else buy out the business interest. Indeed, it may be better for the sole proprietor to just own enough life insurance payable for the benefit of family members and then pass the business to them by will. This way, the beneficiaries may be economically independent of the business. If they can get anything out of it, fine; but if not, they'll be all right anyway. It is important for sole proprietors to understand that either they come up with an equitable buyout arrangement or their families get what is left when business assets are sold, possibly at forced-sale liquidation values. Once the business owner understands that *there is indeed a cost for doing nothing*, creative solutions for funding the life insurance, with the assistance of those with the necessary resources, can be found. (See "Split-Dollar Life Insurance" later in this chapter.)

Partnerships

A partnership is one of the most legally fragile business forms. In the event of the death of a partner, the partnership legally is terminated, and the surviving partner or partners are bound in a fiduciary capacity to wind up the affairs of the partnership, terminate business, and pay out the remaining assets to the deceased partner's survivors based on their partnership shares. During the process of winding up the business, the deceased partner's survivors have a right to the deceased's distributable share of partnership profits or gains; however, survivors of the deceased partner are not to be charged with any partnership losses. This is so, even though while all partners are alive and well, each is totally liable for not only his or her own acts, but the acts and liabilities of the partnership and all other partners as well. Of all business structures, the partnership is the one most in need of proper liability insurance and legally binding business-continuation agreements. Without such arrangements, partnerships can be very hazardous to your economic health.

Cross-Purchase Agreement

In the simple two-person, equal-interest business, a legally binding cross-purchase buy-sell agreement between the individual owners provides that at the death of the first, the surviving partner will buy out the deceased's share for a stipulated sum (Exhibit 11.4). This same sum would be the price of a living buyout under the same agreement. Having each owner become the owner and beneficiary of a policy on the other's life funds the agreement. This is referred to as a cross-purchase agreement because the *individuals* are the ones bound by the agreement. They are the ones who own the insurance policy and the ones who pay out the proceeds to the family of the deceased in completion of the agreement to buy out the business interest. Such an agreement is beneficial to the economic health of both parties. Each knows what the family will realize in the event of death, and each knows that the surviving owner may carry on the business without interruption or interference, continuing to earn a living in the event of the co-owner's death.

This arrangement becomes somewhat more complicated as the number of business owners involved grows. With six, each

EXHIBIT 11.4

Buy-Sell Cross-Purchase Plan (Individual Buyout)

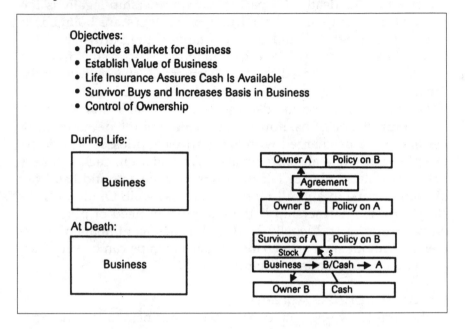

Objectives:
- Provide a Market for Business
- Establish Value of Business
- Life Insurance Assures Cash Is Available
- Survivor Buys and Increases Basis in Business
- Control of Ownership

During Life:

Business

Owner A	Policy on B
Agreement	
Owner B	Policy on A

At Death:

Business

Survivors of A	Policy on B
Stock / $	
Business → B/Cash → A	
Owner B	Cash

would be required to own a life insurance policy on each of the other five lives. There would be five life insurance policies per owner, and thirty policies in all, to maintain and manage in order to carry out the agreement. The advantage of the cross-purchase agreement is that as each survivor buys out a deceased's interest, the cost basis in the business of each is increased by the amount of the purchase price, which, upon sale, would reduce gain and therefore taxes. This advantage may be offset by the disadvantages of managing and paying for multiple life insurance policies. An alternative is to turn to an entity buyout agreement.

Entity Buy-Sell Agreement

Under an entity buy-sell agreement, the obligation to purchase would be turned over to the entity (Exhibit 11.5). The business itself would own and be the beneficiary of the life insurance. The business would carry out the agreement by paying the agreed-upon amount to the deceased's heirs in order to retire that interest.

EXHIBIT 11.5

Buy-Sell Stock Redemption Plan (Entity Buyout)

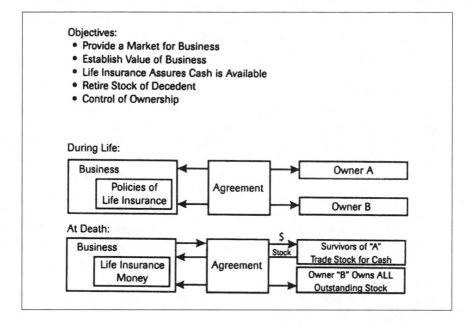

Objectives:
- Provide a Market for Business
- Establish Value of Business
- Life Insurance Assures Cash is Available
- Retire Stock of Decedent
- Control of Ownership

During Life:

Business		
Policies of Life Insurance	Agreement	Owner A / Owner B

At Death:

Business		
Life Insurance Money	Agreement	Survivors of "A" Trade Stock for Cash / Owner "B" Owns ALL Outstanding Stock

Using the example just given, the entity would now own and be the beneficiary of six life insurance policies, one on each co-owner. In the event of the death of an owner, the interest of each surviving owner would go from a one-sixth interest to a one-fifth interest in the business with *no change in cost basis*. This would mean that higher taxes would be due upon sale because the entity buyout arrangement would not increase the cost basis of the survivors.

Corporations

The corporation is a less risky way of doing business than is a partnership. To some extent you are protected from liability by the corporate veil, and you do not pick up additional liability from fellow stockholders. However, in the closely held business made up of owner-operator shareholders, the death of one can bring about a host of problems for those surviving. Inactive, surviving shareholders with minority interest in the company do not have the same interests as the active shareholder-employees. The inactive will want dividends as a result of their ownership or will want to be bought out. Although the majority owner-operator shareholders probably can freeze them out, the minority shareholders may turn to the courts to make life miserable for the owner-operators. You can be on either side of this battle, and both sides lose.

In the corporate situation, the cross-purchase arrangement, discussed previously, could be used to solve this problem and make sure that only shareholders active in the business buy the deceased shareholder's stock. Alternatively, the entity purchase arrangement—which, in the corporate situation, is referred to as a stock redemption plan—might be the preferred choice. In this case, the corporate entity purchases the stock of the deceased shareholder, is the owner and beneficiary of insurance on the life of each shareholder, and buys the stock at a shareholder's death. Such agreements work well for both sides since the survivors of the deceased shareholder get cash at a fair price from the sale of the business interest that they inherited and the surviving owner-operators can continue the business free of concern for the interests of inactive shareholders.

Section 303 Partial Stock Redemptions

Section 303 partial redemptions work well when the issue is *not disposing of the business*. Indeed, the business is to be retained. The issue instead is having enough cash to pay expenses and estate taxes. If the business represents over 35 percent of the deceased's gross estate, Section 303 may be used as a solution since it allows for a partial redemption of stock sufficient to provide the stipulated liquidity needed without having the redemption characterized by the government as a nondeductible dividend for the corporation and ordinary income to the shareholder (Exhibit 11.6).

LIFE INSURANCE AS COMPENSATION
Section 162 Bonus Plans

A Section 162 plan is a bonus plan for an employee (Exhibit 11.7). Such a bonus can be used to pay a life insurance policy premium.

EXHIBIT 11.6

Section 303 Partial Stock Redemption

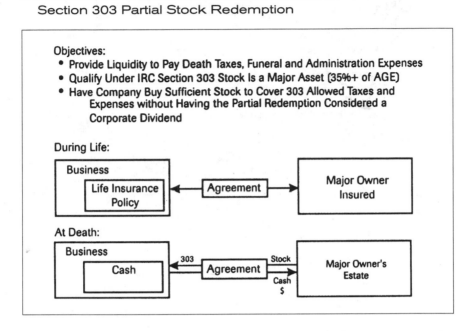

Objectives:
- Provide Liquidity to Pay Death Taxes, Funeral and Administration Expenses
- Qualify Under IRC Section 303 Stock Is a Major Asset (35%+ of AGE)
- Have Company Buy Sufficient Stock to Cover 303 Allowed Taxes and Expenses without Having the Partial Redemption Considered a Corporate Dividend

During Life:

Business — Life Insurance Policy ← Agreement → Major Owner Insured

At Death:

Business — Cash ← 303 — Agreement — Stock → Major Owner's Estate — Cash $

The cost to the employee is the income tax on the premium paid by the employer for the life insurance. This plan is popular because *once paid, the plan belongs to the employee* and is not subject to the creditors of the employer. Further, to the extent that your state shelters life insurance assets from the claims of creditors, it also is protected from the creditors of the employee. The employer could limit the plan benefits by a vesting agreement that would stretch out the time before the plan belonged entirely to the employee. These plans can be less expensive to employees because marginal tax brackets *now* may be lower than in the future upon retirement. They are a way for a corporate employer to pay something to employees other than straight compensation. They also complicate things for competitors trying to hire away the employees since they do indicate special consideration by the employer. Today's variable universal contracts can offer attractive benefits to the right employees.

EXHIBIT 11.7

Bonus Plan Section 162 Life Insurance

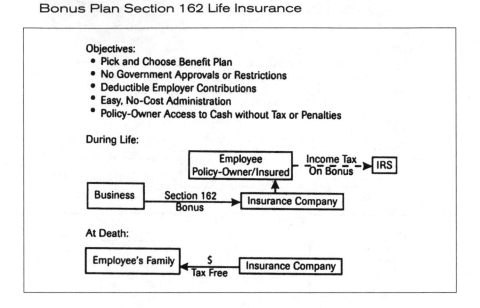

Objectives:
- Pick and Choose Benefit Plan
- No Government Approvals or Restrictions
- Deductible Employer Contributions
- Easy, No-Cost Administration
- Policy-Owner Access to Cash without Tax or Penalties

During Life:

At Death:

SPLIT-DOLLAR LIFE INSURANCE

Split-dollar life insurance is an arrangement whereby both the death benefit and premium payments of a life insurance policy are split between two parties, frequently the employer and the employee (Exhibit 11.8). In split-dollar arrangements using variable universal life policies that are transparent, the employee can pay the mortality costs (COIs) and expenses and have the right to name the beneficiary of the death benefit. The employer, on the other hand, will pay the *plus* dollars going into the investment account and be the owner of these funds. In the event of the insured's death, the employer can collect an amount equal to what the corporation has contributed or the policy surrender value.

In any of these plans the business tax advisor will need to be consulted on plan structure and tax reporting issues, but this is particularly true of split-dollar plans. While basic split dollar has been well accepted by the Internal Revenue Service since 1964, a Notice 2001–10 issued by the IRS in January 2001 has created some

EXHIBIT 11.8

Split-Dollar Life/Disability Insurance

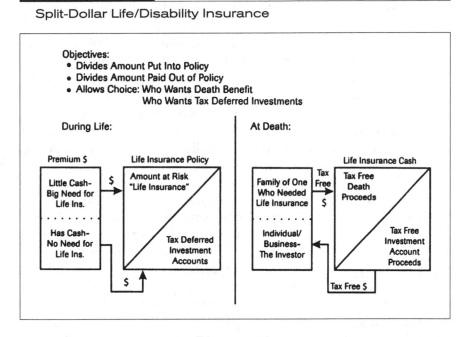

controversy. The controversy has to do with the income tax reporting each year of the employer's and the employee's interests in the split-dollar policy account value and the employers interest in the life insurance. If, for example, the employer is satisfied with its interest as specified in the split-dollar agreement as being limited to the amount that it has paid into a VUL split dollar, then there will be an income tax issue when the account value exceeds what the employer has paid in.

Prior to the Notice, such events were not reported or taxed. The employee was not taxed until the split-dollar agreement was terminated and the unencumbered policy became entirely the employee's. At that time, the employee included in income the value of the property distributed from the company to the employee, and the employer deducted the distribution as compensation to the employee. Many still feel that this is what should be done. The Notice has people worrying that the employee must include in income the excess of the cash surrender value over the interest the employer has in the policy as soon as it occurs. Also, in all years thereafter, whenever the account value growth exceeds employer contributions to the policy, the employee is to include it in income.

There are all sorts of arguments against the Notice procedure, including those that argue that the gain may disappear; that is, the market could give the VUL policy a big boost on which the employee would have to pay income taxes, only to have that gain taken away when the market goes down. To some, this reporting uncertainty is considered an annoyance, but to others it is an opportunity to structure and report a split-dollar plan in a way that is most advantageous to the situation.

If my accountant agreed that the following procedure was justifiable, we might report a split-dollar plan as follows. Suppose I wanted to provide a special compensation package for you to keep you from accepting all those great offers you have been receiving from my competitors. I first would make sure that the wage I was paying you was competitive, and then I would add on a split-dollar plan for you, promising substantial security to your family in the event of your death. I then, with you, would set the living objective of the plan. The living objective would be to build up, over the years of your employment, a substantial accumulation of previously taxed capital. In order to do this, we would want you to pay income taxes on as much as possible of what went into the plan. We would report the economic value of the death benefit using the high New Table 2001 rates as required by notice 2001–10, rather than searching for some lower acceptable term rate, and would report and pay income taxes as the Notice says we should. Doing this increases your cost basis in the plan, which you can withdraw income tax–free in the future.

What is wrong with this plan? It's the fact that you are going to have to pay all those income taxes. The solution is that I, your employer, will pay them for you. We will have an agreement in which I guarantee you bonuses sufficient to pay the income tax liability incurred by the plan and the income taxes on the bonuses, so that we eliminate your concern. As an employer, my interest is in keeping you, and I hope that the unique security that this type of plan gives to you and your family in the way of providing death benefits and building net worth will be enough to keep you.

Of course, I am now going to my corporate accountant, and I will ask that a corporate income tax deduction be made for all funds that go into the plan, as well as for all increases in value that the Notice may require I report as taxable income to you. The inside buildup in excess of employer contribution is to be reported as income to you, and therefore, it should be deductible to your employer who made it happen. If your tax advisor feels that this procedure can be justified, then a profitable employer may be able to obtain some tax deductions without spending any cashflow to get them. However, knowing how the IRS hates it when tax advisors turn its lemons into lemonade, this is an area in which competent legal and tax advice is essential.

In short, split-dollar works because it can provide large amounts of investment types of life insurance for the employee, with the employer coming up with most if not all of the investment capital.

The fact that the employee has received an insurance benefit at little or no cost has not escaped Uncle Sam's attention. Uncle Sam sees an economic benefit that is taxable. The measure for taxability of split-dollar benefits may be taken from the New Table 2001 rates (that replace PS-58 tables) or the actual cost of standard issue life insurance offered by the company providing the coverage. The Table 2001 rates in Exhibit 11.9 show the amount of money on which an employee will have to pay taxes as a result of the death benefit payable to beneficiaries. Any amount actually paid by the employee toward the death benefit is deducted from the Table 2001 calculated imputed income figure.

The currently popular second-to-die or survivorship life policies also can be arranged on split-dollar plans. Imputed income on these contracts is measured by the US-38 tables while both insureds are living (see Exhibit 11.10). It is essential that plans be made to unwind the split-dollar arrangement at the death of the first insured because it can cause problems thereafter, e.g., imputed income to nonemployee insureds.

Reverse Split Dollar

Another twist to the split-dollar policy is to change who typically gets and pays for the account value of the policy. What if your

EXHIBIT 11.9

PS 58 to be replaced by Table 2001 Rates*

The PS 58 rates were used in computing the "cost" of pure life insurance protection that was taxable to the employee under qualified pension and profit sharing plans and tax-sheltered annuities. Revenue Ruling 55-747. 1955-2 CB 228: Revenue Ruling 66-110. The Table 2001 rates were published by the IRS in Notice 2001-10 in January 2001 as the "Interim Table of One-Year Term Premiums for $1000 of Life Insurance Protection" to replace the PS 58 rates for use with split-dollar insurance plans.

One-Year Term Premiums for $1000 of Life Insurance Protection

Age	P.S. 58 Premium	Table 2001 Premium	Age	P.S. 58 Premium	Table 2001 Premium
29	$2.31	$.83	53	$11.69	$3.20
30	2.43	.87	54	12.67	3.65
31	2.57	.90	55	13.74	4.15
32	2.70	.93	56	14.91	4.68
33	2.86	.96	57	16.18	5.20
34	3.02	.98	58	17.56	5.66
35	3.21	.99	59	19.08	6.06
36	3.41	1.01	60	20.73	6.51
37	3.63	1.04	61	22.53	7.11
38	3.87	1.06	62	24.50	7.96
39	4.14	1.07	63	26.63	9.08
40	4.42	1.10	64	28.98	10.41
41	4.73	1.13	65	31.51	11.90
42	5.07	1.20	66	34.28	13.51
43	5.44	1.29	67	37.31	15.20
44	5.85	1.40	68	40.59	16.92
45	6.30	1.53	69	44.17	18.70
46	6.78	1.67	70	48.06	20.62
47	7.32	1.83	71	52.29	22.72
48	7.89	1.98	72	56.89	25.07
49	8.53	2.13	73	61.89	27.57
50	9.22	2.30	74	67.33	30.18
51	9.97	2.52	75	73.23	33.05
52	10.79	2.81	76	79.63	36.33

*The rate at the insured's attained age is applied to the excess of the *amount payable at death* over the *cash value of the policy at the end of the year*, the amount at risk.

objective as an employee is not a substantial amount of life insurance, but rather a substantial buildup of assets? Why not reverse the normal split-dollar situation? Why not have the corporation pay the expenses and mortality costs of a policy and turn the investment account over to you? The employer would take the death benefit, and you would take the cash or account value. The employer gets key employee life insurance, and you get the tax-free buildup of the insurance policy without the normally associated expenses. You could even do this in a family situation where one party wants life insurance and the other wants an annuity without pre–age 59½ penalties or income taxes, i.e., the account value of the VUL policy.

With the typical whole life insurance policies of the past, reverse split-dollar arrangements did not work very well. There was no excitement about the investment value in spite of the fact that, in many cases, it offered a reasonable rate of return in relation to the risk entailed. The reason for current excitement regarding reverse split-dollar plans is the new variable universal life insurance policies with their array of different investment subaccounts offering diversification, the opportunity to dollar-cost-average, and the opportunity to shift among these accounts without current income taxation or transaction costs. These policies give you the ability to manage investments, earn dividends, earn interest, and take capital gains when desired, without concern for any income tax liability. If the expenses and management fees associated with the policy are reasonable, and the investment performance of the subaccounts is competitive, the policy can offer an attractive arrangement.

The corporation gets the death benefit in this case, so the corporation is supposed to pay for the life insurance. The question is how to charge the corporation for the term insurance. The January 2001 IRS Notice 2001-10 leads us to believe that the use of the New Table 2001 rates would be the term costs to use.

SUMMARY

Every life insurance policy strategy discussed in this chapter works better with policy owner control and flexibility of policy

EXHIBIT 11.10

Second-to-Die US 38 Rates per $1000

First Age	Second Age														
	40	41	42	43	44	45	46	47	48	49	50	51	52	53	54
40	0.02	0.02	0.02	0.02	0.03	0.03	0.03	0.03	0.04	0.04	0.04	0.05	0.05	0.05	0.06
41	0.02	0.02	0.02	0.03	0.03	0.03	0.03	0.04	0.04	0.04	0.04	0.05	0.05	0.06	0.06
42	0.02	0.02	0.03	0.03	0.03	0.03	0.04	0.04	0.04	0.04	0.05	0.05	0.06	0.06	0.07
43	0.02	0.03	0.03	0.03	0.03	0.04	0.04	0.04	0.04	0.05	0.05	0.06	0.06	0.07	0.07
44	0.03	0.03	0.03	0.03	0.04	0.04	0.04	0.04	0.05	0.05	0.06	0.06	0.06	0.07	0.08
45	0.03	0.03	0.03	0.04	0.04	0.04	0.04	0.05	0.05	0.06	0.06	0.06	0.07	0.08	0.08
46	0.03	0.03	0.04	0.04	0.04	0.04	0.05	0.05	0.05	0.06	0.06	0.07	0.08	0.08	0.09
47	0.03	0.04	0.04	0.04	0.04	0.05	0.05	0.05	0.06	0.06	0.07	0.07	0.08	0.09	0.09
48	0.04	0.04	0.04	0.04	0.05	0.05	0.05	0.06	0.06	0.07	0.07	0.08	0.09	0.09	0.10
49	0.04	0.04	0.04	0.05	0.05	0.06	0.06	0.06	0.07	0.07	0.08	0.09	0.09	0.10	0.11
50	0.04	0.04	0.05	0.05	0.06	0.06	0.06	0.07	0.07	0.08	0.09	0.09	0.10	0.11	0.12
51	0.05	0.05	0.05	0.06	0.06	0.06	0.07	0.07	0.08	0.09	0.09	0.10	0.11	0.12	0.13
52	0.05	0.05	0.06	0.06	0.06	0.07	0.08	0.08	0.09	0.09	0.10	0.11	0.12	0.13	0.14
53	0.05	0.06	0.06	0.07	0.07	0.08	0.08	0.09	0.09	0.10	0.11	0.12	0.13	0.14	0.15
54	0.06	0.06	0.07	0.07	0.08	0.08	0.09	0.09	0.10	0.11	0.12	0.13	0.14	0.15	0.16
55	0.06	0.07	0.07	0.08	0.08	0.09	0.10	0.10	0.11	0.12	0.13	0.14	0.15	0.16	0.18
56	0.07	0.07	0.08	0.08	0.09	0.10	0.10	0.11	0.12	0.13	0.14	0.15	0.16	0.18	0.19
57	0.07	0.08	0.08	0.09	0.10	0.10	0.11	0.12	0.13	0.14	0.15	0.17	0.18	0.19	0.21
58	0.08	0.09	0.09	0.10	0.11	0.11	0.12	0.13	0.14	0.15	0.17	0.18	0.19	0.21	0.23
59	0.09	0.09	0.10	0.11	0.11	0.12	0.13	0.14	0.15	0.17	0.18	0.19	0.21	0.23	0.25
60	0.09	0.10	0.11	0.12	0.12	0.13	0.14	0.16	0.17	0.18	0.20	0.21	0.23	0.25	0.27
61	0.10	0.11	0.12	0.13	0.14	0.15	0.16	0.17	0.18	0.20	0.21	0.23	0.25	0.27	0.29
62	0.11	0.12	0.13	0.14	0.15	0.16	0.17	0.18	0.20	0.21	0.23	0.25	0.27	0.29	0.32

	0.12	0.13	0.14	0.15	0.16	0.17	0.19	0.20	0.22	0.23	0.25	0.27	0.29	0.32	0.35
63	0.12	0.13	0.14	0.15	0.16	0.17	0.19	0.20	0.22	0.23	0.25	0.27	0.29	0.32	0.35
64	0.13	0.14	0.15	0.16	0.17	0.19	0.20	0.22	0.23	0.25	0.27	0.30	0.32	0.35	0.38
65	0.14	0.15	0.16	0.18	0.19	0.20	0.22	0.24	0.25	0.28	0.30	0.32	0.35	0.38	0.41
66	0.16	0.17	0.18	0.19	0.21	0.22	0.24	0.26	0.28	0.30	0.32	0.35	0.38	0.41	0.45
67	0.17	0.18	0.19	0.21	0.22	0.24	0.26	0.28	0.30	0.33	0.35	0.38	0.41	0.45	0.48
68	0.18	0.20	0.21	0.23	0.24	0.26	0.28	0.30	0.33	0.35	0.38	0.41	0.45	0.49	0.53
69	0.20	0.21	0.23	0.25	0.27	0.29	0.31	0.33	0.36	0.39	0.42	0.45	0.49	0.53	0.57
70	0.22	0.23	0.25	0.27	0.29	0.31	0.33	0.36	0.39	0.42	0.45	0.49	0.53	0.58	0.62
71	0.24	0.25	0.27	0.29	0.31	0.34	0.36	0.39	0.42	0.46	0.49	0.53	0.58	0.63	0.68
72	0.26	0.28	0.30	0.32	0.34	0.37	0.40	0.43	0.46	0.50	0.54	0.58	0.63	0.68	0.74
73	0.28	0.30	0.32	0.35	0.37	0.40	0.43	0.46	0.50	0.54	0.58	0.63	0.68	0.74	0.80
74	0.31	0.33	0.35	0.38	0.40	0.43	0.47	0.50	0.54	0.59	0.64	0.69	0.74	0.81	0.87
75	0.33	0.36	0.38	0.41	0.44	0.47	0.51	0.55	0.59	0.64	0.69	0.75	0.81	0.88	0.95
76	0.36	0.39	0.41	0.44	0.48	0.51	0.53	0.60	0.64	0.70	0.75	0.81	0.88	0.95	1.03
77	0.39	0.42	0.45	0.48	0.52	0.56	0.60	0.65	0.70	0.76	0.82	0.88	0.96	1.05	1.12
78	0.43	0.46	0.49	0.53	0.56	0.61	0.65	0.71	0.76	0.82	0.89	0.96	1.04	1.13	1.22
79	0.46	0.50	0.53	0.57	0.61	0.66	0.71	0.77	0.83	0.89	0.97	1.04	1.13	1.22	1.33
80	0.50	0.54	0.58	0.62	0.67	0.72	0.77	0.83	0.90	0.97	1.05	1.13	1.23	1.33	1.44
81	0.55	0.58	0.63	0.67	0.72	0.78	0.84	0.90	0.98	1.05	1.14	1.23	1.33	1.44	1.57
82	0.59	0.63	0.68	0.73	0.79	0.84	0.91	0.98	1.06	1.14	1.24	1.34	1.45	1.57	1.70
83	0.64	0.69	0.74	0.79	0.85	0.92	0.99	1.06	1.15	1.24	1.34	1.45	1.57	1.70	1.84
84	0.70	0.75	0.80	0.86	0.92	0.99	1.07	1.15	1.25	1.35	1.45	1.57	1.70	1.84	2.00
85	0.76	0.81	0.87	0.93	1.00	1.08	1.16	1.25	1.35	1.46	1.58	1.70	1.84	2.00	2.17

EXHIBIT 11.10 (Continued)

| First Age | \multicolumn{15}{c}{Second Age} | | | | | | | | | | | | | | |
	55	56	57	58	59	60	61	62	63	64	65	66	67	68	69
40	0.06	0.07	0.07	0.08	0.09	0.09	0.10	0.11	0.12	0.13	0.14	0.16	0.17	0.18	2.00
41	0.07	0.07	0.08	0.09	0.09	0.10	0.11	0.12	0.13	0.14	0.15	0.17	0.18	0.20	0.21
42	0.07	0.08	0.08	0.09	0.10	0.11	0.12	0.13	0.14	0.15	0.16	0.18	0.19	0.21	0.23
43	0.08	0.08	0.09	0.10	0.11	0.12	0.13	0.14	0.15	0.16	0.18	0.19	0.21	0.23	0.25
44	0.08	0.09	0.10	0.11	0.11	0.12	0.14	0.15	0.16	0.17	0.19	0.21	0.22	0.24	0.27
45	0.09	0.10	0.10	0.11	0.12	0.13	0.15	0.16	0.17	0.19	0.20	0.22	0.24	0.26	0.29
46	0.10	0.10	0.11	0.12	0.13	0.14	0.16	0.17	0.19	0.20	0.22	0.24	0.26	0.28	0.31
47	0.10	0.11	0.12	0.13	0.14	0.16	0.17	0.18	0.20	0.22	0.24	0.26	0.28	0.30	0.33
48	0.11	0.12	0.13	0.14	0.15	0.17	0.18	0.20	0.22	0.23	0.25	0.28	0.30	0.33	0.36
49	0.12	0.13	0.14	0.15	0.17	0.18	0.20	0.21	0.23	0.25	0.28	0.30	0.33	0.35	0.39
50	0.13	0.14	0.15	0.17	0.18	0.20	0.21	0.23	0.25	0.27	0.30	0.32	0.35	0.38	0.42
51	0.14	0.15	0.17	0.18	0.19	0.21	0.23	0.25	0.27	0.30	0.32	0.35	0.38	0.41	0.45
52	0.15	0.16	0.18	0.19	0.21	0.23	0.25	0.27	0.29	0.32	0.35	0.38	0.41	0.45	0.49
53	0.16	0.18	0.19	0.21	0.23	0.25	0.27	0.29	0.32	0.35	0.38	0.41	0.45	0.49	0.53
54	0.18	0.19	0.21	0.23	0.25	0.27	0.29	0.32	0.35	0.38	0.41	0.45	0.48	0.53	0.57
55	0.19	0.21	0.23	0.25	0.27	0.29	0.32	0.34	0.38	0.41	0.44	0.48	0.53	0.57	0.62
56	0.21	0.23	0.25	0.27	0.29	0.32	0.34	0.37	0.41	0.44	0.48	0.52	0.57	0.62	0.67
57	0.23	0.25	0.27	0.29	0.32	0.34	0.37	0.41	0.44	0.48	0.52	0.57	0.62	0.67	0.73
58	0.25	0.27	0.29	0.32	0.34	0.37	0.41	0.44	0.48	0.52	0.57	0.62	0.67	0.73	0.80
59	0.27	0.29	0.32	0.34	0.37	0.41	0.44	0.48	0.52	0.57	0.62	0.67	0.73	0.79	0.86
60	0.29	0.32	0.34	0.37	0.41	0.44	0.48	0.52	0.57	0.62	0.67	0.73	0.79	0.86	0.94
61	0.33	0.34	0.37	0.41	0.44	0.48	0.52	0.57	0.62	0.67	0.73	0.79	0.86	0.94	1.02
62	0.34	0.37	0.41	0.44	0.48	0.52	0.57	0.62	0.67	0.73	0.79	0.86	0.94	1.02	1.11

63	0.38	0.41	0.44	0.48	0.52	0.57	0.62	0.67	0.73	0.79	0.86	0.94	1.02	1.11	1.21
64	0.41	0.44	0.48	0.52	0.57	0.62	0.67	0.73	0.79	0.86	0.94	1.02	1.11	1.21	1.31
65	0.44	0.48	0.52	0.57	0.62	0.67	0.73	0.79	0.86	0.94	1.02	1.11	1.20	1.31	1.43
66	0.48	0.52	0.57	0.62	0.67	0.73	0.79	0.86	0.94	1.02	1.11	1.20	1.31	1.43	1.55
67	0.53	0.57	0.62	0.67	0.73	0.79	0.86	0.94	1.02	1.11	1.20	1.31	1.43	1.55	1.69
68	0.57	0.62	0.67	0.73	0.79	0.86	0.94	1.02	1.11	1.20	1.31	1.43	1.55	1.69	1.84
69	0.62	0.67	0.73	0.80	0.86	0.94	1.02	1.11	1.21	1.31	1.43	1.55	1.69	1.84	2.00
70	0.68	0.73	0.80	0.87	0.94	1.02	1.11	1.21	1.31	1.43	1.55	1.69	1.84	2.00	2.18
71	0.74	0.80	0.87	0.94	1.02	1.11	1.21	1.31	1.43	1.55	1.69	1.84	2.00	2.18	2.37
72	0.80	0.87	0.94	1.02	1.11	1.21	1.31	1.43	1.55	1.69	1.84	2.00	2.18	2.37	2.58
73	0.87	0.95	1.03	1.11	1.21	1.32	1.43	1.55	1.69	1.84	2.00	2.18	2.37	2.57	2.80
74	0.95	1.03	1.12	1.21	1.32	1.43	1.55	1.69	1.84	2.00	2.17	2.37	2.57	2.80	3.05
75	1.03	1.12	1.21	1.32	1.43	1.56	1.69	1.84	2.00	2.17	2.37	2.57	2.80	3.05	3.31
76	1.12	1.22	1.32	1.43	1.56	1.69	1.84	2.00	2.17	2.36	2.57	2.80	3.04	3.31	3.60
77	1.22	1.32	1.44	1.56	1.69	1.84	2.00	2.17	2.36	2.57	2.80	3.04	3.31	3.60	3.92
78	1.32	1.44	1.56	1.69	1.84	2.00	2.17	2.36	2.57	2.79	3.04	3.31	3.60	3.91	4.26
79	1.44	1.56	1.70	1.84	2.00	2.17	2.36	2.57	2.79	3.04	3.30	3.59	3.91	4.25	4.63
80	1.56	1.70	1.84	2.00	2.17	2.36	2.56	2.79	3.03	3.30	3.59	3.90	4.25	4.62	5.03
81	1.70	1.84	2.00	2.17	2.36	2.56	2.78	3.03	3.29	3.58	3.89	4.24	4.61	5.02	5.46
82	1.84	2.00	2.17	2.36	2.56	2.78	3.02	3.29	3.57	3.89	4.23	4.60	5.00	5.44	5.92
83	2.00	2.17	2.35	2.56	2.78	3.02	3.28	3.56	3.88	4.22	4.59	4.99	5.43	5.91	6.43
84	2.17	2.35	2.55	2.77	3.01	3.27	3.55	3.86	4.20	4.57	4.97	5.41	5.88	6.40	6.97
85	2.38	2.55	2.77	3.00	3.26	3.54	3.85	4.19	4.55	4.95	5.39	5.86	6.38	6.94	7.55

EXHIBIT 11.10 (Continued)

First Age	Second Age													
	70	71	72	73	74	75	76	77	78	79	80	81	82	83
40	0.22	0.24	0.26	0.28	0.31	0.33	0.36	0.39	0.43	0.46	0.50	0.55	0.59	0.64
41	0.23	0.25	0.28	0.30	0.33	0.36	0.39	0.42	0.46	0.50	0.54	0.58	0.63	0.69
42	0.25	0.27	0.30	0.32	0.35	0.38	0.41	0.45	0.49	0.53	0.58	0.63	0.68	0.74
43	0.27	0.29	0.32	0.35	0.38	0.41	0.44	0.48	0.53	0.57	0.62	0.67	0.73	0.79
44	0.29	0.31	0.34	0.37	0.40	0.44	0.48	0.52	0.56	0.61	0.67	0.72	0.79	0.85
45	0.31	0.34	0.37	0.40	0.43	0.47	0.51	0.56	0.61	0.66	0.72	0.78	0.84	0.92
46	0.33	0.36	0.40	0.43	0.47	0.51	0.55	0.60	0.65	0.71	0.77	0.84	0.91	0.99
47	0.36	0.39	0.43	0.46	0.50	0.55	0.60	0.65	0.71	0.77	0.83	0.90	0.98	1.06
48	0.39	0.42	0.46	0.50	0.54	0.59	0.64	0.70	0.76	0.83	0.90	0.98	1.06	1.15
49	0.42	0.46	0.50	0.54	0.59	0.64	0.70	0.76	0.82	0.89	0.97	1.05	1.14	1.24
50	0.45	0.49	0.54	0.58	0.64	0.69	0.75	0.82	0.89	0.97	1.05	1.14	1.24	1.34
51	0.49	0.53	0.58	0.63	0.69	0.75	0.81	0.88	0.96	1.04	1.13	1.23	1.34	1.45
52	0.53	0.58	0.63	0.68	0.74	0.81	0.88	0.96	1.04	1.13	1.23	1.33	1.45	1.57
53	0.58	0.63	0.68	0.74	0.81	0.88	0.95	1.04	1.13	1.22	1.33	1.44	1.57	1.70
54	0.62	0.68	0.74	0.80	0.87	0.95	1.03	1.12	1.22	1.33	1.44	1.57	1.70	1.84
55	0.68	0.74	0.80	0.87	0.95	1.03	1.12	1.22	1.32	1.44	1.56	1.70	1.84	2.00
56	0.73	0.80	0.87	0.95	1.03	1.12	1.22	1.32	1.44	1.56	1.70	1.84	2.00	2.17
57	0.80	0.87	0.94	1.03	1.12	1.21	1.32	1.44	1.56	1.70	1.84	2.00	2.17	2.35
58	0.87	0.94	1.02	1.11	1.21	1.32	1.43	1.56	1.69	1.84	2.00	2.17	2.36	2.56
59	0.94	1.02	1.11	1.21	1.32	1.43	1.56	1.69	1.84	2.00	2.17	2.36	2.56	2.78
60	1.02	1.11	1.21	1.32	1.43	1.56	1.69	1.84	2.00	2.17	2.36	2.56	2.78	3.02
61	1.11	1.21	1.31	1.43	1.55	1.69	1.84	2.00	2.17	2.36	2.56	2.78	3.02	3.28
62	1.21	1.31	1.43	1.35	1.69	1.84	2.00	2.17	2.36	2.57	2.79	3.03	3.29	3.56

63	1.31	1.43	1.55	1.69	1.84	2.00	2.17	2.36	2.57	2.79	3.03	3.29	3.57	3.88
64	1.43	1.55	1.69	1.84	2.00	2.17	2.36	2.57	2.79	3.04	3.30	3.58	3.89	4.22
65	1.55	1.69	1.84	2.00	2.17	2.37	2.57	2.80	3.04	3.30	3.59	3.89	4.23	4.59
66	1.69	1.84	2.00	2.18	2.37	2.57	2.80	3.04	3.31	3.59	3.90	4.24	4.60	4.99
67	1.84	2.00	2.18	2.37	2.57	2.80	3.04	3.31	3.60	3.91	4.25	4.61	5.00	5.43
68	2.00	2.18	2.37	2.57	2.80	3.05	3.31	3.60	3.91	4.25	4.62	5.02	5.44	5.91
69	2.18	2.37	2.58	2.80	3.05	3.31	3.60	3.92	4.26	4.63	5.03	5.46	5.92	6.43
70	2.37	2.58	2.80	3.05	3.32	3.61	3.92	4.26	4.63	5.04	5.47	5.94	6.45	6.99
71	2.58	2.80	3.05	3.32	3.61	3.92	4.27	4.64	5.04	5.48	5.95	6.46	7.01	7.61
72	2.80	3.05	3.32	3.61	3.93	4.27	4.64	5.05	5.49	5.96	6.48	7.03	7.63	8.28
73	3.05	3.32	3.61	3.93	4.27	4.65	5.05	5.49	5.97	6.49	7.04	7.65	8.30	9.01
74	3.32	3.61	3.93	4.27	4.65	5.05	5.49	5.97	6.49	7.06	7.66	8.32	9.03	9.80
75	3.61	3.92	4.27	4.65	5.05	5.50	5.98	6.50	7.06	7.67	8.33	9.05	9.82	10.65
76	3.92	4.27	4.64	5.05	5.49	5.98	6.50	7.07	7.68	8.34	9.06	9.84	10.68	11.59
77	4.26	4.64	5.05	5.49	5.97	6.50	7.07	7.68	8.35	9.07	9.85	10.70	11.61	12.60
78	4.63	5.04	5.49	5.97	6.49	7.06	7.68	8.35	9.07	9.86	10.71	11.63	12.62	13.69
79	5.04	5.48	5.96	6.49	7.06	7.67	8.34	9.07	9.86	10.71	11.64	12.63	13.71	14.87
80	5.47	5.95	6.48	7.04	7.66	8.33	9.06	9.85	10.71	11.64	12.64	13.72	14.89	16.16
81	5.94	6.46	7.03	7.65	8.32	9.05	9.84	10.70	11.63	12.63	13.72	14.90	16.17	17.54
82	6.45	7.01	7.63	8.30	9.03	9.82	10.68	11.61	12.62	13.71	14.89	16.17	17.55	19.04
83	6.99	7.61	8.28	9.01	9.80	10.65	11.59	12.60	13.69	14.87	16.16	17.54	19.04	20.65
84	7.58	8.25	8.98	9.76	10.62	11.55	12.56	13.66	14.84	16.13	17.52	19.02	20.64	22.39
85	8.21	8.94	9.72	10.58	11.51	12.52	13.61	14.80	16.08	17.48	18.98	20.61	22.37	24.27

face amount, premium input, and investment choice. Diversification is essential in these long-term contracts. The opportunity to invest in various subaccounts, so that the contract can be adapted to both the economic environment and policy owner circumstances throughout the policy's existence, is a paradigm shift in a very basic financial product that a few finally have begun to appreciate. Its usefulness is limited only by your imagination.

In addition, insurance company products enjoy a degree of creditor protection that is unique among assets. Look at Exhibit 11.11 to see how your state protects life insurance and annuity assets from the claims of your creditors. You will find that for residents of certain states, valuable asset protection and prebankruptcy planning opportunities exist using life insurance and annuity contracts, provided that the movement of assets into the contracts is not made with the intent to hinder, delay, or defraud creditors. Keep in mind that the determination of whether assets were moved into a contract to defraud creditors will be made in court based on the facts and circumstances of the case and the applicable law in that jurisdiction. It is prudent for each of us to have substantial liability insurance, to plan our estates, and to safeguard our assets in appropriate and legal ways from unknown creditors, from the threat of lawsuit, and from anything that threatens the financial security of our families and us. In the opinion of lawyers Gideon Rothschild and Daniel S. Rubin,* since there are numerous reasons for placing assets into life insurance and annuity contracts that have nothing to do with avoiding an individual's creditors, the finding of an intent to hinder, delay or defraud creditors probably is unlikely except in the most egregious transactions.

Please keep in mind that the chart shown in Exhibit 11.11 was only accurate on the day it was prepared. States and courts frequently change their laws and opinions, and so competent legal advice should be sought in your state of residence.

---

*"Creditor Protection for Life Insurance and Annuities," *The Journal of Asset Protection*, May 1999.

Creditor's Rights in a Nonbankruptcy Context

State Name	Life Insurance Proceeds	Annuity Proceeds	Applicable Section(s)
Alabama	Beneficiary's interest in "proceeds and avails" wholly protected from creditors of owner and insured. Owner's interest in "proceeds and avails" wholly protected from creditors of insured if owner (or owner's spouse) is insured, and spouse and/or children (or owner and/or children) are beneficiaries.	Maximum $250 per month of benefits under all annuity contracts exempt from creditors.	Ala. Code §§ 6-10-8 and 27-14-32
Alaska	Owner's interest in up to $10,000 of value of unmatured policy is exempt. Maximum interest of $350 per week of spouse or dependent beneficiary is exempt.	Owner's interest in up to $10,000 of value of unmatured policy is exempt.	Alaska Stat. §§ 09.38.025 and 09.38.030
Arizona	Maximum interest of $20,000 of spouse or child beneficiary in death benefit is exempt. Owner's interest in up to $25,000 of cash surrender value is exempt if (i) policy held for at least 2 years and (ii) spouse, child, parent, sibling, or other dependent family member is beneficiary. Beneficiary's interest in proceeds wholly protected from creditors of owner.	Exempt only if qualified under Code §§ 401(a), 403(a), 403(b), 408, or 409.	Ariz. Rev. Stat. §§ 20-1131 and 33-1126(A)(1) and (6), and (C)
Arkansas	Beneficiary's interest in all monies paid under policy wholly protected from creditors.	Benefits due annuitant are exempt to extent not in excess of reasonable requirements of annuitant and dependent family members.	Ark. Code Ann. §§ 16-66-209, 16-66-218(b)(7), and 23-79-134

EXHIBIT 11.11 (Continued)

State Name	Life Insurance Proceeds	Annuity Proceeds	Applicable Section(s)
California	Unmatured policy wholly exempt from creditors, provided, however, that loan value of only $8000 ($16,000 if debtor married) is exempt. Death benefits exempt to extent reasonably necessary for support of debtor, and spouse and dependents of debtor.	Unmatured policy wholly exempt from creditors.	Cal. Civ. Proc. Code § 704.11
Colorado	Interest in up to $25,000 of cash surrender value (except for increases attributable to previous 24 months' contributions) exempt from creditors of insured except where beneficiary is estate of insured. Death benefit payable to beneficiary (other than estate of insured) wholly exempt from creditors of insured.	Funds held in or payable from annuity wholly exempt.	Colo. Rev. Stat. §§ 13-54-102(1) and (s)
Connecticut	Interest of owner of unmatured policy in up to $4000 of accrued interest or dividend, or loan value, is exempt provided insured is owner or person upon whom owner is dependent.	Only if ERISA qualified.	Conn. Gen. Stat. §§ 13-54-102(s), 38a-453, and 52-352b(s)
Delaware	Beneficiary's interest in "proceeds and avails" wholly protected from all creditors.	Maximum $350 per month of benefits under all annuity contracts exempt from creditors.	Del. Code Ann. Tit. 18 §§ 2725 and 2728
District of Columbia	Maximum exemption of $200 per month for a beneficiary providing principal support of a family or $60 per month for a beneficiary not providing principal support of a family.	Maximum exemption of $200 per month for a beneficiary providing principal support of a family or $60 per month for a beneficiary not providing principal support of a family.	D.C. Code Ann. § 15-503

State Name	Life Insurance Proceeds	Annuity Proceeds	Applicable Section(s)
Florida	Beneficiary's interest in proceeds wholly protected from insured's creditors unless policy payable to insured or his estate. Owner's interest in cash surrender value wholly exempt.	Interest in proceeds of policy wholly exempt.	Fla. Stat. §§ 222.13 and 222.14
Georgia	Owner's interest in unmatured policy (except credit life insurance) wholly exempt, provided that only · $2000 maximum accrued dividend or interest, or loan value, exempt (provided insured is debtor or individual upon whom debtor is dependent). Beneficiary's interest in death benefit exempt to extent reasonably necessary for support of debtor and dependents	Proceeds of policy exempt to extent reasonably necessary for support of debtor and dependents.	Ga. Code Ann. §§ 44-13-100(a)(2)(E), 44-13-100(a)(8), 44-13-100(a)(9), and 44-13-100(a)(11)(C)
Hawaii	Proceeds and cash value payable to insured's spouse, child, parent, or other dependent are wholly exempt from insured's creditors.	Proceeds payable to spouse, child, parent, or other dependent are wholly exempt from insured's creditors.	Haw. Rev. Stat. § 431:10-232
Idaho	Beneficiary's interest in "proceeds and avails" wholly protected from all creditors.	Maximum $350 per month of benefits under all annuity contracts exempt from creditors.	Idaho Code §§ 41-1833 and 41-1836
Illinois	Proceeds and cash value payable to insured's spouse, child, parent, or other dependent are wholly exempt from insured's creditors. Beneficiary's interest in payment under policy insuring individual of whom beneficiary was a dependent is exempt to extent reasonably necessary for support of beneficiary and dependents.	Proceeds payable to spouse, child, parent, or other dependent are wholly exempt from insured's creditors.	215 Ill. Comp. Stat. § 5/238, 735 Ill. Comp. Stat. § 5/12-1001(f) and (h)(3)

EXHIBIT 11.11 (Continued)

State Name	Life Insurance Proceeds	Annuity Proceeds	Applicable Section(s)
Indiana	If contract so provides, benefits payable to person other than person effecting policy are wholly exempt from creditors.	If contract so provides, benefits payable to person other than person effecting policy are wholly exempt from creditors.	Ind. Code § 27-2-5-1
Iowa	Interest in accrued dividend or interest, or loan or cash surrender value, wholly exempt if beneficiary is spouse, child, or dependent, provided that increases attributable to prior 2 years limited to $10,000. Maximum $15,000 of death benefit exempt if payable to spouse or dependent.	Proceeds wholly exempt except for payments resulting from excessive contributions within prior year.	Iowa Code §§ 627.6(6) and (8)(e)
Kansas	Policy and its reserves, or their present value, wholly exempt from claims of all creditors unless purchased within past year.	Annuities qualifying under certain Kansas statutes wholly exempt.	Kan. Stat. Ann. §§ 40-441(a) and (f), and 60-2313
Kentucky	Beneficiary's interest in "proceeds and avails" wholly protected from all creditors. Owner's interest in policy wholly exempt.	Maximum $350 per month of benefits under all annuity contracts exempt from creditors.	Ky. Rev. Stat. Ann. §§ 427.110(1), 304.14-300, and 304.14-330
Louisiana	Interest of beneficiary (including estate of insured) in "proceeds and avails" wholly protected from all creditors.	Interest in proceeds of policy wholly protected from all creditors, provided that maximum $35,000 exempt if bankruptcy filed within 9 months of policy issuance.	La. Rev. Stat. Ann. § 22:647
Maine	Beneficiary's interest in "proceeds and avails" wholly protected from all creditors.	Maximum $350 per month of benefits under all annuity contracts exempt from creditors.	Me. Rev. Stat. Ann. Tit. 24-A, §§ 2428 and 2431, Tit. 14 §§ 4422(10) and (11).

EXHIBIT 11.11   (Continued)

State Name	Life Insurance Proceeds	Annuity Proceeds	Applicable Section(s)
	Owner's interest in unmatured policy (except credit life insurance) wholly exempt, provided that only $4000 maximum accrued dividend or interest, or loan value, exempt (provided insured is debtor or individual upon whom debtor is dependent).		
Maryland	Proceeds wholly exempt if payable to the spouse, child, or dependent relative of the insured.	Proceeds wholly exempt if payable to the spouse, child, or dependent relative of the insured.	Md. Code Ann., Ins. § 16-111
Massachu-setts	Beneficiary's interest in "proceeds" wholly protected from creditors of owner.	None.	Mass. Gen. Laws ch. 175 § 125
Michigan	Proceeds (including cash value) wholly exempt from creditors.	Proceeds wholly exempt.	Mich. Comp. Laws § 500.2207
Minnesota	Proceeds wholly exempt from creditors of person effecting the policy. Maximum $20,000 of proceeds payable to a spouse or child is exempt from other creditors (increased by $5000 for each dependent of the spouse or child). Maximum $4000 interest in any accrued dividend or interest, or loan value, exempt (provided insured is debtor or individual upon whom debtor is dependent).	Proceeds wholly exempt from creditors of person effecting the policy.	Minn. Stat. §§ 61A.12 and 550.37(10) and (23)
Mississippi	Proceeds (including cash surrender and loan value) wholly protected from creditors of insured, provided maximum $50,000 cash surrender or loan value exempt if from premiums paid in past 12 months.	Exempt to extent reasonably necessary for support of debtor and dependent if on account of illness, disability, death, age, or length of service and qualifies under Code §§ 401(a), 403(a), 403(b), 408, or 409.	Miss. Code Ann. §§ 85-3-1 and 85-3-11

EXHIBIT 11.11 (Continued)

State Name	Life Insurance Proceeds	Annuity Proceeds	Applicable Section(s)
Missouri	Owner's interest in unmatured policy (except credit life insurance) wholly exempt; provided that only $5000 maximum accrued dividend or interest, or loan value, exempt (and provided insured is debtor or individual upon whom debtor is dependent).	Exempt to extent reasonably necessary for support of debtor and dependents, provided benefits are by reason of age, illness, disability, death, or length of service.	Mo. Rev. Stat §§ 513.430(7), (8), and (10)(e)
Montana	Beneficiary's interest in "proceeds and avails" wholly protected from creditors of owner and insured. Maximum $4000 in value of unmatured life insurance contract is exempt.	None.	Mont. Code Ann. §§ 33-15-511 and 25-13-609(4)
Nebraska	Maximum $10,000 of proceeds, cash value, and benefits exempt from insured's creditors (unless beneficiary is estate of insured); also exempt from beneficiary's creditors if beneficiary related by blood or marriage to insured.	Maximum $10,000 proceeds of policy exempt.	Neb. Rev. Stat. §§ 44-371
Nevada	Beneficiary's interest in "proceeds and avails" wholly protected from all creditors. Owner's interest in all money, benefits, privileges, or immunities exempt to extent premium not in excess of $1000 per year.	Maximum $350 per month of benefits under all annuity contracts exempt from creditors.	Nev. Rev. Stat. §§ 21.090 (1)(k), 687B.260 and 687B.290
New Hampshire	Beneficiary's interest in proceeds wholly protected from creditors of person effecting policy unless policy payable to insured's estate.	None.	N.H. Rev. Stat. Ann § 408:2

EXHIBIT 11.11 (Continued)

State Name	Life Insurance Proceeds	Annuity Proceeds	Applicable Section(s)
New Jersey	Beneficiary's interest in "proceeds and avails" wholly protected from all creditors, provided beneficiary is not owner or insured.	Maximum $500 per month of benefits under all annuity contracts exempt from creditors.	N.J. Stat. Ann. §§ 17B:24-6 and 17B: 24-7
New Mexico	Cash surrender value and withdrawal value wholly exempt from all creditors.	Proceeds of policy wholly exempt from all creditors.	N.M. Stat. Ann. §§ 42-10-3 and 42-10-5
New York	Beneficiary's interest in "proceeds and avails" wholly protected from all creditors, provided beneficiary is not owner or insured. Owner's interest in "proceeds and avails" of policy insuring another is exempt as against creditors of insured (and owner's own creditors if insured is owner's spouse).	Court has discretion to order "just and proper amount" paid to creditors with due regard to reasonable requirements of debtor and dependent family, provided maximum $5000 exempt if annuity purchased within prior 6 months.	N.Y. Ins. Law § 3212; N.Y. Debtor & Creditor Law § 283
North Carolina	Beneficiary's interest in proceeds wholly protected from creditors of insured, provided beneficiary is not owner or insured.	Only individual retirement annuity under Code § 408 is exempt.	N.C. Const. § 5; N.C. Gen. Stat. §§ 1C-1601 and 58-58-115
North Dakota	Maximum exemption of proceeds or cash surrender value of $100,000 per policy and $200,000 aggregate (unless more is reasonably necessary for the support of insured and dependents), provided payable to spouse, children, or any dependent relative.	Maximum exemption of $100,000 per policy and $200,000 aggregate (unless more is reasonably necessary for the support of insured and dependents), provided payable to spouse, children, or any dependent relative.	N.D. Cent. Code § 28-22-03.1
Ohio	"Proceeds and avails" wholly protected from creditors of insured, provided beneficiary is spouse, child, or dependent.	Wholly protected from creditors of annuitant, provided beneficiary is spouse, child, or dependent.	Ohio Rev. Code Ann. § 3911.10

EXHIBIT 11.11 (Continued)

State Name	Life Insurance Proceeds	Annuity Proceeds	Applicable Section(s)
Oklahoma	Policy proceeds and cash values wholly protected from all creditors.	Wholly protected from all creditors.	Okla. Stat. Tit. 36 § 3631.1(A)
Oregon	Beneficiary's interest in proceeds wholly protected from creditors of insured, provided beneficiary is not owner or insured. Owner/insured's interest in cash value wholly exempt, provided beneficiary is not owner/insured's estate.	Maximum $500 per month of benefits under all annuity contracts exempt from creditors.	Or. Rev. Stat. §§ 743.046 and 743.049
Pennsylvania	Proceeds payable to spouse, child, or dependent relative of insured wholly exempt from creditors of insured. Proceeds exempt from own creditors to extent necessary to provide for maximum income or return of $100 per month.	Proceeds payable to spouse, child, or dependent relative of insured wholly exempt from creditors of insured. Proceeds exempt from own creditors to extent necessary to provide for maximum income or return of $100 per month.	42 Pa. Cons. Stat. § 8124(C)
Rhode Island	Beneficiary's interest in "proceeds and avails" wholly protected from creditors of insured, provided beneficiary is not owner or insured.	Only individual retirement annuity under Code § 408(b) is exempt.	R.I. Gen. Laws §§ 9-26-4(11) and 27-4-11
South Carolina	Beneficiary's interest in proceeds and cash surrender values wholly protected from creditors of insured, provided beneficiary is spouse, child, or dependent of insured. Maximum $4000 exemption for owner's interest in accrued dividend or interest under, or loan value of, unmatured policy under which insured is debtor or individual on whom debtor is dependent.	Exempt if on account of illness, disability, death, age, or length of service and qualifies under Code §§ 401(a), 403(a), 403(b), 408, or 409.	S.C. Code Ann. §§ 14-41-30(8), 15-41-30(10)(E) and 38-63-40

EXHIBIT 11.11 (Continued)

State Name	Life Insurance Proceeds	Annuity Proceeds	Applicable Section(s)
South Dakota	Maximum $10,000 exemption for proceeds payable to estate or maximum $20,000 exemption for proceeds payable to spouse or children.	Maximum $250 per month of benefits under all annuity contracts exempt from creditors.	S.D. Codified Laws §§ 43-45-6, 58-12-4, 58-12-6, and 58-12-8
Tennessee	Beneficiary's interest in amounts payable under policy wholly protected from creditors of insured, provided beneficiary is spouse, child, or dependent relative of insured.	Beneficiary's interest in amounts payable under policy wholly protected from creditors of insured, provided beneficiary is spouse, child, or dependent relative of insured.	Tenn. Code Ann. § 56-7-203
Texas	Policy proceeds and cash values wholly protected from all creditors (subject to disagreement among courts on interpretation and interaction of statute).	Policy proceeds wholly exempt from all creditors.	Tex. Ins. Code § 21.22
Utah	Exemption for proceeds or benefits paid to a spouse or dependent upon death of insured to extent reasonably necessary for support of beneficiary and dependents. Maximum $1500 exemption for owner's interest in unmatured life insurance.	Assets held and proceeds paid to extent reasonably necessary for support of beneficiary and dependents.	Utah Code Ann. §§ 78-23-6, 78-23-7
Vermont	Owner's interest in unmatured policy (except credit life insurance) wholly exempt. Beneficiary's interest in payment under policy insuring life of individual on whom debtor was dependent wholly exempt; otherwise exempt from creditors of owner and insured only.	Maximum $350 per month of benefits under all annuity contracts exempt from creditors.	Vt. Stat. Ann. Tit. 12 §§ 2740(18) and (19)(H); Tit. 8 §§ 3706 and 3709

EXHIBIT 11.11 (Continued)

State Name	Life Insurance Proceeds	Annuity Proceeds	Applicable Section(s)
Virginia	Beneficiary's interest in proceeds wholly protected from creditors of owner and insured, provided that beneficiary is not owner or insured.	None.	Va. Code Ann. § 38.2-3122
Washington	Beneficiary's interest in "proceeds and avails" wholly protected from all creditors.	Maximum per month of benefits under all annuity contracts exempt from creditors.	Wash. Rev. Code §§ 48.18.410 and 48.18.430
West Virginia	Beneficiary's interest in "proceeds and avails" wholly protected from all creditors of owner and insured, provided that beneficiary is not owner or insured.	None.	W. Va. Code § 33-6-27
Wisconsin	Maximum $4000 exemption for debtor/owner's interest in unmatured policy (other than credit life insurance), if debtor, dependent, or individual of whom the debtor is a dependent of insured. Beneficiary's interest in payment under policy insuring individual on whom debtor was dependent is exempt to extent reasonably necessary for support of debtor and dependents.	Wholly exempt, provided benefits are by reason of age, illness, disability, death, or length of service.	Wis. Stat. § 815.18
Wyoming	Beneficiary's interest in proceeds wholly protected from all creditors of owner and insured, provided that beneficiary is not owner or insured.	Maximum $350 per month of benefits under all annuity contracts exempt from creditors.	Wyo. Stat. Ann. §§ 26-15-129 and 26-15-132

CHAPTER 12

Variable Universal Life in Action

A Financial Tool—But Which End Do I Grab?

This chapter provides information on actual VUL policies, showing how they have worked for their policy owners over the years and what the actual expenses of the policies are. The data are verifiable. This is the place to examine these policies, their expenses, their performance, and the way they have been used by policy owners. Identify the expenses you feel are out of line and indicate what you feel would be a more equitable expense. The objective is to challenge your general conclusions with facts.

A variable universal life insurance policy is a financial tool that, when used correctly, provides positive financial results that cannot be duplicated by any other financial product. Implicit in this statement is the assumption that the expenses within the product are fair and acceptable. You do have to want the life insurance provided by the product, and the cost of the life insurance must be competitive and acceptable. The policy must offer a broad array of competitive subaccounts in the family of funds available so that the policy owner can profitably manage money within the contract *for a lifetime*. The number of variable universal products that fit that description will continue to increase, as the competitive market invents products that, at one end of the spectrum, are too expensive and, at the other end, are too cheap. If the contract is too cheap, it may not be profitable enough for the insurance company to support.

To use these products profitably, you have to understand them and know how to apply them to your situation and objectives. A major goal of this book, is to continually provide this information. However, you will find that very often an advisor can help you to focus on your objectives and needs, and show you how to meet those needs using all the financial tools at your disposal, including VUL. Understand that there is a cost (whether it is called a financial planning fee or a commission) associated with this service, just as there is with any other. You are paying for help in the selection and delivery of the product and for assistance in managing the money within the product. In this case, you may find that the return on your investment as a result of this assistance makes it the most profitable money you have ever spent. This is much the same as in mutual fund purchases. There are more than 12,000 funds from which to choose, so the person who helps you find a suitable family of funds and then shows you how to use them can be very valuable. That educated and informed person cannot work for nothing. You will pay a fee when using no-load funds, and and you will pay a commission when using mutual funds that have sales loads. The point is, get qualified help when you need it, and don't be afraid to pay for it. Use it profitably.

Many people have been hurt by the financial press. Writers of books, magazines, and newspaper articles bombard us, advising, "Buy only *no load!*" Those who are not sure how to choose among the no-loads end up paying in lost returns that are often higher than the costs they are seeking to avoid. Even worse, we may not do anything. As a result of confusion about financial products and the desire to avoid commissions or fees, too many of us have been frozen into economic inertia. Doing nothing presents the biggest threat there is to our economic future. The encouragement, motivation, expertise in matching product to person and objectives, and coaching in the use of financial products by a paid professional are well worth every dollar investors spend. We can all use a good financial coach, so be prepared to pay for one as you go about your search for the variable universal product right for you.

Let's look at a case study. Pete does not need life insurance! But his grandfather bought him a $10,000 whole life policy when he was 2, and his dad bought him a $25,000 fixed-premium variable life policy when he reached 18 in 1979. The variable life was one of the very early contracts of that kind (the first were issued in 1976). His dad put $266.50 into it for each of the first 7 years, for a total of $1865.50. By 1986, it had a value of $2328.15. This represented a return on that $266.50 annual investment of about 7.3 percent. Not great, but by the life insurance standards of the day, it was spectacular.

By 1986 these two policies just were not what Pete wanted. He knew that an alternative called variable universal life had arrived in the life insurance marketplace. Pete had married Susie, and they had become DINKs.

With a mortgage that took both of their incomes to service, and with hope in their hearts for children in the future, Pete and Susie had become economically interdependent. The death of either would leave the survivor in both economic trouble and an emotional state likely to exacerbate the economic problems. They needed to save money as quickly as possible because children would likely increase expenses and possibly reduce income.

THE 1035 TAX-FREE EXCHANGE–TRADING LIFE INSURANCE POLICIES TAX-FREE

The decision was made to trade Pete's two old policies for a single variable universal life policy. But Pete did not wish to pay income taxes on the profit accumulated in the old variable life policy and the 23-year-old whole life policy.

In September 1986, Pete turned in the application, requisite forms, and medical information that proved he was insurable. He told the insurance company to trade the two old policies for the new one. The insurance company credited $4380 from the two old policies to a new policy insuring Pete's life for $250,000. A term insurance rider of $100,000 was added for Susie. Interestingly enough, 9 months later their first child, Meg, was born.

The first-year costs they incurred in September 1986–September 1987 to start the new policy were $750, as shown in Exhibit 12.1. The earnings inside the policy that first year were $512, and so the earnings did not quite cover costs.

Pete and Susie worked hard that first year putting in as much

EXHIBIT 12.1

First-Year Costs

Setup cost	$250
State premium tax—Colorado	65
Administrative expenses	48
Pete's $250,000 life insurance	285
Susie's $100,000 life insurance	102
Total year 1 costs	$750

as they could each month. They sent in $135 most months, and one month they were able to put in $435. By the end of the first year their policy value was $5928, and they were pretty proud of themselves. Most of the money, $4417, was in the guaranteed interest account that first policy year, 1986–1987 earning 8.75 percent. By February 1987, they were putting their monthly checks into the aggressive stock account within their policy. They paid $161 for their first unit of stock in that account.

They chose the aggressive account because they had studied dollar cost averaging (see Chapter 9 for a refresher) and concluded that volatility in a mutual fund was their friend, not their enemy. They knew that dollar cost averaging was most effective when used in a volatile fund likely to provide the highest highs and lowest lows.

In the second policy year (1987–1988), costs for these two 26-year-olds were as shown in Exhibit 12.2.

DUAL INCOME, ONE KID

During the second policy year, they were able to send in $135 in nine of the months, $270 one month, and a check for $1385 another month, for a grand total that year of $2870. Our dual-income, one-kid family was doing a great job—*but* the aggressive stock account did what aggressive stock accounts do; it went *down*. On October 19, 1987, the market went down over 500 points in one day, losing over 20 percent of its value. Well, this couple was in the market. During that second year, they saw the aggressive fund share

EXHIBIT 12.2

Costs for the Second Year

State premium tax	$65
Administrative expenses	48
Pete's $250,000 life insurance	285
Susie's $100,000 life insurance	104
Total year 2 costs	$502

value drop from the original $161 to a low as $138 per share! Pete and Susie were learning about volatility, but at this point they had redefined volatility as "it goes down!" They were not very pleased when they looked at their annual report and saw that their investment results for the year were − $114. Their financial advisor advised them to keep on keeping on—the market does what it will do. Keep on dollar-cost-averaging.

ONE INCOME, TWO KIDS!

Checks into their policy did slow down, and they soon learned that another baby would arrive in early 1989. Pete and Susie were concerned! There was the loss of Susie's income for at least some period of time; there were more expenses; and to top it off, they knew that Susie was becoming ever more dependent on Pete's income—he needed more life insurance. They no longer felt like aggressive investors.

INCREASING YOUR FACE AMOUNT

The decision to double the amount of insurance on Pete's life made them anxious, but that feeling was soon replaced by one of relief. They looked at their flexible-premium, flexible-face-amount policy and found that the cost for the extra $250,000 on Pete's life was about $25 per month. Monthly costs in the policy would increase to $50 a month. They also would have a one-time fee of $250 for the change to the policy. What a relief! A one-time cost of $250 to change, and $300 per year for the extra $250,000 of life insurance. The interior costs were going to be a little over $750 in the coming year, instead of the $502 of the year before. But they could afford the increase! They began to understand the power of their policy.

HOW DO YOU DECIDE HOW MUCH?

They made the changes. Pete's life insurance was increased from $250,000 to $500,000. The thinking behind the amount of the increase was that each $100,000 of death benefit could provide between $5000 and $6000 of investment income for Susie and the children. The first $250,000 would give Susie a supplemental income stream of $12,500 per year, which, with Pete's group life insurance and the social security benefits for one child, would leave Susie okay, but not great.

But with the second child further hampering Susie's ability to earn, they wanted the extra $250,000 of insurance. The $500,000 would generate about $25,000 in supplemental income. The extra insurance was absolutely essential for his family's economic survival if Pete died.

INVESTMENT MANAGEMENT

After the policy was increased, which was a material change, in order to keep the policy from becoming a modified endowment contract, Pete would have to keep his investments each year below $15,000. "No problem!" said Pete. They went back to their dollar cost averaging, but the 1988–1989 year was tougher for them. They put in seven checks for $135, one for $235, and one for $270, for a total of $1450. This was about half of what they had invested in the previous year. Approximately $910 of what they paid in 1988–1989 was directed to the guaranteed interest account. As the second baby's birth approached, they got more conservative. The volatility (downward trend) of the aggressive stock account was not comfortable for them during this period.

Ella was born! Susie decided to put her career aside because she wanted to spend more time with their two children. As a result, income was cut. They were concerned. Pete and Susie talked over their concerns with their insurance agent, who suggested that they look for an opportunity to move to the *tax-free funding level*.

TAX-FREE FUNDING

This is the funding level within an account that generates enough tax-free interest to pay the expenses of the policy in full. *How much do you need, and which account shall you use?*

The account best designed to provide this steady stream of interest payments, with no change in market value, is the guaranteed interest account. The good news for Pete and Susie was that the interest was guaranteed at 8.25 percent in the 1988–1989 year, so if they could get $10,000 into that account, it would earn $825. This would be more than enough to cover the $750 of anticipated costs.

Pete and Susie were going to have to deal with the following considerations as they decided whether to move their money into this guaranteed interest, guaranteed principal account.

1. This is a general account of the life insurance company, and the guarantees are only as strong as the company. The account is subject to the claims of its creditors, so ratings by Standard and Poor's, Moody's, Best's, Fitch, and maybe even Marvin Weiss were important to them. It also meant that whatever information they could have gotten on the company's risk-based capital rating would have been important to them, had it been in existence in those days. Today, they may feel frustrated in trying to get the same information from their agent. They would have trouble understanding or believing that their agent is under a *gag order* that makes it illegal to talk about the risk-based capital ratio of any company. The gag order applies only to agents; the press, the Internet, and everyone else is not so restricted. If Pete and Susie were able to get at John Ward's brilliant *Ward's Results Life-Health* for the current year (ask at your local library), they could find out exactly what the insurance company's risk-based capital rating is and a good deal more about the financial structure of the company. Pete

and Susie decided that as long as their company was considered investment grade by the major rating services, they were not worried about the general account nature of the guaranteed interest account investment.

2. Once their money went into this guaranteed interest account, there would be some limitations on how quickly and when they could move it out. This is a mechanism wisely set up by most insurance companies to prevent a run on this account, no matter if it was caused by a necessary reduction in interest rates or by policy owners being put in a state of panic by the press. Pete and Susie could remove 25 percent of the amount in the guaranteed interest account during one 90-day period each year. This they also found acceptable.

MOVING MONEY

On August 4, 1989, they instructed their insurance company to sell their aggressive stock account and move the money into the guaranteed interest account. The aggressive account unit value on that day was $197.19. They sold 20.97 units and moved $4136.08. They now had more than $10,000 in the guaranteed interest account ready to earn enough interest to cover policy costs. Pete and Susie would not have to worry if they could not put more money into their policy in the coming year!

They had two questions:

1. How did their policy do in the third year of its existence? Financial writers love to tell you that it will take 10 years for your policy to be a good investment.

2. How did their dollar-cost-averaging into the aggressive stock account work up to August 4, 1989, when they moved it out?

Third-Year Policy Results (1988–1989)

During the third policy year, September 1988–September 1989, their policy costs were as shown in Exhibit 12.3. The policy's gross

EXHIBIT 12.3

Third-year Costs

State premium tax	$33
Administrative expenses and waiver	49
Pete's life insurance	
$250,000 until February 1989	
$500,000 thereafter	463
Susie's $100,000 life insurance	111
Total year 3 costs	$656

investment results for the year were a plus $1556. Net of the expenses shown in the exhibit, Pete and Susie made $900 tax-free on their total policy investment, which, during that year, averaged $9258. This gave them a *net* return on the capital in their policy of 9.7 percent *plus* the tax-free earnings that paid for the life insurance! Three years, not ten years! It makes you think that many of those writers have never looked at a real-life variable universal policy in action.

AGGRESSIVE STOCK DOLLAR-COST-AVERAGING RESULTS

Exhibit 12.4 presents the actual results of Pete and Susie's investments in the aggressive stock account. Looking at this exhibit, you might question whether Pete and Susie should have sold or not. But at the time, it was like trying to see what's around the next bend in the road. They sold into the market euphoria that existed after the United States won the Gulf War. They sold because they were different investors for a time. With two incomes–no kids, they could be aggressive investors, but with one income–two kids, they were not aggressive investors. The policy structure that was suitable for them one year was not suitable for them the next year, and so they morphed the policy into current suitability. They did the right thing *for them.*Their investment capital had a very near-term important purpose: to pay the cost of their life insurance from the pretax earnings in the investment account so that they did not have to worry about those costs until their lives settled

EXHIBIT 12.4

Pete and Susie's Dollar Cost Averaging

Date	Gross Investment	Aggressive Stock Unit Value	Aggressive Stock Total No. of Shares
2-9-87	$435	161.06	2.67
3-6-87	135	168.26	3.47
4-6-87	135	174.25	4.23
5-4-87	135	174.14	5.00
6-8-87	135	177.05	5.76
7-13-87	135	182.40	6.49
8-3-87	135	184.95	7.20
9-3-87	135	188.92	7.9
10-5-87	135	205.96	8.54
500-point drop in the Dow, 11-19-87			
11-10-87	$135	138.23	9.5
1-4-88	270	146.91	11.3
2-5-88	135	142.72	12.22
3-7-88	135	157.16	13.06
4-4-88	135	155.48	13.91
5-2-88	135	155.88	14.75
6-24-88	135	160.44	15.58
7-18-88	1385	159.52	24.06
8-8-88	135	152.72	24.93
9-6-88	135	149.53	25.81
10-6-88	135	146.62	26.71
11-29-88	135	137.39	27.67
12-5-88	135	142.86	28.59
Total investment	$4655	162.82 average cost per share	
4-3-89	Sell $1250	164.06	−7.62
		Bought high yield at $115.53 per unit	
8-4-89	Sell $4136.08	$197.19	−20.97
Total sales proceeds	$5386.08	Bought guaranteed interest	
Less cost of shares	$4655.00		
Net nontaxable gain	$731.08		
Cost of sale = 0			
Cost of purchase = 0			
Capital gains/income tax = 0			

down again. It is not relevant that the aggressive stock account went to $462 per share by January 1994 and $704 in February 2001.

VARIABLE UNIVERSAL LIQUIDITY
Policy Loans to the Rescue

By 1989–1990, the fourth policy year, things are tight for Pete and Susie. In fact, they put only five $135 checks into the policy, totaling $675 for the year. Susie is happily at home with the two kids, doing some part-time work, but really concentrating on the family.

Income tax time arrives, and they qualify for tax-deductible IRAs, but it is April 9 and they don't have the $4000 needed. They call their life insurance–investment advisor. What do they do? Here is the advice they get. For each $1000 they put into one of the IRAs, they will reduce their income tax burden by $300. They should borrow $4000 from their policy and put $2000 into each of their IRAs to reduce income taxes by $1200. This is exactly what they do on April 9, 1990. The check from the insurance company is dated April 11 and Express-Mailed to them so they have the money April 12, in time to make the IRA deposits. The loan will cost 8 percent annually. The $4000 is not actually taken from the policy. This insurance company issues it's check for $4000. The policy asset value is merely pledged as collateral to the insurance company for a personal loan, and the collateralized $4000 is put into the loan guarantee fund in their policy, where it earns 7 percent, 1 percent less than the insurance company will charge.

More good news! Pete and Susie, upon completing their income taxes, find that their reduced earnings for the previous year and the $4000 IRA deduction have lowered their taxes enough so they now have a $4000 income tax refund to pay off the loan. On April 23, they sent a check to the insurance company for $4011.65 to pay off the loan and pay the interest for the 13 days involved. Pete and Susie want to get that money back to work in their policy as soon as possible. While they are feeling better about their financial situation, they want all the money back in the guaranteed interest division for this policy year anyway.

EXHIBIT 12.5

Fourth-Year Costs

State premium tax	$15
Administrative expenses and waiver	50
Pete's $500,000 of life insurance	590
Susie's $100,000 of life insurance	117
Total year 4 costs	$772
Gross policy earnings for the year	$742
Earnings shortfall to cover policy expenses	$30
Total account value by year-end	$10,929.33
Investment allocation	100% guaranteed interest division; 8% interest for next policy year

Fourth-Year Policy Results (1989–1990)

During the fourth year, their policy costs were as shown in Exhibit 12.5.

Fifth Policy Year (1990–1991)

Things are looking up! On October 3 Pete and Susie take advantage of the opportunity to move 25 percent out of the guaranteed interest division. They park $2725 in the money market division while they decide where to invest it within their policy. They are feeling more comfortable with their reduced family income and increased family size.

VARIABLE UNIVERSAL AS A PLACE FOR FAMILY GIFTS

Susie's parents are thrilled to have two grandchildren and decide to make a gift to Pete and Susie for the future education of the grandchildren. They give them $550, not enough to bother fooling around with a Uniform Gift to Minors Act gift, and Pete and Susie really don't want the money to belong to the kids at age 18 anyway. They also don't want to have to worry about income taxes on what the money earns each year, and so the gift is put into the life insurance policy. On October 12, 1990, the $550 check is split:

> $275 to the common stock fund. It buys 1.8 units at $146.56 per share. The June 2001 market value is $795.71 per unit. $275 to the aggressive stock fund. It buys 1.5 units at $178.13 per share. The June 2001 market value is $646.71 per unit

Pete and Susie are getting back into their consistent saving and investing mode as things settle down to normal frantic. They are able to put in seven checks in the amount of $135, one for $150, and one for $450, for a grand total of $1545, which, when added to the grandparents' gift, comes to $2095. All of Pete and Susie's money went into the guaranteed interest division.

Fifth-Year Policy Results (1990–1991)

Exhibit 12.6 shows policy costs in the fifth year.

On June 20, 1991, Pete and Susie move $1000 out of the money-market fund to a growth asset allocation account; the fund's basic strategy is 70 percent stock (equities) and 30 percent bond (debt). The $1000 purchases 7.5 units at a cost of $133.41 per unit. The June 2001 market value is $401.43 per unit.

The gross earnings within this policy, for this policy year, total $1306, which is sufficient to cover the $807 in policy costs. Their earnings on a very conservative investment for that policy year are $499. This means that they have a 4 percent net cash-on-

EXHIBIT 12.6

Fifth-Year Costs

State premium tax	$ 47
Administrative expenses and waiver	50
Pete's $500,000 life insurance policy	591
Susie's $100,000 life insurance policy	119
Total year 5 costs	$807

cash, tax-free return on the policy for the year *plus* the value of the life insurance protection for the year.

Sixth Policy Year (September 1991–September 1992)

Pete and Susie put in five checks for $150 and one check for $300. The $300 went to the guaranteed interest division. Of the five $150 checks, three went to guaranteed interest and two to the aggressive stock account. On December 12, they empty the money-market account into the aggressive stock account and pay $1896.75 ($373.01 per unit) for 5.084 units.

On January 28, they take some more grandparent gift money and some of their own and send in a check for $6780. They buy 22.6 units of the global fund at 146.56 per unit and 26.1 units of the conservative asset allocation account at $126.84 per unit that uses a basic investment strategy exactly opposite the one used by the growth asset allocation account (70 percent bond, 30 percent stocks).

Sixth-Year Policy Results (1991–1992)

During the sixth year, their policy costs were as shown in Exhibit 12.7.

Seventh Policy Year (1992–1993)

On February 16, Susie obtains a variable universal policy on her own, so they terminate the $100,000 rider insuring Susie's life under Pete's policy.

Seventh-Year Policy Results (1992–1993)

Exhibit 12.8 presents the costs for this policy year. The gross investment gain for the year September 1992 to September 1993 was $3131. Of this amount, $752 was allocated to pay life insurance costs and expenses. This *left* a net gain for Pete and Susie of $2379 which, when calculated on the amount they had in their policy account at the beginning of the year ($21,368), was a net, nontax-

EXHIBIT 12.7

Sixth-Year Costs

State premium tax	$176
Administrative expenses and waiver	60
Pete's $500,000 life insurance	592
Susie's $100,000 life insurance	126
Total costs for year 6	$954
Gross policy earnings for the year	$969
Earnings excess over policy expenses	$ 15
Total account value by year-end	$21,368
Investment allocation:	
Common stock	$405
Global	$3,157
Aggressive	$2,612
Conservative asset allocation	$3,547
Growth asset allocation	$1,261

able return of about 11 percent. The asset allocation that generated this return is illustrated in Exhibit 12.9.

Their policy prospectus indicates the theoretical split between stocks and bonds in each investment account (growth: 70 percent stock, 30 percent bonds; conservative: 70 percent bonds, 30 percent stock). Adding this to the amount they have in the guaranteed interest account tells us how much is in stocks and how much is

EXHIBIT 12.8

Seventh-year Costs

State premium tax	$ 0	(no money was invested while they were funding Susie's new policy)
Administrative expenses and waiver	62	
Pete's $500,000 life insurance	635	
Susie's $100,000 life insurance for 5 months	55	
Total costs for year 7	$752	

EXHIBIT 12.9

VUL Policy Asset Allocation 1993–1994

September 1993			September 1994	
Dollars	Percent	Investment Account	Dollars	Percent
$10,386	49	Guaranteed interest (6.5%)	$7,508	31.6
3,547	16	Conservative asset allocation	6,818	28.7
1,261	6	Growth asset allocation	1,483	6.2
405	2	Common stock	519	2.2
3,157	15	Global	4,211	17.7
2,612	12	Aggressive stock	3,208	13.5
$21,368	100		$23,747	100

in bonds. The asset allocation within their policy moved from 38 percent stock and 62 percent bonds at the beginning of the year to 46 percent stock and 54 percent bonds at the end of the year. This occurred for two reasons. First, they moved $2585 out of the guaranteed interest account into the conservative asset allocation account at the beginning of the year, and second, the overall return on the stocks outperformed the bond investments.

Their strategy for the coming year will depend upon how Pete and Susie feel this year. Are they secure in their employment, income, and family situation, or somewhat insecure because of uncertain employment, etc.? At this point a good strategy might be to start dollar-cost-averaging the money from their conservative asset allocation account into the common, global, aggressive, and growth asset allocation accounts, moving $100 per month into each. It would take about 18 months to move the bulk of that fund using this strategy. It also would move this young family toward an asset allocation more directed to equities and long-term growth, preparing for the college education years when it is likely that their policy will be called upon to fund some of those expenses.

However, they may choose a different path. Remember, they have been using the conservative asset allocation account to hold gifts from Susie's parents for the children's education, and they may want to keep the funds where they are or decide to transfer them into Susie's policy so her folks can watch them grow there. Isn't it nice that they have a choice?

Eighth-Year through Fourteenth-Year Policy Results (1994–2000)

This 6-year period has gone by quickly, and during that time Pete and Susie have devoted their efforts to raising two talented daughters and being a great family. They have gone to lots of soccer games; bought new cars to replace the ones that have broken down; experienced the excitement of moving to a new and bigger house; said a sad farewell to their old dog Chamois, and in time welcomed a new Airedale, Lucy; and even maximized employee benefit contributions (even the unmatched and the nondeductible). All those events in life that can cause you to focus on things other than your life insurance have gone on in Pete and Susie's lives. Although that is not what would be recommended, it is what happens. In fact, the last time they put any money into their policy was March 12, 1992, some 8½ years ago. Let's look at Exhibit 12.10 to see how it is doing.

The policy managed to pay all its expenses out of the guaranteed interest account. The guaranteed interest (GIA) account has been reduced by $3771. This indicates policy expenses over the last 6 years have averaged about $630 per year, net of GIA earn-

EXHIBIT 12.10

September 1994			September 2000	
Dollars	**Percent**	**Investment Account**	**Dollars**	**Percent**
$7,508	31.6	Guaranteed interest (6.5%)	$3,737	9.6
6,818	28.7	Conservative asset allocation	11,821	30
1,483	6.2	Growth asset allocation	3,640	9.4
519	2.2	Common stock	1,768	4.6
4,211	17.7	Global aggressive stock	11,225	28.6
3,208	13.5		6,993	17.8
$23,747	100		$39,184	100

ings, which were between 5.3 and 6 percent. The current expenses are running $864 for the year. The asset allocation has moved from about 50 percent bond–50 percent stock in 1994 to about 30 percent bond–70 percent stock currently as a result of the growth in the equities and the use of the GIA as the fund from which expenses were drawn. This ability to direct that expenses be paid from a specific account has been a profitable feature for Pete and Susie. During these 6 years the account value has increased $15,437, or 65 percent over its 1994 base of $23,747. Could they have done better? Sure with 20/20 hindsight, they could have taken more risk and received greater rewards. They could have driven faster and gotten there more quickly, but you know what? They did not want to drive that fast. The next question is, could any other type of life insurance have done as much for them and put them in the position of control that they now enjoy? In the coming year, the $864 that the policy must earn to cover its expenses represents 2.2 percent of their current account value, an amount less that the 2.5 percent it could cost them in income taxes if they were managing this money in taxable mutual funds. Years ago they took into consideration another advantage of having these funds inside their life insurance policy, besides the fact that they do not have to pay income taxes or report what goes on within their policy. The account value currently is not counted on college aid forms so it will not count against them in getting aid or scholarships for the college education of their two girls. As the account value grows, this advantage grows in importance. An update on how this real life policy is doing is available to anyone at any time as long as Pete and Susie give me permission.

HOW DOES THE POLICY WORK FOR MATURE FOLKS?

Ken called again today. Asked how much room he has in his policy.

He has *room* for $4054. That is, he can invest that much more in his policy and still enjoy *all* the tax benefits of the policy. He sent in the $4054 because, as he said, "My investments in my policy are doing better than my investments anywhere else." Ken is age 62. His expenses, including the cost of $80,000 worth of life insurance, are $92 per month. They *did not* change when he added the $4054, which he split among five accounts: balanced, common stock, global, aggressive, and growth. Ken now has more than $30,000 in his policy that would be paid out, in addition to the $80,000 of life insurance his policy would provide to his beneficiary in the event of his death. The policy is working for Ken at age 62.

BUSINESS OWNER PREPARING FOR RETIREMENT

Jerry is age 57 now. He is a business owner who must rely on himself for retirement. He is in those years when capital accumulation is important and possible, now that the kids are out on their own. He is using his variable universal life to accumulate money for retirement. That is, he is using it as a place to build capital as fast as he can so it is available when he and Janice finally really do retire. His September 1993 statement is shown in Exhibit 12.11. The gross earnings in the policy were $25,580. The costs were charged against the guaranteed interest account that earned $3650. The result was that the *net* investment earnings were $22,000.

The asset allocation within the policy is shown in Exhibit 12.12. Jerry probably will continue with this asset allocation for the coming year. It is comfortable, it is doing what he wants it to do, and it is working!

THE BUSINESS OWNER RETIREE

Scenario 1

He is 73. I'll bet you think he is retired! Not by a long shot. He's the patriarch of the family business. His policy has a death benefit of $500,000. It has $100,000 of investment capital in it. The cost for life insurance for the year was $9000, and the investment gain in the policy was $10,000.

Result

The tax-free earnings within the policy were sufficient to cover all policy costs.

EXHIBIT 12.11

Jerry's VUL (Age 57)

Total death benefit	$708,000	
Amount at risk/life insurance	500,000	(Option B)
End-of-year account value	208,000	
Beginning-of-year account	176,000	Average account balance $192.00
Increase in account value	$ 32,000	
Amount Jerry invested	$ 10,000	
Account net investment earnings	$ 22,000	
Net cash-on-cash rate of return on average account balance of	$192,000	11.5%
		17.4%
		Equivalent taxable return
Additional benefits:		
$500,000 life insurance		
Investments protected from income taxes		
Expenses figured in the preceding numbers:		
State premium tax		$ 200
Administrative expenses		60
Cost of $500,000 life insurance		3320
Total costs		$3580

Alternatives

What were this policy owner's alternatives? He could buy just term insurance—if he could get it for $9000—which he can't. If he could, he would have to earn $13,637 [$9,000/(1 − 0.34)] in order to have enough to send $9000 to pay for his life insurance and $4637 to the IRS. He would have to earn 13.6 percent on his investment capital of $100,000 to earn enough outside of the policy to pay for his insurance.

Conclusion

It is easier and less risky to earn the $9000 within the policy. Yes, variable universal is working well for this business owner. And looking at the big picture—yes, variable universal can work very well for mature individuals.

EXHIBIT 12.12

Jerry's VUL Asset Allocation

Guaranteed interest	$58,000	Pays expenses
Balanced division bond	$ 5,000	Bond
Balanced division stock	$ 5,000	Stock
Common stock division	$ 2,000	Stock
Global stock division	$22,000	Stock
Aggressive stock division	$49,000	Stock
Growth investors division		
30% bond	$20,000	Bond
70% stock	$47,000	Stock
Total	$208,000	Stock
Bond	$ 83,000	40%
Stock	$125,000	60%

Scenario 2

Adam is 45 and has just completed the sale of his business. He has owned his VUL since 1987, only 2 years after the policies were made available to the public. As a business owner, he has always been aware of the possibility of a lawsuit and has always done financial and estate planning to make sure his family was protected against all risks to its security. He lives in a state in which the laws protecting the assets inside a life insurance policy are very strong, so this gave him an extra reason to keep his policy funding level up as high as he could.

It has been said that VUL is the last bastion of financial privacy. The information is between you and your insurance company. It does not appear on any income tax returns. Adam and I had to use that feature in this policy once. Times were not good a number of years ago for Adam. So he took on a partner who was to be a rainmaker—bring in lots of business—and he sold him one-half of his company. The partnership did not work out. Adam wanted to buy back the other half of his business with an offer that was substantial enough so that the new partner would not exercise his option under the buy-sell agreement to buy out Adam at the price Adam was offering the partner. Adam decided to make a substantial all-cash offer and make the time frame very short so that the partner would not think it was feasible. We knew that the partner thought Adam was too young to be able to raise that much money so quickly. The partner accepted the offer. It took 5 days to get the settlement on his brokerage account. The income taxes on the liquidation of that account were painful the next April. As I'm sure you have surmised, Adam planned to borrow against his VUL. We faxed the loan form into the insurance company, which cut the policy loan check. The insurance company Express-Mailed the check to Adam so that he received it the next day. There were no income taxes as a result of the policy loan. The bank holding the stock in escrow accepted the funds and exchanged the stock for the cash, and Adam had his company back. The bank was so impressed with Adam's dexterity that it offered him a generous line of credit that he used to pay off his policy loan. Adam's cost for the loan was 1 percent simple interest for about 10 days.

As I said at the beginning, now Adam has sold his business entirely and is going to figure out what he really wants to do next. In the meantime, he has max-funded one of his VUL policies with a check for $135,000, which he put into the money market in the policy and has directed that it be moved into five of his favorite subaccounts in the policy over the next 13 months. The policy now has $262,000 in it, and the amount deducted from the guaranteed interest account to cover COIs and expenses is $78.45 per month, which comes to about $942 for the year. This means this $262,000 will pay 36 basis points (0.36 percent) for life insurance to benefit his family. How much do you think he would have to pay in income taxes each year if these funds were in taxable growth mutual funds? We have been using the figure quoted on the SEC web site (www.sec.gov) of about 2½ percent as an average. If that were the case, the income taxes on this $262,000 investment would be about $6550. Which would you rather pay: $942 for the benefit of your family or $6550 to benefit the public?

Other businesspeople who have been instrumental in helping this author understand and appreciate the value of storing significant amounts of capital in their VUL policies are Mike, whose life insurance costs and expenses require 41 basis points (0.41 percent); Curt at 80 basis points; and Chuck at 97 basis points. Although all these policy owners have kept personal control over their policies in the event that they need them for retirement capital, I do not expect that they will need them. If the estate tax remains an issue, which it probably will, most likely we will move the policies out of their estates when they are sure they do not need the capital inside the policies for retirement and know where they want it to go. And we will do this, working closely with their legal and accounting advisors, without ever having to pay income taxes, gift taxes, or estate taxes. No one has ever shown me any type of property that can do as much for so many at so little cost. The challenge remains to all financial advisors and authors: Please show us a financial product that can do more for people than VUL. If such a product exists, people need to know about it. Properly managed VUL can do more for families providing tax efficient management, diversification and delivery of capital at less cost than any other financial product.

CHAPTER 13

Life Insurance Wrap Up

Life Insurance Policy Owner's Bill of Rights

Life insurance contracts offer you, the policy owner, a bundle of rights. The rights in each basic policy design—whole life, universal life, fixed-premium variable life, and variable universal life—are unique. You and your advisors should examine the rights in these various policies as one of the first steps in choosing a life insurance policy design. In practice today, this issue is seldom examined at all, so it may be up to you to bring it up. The Life Insurance Policy Owner's Bill of Rights provides a checklist and description of the important rights available in the various life insurance policy designs to make it as easy as possible for you to address this important issue.

This chapter presents the Life Insurance Policy Owner's Bill of Rights (see Exhibit 13.1) and discusses the reasons for the answers given in the checklist. However, you and your advisors might take issue with some of the answers given here. Your best course of action is to copy the Life Insurance Policy Owner's Bill of Rights checklist in Exhibit 13.1 without the answers and, with your advisors' help, fill in your own answers, answering yes or no about whether you think a right does or does not exist in each type of policy. Once you have filled in the checklist, decide which rights you require in your life insurance policy.

EXHIBIT 13.1

Life Insurance Policy Owner's Bill of Rights

Policy Owner Rights	Whole Life	Universal Life	Fixed-Premium Variable Life	Variable Universal Life	Right is Required/ Not Required
1 Guaranteed cash value	Yes	No	No	No	
2 Guaranteed premium	Yes	No*	Yes	No*	
3 Guaranteed death benefit	Yes	No*	Yes	No*	
4 Maximize, minimize, and skip premiums	No	Yes	No	Yes	
5 Increase or decrease death benefits	No	Yes	No	Yes	
6 Choose death benefit option A(1) or B(2)	No	Yes	No	Yes	
7 Access policy values by withdrawal	No	Yes	No	Yes	
8 Have a choice of general and/or separate accounts	No	No	Yes	Yes	
9 Change investments	No	No	Yes	Yes	
10 Diversify policy assets	No	No	Yes	Yes	
11 Choose separate account protection from life insurance company creditors	No	No	Yes	Yes	
12 Convert the contract into an annuity without immediate taxation on the gain	Yes	Yes	Yes	Yes	

*Many universal types of policies include riders that provide for a guaranteed death benefit if stipulated levels of premium payments are made.
©Ben G. Baldwin 1999.

1. GUARANTEED CASH VALUE

This right exists in whole life, but does not exist in the other three contracts. However, in each of the other three contracts there often is a general account alternative that provides a guaranteed minimum interest rate, e.g. 3 or 4 percent; and if this account were funded with a specific amount of investment capital, an account similar to the guaranteed cash-value account could be built.

2. GUARANTEED PREMIUM

Guaranteed premiums are a part of both a whole life contract and a fixed-premium variable life contract. Universal and variable universal contracts do not have fixed premiums.

While a fixed premium is referred to as a policy owner's right, it really is a policy owner's obligation. If the policy owner is ever unable or unwilling to meet the fixed-premium obligation set by the insurance company, the policy is liable to go into its nonforfeiture guarantee of extended term insurance until expenses eat up the policy account.

3. GUARANTEED DEATH BENEFIT

A guaranteed minimum death benefit is a part of whole life and fixed-premium variable life policies. In the generic form of universal and variable universal policies, a guaranteed minimum death benefit does not exist. As a result of consumer demand for guaranteed death benefits, most insurance companies now provide them by rider within both universal and variable universal life policies. It is relatively easy for an insurance company to build such a death benefit guarantee by requiring the policy owner to put a certain level of investment capital into the policy. If a policy owner will guarantee a certain level of premium, then the company will provide a guaranteed death benefit.

4. MAXIMIZE, MINIMIZE, AND SKIP PREMIUMS

This right does not exist in the two fixed-premium contracts, whole life and fixed-premium variable life, but does exist in the two universal design policies. Participating whole life policies allow for the use of dividends to reduce premium, which is not the same as the full right to increase, decrease, or skip a premium payment.

5. INCREASE OR DECREASE DEATH BENEFITS

This right does exist in universal design policies, but not in guaranteed premium, guaranteed face-amount policies, such as whole life or fixed-premium variable. In order to increase the death benefit, financial and medical underwriting normally will be required. A change to decrease the death benefit of a policy merely requires a written request; however, decreases in death benefits can expose you to surrender charges, so make sure the savings in COIs are not offset by the imposition of a surrender charge. Under some circumstances, decreases in death benefits also can create an income tax liability, and so you will want to make sure that is not a problem in your case prior to making a reduction in policy face amount.

6. CHOOSE DEATH BENEFIT OPTION A (1) OR B (2)

The right to use these two death benefit options is unique to universal design policies and does not exist in the fixed-premium contracts. Under the level death benefit option commonly called option A, or 1, typically the beneficiary will receive a death benefit that is the face amount of the policy, made up of two parts. One part is the insurance company's money, referred to as the *amount at risk*, and the other part is the account value of the underlying investment account. As the account value grows, the amount at risk decreases, and the cost for the amount at risk also decreases. This option emphasizes accumulation of account value more than current death benefit.

The death benefit in an option B, or 2, policy pays the beneficiary a stipulated amount at risk (face amount) plus whatever is in the investment account. This option means that more policy owner money will be spent on the amount at risk, but also gives the policy owner control over whether the amount at risk is to be reduced or not, rather than have it automatically reduced when investment capital is added or when the account value grows as a result of good investment returns.

7. ACCESS POLICY VALUES BY WITHDRAWAL

The right to borrow from a policy exists in all four investment forms of contracts although the cost of borrowing varies from contract to contract. Borrowing from a policy is not the same as a right to make outright withdrawals from a policy. The right to withdraw from the contract exists only in universal design policies. Some will argue that accumulated dividends in a participating whole life policy may be withdrawn, which is true, but technically that is not the same as an outright withdrawal right.

8. HAVE A CHOICE OF GENERAL AND/OR SEPARATE ACCOUNTS

Whole life and universal life contracts are general account–only contracts. Policy owners of whole life insurance and universal life insurance have no access to the separate account and its underlying subaccounts. The separate account is unique to variable life contracts. You can tell the difference because if you are offered a general account–only product, you will not receive a prospectus. If you are offered a variable product containing a separate account and its underlying subaccounts, you must receive a prospectus, and the individual who is offering it must be properly licensed. You will be asked many questions regarding your investment objectives in order to determine if the product is suitable for you and if the contract provides subaccount investment alternatives that will provide an investment allocation suitable for your objectives.

9. CHANGE INVESTMENTS

There is no ongoing right to change or choose between investments in general account–only products, whereas this right does exist in variable products offering a general account option and an array of subaccounts similar to mutual funds.

10. DIVERSIFY POLICY ASSETS

Some will say that the asset value of a general account–only life insurance policy could be considered the bond portion of an individual's portfolio. This brings up a number of issues. For instance, as an insured ages and the asset value of a whole life policy grows, it may become too great a portion of a policy owner's invested assets. The guaranteed cash value of a whole life policy will be the policy's face amount when the insured is age 95 or 100. With people living longer, more and more people will find themselves in this situation. Also, the bond and mortgage account of an insurance company is exposed to some unique risks to which a typical bond portfolio is not exposed. For example, it is subject to the creditors of the life insurance company, which someday could create unsuitable risks to family security. It is also a "blind pool" bond fund, a bond fund over which the policy owner has no control—and no ability to adjust to his or her personal level of risk tolerance.

People criticize variable contracts by saying that they shift all the risk to the policy owners. However, when the policy owners accept the responsibility of directing the investment capital within the policy, the policy owners also pick up the right to match the investment accounts available within the policy to their risk tolerance and to diversify the assets. Diversification now is required by fiduciary policy owners in many states under the Uniform Prudent Investor statutes.

11. CHOOSE SEPARATE ACCOUNT PROTECTION FROM LIFE INSURANCE COMPANY CREDITORS

The two general account–only products, whole life and universal life, have no account that is protected from the creditors of the insurance company. Separate accounts do have protection from the creditors of the insurance company. Evidence of this can be found in the prospectus, where it will confirm that separate account assets are not subject to the claims of any of the insurance company's other creditors.

12. CONVERT THE CONTRACT INTO AN ANNUITY WITHOUT IMMEDIATE TAXATION ON THE GAIN

This right is stipulated under Internal Revenue Code Section 1035 and is available for all investment types of life insurance. This is an important right. You may no longer need the death benefit for your beneficiaries, but you may need the cash accumulation within the contract to assure a life income for yourself.

SUMMARY

You need to understand the rights under the various contract forms and to know what policies can and cannot do. Once a suitable contract design has been selected, then illustrations can be used to identify policy costs and funding options.

You and your advisors must recognize that there are potential risks and returns in all investment types of life insurance policies that need to be addressed prior to making a choice between contracts. In making that choice, each policy should be examined from the standpoint of suitability to the policy owner and the financial job that the policy may be required to do over the life of the insured. Suitability is not just a one-time thing. It is forever an issue.

The performance of any investment type of life insurance policy, and its ability to use policy earnings to offset some or all of the policy's costs, is dependent upon the following:

- The amount of capital that is put into the policy
- The return that the economy allows that capital to earn
- The constraints that the lawmakers choose to put on the insurance company's ability to manage that capital profitably

The NAIC mandates multipage illustrations containing long lists of numbers, including dividends for whole life, excess interest for universal life, and investment return for variable life. Prospective policy owners and agents must sign these illustrations. This creates the perception that the illustrations are even more credible than those of the past. Perhaps instead of mandating such illus-

EXHIBIT 13.2

WARNING

This is an investment type of life insurance policy.

An investment type of life insurance policy is that type of policy into which a policy owner puts more money than that needed to cover policy costs. The extra money is to earn a return for the policy owner. This untaxed return may be used in whole or in part to cover policy costs. If the amount of the return is insufficient to cover policy costs, the capital in the policy will be used to do so. If the capital is used up by costs, the policy owner will have to pay more money into the policy or the policy will terminate.

Whole life, universal life, equity-indexed life, variable life, and variable universal life are investment types of policies. The performance of any investment type of life insurance policy and its ability to use policy earnings to offset some or all of the policy's costs is dependent upon the amount of capital you put into it, the earnings that the economy allows that capital to earn, and the constraints that the lawmakers choose to put on the insurance company's ability to manage that capital profitably.

It is up to *you* to know the risk and return potential of this policy, as well as the constraints that the regulators and the market put on it.

---

trations, the NAIC should require that policies carry a warning label. Advisors may want to use the warning shown in Exhibit 13.2 on any investment type of life insurance policy. Once the information in the warning is clear in your mind, you will be in a position to evaluate the risks and returns inherent in a policy.

GENERAL ACCOUNT ONLY OR GENERAL AND SEPARATE ACCOUNT

The first distinction between investment types of life insurance that must be made is whether the product is a general account–only product or whether it offers the policy owner a choice between the general account and a separate account containing a family of subaccounts.

- General account only
  Whole life: Long-term bond portfolio
  Universal life: Short-term bond portfolio

- General account and separate account
  Variable life
  Variable universal life

Investment Types of Life Insurance Policy Design

The generic names for the primary general account–only life insurance products are *whole life* and *universal life*. You also may hear names such as *interest-sensitive whole life* and *equity index life*, which are hybrid general account products. The investment types of policies that offer you the opportunity to use both the general account and separate accounts are *fixed-premium variable life* and *variable universal life*, also known as *flexible-premium variable life*. See Exhibit 13.3 for a brief look at the different investment types of life insurance design.

The Nature of the General Account

The general account of a life insurance company is subject to the claims of all the company's creditors. This means that the asset value of your policy is subject to the claims of creditors other than you if the insurance company has financial difficulties. The existence of this risk to you and other policy owners has made the insurance commissioners of each state and their national organization, the National Association of Insurance Commissioners, establish many rules and regulations about how insurance companies should manage their general accounts. The most notable of these rules is the risk-based capital ratio (RBC) regulation that mandates regulatory action should a company's RBC deteriorate to a certain level. These RBC regulations cause an insurance company to invest more conservatively in order to get a higher risk-based capital ratio. This, in combination with reducing interest rates and the scrutiny with which the various rating services watch insurance company general accounts, has driven down the return that insurance companies can earn in general account policies for their policy owners.

The general account of the insurance company is managed by the insurance company to meet its liabilities. Primarily, it is a bond and mortgage account. Of the $1.974 trillion in general account assets in 1999 tracked by the American Council of Life In-

EXHIBIT 13.3

Investment Types of Life Insurance Policy Design

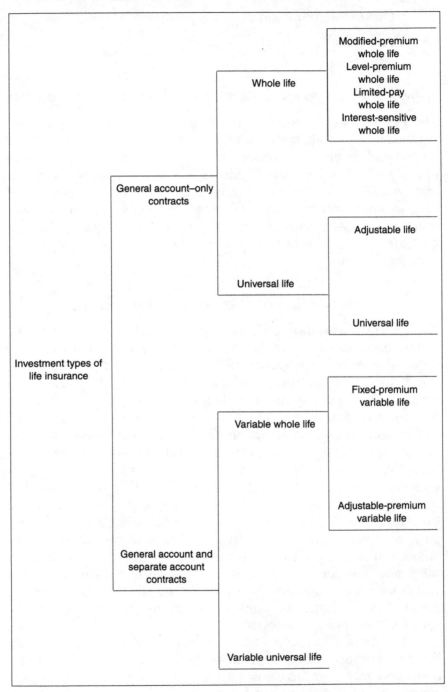

Investment types of life insurance

- General account–only contracts
  - Whole life
    - Modified-premium whole life
    - Level-premium whole life
    - Limited-pay whole life
    - Interest-sensitive whole life
  - Universal life
    - Adjustable life
    - Universal life
- General account and separate account contracts
  - Variable whole life
    - Fixed-premium variable life
    - Adjustable-premium variable life
  - Variable universal life

Thanks to Lawrence J. Rybka, J.D., CPP, for his contribution of this exhibit.

EXHIBIT 13.4

The General Account of the Life Insurance Industry, 1999

Bonds	$1.406 trillion	71.2%
Mortgages and real estate	$0.250 trillion	12.7%
Policy loans, cash, short term and miscellaneous	$0.218 trillion	10.9%
Common and preferred stock	$0.100 trillion	5.1%
Total	$1.974 trillion	100%

surance, 71.2 percent was in bonds, 12.7 percent was in mortgages and real estate, 5.1 percent was in policy loans, 5.8 percent was in miscellaneous assets, and 5.1 percent was in stock.* (See Exhibit 13.4)

It can be seen in Exhibit 13.4 that the insurance industry general account shown in the exhibit it is composed of 95% interest-earning types of investments only about 5 percent stock. General account–only life insurance policies are primarily interest rate–driven policies. That is, they run on the interest that insurance companies are able to earn on the assets in their general accounts. Life insurance company general account earnings not only are dictated by the interest rate environment but also are constrained by the regulators and the rating services. An investment account made up of 95 percent bonds and only 5 percent stock can be expected to provide a long-term gross return of between 5 and 7 percent, which, reduced by expenses, could drive the return down to between 3 and 5 percent.

Risks and Rewards of Whole Life Insurance

Whole life is the original investment-oriented life insurance policy. It is a general account–only policy. It has risks and rewards like every other investment type of policy. People like whole life for its guaranteed premium, guaranteed death benefit, and guaranteed cash value. People dislike whole life when dividends are re-

---

*The American Council of Life Insurance Life Insurance Fact Book, 2000, pp. 114–115 (www.acli.com).

duced or eliminated, when the insurance company has financial difficulties, and when they desire flexibility.

Risks and Rewards of Universal Life Insurance

The high interest rates in the 1980s gave birth to universal life. It was the high interest rates of the day that drove the demand for the product. The scathing Federal Trade Commission report in 1976, which severely criticized the insurance industry for low returns in whole life insurance, brought universal life into existence. Universal life promised interest rates that would be competitive with the money-market rates that were so popular in the early 1980s. Universal life was an important innovation. You finally could see all the working parts of an investment type of life insurance policy. Prior to universal life, the only investment life insurance available—whole life—was a black box in that you could not identify costs of investment return. Universal life disclosed the three parts that it comprised: term life insurance or amount at risk, expenses, and an investment account earning a return. Although this sounds rather simple now, it was revolutionary at the time. However, universal life still is a general account product and has the problems of the general account:

1. Insurance company creditors have access to the general account.
2. The account is interest rate–driven so that decreasing interest rates and increasing regulatory pressure for conservatism continue to drive down interest crediting rates in the policies.

The risks of universal life are the same as those of whole life. People like universal life for its flexible premium, flexible death benefit, and—when conditions are favorable—generous interest rates. People dislike universal life when interest rates are reduced or when their insurance company has financial difficulties.

Risks and Rewards of Fixed-Premium Variable Life

The year 1976 was the first year that a variable life insurance policy could be purchased in the United States. Variable life allowed you to choose among subaccounts (which act like mutual funds) within the separate account of an insurance company. The separate account allowed the insurance company to segregate this account from the general account. It could now specify that, although the funds in it legally belonged to the insurance company, the assets were being held for the benefit of the policy owner, and were not subject to the claims of the insurance company's other creditors. Fixed-premium variable life policies are built with a specified premium payable for a specified period, from a single payment to payments until age 100, and with a stated face amount. The death benefit in fixed-premium variable life can exceed the stated face amount, and generally will when investment results are positive, but the death benefit cannot go below the face amount even if investment results are negative. The mid-1970s proved to be an unfavorable environment for stocks. People had watched the stock market decline 40 percent in 1974. Variable life was criticized for passing all the investment risk to naive policy owners. Growth and acceptance of the product was slow. Eleven years later when variable universal life was introduced, the market share of the entire premium taken in for variable life insurance in that year was 3 percent of the total premiums for all life insurance. In 2000, it accounted for about 4 percent. Most of the growth in variable life insurance has gone to variable universal life.

People like fixed-premium variable life for its guaranteed premium, guaranteed minimum death benefit, and the opportunity to use the general or separate account for investment with little downside risk. That is, no matter how poorly your investments perform, you do not have to pay more and your death benefit is guaranteed. People dislike fixed-premium variable life when they are unable to meet the fixed-premium obligation or when they want more life insurance but cannot increase the face amount. They are unhappy when they like the investments in the policy but cannot put in more money because the policy cannot accept it, or when they are required to put more money into the policy even though the investments are doing poorly.

Risks and Rewards of Variable Universal Life

Variable universal life insurance entered the life insurance marketplace in 1985. In its first year, it accounted for about 1 percent of life insurance premiums. By 2000, it accounted for about 41 percent. From 1976 to 1985, investment-oriented life insurance consisted of whole life, fixed premium variable life, and universal life. For those 11 years you could see that putting the variable features (diversification of investment) together with the universal life features of face amount and premium flexibility was inevitable. It was not until 1985 that the life insurance industry felt that the technology of the day would handle all the moving parts within VUL and that it could be constructed as a profitable product for the insurance company and the policy owner. The praise and criticism of VUL are directed at the moving parts. The critics say that it is too complex and that it has too many moving parts. The proponents rave about all the financial problems that can be solved *because* this product has all those moving parts. The key word for VUL is *flexibility*, which equates to adaptability to your ever-changing needs.

People like variable universal life for its flexible premium, flexible death benefit, and availability of the general account and separate account for investment. People dislike variable universal life when they are unable to invest sufficient assets in the contract to earn significant income tax–deferred returns or when their investments do poorly.

Equity-Indexed Life Insurance

Equity indexing first began in annuities in 1995 and has had little impact on the life insurance marketplace to date. An equity-indexed life insurance product promises that the contract's asset value will earn some minimum interest rate, such as 3 percent. However, it will be credited with some portion of the equity index it is using (such as 70 percent) to a maximum of a certain amount if the index provides a positive return (e.g., the S&P 500 Index). The message of equity indexing is no downside risk but the possibility of gains that may exceed what a fixed product might earn. It is, to many people's surprise, a general account product, not a registered product. It is not sold with a prospectus, and salespeople require only a life insurance license to sell it. Over the first 5 years, the account values of equity-indexed insurance products have had an average return of from a little under 10 percent to over 12 percent, depending upon the specific product. Equity indexing has, in the main, accomplished what it set out to accomplish—to provide returns somewhere between interest-only products and equity investments. If equity indexing proves to be profitable to consumers and insurance companies, we can expect to see more equity-indexed life insurance, and, possibly, it may be made available as an alternative investment in VUL policies.

Single-Premium Life Insurance

Single-premium life insurance is any type of investment-oriented life insurance that contractually promises to be entirely paid up for life with but a single payment. The death benefit is guaranteed for life. It provides an alternative for money that is to compound income tax-free during the insured's lifetime and be paid to a beneficiary income tax–free at the insured's death. It comes in whole life, direct interest crediting, and variable policy designs.

Multiple-Life Life Insurance Contracts

Insuring more than one life within one life insurance policy is a practice that goes back to the 1960s. Policies can be purchased that pay a death benefit at the death of the first and then let the survivor or survivors continue the policy; or policies can be purchased that do not pay off at the first death but delay payment until the second death. The former usually are referred to as *joint life policies*, whereas the latter are referred to as *second-to-die* or *survivorship life insurance*. Survivorship life policies have been popular for two purposes. One, the payment of the death benefit at the second death makes them a perfect way to provide estate liquidity for a married couple taking advantage of the marital deduction at the first death. The policy pays off when the estate taxes can no longer be avoided. The second purpose is to compound money within a life insurance policy to avoid current taxation and to take advantage of whatever creditor protection is offered to life insurance in the insured's state of residence. The cost of investing in a taxable environment is income taxes and expenses. The cost of investing in annuities is expenses, lack of liquidity, and eventual income taxes. The costs inhibiting investment returns in life insurance are expenses and insurance costs, commonly referred to as *costs of insurance,* or *COIs.* The COIs in a first-to-die life insurance policy typically will be 10 times the COIs in a second-to-die policy. As a result, there is less cost drag on the investment capital in a VUL second-to-die policy, which allows the money to compound more rapidly for the policy owner. The uses for a VUL second-to-die policy are limited only by your imagination and that of your advisors.

DISPOSING OF UNNEEDED LIFE INSURANCE

It is time to explore the opportunities for change if neither you, the policy owner, nor the beneficiary consider an existing life insurance policy necessary and appropriate as it exists currently. Such policies could represent lazy assets on your net worth statement. That is, they have financial value, but that value is no longer doing you and your spouse very much good. For example, could you use the cash value more productively if the policy's cash value is equal to 80 percent of its face amount and is earning less than 4 percent? You and your spouse might very well determine that the 20 percent, which represents insurance company money (amount at risk) payable to the surviving spouse at the insured's death, will not have any impact on that spouse's lifestyle.

What you would like to do is to increase your current income and provide for your long-term care needs. The 80 percent of the policy, which is cash value, could change your standard of living. Let's consider executing a 1035 tax-free exchange of this life policy into either:

1. *A deferred variable annuity.* Then you can diversify among the subaccounts so that you could see some growth, as opposed to the 4 percent current earnings. The annuity contract could exceed the value of the old life insurance policy in a very few years.

Or:

2. *An immediate joint and 100 percent to the survivor annuity.* Then you and your spouse can enjoy the proceeds as income over your remaining lifetime. Go for variable

annuity if you consider the money you are putting into it "found" money, are an optimist, and want to enjoy the varying monthly checks, up and down.

Internal Revenue Code Section 72 governs the income tax treatment of annuities. Amounts received under an annuity contract are includable in income except to the extent that they represent a return of the investment in the contract.

The reason to do a 1035 tax-free exchange rather than just surrendering the policy is to accomplish two things. One, to avoid paying taxes on the gain that may have accumulated in the life insurance policy. And two, to get back the entire cost basis in your life insurance policy, which includes the cost of insurance for all the years the policy has been in force. After getting the report from the insurance company, you may find that the cost basis exceeds the surrender value of the policy and that income taxes are a nonissue. That is, you will not have any to pay. However, it may well be that the bad news of having paid more for the insurance than it was worth can be turned into the good news of a future income tax benefit. The annuity purchased by this transaction will be a nonqualified annuity and, as such, will have a cost basis that will be distributed at some time without being subject to income taxes. If the distribution happens to be by way of a joint and 100 percent to the survivor variable annuity, getting that tax-free distribution of basis could be a very pleasant result.

If payments are to continue for a life or lives, multiplying the sum of 1 year's fixed annuity payments by the life expectancy of the measuring life or lives yields the expected return. The life expectancy multiple or multiples must be taken from the annuity tables prescribed by the IRS in Internal Revenue Code Section 72(c)(3). The result is a *percentage of income* that is the return of basis each year until all the basis is recovered (exclusion ratio). Thereafter the distributions are entirely taxable. (See Chapter 14 "Understanding Annuities," for a more thorough explanation.)

In a variable immediate annuity, the expected return is unknown, and so instead of calculating expected total return, we calculate the time period (life expectancy) over which we expect to recover the investment or cost basis in the contract. The cost basis is divided by that life expectancy figure that results in the *amount that can be excluded* from taxation each year until all the cost basis is recovered. This might have been a policy from one of the companies that had failed and then been reestablished by the insurance commissioner, so that what you had paid into the life insurance policy would exceed the current value that is being paid into the annuity. By annuitizing, you get your cost basis back income tax–free over your life expectancy so that you may not have to pay income taxes on the entire monthly payment.

Many people have held onto life insurance policies when the assets could have been used more productively elsewhere. These are not sacred assets. They should be included among those available to solve your financial problems. You may find that if you get your ever-replaceable income up high enough, you could drop a least one of your long-term care policies. Move the life policies outside your estate by trading them in for an annuity. With a joint and 100 percent to the survivor annuity, there will be nothing left to tax at the death of the surviving spouse because the income stream will stop. This technique may be called turning lemons into lemonade.

SELL YOUR LIFE INSURANCE POLICY?

You may own what you consider to be one of those relatively "worthless" policies. Maybe it is a big unwanted term life insurance policy or an underfunded universal life policy with a huge surrender charge. It may be a life insurance policy with a high face amount that has become a burden to you rather than a benefit. Consider some alternatives before you decide to just terminate it.

Viatical Settlements

The taxation on a life insurance policy that has been turned into cash for a person who is terminally or chronically ill was first defined in statute form in the Health Insurance Portability and Accountability Act of 1996, Section 331(b), also known as the Kennedy-Kassenbaum Act, or HIPAA '96. The act stipulated that if any portion of the death benefit under a life insurance contract on the life of a terminally or chronically ill insured is sold or assigned to a viatical settlement provider, the amount paid for the sale or assignment will be treated as an amount paid under the life insurance contract by reason of the insured's death and thus excluded from income under Internal Revenue Code Sections 101(a) and 101(g)(2)(A). That is a long way of saying that, under certain conditions, you can sell your life insurance policy. There are organizations that will buy that policy, and there may be *no* income taxes to pay on the proceeds you receive.

The proceeds are tax-free if you, the insured, are deemed by a physician to have an illness or physical condition that reasonably can be expected to result in death within 24 months.*

The proceeds are also tax-free if you are chronically ill. To be considered chronically ill, a person has to be certified by a licensed health practitioner as being unable to perform for a period of 90 days or more, without substantial assistance, at least two activities of daily living. The defined activities of daily living are eating, toileting, transferring, bathing, dressing, and continence. If the chronic illness is caused by severe cognitive impairment, a licensed health practitioner must certify it to be threatening health and safety.† The exclusion from income of benefits received will generally be granted only for those funds used for qualified long-term care services that the insured person receives.

Senior Settlements

The business of selling a life insurance policy to a company that is in the business of buying such policies became legitimate when the IRS defined such a business in the tax code. Internal Revenue Code Section 101(g)(2)(B)(I) defined this business as "any person regularly engaged in the trade or business of purchasing, or taking assignments of life insurance on the lives of insureds."†† This has given rise to a market for the sale of life insurance policies on the lives of people who do not meet the strict viatical settlement requirements. The large viatical settlement providers now are willing to look at the purchase of other life insurance policies that policy owners find they no longer need or policies that are no longer affordable if the insured is old enough or sick enough, and the policy is big enough. These senior settlement companies are

*Internal Revenue Code Section 101(g)(4)(A).
†Internal Revenue Code Section 101(g)(4)(B) and 7702B(c) (2)(A) and (B).
††Internal Revenue Code Section 101(g)(2)(B)(i).

creating value for policy owners where previously there was thought to be little or no value. This new market gives you an alternative to 1035 tax-free exchanges, surrenders, or lapsing of unneeded life insurance policies.

This could be of value to you under the following circumstances:

- You are about to surrender a policy and accept the cash surrender value as settlement.
- There has been a change in business ownership that leaves policies that are no longer needed.
- Buy-sell agreements in business are terminated leaving unneeded policies.
- An insured key employee leaves and you no longer need the policy.
- Business reversals or bankruptcy creates a need for money but not old life insurance policies.
- Personal reversals cause a need for money more than life insurance.
- Unaffordable premiums mean a policy will have to be dropped.
- An individual policy is no longer needed and a survivorship policy would be preferred.
- A life insurance policy needs to be eliminated from the estate, now, not 3 years from now. Sell the policy and gift the proceeds.
- Reappearing premiums on so-called vanishing-premium policies aggravate and annoy you and make it impossible to continue a policy.
- A charitable organization has been the recipient of gifted life insurance policies but it would prefer cash now.
- Tax law changes cause old life insurance programs to become uneconomical and unneeded.
- The insured has outlived all appropriate beneficiaries.
- Changes in estate size or makeup or in the tax law cause life insurance policies that were purchased to solve estate liquidity problems to become unwanted or unneeded.

- An irrevocable life insurance trust owns life insurance on an insured donor who no longer wants to make gifts to the trust to pay the premium.
- An 80-year-old still paying substantial premiums who wonders why.
- The policy owner needs or wants money for . . .

The typical transaction is fairly easy. The unneeded in-force policy, along with the insured's medical history, is submitted to the company considering the purchase. The company considers the contract as one that was issued under one set of mortality assumptions that time or an intervening medical event may have changed, and if possible, the company makes an offer. If the offer is acceptable to the policy owner, the company becomes the new owner, beneficiary, and premium payer and the policy owner receives a lump-sum cash payment.

Taxation to the Seller

Prior to the availability of this market, your options with a term insurance policy were to just to drop the policy, receive nothing, and not be able to use any portion of the premium payments as a loss. If it was a cash-value policy, it could be surrendered for its net cash surrender value. If cost basis exceeded net proceeds received, no loss would be allowed. If cost basis was less than net proceeds received, the gain would be taxed as ordinary income.* The one exception to this was a special exception for national service life insurance, the gains on which are entirely tax-free.†

Now comes the viatical settlement provider, who makes an offer exceeding the policy cost basis, and exceeding the policy's net cash surrender value. So now how is the seller taxed? Let's say that the policy in question has a cost basis of $50,000 and a net cash surrender value of $60,000, and the purchasing company has offered to pay $200,000 for it. The taxation on the difference between the cost basis and net cash surrender value is fairly clear, $10,000 of ordinary income to the seller. However, how is the

---

*Reg. 1.61-2(d)(2)(ii), Rev. Rul. 70-38, 1970-1 CB 11, Ltr. Rul. 9443020.
†See 38 USC 3101(a); Rev. Rul. 72-604, 1972-2 CB 35.

EXHIBIT 13.5

Disposal of Unneeded Life Insurance

Viatical Settlement	Senior Settlement
24 months or less to live or chronic	Unwanted life insurance of any kind
Regulated in at least 18 states	Age 72-plus—no illness necessary
State license may be required	No license regulations
Cash paid 50 to 85% of face value	Cash paid 30 to 50% of face value
Federal income tax–free distribution. Also most state income tax–free distribution	Capital gains and some ordinary

$140,000 difference between the net cash surrender value and the sale price to be taxed? The purchasing company of this contract and its tax counsel are arguing that the sale of the policy in this manner is the sale of a capital asset, and the $140,000 should be taxed at the lower capital gains tax rate.

Summary

Whether it is ordinary income or capital gains, if you were the policy owner who received $140,000 more than you expected from the sale of your policy, you probably would be pleased. Here is what to watch for.

- Unneeded, unwanted life insurance of any kind, including term life contracts
- Face amounts of $500,000 or more—larger policies create greater purchaser interest
- Insureds age 72-plus (younger, if in ill health)

For a review of the important points for both kinds of settlements—viatical settlement and senior settlement—see Exhibit 13.5. For additional information and a listing of organizations, contact the Viatical Association of America at 800–842-9811 or www.viatica.org/viatical or the National Viatical Association at 800-741-9465.

CHAPTER 14

Understanding Annuities

Don't Let Me Run Out of Money!

*Everyone over age 60 has a nagging fear
they will run out of money.*

PETER DRUCKER

*Annuity: The annual payment of an
allowance or income. The right to receive
this payment or the obligation to make this
payment. An investment on which a person
receives fixed payments for a lifetime or a
specified number of years.*

THE AMERICAN HERITAGE DICTIONARY,
SECOND COLLEGE EDITION, 1985

An annuity is a written contract between an annuity contract owner, an annuitant, and an insurance company. Frequently, the contract owner and the annuitant are the same individual. The contract can be for accumulation of capital without current income taxation, or for the distribution of capital over some period of time, life, or lives, or for both accumulation and distribution.

More people are beginning to think of an annuity as a distribution plan during retirement, a series of payments for life, or a way to receive monthly income from a pension plan. With lifetime annuitization, a sum of money is paid out as continual income with the assurance that the payments will go on for the rest of the annuitant's life. At present it has been reported that less than 1 percent of annuities ever annuitize. The other 99 percent are merely asking for withdrawals from their contracts on an as-needed basis. In the *lifetime annuitization mode*, an annuitant can protect against the risk of running out of income during life. The economic risk of living too long is a growing concern as a result of people living longer. A generation of pre-retirees are becoming more and more concerned that their parents may run out of money or have a severely diminished standard of living as a result of the dramatically increasing cost-of-living during their 30-plus years of retirement. Many of their parents retired with social security and pension plans and felt much more secure the day they retired than they do now. With 20/20 hindsight, had their parents used a portion of their capital when they retired to purchase a joint and 100 percent to the survivor variable annuity, they would be better off today. As retirees and their grandchildren quickly learn, it is not the size of your pile that makes you rich; it is the amount of your ever-replaceable income. We must all keep in mind that one of the most devastating risks we face is outliving our income.

Annuities, in their payment mode, can protect us from outliving our income. However, that is just half the story. Annuities also may be accumulation and investment vehicles.

If you want to use the annuity contract as a payout vehicle, you purchase an *immediate annuity*. You give the insurance company a lump sum of money, and the company will commence making periodic payments in accordance with your instructions within a period of time, usually ranging from 1 month after deposit to as long as 1 year after deposit.

Alternatively, you can use the *deferred annuity* as an income tax–deferred accumulation vehicle by making deposits—a series of deposits or irregular deposits. You then ask the insurance company to invest those funds on your behalf until further notice, with the objective of earning the highest return possible consistent with your risk-tolerance level.

In the pages that follow, we will deal with annuity contracts in terms of both functions, as payout vehicles and as accumulation vehicles. Exhibit 14.1 is a decision tree that helps in selecting an annuity contract appropriate for the contract owner's objectives and risk tolerance.

IMMEDIATE ANNUITIES: PAYOUT VEHICLES

The purpose of purchasing an immediate annuity is to protect yourself and your spouse against the risk of running out of income during life or, alternatively, to assure a series of payments for a

EXHIBIT 14.1

Annuities

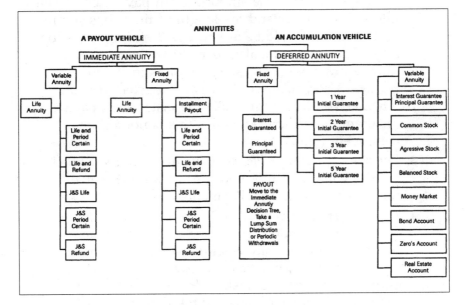

fixed period of time or in a fixed amount. The first decision you have to make when purchasing an immediate annuity is the choice between a *fixed* and *variable* annuity.

Fixed Immediate Annuities

The fixed immediate annuity provides fixed-dollar periodic payments as a result of a deposit. It gives you a safe, secure feeling that, for example, the $1000-per-month check will be arriving every month for the time period chosen. After deciding on a fixed annuity, you will be asked what guarantees you would like regarding the annuity's continued payment of checks in the event of the annuitant's death.

The immediate annuity guarantees available are as follows.

1. *Installment payment—fixed amount.* You dictate the amount, and the insurance company tells you how long it will be paid, no matter whether you live or die. This is not a life-contingent option.

2. *Installment payment—fixed period.* You dictate the period of time for the periodic payments, and the insurance company tells you the amount it can pay based on the interest it will pay and the length of time chosen. The period chosen could be as short as 2 months or as long as you desire (payments must satisfy the company's minimum payment rules, e.g., no less than $20 per payment). Payments continue for the fixed period whether you live or die. Like the installment payment–fixed amount described above, this is not a life-contingent option.

3. *Life annuity (straight life, pure annuity).* Your specified income continues until your death. (Risk: Receive 1 month's payment. Die: Payments terminate.)

4. *Life and period certain (10 or 20 years).* This is similar to the preceding option. The payments continue for your life; however, you may wish to assure that someone other than the insurance company benefits if you die early. The company is instructed to make the payments to your named beneficiary for the remainder of the guarantee period, at least 10 or 20 years, even if you die before that time.

5. *Life and refund certain.* In this case, you again are trying to protect against early termination of payments in the event that you die before you at least get your principal back. The company is instructed to pay you for life. However, should you die early, the company is instructed to refund your deposit in continuing monthly payments to your named beneficiary until the amount of deposit is returned. If it is a cash refund, the payout will be the discounted present value of the future payments.

6. *Joint and survivor life annuity.* The annuity pays for the whole of the lives of two individuals. It continues to provide level payments until the death of the second-to-die annuitant. Variations of this form of payout include a joint and 75 percent survivor annuity, in which the surviving annuitant will receive 75 percent of the

original monthly payment, and joint and 50 percent survivor annuity.

7. *Joint and survivor life annuity with period certain.* This is to protect against the early termination of payments if both of the annuitants die early. The insurance company is instructed to continue payments until the death of the last to die, with a minimum payout period of at least 10 or 20 years.

8. *Joint and survivor life annuity with refund certain.* This protects against the early termination of payments due to the death of both annuitants. If both the annuitants die, the insurance company is instructed to refund the remaining balance of the deposit by continuing monthly payments to the named beneficiary until the amount deposited is returned. If it is to be a cash refund, the payout is the discounted present value of the remaining payments.

Fixed Immediate Annuity Cost

The cost of an immediate annuity is primarily dependent on the prevailing level of interest rates at the time it is purchased, for it is at that time the insurance company will invest the reserves to guarantee the payments promised by the contract. The insurance company expects to use up the reserves and the interest earned on those reserves over your lifetime. Within the insurance company's total life annuity business, certain annuitants will die before the reserves are expended. This makes up for the annuitants who live beyond their life expectancy, and those reserves will be used to assure their continued life income. The annuitants get peace of mind. Now it is the insurance company's problem to deal with the fact that they may live as long as their parents, or longer. The annuitants know their income will continue for life. The insurance company factors in the costs associated with issuing the contract and an allowance for profit. What you pay to purchase the annuity can be influenced by where you live. Each state may have different rules regarding what annuities can be offered to the residents of that state and the costs of those annuities (see Exhibit

EXHIBIT 14.2

Immediate Annuity Purchase State Taxes

	Nonqualified Annuities, %	Qualified Immediate Annuities, %
Alabama	1.00	1.00
California	2.35	0.5
District of Columbia	2.25	2.25
Kansas	2.00	0
Kentucky	2.00	2.00
Maine	2.00	0
Nevada	3.50	0
South Dakota	1.25	0
West Virginia	1.00	1.00
Wyoming	1.00	0

14.2). You may find the annuity you want is not available to you in your state or costs more or less than it does in another state. For instance, some states levy a tax on annuity contracts. The point of all this is that you will find the cost of purchasing an annuity for some ages in the following pages, but you must not depend on them being accurate for you. These rates are only given so that you can see the relative costs of an annuity that stops when you die and an annuity that continues paying after your death.

In addition to the variations of availability and cost from state to state, immediate annuities today may depend upon your health. Now don't complain. Think about it. You just got turned down for life insurance or long-term care insurance. You are worried about income and long-term care, and your folks were not considered healthy either, but they lived well into their nineties. You were going to buy a long-term care policy that would pay $100 per day, $36,500 per year. Now, you go to an annuity company and cough and look as unhealthy as you can. They offer you an income of $36,500 per year for life, starting now, for the rest of your life. The cost would have been about $400,000 if you were a 65-year-old healthy male. However, because the insurance company estimates your life span is 5 years less, the cost for the same income is reduced to $360,000. So you buy the annuity and take your $100 per day now, and then join a health group that extends your active quality of life. Things could be worse. Again, the point is that we do not know how much an immediate annuity might cost you or be worth to you. It is a financial product that makes many people sleep better at night, and the income improves their standard of living and quality of life.

Fixed-Period and Fixed-Amount Installment Annuities

You may direct the insurance company to make payments for fixed specific dollar amounts at equal intervals until both principal and interest are exhausted or, alternatively, for a fixed period of time. The time chosen would determine the amount of each payment. These annuities are useful in situations where there is an income tax liability on a lump sum that otherwise would be distributed and taxed all in 1 year. You can spread the tax liability over a period of years convenient for the annuitant, e.g., 5 years. Also, you can purchase such contracts for a specific purpose, such as an annuity payment commencing when a parent enters a nursing home to assure payments for a specified period.

Whenever funds are needed to provide for a specific need, an annuity can be designed to provide those funds. But there is one caution: The Tax Reform Act of 1986 imposed a 10 percent penalty tax on any annuity distributions to an annuitant prior to age 59½ not based on life contingencies. Fixed-period and fixed-amount installments are *not* life-contingent annuities.

Life Annuity, Straight Life Annuity, Pure Annuity

The process of selecting from among life annuity alternatives starts with a question to the insurance company: "I want a $1000 check every month for the rest of my life. I am 65. What will such a contract cost me, and what alternatives are available to me?"

A life annuity costs the least. In other words, this type of annuity will provide the largest possible monthly payment based on a given deposit. It is low in cost because of the high risk of the loss of capital. The risk in a life annuity is that if you die prior to the time the deposit in the annuity has been used up, the balance of the deposit is forfeited to the insurance company or pension plan from which it was being paid. This would occur even if only one monthly check had been paid prior to your death. Most buyers of annuities consider this too great a risk. They want greater safety and assurance that the payout stream will continue to their beneficiaries in the event of their deaths.

Life and Period Certain Annuity

This is one method of assuring the continuation of the payout stream in the event of the primary annuitant's death. Under this election, you would purchase a guarantee of payments for some minimum time period, such as 10 or 20 years. In Exhibit 14.3, you will note that this guarantee increases the purchase price of the annuity by about 6 percent for a 10-year minimum guarantee and about 22 percent for a 20-year guarantee. The purchaser is buying insurance that costs $8039 ($136,695 − $128,656 − $143,825 = $8039) to assure that payments continue for at least 10 years, or $26,778 ($155,434 − $128,656 = $26,778) to assure that payments continue for 20 years.

Life and Refund Certain Annuity

Under this alternative you elect to receive a life income. However, if you don't live long enough to receive all the principal, it will be refunded to your named beneficiary in continued monthly in-

E X H I B I T   14.3

Costs for Single-Life Annuities Providing $1000 per Month for Life (Male Age 65)*

Type	Cost to Purchase	Increase
A life annuity	$128,656	
Life 10-years certain	136,695	6.2%
Life refund certain	139,836	8.7%
Life 20-years certain	155,434	21.0%

*Representative 2000 rates.

stallments or in a cash settlement (discounted present value of the payments due).

Joint and Survivor Life Annuity

The joint and survivor life annuity is designed to function as an assured payout vehicle during the lives of two people. It is to continue the level monthly payments through the life of the last to die. It normally is used by married couples for pension income to ensure that the income stream will not terminate at the death of the first annuitant.

Under the joint and survivor annuity option, there also are a number of alternatives. A refund certain or period certain guarantee could be selected for 10 to 20 years. You may adjust the continued payments to the surviving annuitant consistent with the survivor's needs. During both the annuitants' lives, the income will be one amount, but after the death of the first, that income could be reduced to 75 percent, 66 percent, or 50 percent of the amount of the original payment. Such an election reduces the cost for the income guaranteed. For instance, to assure $1000 *level* payments for both lives, the cost is $165,375 (see Exhibit 14.4)

Alternatively, providing only $500 per month to the survivor reduces the cost to $141,333, a saving of $24,042. The extra $24,042 could be used to increase the monthly payments to $1,170, leaving $585 to the survivor, if such an arrangement fits the couple's needs.

EXHIBIT 14.4

Costs for Joint Life Annuities Providing $1000 per Month for Life (Male Age 65, Female Age 62)*

Type	Cost to Purchaser	Cost Difference
Joint and survivor life	$165,375	100%
Joint and survivor refund	166,649	100.77%
Joint and 75% to the survivor	153,354	92.7%
Joint and 66% to the survivor	149,026	90.1%
Joint and 50% to the survivor	141,333	85.5%

*Representative 2000 rates.

If you have determined that the greatest need for income is while both annuitants are living, and that the single surviving annuitant will not have as great a need, then this reduction in income to the survivor may be appropriate. The problem is inflation. Enough today is often not enough for tomorrow!

Exhibit 14.5 illustrates the annuity income that could be purchased with a deposit of $100,000 in 2001 for a male age 65 and also the joint and survivor annuity income that could be purchased for annuitant and spouse age 62. For illustration purposes, we have assumed that they will be in the 28 percent tax bracket. The temptation when looking at this exhibit is to convert the annual income figures to a percentage return on the $100,000 of capital invested. That, of course, is invalid, because what is being paid out is a combination of both interest and principal. It would be misleading to calculate percentage return in that fashion.

However, from a practical standpoint, you may purchase an annuity because you cannot afford to live on just the interest earnings of your $100,000 of capital. You may be reluctant to invest aggressively to earn higher yields for fear of losing your capital during that time. It may be very comforting to seek the shelter of

EXHIBIT 14.5

Annual Incomes Purchased by an Immediate Life Annuity Investment of $100,000

Male Age 65*	Gross Annuity Annual Income	Percentage Tax-Free
Life income	$9,324	53.6
Life income refund certain	$8,581	59.6
Life income 10-years certain	$8,779	54
Life income 20-years certain	$7,720	53.1
Male Age 65, Female Age 62		
Joint and survivor 100% to the survivor	$7,256	52
Joint and survivor refund certain	$7,201	52.4
Joint and survivor 75% to the survivor	$7,825	53.6
Joint and survivor 66% to the survivor	$8,052	54.2
Joint and survivor 50% to the survivor	$8,491	55.6

*Representative 2000 Rates

an annuity that promises an income stream that cannot terminate during your lifetime. Your security would be in a constant stream of freely usable, ever-replaceable income rather than capital sitting in a bank providing fluctuating interest.

As you review the net after-tax spendable income from the investment of $100,000, you may have one of two reactions. You may think that it assures a pretty good income for the rest of your life, or you may think that you could generate that much income today with $100,000 in some other investment. Your reaction will be based upon the currently available interest rates. In an economic environment in which prevailing short-term interest rates are relatively high, you are not likely to find the annuity principle very appealing. Also, the younger you are, the less appealing it will be. However, in an economic environment in which prevailing interest rates are fairly low, it may look pretty good to you. The reason for this is that when an insurance company guarantees a fixed income for the life of an annuitant, it is looking at a long-term obligation that must be conservatively met with long-term investments. In short, the company must forecast prevailing interest rates available for this block of capital (your investment) for the rest of your life. It will do so in a conservative fashion and will likely use long-term bonds and mortgages as a reserve for the annuity liability, i.e., its obligation to pay you.

OBTAINING ANNUITY QUOTES

Insurance company annuity rates are competitive and constantly changing. The rates shown in these Exhibits (Exhibits 14.3, 14.4, and 14.5) are based on the prevailing rates effective November 2000. You would be wise to shop carefully for your general account fixed annuities and to look not only for a competitive rate, but also for a *quality company* that can be expected to perform well *for the rest of your life.* You probably would not even consider an immediate-payout life annuity unless you expected to live a long time, and so company selection is very important because future performance will have to be good. There are people out there who did not heed this warning and have had their life income payments interrupted, at best, or lost them, at worst, because of insurance company failures. Remember, once a contract is annu-

E X H I B I T   14.6

Immediate Fixed Annuity Quote Request

Date of birth _____	Sex _____
If joint: Date of birth _____	Sex _____
Marginal tax bracket _____	State of residence _____
Single	Monthly life
consideration _____ and/or	income _____

Nonqualified (personal) funds _____
Qualified funds (from an IRA or other qualified retirement plan) _____
Insurance company will receive the proceeds by _____ (date).
Please commence payout of the proceeds by _____ (date).
We are interested in applying for an impaired risk annuity. _____ Yes _____ No
Please mail the information to:
Name: _____
Address: _____
_____
Phone number: _____
Fax number: _____
E-mail address: _____

itized (payments have commenced), there may be no turning back; there are no 1035 exchanges, and you *are* dependent on the company you have chosen. When your employer terminates a retirement plan and funds your benefits by buying an immediate-payout annuity, the insurance company risk is being transferred to you. Make sure you have some say in where the employer buys your annuity contract. If you would like to find out what income may be available to you, you may obtain quotes from insurance companies by providing the information shown in Exhibit 14.6 to any company that sells annuities.

Exclusion Ratio (Nonqualified Annuities)

You may purchase *nonqualified annuities* [obtained using after-tax capital rather than pretax capital in retirement plans such as deductible IRAs and 401(k) plans]. A greater portion of your annuity income is usable than if you were living on interest income alone. That is because a part of your income is the return of your personal after-tax capital which is factored into the federal income tax exclusion ratio. The proportion of the annuity income that is tax-free (the return of capital) is determined in accordance with Section 72 of the Internal Revenue Code.

The exclusion ratio is determined by dividing the *investment in the contract* by the *expected return* as of the annuity starting date, the day the income stream commences. You might invest $60,000 in an annuity and expect $100,000 as the payout. Therefore, 60 percent of each payment would be a nontaxable return of capital, while the balance would be taxable interest.

$$\text{Exclusion ratio} = \frac{\text{investment}}{\text{expected return}}$$

$$= \frac{\$60,000}{\$100,000} = 60\% \text{ exclusion ratio}$$

60% × $1000 = $600, which is income tax–free

Exclusion ratio × payment received

= amount excluded from taxation

You know the investment you have put into the contract. However, determining the expected return is complicated by the fact that no one knows how long you are going to live. If we assume you're not going to live long, this would result in a greater portion of your payments being tax-free return of principal. You might be trying to prove to Uncle Sam how sick you are to minimize your income taxes.

To solve this problem, the IRS has provided four life-expectancy tables in Internal Revenue Regulation Section 1.72. These are to be used in determining expected returns. Exclusion ratios vary depending upon the type of annuity purchased. The higher the guaranteed return of capital after the death of the annuitant, the lower the exclusion ratio. It will also vary based upon the age and sex of the annuitant.

The exclusion ratio results in a greater portion of your income stream being usable income, because it is not subject to current income taxes. A comparable stream of fully taxable income would result in increased taxes, thus reducing your spendable income.

Exclusion Ratio TRA-86 Change

One final point concerning the taxation of annuity income: One of the advantages of the annuity was the federal income tax exclusion ratio. In the above examples it was approximately 60 percent of the annuity income. This exclusion ratio used to apply throughout the annuitant's lifetime. Therefore, even if you lived far be-yond the time predicted in the life expectancy tables, and had gotten all your tax-free principal back, you continued to receive approximately 60 percent of your income without taxation throughout your lifetime. The Tax Reform Act of 1986 changed this situation for annuities not yet annuitized on January 1, 1987. Under that law, once the annuitant has received the investment back without taxation, the exclusion ratio ceases to apply. Pay-ments continuing beyond that point are taxed entirely as ordinary income. In our example, this would result in increased income tax for the annuitants at approximately age 85. This means that in-dividuals who have lived on a level monthly income unadjusted for inflation for 20 years, who took the annuity because of their need for spendable income, will be blindsided by Uncle Sam with additional income tax at age 85. Do you suppose our politicians will use those additional tax dollars for the indigent elderly? The politicians' mothers should know what they have done to them!

VARIABLE IMMEDIATE ANNUITY

With fixed annuities, the insurance company accepts the mortality risk, the expense risk, and the interest risk and you accept the purchasing power risk. With the variable annuity, you trade in-terest guarantees for variable, increasing (we hope) payments, which leaves the mortality and expense risks with the insurance company.

A variable annuity is one in which the periodic payments received from the contract vary with the investment experience of the underlying investment vehicle. The variable immediate an-nuity was developed to answer the problem of conventional fixed annuities. The purchasing power of a conventional-payment fixed annuity is eroded by inflation. It was hoped that the variable an-nuity, with a fluctuating income based on its underlying equity accounts, would adjust itself to current purchasing power and off-set the eroding effects of inflation on annuity income. The variable immediate annuity can accomplish this objective, but not without risk to the annuitant. The risk is that the payments can decrease as well as increase. Keep in mind that once you annuitize, there may be no turning back. The inflexibility of annuitization has led many to shun them. As a result, more and more companies are building liquidity provisions into their contracts and allowing for changes even after annuitization has begun.

The Teacher's Insurance and Annuity Association (TIAA) and the College Retirement Equities Fund (CREF) are *nonprofit* organizations providing insurance and annuities to academic personnel. These organizations did a great deal to develop the concept of the variable annuity and were the original source of such contracts. They fought the original regulatory battles starting in 1952. In 1959, the variable annuity contract became subject to dual supervision by the Securities and Exchange Commission and the state insurance departments.

The investment vehicle in a variable immediate annuity has to be a property that is easy to purchase and sell and that moves with the economy, reflecting the general economic trend on a long-term basis. TIAA's extensive studies covering common stock history from 1880 to 1952 showed that common stock was closest to the ideal investment vehicle. More recent studies confirm this conclusion.

The market for variable *immediate* annuities is currently small but is expected to increase as the baby boomers deal with their retirement income problems. Trying to live on a lump sum of money left from a 401(k) plan can be stressful and difficult. It is likely that those with extreme longevity in their families will opt to have some portion of their income guaranteed for life and capable of standing up to inflation. They will, in effect, buy a pension. The annuity payout principle typically appealed to conservative older individuals who had a substantial need for income and a desire to ensure that the income will not terminate during their lifetimes. It was relatively unusual to find this same risk-averse individual willing to have funds paid out as a variable annuity, because there is the potential for a decrease in income as well as the hoped-for reward of increased income. The baby boomers have watched their parents live a lot longer than their parents expected and watched their parents' pensions that were sufficient when they retired become insufficient to maintain their standard of living. That lesson will not be lost. It will cause more and more people to have a portion of their retirement income provided by variable annuities. The exploding market for variable annuities is currently in the accumulation annuity arena. As the owners of those accumulation annuities reach retirement, it is expected that the insurance industry will make annuitization, both fixed and variable, more and more attractive to minimize your financial concerns. Variable annuitization is not without risk, however.

In an actual case, Aunt Gen deposited $15,288.80 on March 15, 1972, with an insurance company. She was guaranteed a variable monthly income starting at $100 per month, based on the number of units she purchased. As those units varied in value, so did her monthly income. Starting in 1974, the stock market dropped more than 40 percent over a period of 21 months, causing a drop in the underlying investment account of her annuity, and the monthly payments dipped to a low of $63 in 1974. By the time the last payment was made when Aunt Gen died in October 1986, the monthly payment was up to $234. An ironic twist of this particular variable annuity was that by the time the 1980s arrived, and the monthly payments were consistently over $100 per month, most of Aunt Gen's other assets had been used up. Her fear of running out of assets prior to her death was realized. Her annuity income and social security were about all that was available, and as a result she lived in low-income housing. Every time she received an increase in her monthly payment from the variable annuity, the low-income housing authorities raised her rent an equivalent amount. All she would have needed to complete the picture would have been loss of her exclusion ratio and the increased taxation Uncle Sam imposed on post–January 1, 1987 annuitants who managed to live long enough to receive a full return of basis. The actual results from Aunt Gen's immediate variable annuity contract are shown in Exhibit 14.7.

Variable Immediate Nonqualified Annuity Exclusion Ratio

The exclusion ratio for a variable immediate annuity is determined in a similar fashion to that used for fixed annuities. However, you run into the complication of not knowing your "expected return" since your income will vary based upon the actual performance of stock investments supporting the annuity pay-

EXHIBIT 14.7

Variable Immediate Annuity with Period Certain
Actual Case: February 28, 1972–October 28, 1986

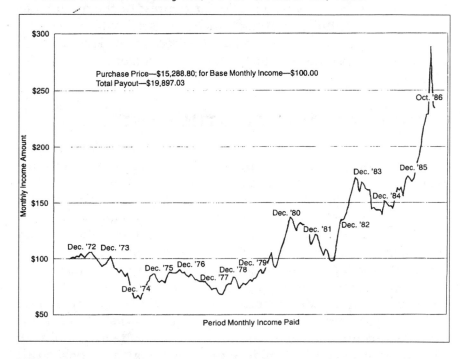

Purchase Price—$15,288.80; for Base Monthly Income—$100.00
Total Payout—$19,897.03

ments. Payments will vary, probably with each check. Life expectancy tables that the government provides dictate that you can recover your investment (cost basis) over your life expectancy (the tables are provided in Exhibits 13.21 and 13.22). The procedure is to take your life expectancy in years and divide it into your cost basis to determine "how much" rather than what percentage you can recover tax-free each year. If you ever have a particularly bad year and receive an amount of income less than the amount you can recover tax-free, you are allowed to continue your recoveries until such time that 100 percent of your investment in the contract has been recovered.

If you outlive the annuity tables, there may come a time when you have received your entire cost basis back from your annuity contract. When that time arrives, all subsequent payments will be subject to ordinary income tax in their entirety. As noted earlier, this rule was incorporated in the Tax Reform Act of 1986 and applies to annuities that had not been annuitized as of January 1, 1987. Annuity contracts that had been annuitized before that date enjoy the exclusion ratio for the rest of the annuitant's life and may continue to exclude the same percentage even after the annuitant's entire cost basis has been recovered. The rule adds an additional income tax burden for senior citizens in their mid-eighties.

IMMEDIATE ANNUITY ACTION LETTER

Now that you have a basic understanding of immediate annuity contracts, it's time to go shopping. The appropriate annuity depends upon your objectives and those of your spouse, in addition to your health situation and the capital available. With all this in mind, you need to know the actual dollar amounts the annuity could provide to you in your situation. This information is easy to obtain by adapting the action letter (Exhibit 14.8) to your personal situation and sending it to the insurance companies from whom you would consider purchasing an annuity contract. Based upon the information you provide, they will be happy to give you a quote to provide you, free of charge, information regarding what their contracts will do for you. Don't hesitate to ask all your questions; you need to understand what you are considering buying.

The information you gather as a result of sending the action letter will assist you in making a decision regarding your employer-provided retirement plan options. It also will give you the information you need in order to purchase an immediate annuity. Discuss the plans that seem to meet your family objectives with your financial advisors and insurance professional. Since interest rates change frequently, the quotes that you receive will only be valid for a short period of time. Last month's quote—or even last week's—may no longer be good today.

An immediate fixed annuity contract is relatively simple because it is so inflexible. It promises you only how much you are going to receive, how often you are going to receive it, and for how long. Therefore, you will be looking for the maximum amount of income based on the guarantees that you require from

EXHIBIT 14.8

Immediate Annuity Action Letter

To Whom It May Concern:
I am considering the purchase of an immediate annuity contract. I am interested in purchasing a single-premium immediate *fixed/variable* annuity contract. The annuitant is a male / female born _____. I also would like a quote on a male / female born _____.

In addition to the above quotes, I would like a quote on a joint life annuity for a male / female born _____and a male / female born _____. We are residents of the state of _____, and our personal marginal state and federal income tax bracket is _____%. Please base your quotes on a single consideration of $ _____and / or a monthly income of $ _____per month. The monies that I would be investing in this immediate annuity contract are coming from my personal funds / IRA funds /TSA funds / lump-sum distribution from my employer's qualified retirement plan or _____.

For quote purposes, please assume the insurance company would receive these proceeds by _____ [date]. I would ask that my monthly payments begin _____ [date]. (This date should be at least one month after the date that the insurance company receives the proceeds.)

Please provide me with quotes from _____ [number of] insurance companies and send all the financial ratings available on each insurance company that is providing a quote.

Mail the information to me at the following address. I will call you with my questions after I have had a chance to review the information. If you have any questions, please call me at _____.

Thank you very much for your assistance.
Sincerely,
Name
Address
Phone number
Fax number
E-mail address

an insurance company (that you are sure is going to last as long as you do).

FIXED DEFERRED ANNUITIES

Fixed deferred annuities are invested in the general account of the insurance company that guarantees the principal and pays a current rate of interest. These were very popular in the 1980s and 1990s when interest rates were high. As interest rates have come down and as the returns on stocks have continued to be generous, their popularity has diminished. Many who purchased deferred annuities were not the least bit concerned about *annuitizing* their annuity, that is, changing it into an immediate annuity. Their primary concern was to accumulate as much wealth as possible within the contract. They may have purchased it just because the interest rates offered initially were higher than they could get at the bank. This has led to some being disappointed in the product. In the years after initial issue the interest rate paid by the insurance company may have been less than what was available in the current marketplace; but because the annuity had contingent deferred sales charges (back-end loads), the policyholders could not move their money to the higher-interest-rate alternatives.

The inside buildup in an annuity is not subject to current taxation when owned by an individual. Your returns are not diminished by income taxes, which is the key to the deferred annuity's appeal. There is no reason to make deposits to a nondeductible IRA when, if you do, you're limited to a maximum of $2000 per year, and are required to fill out special income tax forms, make special annual tax calculations at eventual payout, and continue to account for those nondeductible contributions for the rest of your life. Why not use a deferred annuity or Roth IRA, if you qualify, and thus avoid these problems? The fixed deferred annuity can provide the following benefits.

1. *Safety.* The insurance company offering a general account fixed annuity guarantees the originally invested capital. Pick carefully among highly rated companies, because fixed annuities are part of the insurance company's general account and subject to the general creditors of

the insurance company. Your guarantee is only as good as your guarantor. Always be aware of expenses and the restrictions of back-end loads.

2. *Liquidity/marketability.* You may recover the capital invested subject to insurance company back-end loads, current taxation on interest earnings in the contract, and a 10 percent penalty if you are less than 59 ½ years old.

3. *Tax benefits.* Taxation is deferred on the interest until withdrawal, at which time ordinary income tax will be due on all earnings. This is identical to the benefits of the nondeductible IRA.

4. *Flexibility.* All the *immediate* annuity payout options previously discussed are available to you with the accumulation in your deferred annuity, which could be an advantage in an old annuity that provides lifetime payouts based upon old life expectancy tables.

You have the right to make tax-free 1035 exchanges from one annuity contract to another. You may also make a tax-free exchange from a life insurance policy to an annuity, but you may not make a tax-free exchange from an annuity to a life insurance policy.

Deferred annuities come in all varieties. There are single-premium deferred annuities, scheduled-premium deferred annuities (the contract states how much and how often you must pay premiums), and flexible-premium annuities.

The old-fashioned scheduled-premium contract, which required a stated premium at stated times, has fallen out of favor. Its mandatory nature, loads, and penalties for not maintaining payments are unappealing. Single-premium deferred annuities, although marketable and popular, have an unappealing lack of flexibility. There is market appeal for the concept of *single* premium (i.e., no additional payments being required); therefore, marketing departments have been promoting those single-premium annuities that *can accept* additional premiums ("non-single-premium" single premiums). This may be a new definition of *market-driven.* Ask the market what it wants, and then tell it that the product you have on the shelf is just that.

In today's marketplace, annuity contracts with the greatest

appeal give the annuitant the option of making payments when convenient and in amounts determined by the annuitant—in other words, flexible-premium deferred annuities.

SINGLE-PREMIUM DEFERRED ANNUITIES

Single-premium, interest-only deferred annuities appeal to the individual who has a lump sum of capital available at a specific time and who is seeking the highest possible interest rate without current income taxation. Buyers often compare the single-premium, interest-only deferred annuity vehicle with certificates of deposit.

When contemplating a single-premium deferred annuity purchase, you will want to check the following features.

1. *The company issuing the contract.* The financial strength and track record of the insurance company are of paramount importance in today's financial world. An annuity contract is only successful when the relationship is long term, i.e., lifetime.

2. *Current interest rate if you choose a fixed annuity. Or investment accounts, investment management, and competitive current interest and guaranteed principal accounts if you are choosing a variable annuity.*

3. *Guarantee period for the guaranteed interest rate.*

4. *Minimum guaranteed rate of interest after the initial guarantee period is completed.*

5. *Bailout provisions.* These provisions allow you to surrender the annuity contract without penalty if the interest rate falls below a contractually stated amount.

6. *Cost of bailout provision.* That is, do you have the option of accepting higher interest and no bailout provision or lower initial interest with a bailout provision?

7. *Interest rate track record.* Interest rate track records for fixed annuities are as important as investment account track records for variable annuities. You will want to check the interest rate renewal rates after the first contract year. Make sure the company keeps its rates

competitive rather than enticing you in with a high rate just to lower it in the future while you are prevented from leaving as a result of surrender charges.

8. *Free withdrawal privilege.* How much cash can you withdraw from a contract each year without being subject to company-imposed withdrawal charges? Withdrawal from any annuity would be subject to income taxes to the extent of gain and a 10 percent penalty if taken prior to age 59½.

9. *Front-end charges.* Are sales charges applied against your initial deposit, thereby reducing it?

10. *Surrender charges (back-end loads).* What percentage of the annuity would be left with the insurance company to cover deferred sales charges if you surrendered the annuity, and at what point would such surrender charges no longer exist?

11. *Surrender charges waived.* Under what circumstances are the surrender charges waived—death, disability, long-term care, an annuity payout?

12. *Market value adjustment.* If the annuity contract is surrendered, is the surrender value adjusted as a result of changes in prevailing interest rates? This would be typical of a variable-annuity bond account. It is found in some fixed annuities and can cause surprises if you do not make sure you know how it works.

13. *The situation for your named beneficiary.* With fixed annuities, it would be unusual for there to be a situation where the amount to be paid out to your beneficiary is less than the amount invested. However, with variable annuities, a significant drop in the stock market could expose an annuitant-owner to significant principal risk. You will find with most variable annuities that the beneficiary will receive the annuity at market value or the owner's gross investments in the contract, whichever is greater. The death benefit offered to the beneficiaries has become a competitive feature. Companies will now ratchet the death benefit up over time in different ways to make their contract more

competitive. You can expect to find approximately a ¼ percent charge for this guarantee within the prospectus for the variable annuity.

14. *Guaranteed minimum income benefits.* Another competitive feature that has gained popularity in variable annuities is the guaranteed minimum income benefit. Insurance companies observed that contract owners with significant balances in their contracts invested very conservatively because of their fear of market losses. As a result the insurance companies now offer a guaranteed minimum lifetime income based upon some minimum fixed return if the contract owner leaves the contract capital in the equity accounts for some minimum period of time, such as 7 years. To the contract owner this is like a guaranteed minimum pension benefit that you can fall back on if your equity investment does not do well. This underlying guarantee gives you the courage to remain fully invested, which should cause your investments to do well. The insurance company will likely charge you about ¼ of 1 percent per year for this guarantee.

15. *Annual and other fees.* If there are other fees, you will want to know how much and what for.

16. *Commission paid, if any.* You will want to know what impact commissions (if there are any) will have on your account. A segment of the insurance industry markets its products to agents based upon the high commission it pays them as opposed to the value the product provides to you, the consumer. You will want to avoid that type of product because you pay all the expenses.

FLEXIBLE-PREMIUM DEFERRED VARIABLE ANNUITIES

These contracts are recommended because they give you the option of making payments when convenient and in amounts that you determine. Flexible-premium deferred variable annuities offer you many different types of investment accounts. They can have investment accounts that guarantee principal and interest similar to a fixed annuity, while offering you the flexibility of adding to that account in the future if you want to do so. In other words, you could have your flexible-premium variable annuity emulate a single-premium fixed annuity by directing your investment to a guaranteed interest account within the variable annuity and choosing to make only a single payment. In most cases, the variable contract with flexible-premium options offers you greater opportunity to adjust the contract to changing future needs.

Flexible-premium deferred variable annuities also offer various investment funds that range from common stock accounts of the aggressive, blue-chip, and balanced varieties, to bond funds, zero coupons, Ginnie Maes, and real estate accounts. You have the option of moving among these funds, switching your contributions and accumulations from one fund to the other, and managing the fund in accordance with your particular objectives.

However, these accounts may contain restrictions on your ability to move funds, such as limitations on the number of moves you can make during a particular time period or charges for making moves from one account to another. People who fear the stock market love the ability to put their money into a guaranteed interest account and then just move their interest into the stock accounts each month. This strategy assures that they will have no loss to their principal investment, and can still participate in stock market gains. Since a variable annuity is similar to mutual fund investing, you will also be interested in the performance of the investment divisions and their management.

The features to be evaluated in variable deferred annuities are these:

1. Professional management
2. Investment diversification (the availability of various investment alternatives)
3. Flexible payments (including the opportunity to dollar-cost-average with small deposits and minimum expense)
4. Economy of investing and reasonableness of management fees
5. The variety of payout options available to conform future withdrawals with future needs

The disadvantages of flexible-premium deferred annuities occur when they are purchased or sold inappropriately or when they are subject to excessive expenses. If you buy an annuity without being aware of the tax consequences, it may cost you at withdrawal, annuitization, or death. If you buy the annuity with the highest interest rate available, without consideration of the other features within the contract or the company behind it, you may set yourself up for a disappointment. The customers in the fixed annuities of Baldwin United (not related to the author), Executive Life, Mutual Benefit, etc., went for long periods of time not knowing when their capital may be made available to them, let alone if they would receive any interest on that capital.

Accumulation Units

When you buy into a deferred variable annuity, the purchase of the accumulation unit is similar to the purchase of a share in a mutual fund. Your money arrives at the insurance company, and the company calculates the value of the account accumulation unit at the "closing price" the day the money is received or the next business day of the New York Stock Exchange. Your money purchases units of the fund based on that unit value. This procedure is referred to as *forward pricing* to distinguish it from the way stock is purchased based on a quoted price prior to the receipt of payment.

INVESTMENT RESULTS
IN VARIABLE ANNUITIES

Variable annuities are similar to fixed annuities. They have the same policy forms, general provisions, and nonforfeiture rights. The settlement options and option tables, actuarial principles, and mortality and expense assumptions are the same. They are subject to similar income tax treatment but differ in underlying investment vehicle. With a variable annuity you accept the investment risk and responsibility, and the insurance company acts as a conduit to pass the investment results on to you.

You purchase accumulation units during the deferred or accumulation annuity stage and receive annuity units at the time you direct the insurance company to annuitize the contract, establishing the payout and/or time guarantees.

VARIABLE ANNUITY SELECTION

Flexible-premium *variable* annuities are the only type of annuity that this book recommends Single-pocket, interest-only annuities are things of the past. The world and your needs change too often to select one investment and think that you will be happy with it for the rest of your life. You must have flexibility, and you must retain control over your investments. You must have multiple-pocket contracts (multiple investments including general account investment options and separate account investments), so that you can make your insurance investments adapt to your needs now and in the future. Put another way, what is suitable for you today because of your circumstances may not be suitable for you tomorrow as a result of changed circumstances. You need financial products that can be morphed to be suitable for you at any time.

When evaluating a variable annuity, keep in mind that your objective is long-term investment growth for your retirement. You have chosen the annuity in order to grow capital faster, since income taxation on interest, dividends, and most importantly capital gains taxes is deferred until you start using your money. Avoiding taxation on profits, as you sell out of very profitable accounts and move to less volatile accounts to safeguard your gains, is very important for two reasons. First, the hope is that your profits will provide a good percentage of your return and exceed the amount you will earn from interest and dividends. Second, if you have ever owned a stock or mutual fund that has increased substantially in value, what would keep you from selling it? Perhaps you don't want to sell it because you think it is going to go higher, or you don't want to sell it because you don't want to give about one-fifth of your profits to Uncle Sam. If you had hesitated and not sold an investment like this in September 1987 just before the 500-point drop in the Dow Jones Average (October 19, 1987), you would know how unwise it can be to let taxation drive your investment decisions. Investments inside variable annuities are not subject to taxation, so remove that from consideration in your annuity investment decisions. The ability to sell various subaccounts and buy into others without taxation or transaction costs is one of the most profitable of annuity features. As a result, you want subaccounts similar to mutual funds within your variable annuity that can accommodate your investment needs over a lifetime and that are profitably managed.

MANAGER OF MANAGERS

What if you were given the opportunity to invest without current income taxation, picking the best managers to manage your money within funds like T. Rowe Price, Scudder, MFS, Alger, Fidelity, Pioneer, Morgan Stanley Dean Witter, Alliance Capital, Janus, Evergreen, Capital Guardian, and Putnam. Your problem could be which ones to choose! Inside variable annuities and variable life insurance you have two levels of assistance working to solve that problem for you. First, the company bringing you the product searches the marketplace for the best managers from a list more extensive than the above to bring to you the best funds the company can find, and then it monitors performance and will replace those that are found lacking. Second, once one of these funds is put into the annuity, the fund company, such as Fidelity, does all it can to make sure its manager is doing the best job possible and will replace a manager if necessary. By the time the funds are brought to you for selection, two sets of professional have worked hard to bring you the best of the best.

SUBACCOUNT SELECTION

Morningstar publishes its *Morningstar Principia Pro* for variable annuity subaccounts, which are similar to mutual funds. This service provides you, or the professional assisting you, with information about the performance, features, and expenses of variable annuities. In mid-2001 its database consisted of 10,998 subaccounts in variable annuities. It is located on the web at www.morningstar.com. Many professionals have the Morningstar data on disk and make a business of helping you search for a variable annuity with acceptable costs, fund diversity, and good performance suitable for you. However, it would be good for you to have an understanding of the expenses and range of expenses you are likely to find in a variable annuity prior to seeking professional help.

EXHIBIT 14.9

Low	Average	Maximum
0.00%	1.29%	1.80%

INSURANCE EXPENSES

Insurance expenses, often referred to as M&E charges for mortality and expense, are charged against the investment subaccounts within your variable annuity (see Exhibit 14.9). These are charges made by the insurance company for the guarantees it provides within the annuity contract, such as a maximum guaranteed interest rate in the general account investment alternative. It also guarantees that in the event of death, the annuitant's beneficiary will receive the greater of the deposits in the contract or the account value, a protection against adverse investment results.

FUND EXPENSE

This may also be referred to as a *management fee* or *operating expense charge* (see Exhibit 14.10.) It is the expense charged against your subaccounts (mutual funds) for paying the fund managers and the operating expenses of the fund. It may not include the brokerage costs.

Note that bond funds within a high-expense variable annuity will not be able to do much for *you*, since their long-term rate of

EXHIBIT 14.10

Low	Average	High
0.00%	0.88%	5.16%

return is about equal to the expenses. It is important to be aware of these expenses as you invest in these products. You are looking for an acceptable net after-expense rate of return. If you have a general account investment within your variable annuity, the interest quoted normally is *net* rather than gross interest from which you have to deduct these charges, and so it may be a better alternative than a bond account, particularly in a potentially increasing interest rate environment.

TOTAL EXPENSE RATIO

The total expense ratio in deferred Variable Annuities, which combines the impact of both M & E and the fund expenses, is the expense ratio you would use to compare expenses inside annuities with the expenses of regular mutual funds and with those of VUL. The average expense ratio in the 10,998 variable annuity subaccounts that Morningstar tracked at year end 2000 is 2.16 percent (see Exhibit 14.11), whereas the average expense ratio in the 12,549 mutual funds it tracked is 1.37 percent. The total expense ratio for annuities averages 79 basis points more than that for regular mutual funds. This is a significant expense over a period of time. You will want to know what features in the annuity are worth this extra cost. When comparing the cost of an annuity with the cost of mutual funds that are subject to income taxes, the income tax savings alone may be enough to justify the additional cost to you. However, if your funds are already inside a tax shelter such as an IRA or 401(k), then the income tax shelter of the annuity is redundant and adds no value. As a result, it would have to be the other features of an annuity that attract you to it, such as the guaranteed death benefit, guaranteed income benefit, guaranteed

EXHIBIT 14.11

Low	Average	High
0.53%	2.16%	6.36%

annuitization factor, guaranteed interest account, access to multiple fund managers without extra cost, and two levels of managers of managers. The average total expenses in Morningstar's database of 5653 variable life insurance subaccounts was 1.56 percent on 03-31-2001, 60 basis points less than for annuities and 19 basis points more than for taxable mutual funds.

SURRENDER CHARGES

A surrender charge is paid from your annuity if you cash it in (surrender it) in the early years of the contract (see Exhibit 14.12). It is usually highest within the first years your contract is in force and then decreases and is eventually eliminated over the years. Be very aware of "rolling" surrender charges. This means that the surrender charge is applicable to each contribution to the contract for the full surrender charge period from the date you put the money into the contract. Even if you have a 15-year-old contract with your surrender charge period completely behind you on the original contract if you make an additional contribution today, that money would be subject to the surrender charge for the next 15 years. The average rolling surrender charge period is 5 years.

If you elect to make an early withdrawal of just part of the funds within your annuity contract prior to the end of the surrender charge period, you may have a free corridor amount you can withdraw without any charge. The norm is about 10 percent; however, some contracts do not allow any withdrawals without charge whereas the most generous allow 15 percent per contract year withdrawals without charge (see Exhibit 14.13).

Amounts in excess of the free corridor amount would be subject to proportional surrender charges. Since most of these are

EXHIBIT 14.12

Short	Average	Long
0 years	7 years	15 years

EXHIBIT 14.13

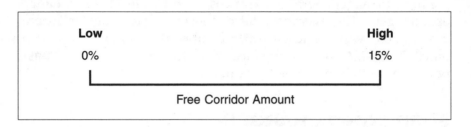

flexible-premium contracts, you may have *rolling surrender charges*, meaning that each investment within the contract must stay within it for a certain period of time before the surrender charge is lifted for that deposit.

Examine these charges carefully to make sure that you can leave your money in the contract long enough so that you do not to have to pay the surrender charge. If you leave your money in the contact long enough, it will be profitable to the insurance company. If you do not, the company will try to recoup the expenses of putting the contract in force through surrender charges. Remember, it is in your best interest to buy products that are profitable to the company. You do not want to be exposed to a disappearing company even though your subaccount investments (similar to mutual funds) within these contracts are not subject to the creditors of the insurance company.

Since variable annuities are a securities product, it is usually easier to identify all expenses within them as opposed to within a fixed annuity that is not subject to the security disclosure regulations. The Morningstar reports on the products you are considering summarize all this information; however, you should also carefully check a current prospectus before buying. You will find the prospectus information surprisingly simple to read. It is fairly easy to find all the expenses and surrender charges carefully itemized and compare them with the ranges in the previous exhibits.

Trading Life Insurance and Annuity Contracts: The 1035 Tax-Free exchange

You have read throughout this book that flexibility is an important feature of the life insurance and annuity contracts that you use to enhance your own and your family's financial security. Change is inevitable for all of us. If the contract you have purchased is adaptable to your economic circumstances as they change and develop, it is more likely you will be happy with it.

However, you may find yourself owning a life insurance or annuity policy that is no longer suitable and is so inflexible you cannot adapt it. If so, don't just surrender that contract—the income taxes and penalties that may result will burden you with unnecessary expenses. Section 1035 of the income tax code allows you to make tax-free exchanges of a life insurance policy for another life insurance policy, or a life insurance policy for an annuity contract, or an annuity contract for another annuity contract. You simply trade annuity contracts. Be aware, however, that you cannot trade an annuity contract into a life insurance policy without taxation.

Caution

Your old annuity contract may have some unique advantages depending on when you purchased it, so do not do a 1035 exchange without carefully considerating it with your advisors. For example:

> Variable annuity contracts purchased before October 21, 1979, are eligible for a step up in basis if the owner dies prior to the annuity starting date—Internal Revenue Code Section 72; Revenue Ruling 79-335, 1979-2 CB 292.

> The IRS Taxes withdrawals from an annuity issued prior to August 14, 1982 as cost basis first (not taxable) and gain next (taxable)—Internal Revenue Code Section 72(q) (2).

Tax-Free Exchange Procedure

To effect a 1035 tax-free exchange, you assign your company A contract to company B, and direct company B, in writing, to put the company A contract proceeds into the company B annuity. If done properly, you should not have to pay income taxes on the transaction. You may, however, have to pay surrender charges to company A and acquisition charges to company B. If these are acceptable and the alternative contract is better suited to fulfilling your needs, then proceed.

The advantage of the tax-free exchange is that you will not have to pay any taxes on the gains earned in the original contract at the time of the exchange. But what if there are no gains in the original contract? Indeed, what if there is a loss?

Surrendering the contract does not allow you to take a deduction for that loss on your income tax return. Losses as a result of surrendering life insurance or annuity contracts are not deductible. The reason you have a loss in the old contract is because your cost basis, your investment, exceeds the capital accumulated in the contract. The advantage of doing a 1035 tax-free exchange in this case is that you would be rolling that high cost basis into the new contract. The higher your cost basis in your new contract, the more you will be able to take out of that contract in living benefits without taxation in the future. Old contracts that have not performed adequately can still be valuable to you in this way. In short, regardless of the gain or loss in your old contracts, the 1035 tax-free exchange is likely to be to your economic advantage.

The 1035 tax-free exchange also is advantageous if you own a life insurance policy and, at some point in the future, determine that it is no longer needed or appropriate. You can reclaim the money that you have put into your contract (your basis) by making a withdrawal if the policy permits. Then, via a 1035 exchange of that policy for an annuity contract you can avoid current taxation on the gain. From that point forward, the investment return within the annuity contract will not be subject to the COI charges of the life insurance policy, and your tax-deferral will continue. Your cost basis in the life contract includes your previously paid life insurance costs and expenses, so if you annuitize more of your income will be considered the income tax-free return of your cost basis.

Many old annuity contracts were less flexible and provided lower investment returns to contract holders than do those being issued today. If you find yourself with such a contract, you may opt for a 1035 exchange into an annuity contract that would better suit your present needs and provide you with greater investment returns and more flexibility.

EQUITY-INDEXED ANNUITIES

The equity-indexed annuity (EIA) was introduced in 1995 and has become a fast-growing alternative to fixed-rate annuities. Fixed annuities offer a specified and company-guaranteed return that you pay for in the form of modest returns. Variable annuities let you place your funds in any number of subaccounts, similar to mutual funds that pass the return they earn plus or minus directly to you less expenses. There is no underlying guaranteed minimum in the typical variable annuity. Equity-indexed annuities were developed to eliminate the downside risk of the variable return but to obtain some of the variable annuity's upside potential as represented in the stock index they use.

Equity-indexed annuities do this by providing a guaranteed minimum interest rate (often about 3 percent) combined with the ability to earn a certain percentage, not all, of certain market-driven indexes such as the S&P 500. The percentage of the index's gain that a customer receives is called the *participation rate*. This rate varies, with some companies offering rates as low as 50 percent; the usual participation rate is approximately 75 percent of the index-linked return. Customers are offered a percentage of how much the index gains over a period of time. Note that this does not include dividends, which have accounted for about 30 percent of the total return of the S&P 500 for the last 20 years. There are many ways insurance companies calculate your index-linked returns, including the following:

- *The point-to-point method* divides the index on the maturity date by the index on the issue date and subtracts 1 from the result. (Other indexing methods use this same formula, with different data points.) This ignores all the fluctuations between start and finish, and makes this method the simplest both to understand and to calculate. One drawback is that market fluctuations can produce very different results for customers who bought the policy just a few days apart. The method comes from European stock markets, where options can be exercised only on their expiration date, and is sometimes referred to as the *European method*.
- *The Asian method* involves averaging several points of the index to establish the beginning and/or ending index. This method can help shield consumers from the risk of a market decline on the maturity date. Some companies

take an average of the 12 monthly indexes to establish the policy's maturity index level. This method takes its name from the Asian stock markets.

- *The look-back* or *high-water-mark method* is another popular approach. On each policy anniversary, the company notes the index level. The highest of these index levels is then taken and figured as the index level on the maturity date.

- *The low-water-mark method* uses the lowest of the indexes on each of the policy anniversaries before maturity as the level of the index at issue. This method tends to lessen the risk of market decline.

- *The annual reset* or *ratchet method* is among the most complicated. The increase in the index is calculated each policy year by comparing the indexes on the beginning and ending anniversaries. Any resulting decreases are ignored. Appreciation is figured by adding or compounding the increases for each policy year.

Equity-indexed annuities offer consumers what could be described as the best of both worlds: a market-driven investment with attractive returns and a guaranteed minimum return. Because EIA returns are tied to indexes of market activity, rather than to the performance of individual stocks or funds, and provide a minimum guaranteed return, they have not been considered an investment product subject to U.S. Securities and Exchange Commission oversight. This could change in the future; however, for the present EIAs do not have to be registered with the SEC, are not sold with a prospectus, and can be sold by anyone with an insurance license.

Insurance companies are required to file their equity-indexed annuities with each state, where they are regulated. Since equity-indexed annuities have been around for a relatively short time and there are so many different product designs, each with its own benefits and disadvantages, developing a regulatory model will not be easy.

Insurance companies construct equity-indexed annuities by investing the premiums they collect in bonds, to cover the guaranteed minimum return, and in call options on the index they are using, to cover market appreciation. Price volatility in the index options has made pricing more difficult, and so companies have used interest rate caps (a maximum return) and a reduction in participation rates to reduce the company's risk.

QUALIFIED RETIREMENT PLANS

Up to this point, we have been discussing nonqualified annuities—after-tax investments in which you establish a cost basis in the contract, which you will receive back tax-free upon distribution. The word *qualified* refers to the fact that tax law qualifies some retirement funds to receive special treatment under the tax law if they are set properly. The key to many qualified plans is that you can set aside money for retirement and not pay taxes on what you put in the plan. IRAs, 401(k) plans, and for teachers, hospital personel, and people who work for charities, tax-sheltered annuities (TSAs), are all examples of qualified plans. Since you never had to pay tax on what went into the plan, there is no cost basis that you can recover income tax–free. This is a major difference between the nonqualified and the qualified annuity. In the qualified plan, you have no cost basis because you have made no taxable contributions into the contract. Therefore, when payout day comes, the tax liability will be on the entire amount coming out.

A principal advantage of the qualified plan is that any investment you make, or that is made by your employer on your behalf, can be exempt from current income taxation. The investment itself will escape current taxation, and in addition, you will have all the benefits of tax-deferred compounding. For example, to make a $1000 investment into a *nonqualified* annuity, you would have to earn $1388.89 (assuming the 28 percent tax bracket). You would pay your 28-percent taxes on those earnings ($1388.89 $\times$ 28 percent = $388.89) and send the remaining $1000 into your annuity contract. If you are fortunate and able to put money into a qualified plan, you don't have to pay taxes on your earnings to net $1000. You just take $1000 off the top of your income without taxation, save the $388.89 that would otherwise have been lost to taxation, and also reduce your current income taxes by $280. Your net cost to put away $1000 is $720, about one-half of what it costs you to save after tax. Your IRA, TSA, 401(k), profit-sharing, and

pension plans are all practical opportunities for qualified plan contributions. If you qualify for any of these, take maximum *advantage
of them.* You will find that in addition to the tax benefit of the
qualified plan, there are often other advantages. There may be
higher interest rates, and in many instances you may find employers making contributions on your behalf without taxation
to you.

For example, a company has a qualified plan. An employee
can choose to contribute up to 5 percent of pay on a pretax basis.
The company will contribute 30 cents for every $1 the employee
contributes. What does that mean to an employee whose combined state and federal tax bracket amounts to 30 percent? As you
can see from Exhibit 14.14, a $1000 investment (costing only $700)
has resulted in $1300 being added to the employee's investment
account—a gain of $600 over the employee's $700 cost of investment and an 86.7 percent gain! How much would this employee
have had to make to add $1300 to his or her own account with
after-tax dollars? Take the amount to be deposited ($1300) and
divide by 1 minus the tax bracket (1 − 0.30, or 0.70). The earnings
required to make this investment on an after-tax basis would be
$1857.14. To check this, merely multiply by the 30 percent tax
bracket figure ($1857.14 × 30 percent). You find that the tax would
be $557.14, leaving $1300 to invest. That is 3.57 times what it cost
through the Company sponsored plan. Qualified plans offer such
a good advantage that you should participate whenever practical
to the maximum extent possible.

Nonqualified annuity contracts offer outstanding investment
and family wealth-building opportunities. Tax-deferred com-

EXHIBIT 14.14

Employee's Gross Investment	Employee's Tax Reduction Due to Contribution	Employee Cost of Investment	Company's Contribution (0.30 per $1.00)	Total Working on Employee's Behalf
$1000	− $300	= $700	$300	$1300

pounding is a powerful tool. Tax-deferred compounding throughout two lives, both husband and wife, is even more powerful. There is no computation, no reporting, and no current dividends, interest, or gains to keep track of or report. Opportunities to change your investment orientation without current taxation are available, as is the opportunity to control your future taxation by controlling payouts from your contracts.

ANNUITY CHANGES IN OWNERSHIP

TRA-86 declares that a change in ownership of an annuity is a taxable event that will be treated, for tax purposes, as if the owner/annuitant had died. In short, it means that unless the recipient beneficiary is the owner's spouse, the tax deferral cannot continue. To avoid this problem, do not make gifts of annuities; rather, make cash gifts into annuities already owned by the individual to whom you wish to make the gift.

Anyone can make a gift into an annuity contract that someone else owns. If the recipient of this gift happens to be a spouse, the gift will be sheltered from gift taxation by the unlimited marital deduction. Nonspousal gifts will have to be considered more carefully.

At the present time, each of us can give $10,000 per year to any individual, and if it is a *bona fide* gift and a gift of a *present interest*, it will be exempt from gift taxation. If you join together with your spouse in making the gift to a third person, then $20,000 may be gifted without the imposition of gift taxes. This is commonly referred to as a *split gift*. If you plan to use the shelter of the split gift, you will have to file a current gift tax form with the IRS.

To qualify for the $10,000-per-year (per individual) gift tax exemption, the payment of the premium into the annuity contract must create a gift of a present interest for the contract owner (ability to control the benefits of the contract currently). If the gift of the premium into the annuity contract is deemed to be a gift of a *future interest* (enjoyment of contract benefits is deferred) or is in excess of $10,000, it will be subject to gift taxes. A gift tax return should be filed, and if the gift giver has used up the current lifetime *unified credit* ($675,000 for 2001; and, as a result of the 2001 tax act, $1,000,000 in 2002 and 2003) available under the Unified Transfer Tax System, then gift taxes would be due as determined under the Unified Transfer Tax Rate Schedule. Once an individual has used up the allowable exemption, additional gifts are taxed at a rate starting at 37 percent and currently increasing to the top tax rate of 55 percent.

If a gift is being given for the payment of tuition or medical expenses, it can qualify for an unlimited exclusion by complying with the regulations controlling such gifts. You might wish to utilize this special exclusion. It would enable you to give a nontaxable gift and would not be drawn back into your estate for federal estate tax purposes. An annuity contract can be useful in providing for a nonspouse's medical expenses, such as an aging parent's nursing home expenses.

NONDEDUCTIBLE IRA OR NONQUALIFIED ANNUITY

Contributions to *qualified* plans are tax deductible to the extent that you qualify to participate in such plans, and it's a good idea to maximize your contributions to such plans. And there are times when you may continue to make contributions to a qualified plan even though you do not qualify for deductible contributions—it's also a good idea maximize your participation in these plans. However, your income may be too high for a deductible IRA contribution, or either you or your spouse is already participating in an employer-sponsored plan, so you may be offered the opportunity to contribute to a nondeductible IRA. Contributions to nondeductible IRAs are limited to $2000 per year ($2250 with a nonworking spouse). Normally it is not a good idea to participate in these plans because nondeductible IRA contributions create a tax reporting and record-keeping requirement that goes on for the rest of your life. You must be able to establish the portion of the funds you put into the IRA that qualify for a tax deduction as well as the portion that does not. You have to be able to do this when you are ready to take the funds out at retirement. An exclusion ratio will be established that will reflect the nondeductible contributions made to the contract, so that these funds may be excluded from taxation at distribution. To avoid the $2000 limitation, the reporting requirement, and the record-keeping problems that non-deductible IRAs could create, you could use a Roth IRA or an individually purchased, nonqualified deferred annuity contract. Upon distribution, in the deferred annuity contract everything in excess of cost basis would be subject to income taxes. If you qualify for a Roth IRA and treat it properly, you will not even have to worry about income taxes on the distributions. Nonqualified annuities are not subject to the $2000-per-year limitation, the reporting requirement, or IRS record-keeping requirements.

The Roth IRA

Named for Senator William Roth, Jr., chair of the Senate Finance Committee in 1997, the Roth IRA is something you will want to consider carefully and probably take advantage of, if you qualify.

What Is a Roth IRA?

It is a nondeductible contribution of $2000 into an account that may be invested and that retains all earnings without federal income taxation. What is entirely unique is that you can withdraw and use those earnings after age 59½ without taxation. Also, you will not be forced to begin to take a percentage of that money out every year after age 70½, and your beneficiaries inherit it income tax–free. Characteristics and advantages of the Roth IRA include the following (see also Exhibit 14.15.):

- Adjusted gross income limits:
  - Singles: less than $95,000 fully qualified—phased out over $110,000.
  - Couples: less than $150,000 fully qualified—phased out over $160,000.
- You can make annual contributions for as long as you qualify (have earned income).
- You are not forced to begin taking out money at age 70½.
- You can establish a Roth IRA after age 70½ as long as you are still working.
- You may make the contribution as late as the due date of

EXHIBIT 14.15

IRA Alternatives

	Regular IRA	Roth IRA	Education IRA
May be suitable for:	*Wage-earners, to save for retirement *Nonemployed spouses who file a joint tax return	*Wage-earners, to save for retirement *Nonemployed spouses who file a joint tax return	Individuals who want to save for a child's post-secondary education
Features:	*Contributions *may* be tax-deductible. *nondeductible* IRAs cause record-keeping problems. *Must start minimum withdrawals or annuity payout by age 70½. *Earnings accumulate tax-DEFERRED *Can be used together with ROTH and EDUCATION IRA (Max. total=$2000)	*Contributions are *not* tax-deductible *Contributions *can continue* after age 70½ if you have earned income *Earnings accumulate tax-free *Can be used together with REG. IRA and EDUCATION IRA (max total=$2000)	*Contributions are *not* tax-deductible *Can be rolled over or transferred to an Education IRA for the benefit of another family member. *Earnings accumulate tax-free *Can be used together with REG. IRA and ROTH IRA
Eligibility	*Under age 70½ *Must have earned compensation/yr. May earn $2000 and contribute $2000=100% of compensation If you participate in a 401(k) deduction limited by AGI Singles AGI <$33,000 = $2000, max less to $43,000 Married AGI <$53,000 = $2000 max less to $63,000	* Single must have AGI <$95,000 to $110,000 Joint <$150,000 to $160,000 *Can convert regular IRA to ROTH if AGI is under $100,000.	*Must have AGI <$95,000 Single (to $110,000) <$150,000 Joint (to $160,000) *Cannot* be contributing to qualified state tuition program.

	Plan 1	Plan 2	Plan 3
Plan Contribution Limits:	*Annual contributions up to $2000 or 100% of compensation, lesser of. *Nonemployed spouses may contribute and deduct up to $2000/yr.	*After-tax contributions up to 100% of compensation up to $2000.	*After-tax contributions up to $500 per child under age 18. *If "excess" (over $500) contribution made—take out in that tax yr. or 6% penalty on excess until taken out
Distributions:	*Taxable income distributions. *IRS 10% penalty. Penalty free distributions if: 1) Age 59½ + 2) Permanent disability 3) Education expenses 4) First time home purchase ($10,000 lifetime cap.) 5) Payment of medical expenses 6) Payment of health insurance (if unemployed) 7) Death. *Minimum distributions required at age 70½. (or lifetime annuity)	*Tax-free income distributions. *IRS 10% penalty. Penalty-free distributions if: 5 YEARS IN PLAN, PLUS: 1) Age 59½ + 2) Permanent disability 3) First-time home purchase ($10,000 lifetime cap.) 4) Higher education costs 5) Death. *NO minimum distribution requirement	*Tax-free income distributions IF used to pay for qualified higher education expenses. (Exceptions to this if using Hope Scholarship or Lifetime Learning Credits). *IRS 10% penalty. Penalty-free distributions if: 1) Used for post-secondary education expenses of named child 2) All money in account must be distributed, or transferred to another (qualifying <18) family member, by the time the named child attains age 30.
Deadline to set up / contribute	*Tax-filing deadline, not including extensions (Usually April 15)	*Tax-filing deadline, not including extensions (Usually April 15)	*December 31 of the current year

Developed by Katie Baldwin Leipprandt CFP, CLU, ChFC. Used with permission.

your income tax return for the previous year not
including extensions.
- Even if you and/or your spouse participates in a
retirement plan at work, you can establish a Roth IRA.

What to Do to Establish a Roth IRA

Put away (invest) up to $2000 per person, $4000 per couple. Hold
the investment for at least 5 years and *never* pay federal income
taxes on the earnings on that investment. This has previously been
unheard of and may not last long. There are some limits on using
the earnings prior to age 59½ without being taxed on them. You
must have held the investment for 5 years (the time period starts
from the date you first set up the account, so get it started quickly)
and you may use only up to $10,000 to purchase your first house,
or a first house for a child or a grandchild. Here you need to know
the definition of "first house" in IRS parlance. If you have not
owned a house within the last 2 years, you will be considered to
be buying your "first house."

You also may use the earnings prior to age 59½ without taxation as a result of a disability. You can use the capital (not earnings) you invested in the Roth at *any* time without taxation. It is
a return to the FIFO method of taxation (first in, first out—that
was taken away from nonqualified annuities in 1982). Your beneficiaries will not have to pay tax on the earnings if they receive
your Roth IRA as a result of your death.

What about Existing IRAs?

You can "Roth" existing IRAs as long as your adjusted gross income does not exceed $100,000. You will have to pay income taxes
on the gain in your traditional IRA in the year of conversion if
you change it to a Roth IRA. Those who converted in 1998, and
1998 only, were allowed to spread that tax liability over the next
4 years. All the deferred income will be taxed in the year of conversion for IRAs converted after 1998. To control your income tax
liability you can convert portions of your IRA each year rather
than "Rothing" the whole IRA all at one time.

How Do I Convert my IRA to a Roth IRA?

There are three ways to convert a traditional IRA to a Roth IRA:

1. Notify your IRA trustee that you would like to convert you IRA account to a Roth IRA. It would be a good idea to make the request in writing so that you have a record of your request.
2. Make a direct transfer of an IRA account from one trustee to another trustee, notifying the new trustee that the account is to be established as a Roth IRA. In a direct transfer, you never take possession of the money yourself.
3. Roll over your IRA, meaning you receive a distribution from your IRA account, and then invest that money into a Roth IRA within 60 days of receipt of the funds. (Rollovers generally are allowed only once per 12-month period, but this rule is eliminated for a rollover to a Roth IRA.)

Planning Tip

This is a great chance for those who qualify to get rid of those onerous IRS reporting problems called nondeductible IRAs. Convert them to Roths!

"IRA" Rules

The annual contribution to any and all IRAs cannot exceed $2000 per person up to earned income. Couples may contribute up to $4000, even if one spouse stays at home and has no earned income. They also may deduct that payment if the employed spouse is participating in a 401(K) plan at work. The ability to deduct IRA contributions phases out for couples after adjusted gross income (AGI) reaches $53,000 and is gone at $63,000. The phaseout range for couples for Roth IRAs are $150,000 to $160,000.

Education IRAs

A total of $500 per year can be put into all such education IRAs for a child. The child, however, may have multiple education IRAs if they are established in different years.

- Adjusted Gross Income qualifications:
  Singles: up to $95,000 fully qualified—phased out over $110,000

Couples: up to $150,000 fully qualified—phased out over $160,000

The income cap pertains to the person starting the IRA. The contribution may be made by a relative (aunts, uncles, and grandparents, take note) or friend, if the person's income is below the cap. Exhibit 14.16 is provided to help you compare nonqualified IRA contributions with annuities, life insurance, and other investments.

INVESTMENT MANAGEMENT INSIDE VARIABLE ANNUITIES

It would have been wonderful to have invested a single large premium into common stocks or other equity investments within an annuity or a life insurance policy in August 1982, when the Dow Jones Industrial average stood at 742. The results would have been almost as exciting if you had invested, with a single-premium deposit, in long-term interest-yielding securities in December 1980 at the top of the interest rate curve, when the prime rate was 21½ percent. Looking back at it from the present, there would not seem to be much opportunity for loss, interest rates continued to go down and the stock market continuing to fluctuate in a generally upward direction although with periods of frightening declines. Therefore the single deposit into a diversified equity portfolio in life insurance or an annuity contract would not have exposed you to excessive risk of loss if you had the courage to hold on during the bad times. It's amazing how clear it all seems looking back and how foggy it always is looking forward.

As this new edition of *The New Life Insurance Investment Advisor* goes to press in the year 2001 with the Dow in the 10,000 to 11,000 range, it is interesting to see what was said in previous editions of this book and how the same thing could be said now. All we need to do is change the year and the level of the Dow.

In an early 1994 economic scenario, the question is, *What do I do now?* From here, with long-term bonds yielding about 6 percent, it appears that interest rates may decline another 1 percent. The stock market, from a level of almost 3,900 on the Dow, appears to offer

EXHIBIT 14.16

Alternatives to a Nonqualified IRA

	Roth IRA	Regular IRA	Nonqualified IRA	Nonqualified Annuities	Variable Universal Life Insurance	Independent Investment
Tax Deductible Contributions	No	Yes	No	No	No	No
Tax Sheltered Investment Results	Yes	Yes	Yes	Yes	Yes	No
Dollar Limit on Contributions	2,000	$2,000	$2,000	No Limit	No Limit	No Limit
Access to Cash	Some Limits	Limited	Limited	Limited	No Limit	No Limit
Loans	N/A	No	No	No	Yes	Yes
Withdrawal Penalties (IRS)						
(A) Pre-age 59½	Some 10%	Yes	Yes	Yes	No	No
IRS Penality	Some 10 %	10%	10%	10%		
(B) IRS Taxation on Gains	No	Yes	Yes	Yes	Owner Controlled	Yes
(C) Cause SS to Be Taxed	No	Yes	Yes	Yes	No	Yes
Mortality Charge from Investment Results	No	No	No	No	Yes	No
Tax-Free Inflated Death Benefit	No	No	No	No	Yes	No
IRS Accounting Difficulties Anticipated	No	No	Yes	No	No	No
Mandatory Taxable Withdrawals past 70½	No	Yes	Yes	No	No	No

Conclusions: Rules of Thumb (ROT) concluded from the above:

1. Regular IRA, if available, should be utilized. The tax deductibility of the contribution is such an advantage that it overwhelms the disadvantages of limited access to the assets.

2. There is but one advantage in the non-qualified IRA column, tax sheltered investment results, versus eleven in the life insurance column.

an opportunity for near-term losses as well as gains. It is interesting to note that six years ago, in 1988 when the first *Life Insurance Investment Advisor* was published, the Dow was at 2,700 and we said the same thing. The clarity of our hindsight and the fogginess of our foresight will always plague us.

1994 edition of *The New Life Insurance Investment Advisor*

But meanwhile the market keeps doing what the market does—goes upstairs like a drunken sailor. Dollar cost averaging (the consistent investment of equal periodic payments into a diversified equity-based investment), rather than large single-sum investing, is a relatively conservative strategy. If you obtain a contract that offers a guaranteed interest, guaranteed principal account from which you can move monies at your discretion into equity accounts, you can put your single-sum deposits in these accounts and then move portions into the equity accounts using the dollar-cost-averaging arrangement.

Dollar cost averaging can best be described by illustration. Exhibit 14.17 indicates what happened when one extremely fearful investor was persuaded to put $100 per month into the stock account of a variable contract for 5 months, even though he was convinced that the entry of his $100 investment was sure to trigger substantial market declines. As you will note in the illustration, he was right. The market had two 50 percent declines before it

EXHIBIT 14.17

A Dollar-Cost-Averaging Example

	Month						Totals
	1	2	3	4	5		
Investment	$100	$100	$100	$100	$100	=	$500
Share value on purchase date	100	50	25	50	100		
Shares purchased	1	2	4	2	1	=	10 shares

Sell all shares at the end of the fifth month:		
10 shares × $100 market price	=	$1000
Less investment		−500
Gain on investment		$500

started to recover during the first 2 months of his participation, and as soon as the market came back to where it was, he got out. Had he made a substantial single-premium deposit, it would have been merely a very agonizing ride with no reward; however, with dollar cost averaging, he was repaid with a 100 percent return on his investment.

The discipline of dollar cost averaging can provide a fairly conservative long-term investment strategy when applied to equity-based annuity and life insurance contracts, as well as mutual funds and other investments. It is a lower-risk strategy than lump-sum investing. If the scenario above had described a market going straight up, it certainly would have been more profitable to go into equities with the whole investment at the outset. But who knows?

As time goes on and your investments build within your annuity or life insurance contract, you may find that you want to cash in some of the gains that have built up over the years in the stock funds. You may move the accumulated funds out of the stock accounts into a more conservative account. If you made this decision with a mutual fund or a personally managed portfolio of common stocks, you would no doubt agitate over the fact that the sale would trigger current taxation. Two things would be on your mind. First, will the stock market keep going higher? If so, you will lose the opportunity to enjoy further gains. Second, if you sell out now, Uncle Sam is going to take his income tax bite. That could be 20 percent of your profits—not an insignificant amount. That is 20 percent less to reinvest to provide for your personal security. If the assets you are considering moving are within the annuity or the life insurance policy, you have only one of these worries to contend with: If you move out now, you will miss the additional potential profits if the market continues to move up. Taxation, however, will not be a consideration. Not having to consider taxation in evaluating your investment alternatives is a substantial advantage.

DEFERRED ANNUITY ACTION LETTER

A deferred/accumulation annuity is a more complex purchase since the contract can be far more flexible. Generally speaking, if you are going to invest in a deferred annuity, you should seek flexibility. The most successful deferred annuity contracts are typically those that stay in existence over a long period of time. Your needs and attitudes inevitably will change over time, so you will want a contract that is adaptable to such change. If the annuity contract is not flexible, it is likely that you will either terminate it, trade it for a variable annuity contract, or put it in a drawer. Any one of these three options might result in fees, penalties, potential tax liability, and the losses that occur due to inattention. The deferred annuity action letter will help you indicate to the insurance company your specifications for a deferred annuity quote based upon your personal situation and requirements (see Exhibit 14.18).

This action letter specifically does not ask for illustrations regarding how your money might compound based on some particular investment or interest rate. The return from your annuity investment will be based upon interest rates and investment returns over a long period of time, as well as minimization of expenses. Your product evaluation should be directed toward the specific information regarding all expenses and charges that may be incurred under a particular contract as well as the investment options and interest rate track record. (See also the annuity purchase checklist shown in Exhibit 14.19.)

ANNUITY TAXATION

The general rule has been that the annuity earnings accumulate within the annuity on a tax-deferred basis. TRA-86 modified the general rule, so that only an annuity that is owned by a natural person will enjoy this tax-deferred income. Code Sections 73(u) and 71(q) provide that an annuity contract issued or added to after February 28, 1986, owned by a corporation, partnership, or other nonnatural person, will not enjoy the tax deferral on the inside buildup. Taxes will have to be paid each year on contract earnings. Contracts contributed to by February 28, 1986, have been grandfathered and will not be taxed on prior or continued earnings on such contributions.

To determine the way funds will be taxed when distributed from tax-deferred annuities, we have to look to the date that the funds were put into the annuity. If the funds were received by

EXHIBIT 14.18

Deferred/Accumulation Annuity Action Letter

I am considering investing in a deferred annuity. I would prefer an annuity contract that allows me the flexibility of investing at my personal convenience when funds became available for investment. I would prefer not to purchase a contract that makes investment in the contract mandatory over some predetermined time. I prefer not to accept the restrictions imposed by a single-premium deferred annuity contract unless such a contract would offer superior returns or features different from those available from a flexible-premium annuity contract. For quote purposes, please use $___ as my initial investment into the contract.

Please provide an explanation of any and all charges that will be made against my investment and the net amount that will go to work for me in the annuity contract. Also, please indicate any surrender charges or contingent withdrawal fees that I could be exposed to should I cash in the annuity contract and the time period during which these charges are applicable.

I am not unfavorably disposed toward variable annuity contracts as long as there is a safe haven account available within the contracts. Please indicate which account is a safe haven account and what guarantees of principal and interest are available within that account. I would also like to know if there are any restrictions on my movement into and/or out of any accounts during the life of the annuity contract. Please provide me with the prospectus and all other information that is available regarding all of the accounts within the contract.

I would like an annuity contract from a quality company with low expense and sales charges. I would prefer surrender charges to front-end sales charges so that all of my money would go to work for me immediately and so that, if I maintain my contract until after the surrender charge period, I may never have to pay such sales charges. I would like maximum flexibility, a good safe haven account providing interest and principal guarantees, and good-performing, alternative mutual fund types of accounts. I seek flexibility and convenience of investment and frequent and convenient reporting regarding account balances. I would like to be able to switch between the various accounts at my convenience, preferably by telephone, fax, or Internet.

At this time, it is my intention to defer the annuity for as long a period as possible, so please let me know at what age the insurance company insists that I begin to take funds. I would like to avoid forced annuitization for as long as possible. Please state explicitly any penalties I could be exposed to if I choose never to annuitize my contract. Please send the information to me at the address indicated below. Call me if there is anything else you need to know in order to provide me with this information.

Thank you for your assistance.

Sincerely,

Name
Address
Phone
Fax
E-mail

EXHIBIT 14.19

Annuity Purchase Checklist

Fixed Annuity			Variable Annuity (Author prefers)	
(Most important) % (125% plus)		Company Rating NAIC—RBC%	(Important) % (125% plus)	
Level	**Trend**		**Level**	**Trend**
		A. M. Best		
		S & P		
		Moody's		
		D & P		
		Weiss		
		Other		
		(Prefer above levels 7 and uptrends rather than downtrends)		
(Most important) %		General Account *Interest Rate* Current	(Important) %	
Months		Guarantee period	Months	
%		Minimum guarantee	%	
%		Bailout interest rate	%	
%		Cost of bailout, %	%	
		Interest rate track record		
		Crediting method		
(None)		*Separate Accounts* Variety and track record (see prospectus)	_____ (Total number) _____	
		Premium Type Single Contractual Flexible		
		Expenses		
	%	Front load		%
	%	Surrender charge		%
	Years	Years surrender applies		Years
Yes/No		Rolling surrender charge	Yes/No	
$		Annual contract charge	$	
	%			%

EXHIBIT 14.19 *(continued)*

Fixed Annuity			Variable Annuity (Author prefers)	
(Most important) % (125% plus)		*Company Rating* NAIC—RBC%	(Important) % (125% plus)	
Level	**Trend**		**Level**	**Trend**
	%	*Withdrawal* free corridor	%	
		Other free corridors Death Disability Terminal illness Nursing home confinement		
Not applicable		Separate account charges	(See your prospectus)	
		Fund Expense Name of account _____ _____ _____ _____ _____	(Note for each fund)	
Not applicable		Mortality and expense risk	%	
		Administration expenses	%	
		Total expense	%	

August 14, 1982, withdrawals will be received by the annuitant as principal first and income second (first in, first out—FIFO). If deposits were received after August 14, 1982, withdrawals are taxed as income first and principal last, to the extent of earnings in the contract (last in, first out—LIFO). The annuitant is exposed to ordinary income tax immediately on withdrawals from such contracts. The ordinary income tax liability is created when a partial withdrawal or lump-sum distribution is made. If the annuity contract is pledged or assigned as collateral for a loan, ordinary income taxes are due on the amount collateralized up to the amount of the accumulated earnings in the pledged contract, and the 10 percent penalty applies if the annuitant has not yet reached age 59½.

TRA-86 also increased the penalty tax from 5 to 10 percent on withdrawals made prior to age 59½ from both nonqualified and qualified deferred annuities. The penalty tax is waived if the owner of the annuity is age 59½ or older, dies, or becomes disabled; or if the annuity contract is being used relative to the periodic payments required under a personal injury suit. The penalty also will be waived if benefits are annuitized, paid out in a series of substantially equal payments over the life of the annuitant or over the joint life of the annuitant and the primary beneficiary. This 10 percent penalty tax is also applicable to withdrawals from pre–August 15, 1982 annuities. These contracts were grandfathered from the standpoint that you may still consider withdrawals to be of principal first and thus not subject to tax up to your pre–August 15, 1982 cost basis. However, you will have to pay the 10 percent penalty tax to take *taxable funds* out prior to age 59½. Once your pre–August 15, 1982 basis has been recovered without taxation, your next withdrawals will be entirely taxable annuity earnings and thus also subject to the 10 percent pre-59½ penalty. (See Exhibit 14.20).

NONQUALIFIED ANNUITY TAXATION AT THE DEATH OF THE ANNUITANT

The taxation of annuity proceeds in the event of the death of the annuitant will depend upon two things:

1. Whether income has commenced or has not yet commenced at the death of the annuitant
2. Whether the beneficiary receiving the proceeds of the annuity contract is the annuitant's spouse

First, let us assume that payments had not yet begun at the annuitant's death, leaving the proceeds of the annuity to the surviving spouse. The spouse has the option of continuing the an-

EXHIBIT 14.20

Nonqualified Annuity Income Taxation

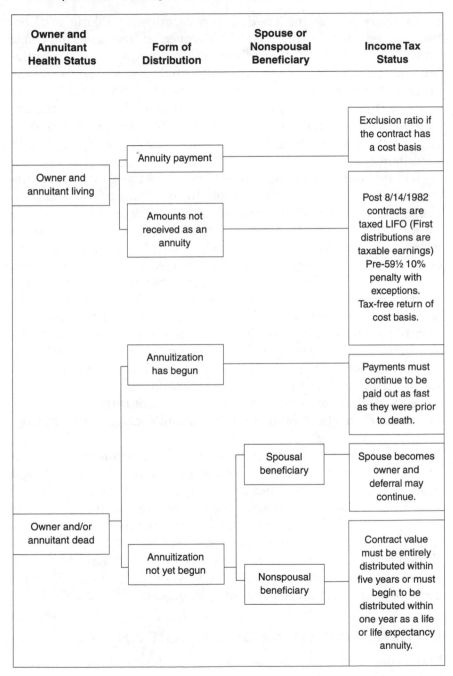

Owner and Annuitant Health Status	Form of Distribution	Spouse or Nonspousal Beneficiary	Income Tax Status
Owner and annuitant living	Annuity payment		Exclusion ratio if the contract has a cost basis
	Amounts not received as an annuity		Post 8/14/1982 contracts are taxed LIFO (First distributions are taxable earnings) Pre-59½ 10% penalty with exceptions. Tax-free return of cost basis.
Owner and/or annuitant dead	Annuitization has begun		Payments must continue to be paid out as fast as they were prior to death.
	Annuitization not yet begun	Spousal beneficiary	Spouse becomes owner and deferral may continue.
		Nonspousal beneficiary	Contract value must be entirely distributed within five years or must begin to be distributed within one year as a life or life expectancy annuity.

nuity and enjoying the tax-deferred earnings or taking a distribution and paying the taxes. However, if the annuitant *had* annuitized and died leaving the annuity payments to the surviving spouse, the benefits would be distributed as stipulated by the annuitant in the annuity contract. Taxation will continue to apply to those proceeds just as prior to the annuitant's death. If the annuitant was just taking periodic withdrawals, then the spouse beneficiary usually has the same distribution control as the deceased annuitant had.

If the nonspousal beneficiary receives the proceeds in the event of the annuitant's death prior to the distribution of any income, the nonspousal beneficiary may elect a lump-sum distribution without penalty but with full taxation on the accrued interest or gain within the contract. Alternatively, the annuitant may elect a series of payments to be made over a period of time not to exceed the beneficiary's life expectancy, beginning within 1 year of the annuitant's death. The nonspousal beneficiary has no option to continue the contract, and although the payment is not subject to a 10 percent penalty tax since it is the result of the annuitant's death, it will be subject to ordinary income tax to the extent of the decedent's earnings in the contract. If the annuity income had started prior to the annuitant's death, then the proceeds would have to continue to come out of the annuity at least as rapidly as the method in effect before the annuitant's death, with normal taxation continuing.

The taxation of annuitized benefits from nonqualified annuities will be based upon the exclusion ratio; that is, the investment in the vehicle will be divided by the expected return to be enjoyed by the beneficiary to determine the exclusion ratio. Each payment to be received by the beneficiary is multiplied by the exclusion ratio to determine the amount of the payment that would be excluded from current taxation as a return of principal, up to a point where basis has been fully recovered. After that, all annuity payments are fully taxable as ordinary income. (See Exhibit 14.20.)

ESTATE TAXATION OF ANNUITIES

Make sure that your qualified annuity contracts (those from your IRAs, retirement plan rollovers, and such) are arranged so that if you are survived by your spouse, your spouse will be allowed to continue the deferred annuity and manage it just as you had during your life. Deferred annuity contracts are not as efficient as life insurance policies in accomplishing the transfer of wealth to a nonspouse beneficiary. The annuity contract, while deferring taxation on earnings within the contract until future use, never escapes that pent-up income tax liability. If the beneficiary of an annuity contract is not a spouse, the income tax liabilities within the contract become the beneficiary's income tax liabilities at the same time that these same funds may be exposed to estate taxes. Income taxes will have to be paid as the funds are paid out. The beneficiary who is a nonspouse is not allowed to continue the deferral but must establish a payout arrangement with the insurance company within 1 year of the death of the survivor of the annuitant. The income tax liabilities will have to be paid based on the payout arrangement your beneficiary selects—annuity, lump sum, or over 5 years.

Retirement plan money and qualified or nonqualified annuity money are to be used up during your and your spouse's lifetime because the taxes it is exposed to are so onerous after both of your deaths that your beneficiaries are unlikely to thank you. This is one reason that joint and 100 percent to the survivor immediate fixed and variable annuities will probably become much more popular. You will learn that even if you do not need the money, even if you do not want to pay the income taxes on it, it will be more profitable for you and your beneficiaries if you take the immediate annuity income and spend it on your beneficiaries, buy survivorship VUL with it and leave them the life insurance money outside your estate, or make gifts to your favorite charities, while you are around and they can thank you personally.

Compare a qualified plan and an annuity with a life insurance policy in which the death benefit is substantially greater than your investment within the life insurance policy (the net amount at risk) and is passed to the beneficiary income tax–free, and, if properly structured, also estate tax–free. The difference in the tax treatment requires you to define your objectives carefully in order to determine which contract—annuity or life insurance—will serve you and your family best.

Usually, you begin to be concerned about estate taxes when

your estate reaches the level that would cause them to be paid. One of the first changes the Reagan administration made was to eliminate taxes on assets passing between husband and wife, either during life or at death. You can be assured that, under current law, no matter how much you leave to your spouse, it will not incur any estate or gift tax. The estate tax or death tax that many are seeking to reduce or eliminate is levied against that which you own at death and leave to those other than your spouse. Under current law, the first $675,000 of assets passed by gift or at death to nonspousal beneficiaries incurs no estate tax (to be increased to $1000 in 2002) since the tax is offset by a credit against the tax for which we are all eligible. Transfers above $675,000 are taxed at a 37 percent rate up to $750,000 and a 39 percent rate from that level to $1 million. Over the $1 million mark, the rate begins at 41 percent and rises to the maximum of 55 percent.

In brief, the Uniform Transfer Tax System established a means of taxing everything that you or I own and pass to others with certain exceptions:

1. If the recipient is your spouse (spousal gifts and marital deduction)

2. If it is a present interest gift of less than $10,000 a year per individual recipient (joint with spouse gifts, $20,000)

3. If the total of all the gifts, not counting the $10,000-per-year gifts, is less than $675,000 as adjusted upward in the future in your whole lifetime including the total of all you passed by inheritance at your death.

Some estate planning strategies suggest that an estate owner arrange his or her estate with the spouse so as to pay some estate taxes at the 37 percent level as rapidly appreciating property, so that at the spouse's death the taxes will not have to be paid at the 55 percent level. The relatively small difference of 18 percent between the lowest bracket and the highest bracket, and the fact that we are all looking forward to some estate tax relief makes it difficult for most estate owners to understand the logic of death tax prepayment. Also, many feel that if they retain the 37 percent, they probably would earn the extra 18 percent and more, and thus justify paying the higher level of estate taxes later. One way to reduce your estate and thus your estate taxes is to make gifts, preferably that qualify as gifts of a present interest and are thus protected from taxation by the $10,000 gift tax exclusion, or split gifts with your spouse, which warrant a $20,000 exclusion. Also, if you are able to give gifts of rapidly appreciating property, you can keep the growth out of your estate.

Just as with any property, you will find the value of the annuity included in the owner's estate at death. Whether it will cause estate taxes or not depends upon the contract owner's total estate. If the beneficiary of the contract happens to be the contract owner's spouse, the annuity is protected from estate taxes by the marital deduction. However, if the beneficiary of the contract is other than the annuitant's spouse, not only will the contract be included in the contract owner's estate for estate tax purposes, but the beneficiary will incur an immediate income tax liability as he or she is forced to begin taking withdrawals from the contract within 1 year of the annuitant's death. Since the single-sum payout could create a substantial ordinary income tax burden, beneficiaries may elect a payout arrangement that stretches out the income tax liability. Annuities in this case have a disadvantage in comparison with other assets owned by the deceased. Other personally owned assets take on a new basis as of the death of the owner which wipes out gain and eliminates income tax liabilities on accumulated gains. This is referred to as *step-up in basis* and it is one of the items that the 2001 tax act eliminates for people dying after December 31, 2009. Step-up in basis at death does not apply to annuity contracts issued after October 20, 1979.

Annuity Contract: Pre–Age 59½ Liquidity

You might as well consider pre–age 59½ annuity accumulation and liquidity as a contradiction in terms. There are three reductions in value to which your annuity can be exposed should you decide to take money out of the post-TEFRA (Tax Equity and Fiscal Responsibility Act of 1982) deferred annuity (issued after August 13, 1982). First, the insurance company that issued the contract may impose charges. Many annuity contracts are back-end-loaded. The insurance company charges little or no upfront fees when you deposit money into the contract, but it does charge for premature withdrawals, referred to as *back-end loads*.

These charges usually disappear after 5 to 15 years. Some companies have what are referred to as *rolling* back-end loads, which, as explained earlier, means that when you put new money is put into the contract, the time period for the back-end load for those new funds starts all over again on the day of the deposit.

In addition to the charges made by the insurance company, there are two potential charges from Uncle Sam. The first is ordinary income tax on the amount of money withdrawn from the annuity contract to the extent that there are earnings within the contract. It is not until all the interest earnings on your annuity contract have been removed and subject to taxation that your principal will come out without further taxation for post–August 13, 1982 contracts.

QUALIFIED PLAN ANNUITY DISTRIBUTIONS

By April 1, following the year you attain age 70½, you must make at least minimum annual distributions from all of your qualified plans. That is, all qualified retirement plans such as your Individual Retirement Accounts (IRA), Self-Employed Plans (SEP), Simple IRA plans, profit sharing, 401(k)s, pension plans, Section 403(b) annuity (TSAs), and Section 457(d) deferred compensation plans.

Most people choose to take their first minimum distribution in the year they attain age 70½, rather than waiting until the first quarter of the following year. If you wait until the following year, you would have to take two minimum distributions, one for the year in which you were 70½ and one for the year in which you were 71½. This could stack too much income into that one year.

On January 11, 2001, the IRS issued new proposed minimum distribution regulations giving us new rules about how we are to comply with the minimum distribution requirements. These still are "proposed" regulations and are subject to an executive "stay" issued on January 20, 2001, effectively "staying" the implementation of all regulations until the White House can "review all new and pending regulations." The stay order requires the IRS to "temporarily postpone the effective date for 60 days." The stay was quickly removed and these new regulations will be effective, as proposed by the IRS, for all qualified plan distributions in 2001. Therefore, we will try to summarize here what the IRS described in 55 pages. We again caution you not to rely on the information in this book when you go to implement your plans. You can see how time sensitive information is. Consult your personal attorney, accountant, and personal financial advisors who are familiar with your personal situation and who are up-to-date on all the changes that are constantly taking place. This book is intended to help you become a better informed consumer of financial products. It is not intended, or capable of, giving you tax or legal advice.

The proposed changes are a great improvement over the minimum distribution rules of the past. They are easier and more straightforward. For example, there are basically just two ways you can comply and you are required to be in compliance by April 1 of the year following your 70½ birthday. The two methods for complying are the Annuity Method and the Account Balance or Minimum Distribution Method.

Annuity Method

Annuitize. That is, ask your qualified plan provider to provide you with a life income from the plan for the rest of your life or the rest of your own and your spouse's life. You will have many of the options already described for annuities both fixed and variable. It will be up to employers, their actuaries, and insurance companies that sell immediate annuity contracts to make sure that they provide annuity payments that comply with the regulations. If you retire from an employer-provided plan that allows retirement at age 55, you could choose an annuity contract at that time. If you want to annuitize an IRA, you could do it as early as you wanted as long as the payments are based upon your life expectancy or that of you and your spouse. You could choose to annuitize even after your required beginning date, beyond that April 1 after the year in which you attain age 70½. Of course you will have to make sure you are taking large enough distributions up to the year you choose to annuitize using the Account Balance Method or Minimum Distribution Method to be in full compliance in the year in which you choose to change to the Annuity Method.

Account Balance Method or Minimum Distribution Method

Scenario One

You have reached age 70½, have retired and want to start your minimum distributions this year, the year of your seventieth birthday, rather than wait until next year. You would have to take out two distributions in the next year to be in compliance if you waited until that April 1 the year after you reach 70½. This would mean increased income taxes because of the two distributions in one year. You have to base your calculations on the gross amount of money in all of your IRAs, 401(k), and other qualified plan balances as of the December 31 of the prior year (prior to your attainment of age 70½). Add up the balances in all of the accounts. Next look up the divisor that coordinates with your age attained in the year of distribution in the following IRS-provided table of account balance divisors (see Exhibit 14.21). Your divisor is 26.2. So, if all of your account balances total $100,000 on December 31 of the preceding year, you divide $100,000 by 26.2 and find that your required minimum distribution is $3802.28. Keep in mind that this represents the *minimum* you must take out. As far as the government is concerned, you are free to take as much out as you wish. In each succeeding year you do the same thing, that is, add up all account balances for the previous December 31, go to the table and, since you had your seventy-first birthday in this distribution year, you would divide the December 31 balance by 25.3.

Exception: You are married to someone more than 10 years younger than you are. In this case, you can use the IRS-provided tables based upon a longer applicable distribution period on a recalculated basis. See your tax advisor.

Scenario Two

You die and your spouse is your sole primary beneficiary with an unlimited right to withdraw from the account. Your spouse must take out what you were required to take out in the year of your death using the calculations shown in Scenario One. For example, take the December 31 balance of the decedent's accounts the year before death, use the divisor for the birthday in the year of death, do the division, and this will be the minimum distribution

EXHIBIT 14.21

IRS-Proposed Applicable Distribution Periods

Birthday of account balance owner in year of distribution	Applicable Distribution Period (Divide previous 12/31 total account balances by this number)	Birthday of account balance owner in year of distribution	Applicable Distribution Period (Divide previous 12/31 total account balances by this number)
70	26.2	93	8.8
71	25.3	94	8.3
72	24.4	95	7.8
73	23.5	96	7.3
74	22.7	97	6.9
75	21.8	98	6.5
76	20.9	99	6.1
77	20.1	100	5.7
78	19.2	101	5.3
79	18.4	102	5.0
80	17.6	103	4.7
81	16.8	104	4.4
82	16.0	105	4.1
83	15.3	106	3.8
84	14.5	107	3.6
85	13.8	108	3.3
86	13.1	109	3.1
87	12.4	110	2.8
88	11.8	111	2.6
89	11.1	112	2.4
90	10.5	113	2.2
91	9.9	114	2.0
92	9.4	115 and older	1.8

amount. Once this is complete, the surviving spouse can treat the inherited plan balances as his or her own and proceed as shown in Scenario One. If the surviving spouse is over 70½, he or she will have to include the inherited plan balances combined with his or her personal plan balances in the minimum distribution calculations.

Scenario Three

You die and leave a person other than your spouse as beneficiary. This would be the same as the situation in which your spouse dies after you do and leaves the plan balances to someone other than a spouse. The year of death distribution to the deceased, for the deceased, must take place as if living. The beneficiary, regardless of age, goes to the IRS-provided table (IRS provides tables for ages younger than 70) and enters the table, with the age that they are in the calendar year after the calendar year of the account owner's death, to find their divisor. The procedure for making the required minimum distribution in the first year after the account owner's death is as has already been described. However, in subsequent years the beneficiary does not have to go back to the table to determine the divisor; rather he or she subtracts one (1) from the initial divisor for each distribution year thereafter and uses that number to calculate the minimum distribution requirement for the year.

Scenario Four

You die, leaving no named beneficiaries, after your required minimum distributions have begun. Don't do this! If this does happen, your remaining plan balances have to come out at a minimum using the divisor for your age based upon your birthday in the calendar year of your death as the divisor for that year. In subsequent years, one (1) is subtracted from that divisor for each year since your death. Although you are not going to have to worry about it, someone is going to have to deal with it.

Scenario Five

You die prior to your required minimum distributions date, leaving no named beneficiaries. Here you really blew it. Now your plan balances have to be paid out within 5-years of your death. That is likely to cause an income tax headache for your survivors. See Exhibit 14.22 (page 391) for a summary of these scenarios.

Beneficiary Designation

Generally speaking, anyone who is married will want to name his or her spouse as the primary beneficiary, with children as equal secondary beneficiaries. If these two selections do not fit your situation, be sure to name those whom you wish to benefit. These accounts are valuable assets. You will hear that the IRS wants the designated beneficiary identified by the December 31 of the year following the employee's death. Although this does give your survivors an opportunity for postdeath planning, it does not mean beneficiaries can be added or subtracted after your death. The IRS will not allow the selection of a beneficiary after the IRA owner's death where none is in place at death. It does mean that all of the named beneficiaries could get together and decide who among them would benefit most by inheriting your IRA. Those not wanting to be a beneficiary could disclaim their interest.

LIFE INCOME AND LIFE CARE

I would try to convey this message myself if I thought I could do it as well as my friend Dave Littell has done it. I have asked him to explain how the annuity financial tool was used by his parents and how his parents taught the two of us so much about peace of mind in retirement.

Dave's story about his parents helps us to understand the positive side effects of long-term care facilities and immediate annuities that those of us, who have not lived through the situation, might not understand.

Lessons from My Parents, the Retirees

David A. Littell, JD*

At The American College, I have been responsible for developing course material in retirement planning for a number of years. I've learned from many people, but one important, and surprising, source of information has been my parents. Like any adult child, I can be skeptical about my parents' expertise, but in the last few years, I've really grown to respect the way they have handled themselves in retirement. After hearing and seeing one horror

---

©David A. Littell, JD. Used with permission.
*David A. Littell, JD, is an associate professor at the American College in Bryn Mawr, Pennsylvania. There he is responsible for the development of course material in the areas of pension and retirement planning in the CLU and ChFC curriculum.

story after another, I'm ready to nominate my parents as "retirees of the year."

To start off, they have done all the basics that you would recommend to your clients. They have used investment professionals for money management, lawyers for appropriate estate planning, and insurance professionals for their insurance needs. In addition, my folks have made many other good decisions that have taught me some important lessons. Here are a few I'd like to share.

Life Care

About seven years ago, my parents (then in their late 70s) announced they were moving into a life-care community. In exchange for a significant entrance fee and a monthly assessment, they are promised lifelong care at a monthly rate that does not vary according to the level of care they are receiving—i.e., whether they are in independent living or the home's nursing facility. The retirement home is solvent and prosperous. It has no significant long-term debt, and looks like it will be around to service its residents for many, many years to come.

They moved into a two-bedroom, newly renovated apartment. With less living space than they had been accustomed to previously, regular maid service, easy access to a fine dining facility, and all new appliances—my mother's first comment was, "Now, *I* get to retire."

Today, their lives are quite comfortable and full. From my position as their child, I am happy that they are well cared for and are enjoying their lives. Also, it's nice to know that they live in a place that is "senior proof," which minimizes their chances of falling or incurring an accident.

One thing I've learned watching their lives is that a good life-care community doesn't mean giving up freedom; it means more freedom. It releases them from the drudgery of the increasingly difficult tasks of daily living, giving them more time and energy to pursue exercise, hobbies, and travel.

I could give numerous examples of this, but one instance stands out in my mind. Recently, my mother began to require daily shots of insulin for diabetes. My father can administer the

EXHIBIT 14.22

Qualified Plan Minimum Distribution Requirements

Account balance owner living at RBD*	Account balance owner dies *before* RBD	Distribution	Account balance owner dies *after* RBD	Distribution
RBD is the April 1 of the year following the year you attain age 70½. If you delay your distribution beyond December 31 of the year in which you attain age 70½, you will have to take the distribution for the year in which you attain age 70½ and for the next year (your 71½ year) in the same year.	Spouse sole unlimited beneficiary IRC Section (a)(9)(B)(iii) and (iv)	RBD is: (1) Calendar year after death (2) Calendar year owner would have been age 70½ (3) Spouse new account owner—RBD spouse's age 70½	Spouse sole unlimited beneficiary IRC Section (a)(9)(B)(iii) and (iv)	RBD is: (1) Calendar year after death (2) Spouse's birthday that year for divisor, and that divisor reduced by one for subsequent years.
	Nonspousal beneficiary IRC Section 401(a)(9)(B)(iii) and (iv)	RBD is: (1) Calendar year after death (2) Use IRS table for beneficiary's life expectancy reduced by one (1) for succeeding years	Nonspousal beneficiary IRC Section 401(a)(9)(B)(iii) and (iv)	RBD is: (1) Calendar year after death (2) Use IRS table for beneficiary's life expectancy reduced by one (1) for succeeding years
Use the IRS Table for your life expectancy using the birthday age in the year of distribution to find your divisor for that year. For each subsequent year, again use the table for the divisor that corresponds to your birthday in the year of distribution.	No named beneficlary IRC Section 401 (a)(9)(B)(ii)	Distribute all by the end of the calendar year that contains the fifth anniversary of the owner's death IRC Section 401(a)(9)(B)(ii)	No named beneficiary IRC Section 401 (a)(9)(B)(ii)	RBD is: (1) Calendar year after death (2) Use IRS table for beneficiary's life expectancy reduced by one (1) for succeeding years

*RBD stands for "required beginning date" and from a practical standpoint for most of us it is the year we attain age 70½, although we may delay our first distribution until the April 1 of the year after we attain age 70½. IRC Section 401(a)(9)(C).

shot, but doesn't see well enough to fill the syringe. At the retirement community, a new supply of properly filled insulin syringes is delivered to them every week. If they were living independently, think how complicated this process could become. Who would do it, where would they go to get it done, how much would it cost, and most importantly, how long would it take to do this each day? I think that the retirement community provides them with an invaluable service. They get health care tailored to their needs. This minimizes the time they spend dealing with health-care maintenance, and allows them to be as independent as they wish to be.

Organized Documentation

As the co-executor of his brother's estate, my father experienced firsthand the difficulty of locating documents after his brother's death. It took several months just to locate all of my uncle's assets. In response, my father has been quite clear that this won't happen to his own heirs. Every year, he sends a complete list to all of his children of where his assets are, who's responsible for what, and so on. He includes addresses, phone numbers, and helpful hints. I know professionals give clients this advice all the time, but do you know anyone who actually keeps these sorts of records?

The Life Annuity

Several years ago my father began worrying a great deal about his financial affairs. From his perspective, annual fees at the home were going up, and the interest earnings on his bond portfolio were dropping. His stock portfolio was appreciating, but dividend yield was extremely low. With only Social Security as guaranteed monthly income, periodically he was having to liquidate assets to pay the bills, and every sale generated significant capital gains tax (then at 28 percent). In reality, my parents have sufficient assets to be able to modestly spend down their assets for a very long time. However, the thought of dwindling assets and a long life at an expensive retirement home was eating at my father. It also caused tension with my mother, because he was becoming increasingly concerned about her favorite hobby—writing checks (for birthdays, anniversaries, etc.) to our extremely large and ever-expanding family.

As strange as this may sound, I suggested to this octogenarian that he consider purchasing an immediate, fixed, joint-life annuity. He looked into it, got some quotes, and ended up purchasing enough to essentially pay his monthly bill at the retirement home. He now sleeps much better knowing that this bill always will be paid.

Over time, it became apparent that this decision had other positive financial and emotional side effects as well. First, my father intends to get his money's worth, and is doing everything he can to live forever—and, given the care he gets at the retirement home, he probably will. Second, my mother is writing checks like mad, and my father is leaving her alone. Third, the annuity income allows him to leave his stock portfolio alone. If he leaves the stock to his heirs, income tax can be avoided (the step-up-in-basis rules) on the large amount of capital appreciation. What seems somewhat unconventional turns out to be my father's favorite investment.

I've seen my parents make decisions in a calm, rational way in their retirement. I see how these decisions have simplified and enriched their lives. They made their decisions, in part, so that they wouldn't end up as a burden on their children. As one of their children, I'll tell you that I appreciate that and am very happy that they are well cared for. To end, let's just say that yes, you can learn a lot from your elders.

SUMMARY

Keep in mind that annuities are for *you* and your retirement income. They are tax-inefficient for your beneficiaries, but not for you and your spouse. They are designed to be used within your own and your spouse's lifetime. Annuities that pass to nonspousal beneficiaries incur income taxes, whereas many other assets may receive a step up in cost basis at the death of the owner and are thus forgiven income tax liabilities that the living owner would have incurred. Income taxes and estate taxes reduce the net benefit to nonspousal beneficiaries of annuities at death.

CHAPTER 15

Where to Go for Products and Assistance

I'm So Confused!

Prior to the mid-1970s, few financial professionals or consumers worried about the financial integrity of insurance companies. Street talk regarding a company and its products, service, and stability served as good enough indicators for most people.

We have learned that such confidence was unjustified. Many of you will remember the Equity Funding fiasco in which the insurance company staff people actually manufactured bogus policies for nonexistent insureds. An alert reporter finally exposed the fraud. Then came the Baldwin-United failure in which the consumer was promised *too good to be true* interest rates and salespeople received *too good to be true* commissions. Many have been shocked by the fact that insurance companies can fail, that they fail to provide service, that their products fail, and that they abandon products. On April 11, 1991, the state insurance commissioner of California placed Executive Life of California in conservatorship and the world learned a new lesson. Other companies that have been taken over by the regulators include Confederation Life, Executive Life of New York, Fidelity Bankers Life, Fidelity Mutual Life, First Capital Life, General American Life, Guarantee Security Life, Kentucky Central Life, Mid-Continent Life, Monarch Life, Mutual Benefit Life, and Old Colony Life. In each of these situations the financial security of the policy owners was put at risk. In the September 2000 issue of his publication,

The Insurance Forum, Joseph M. Belth reports that policy owners of failed companies have to deal with uncertainty, delay, aggravation, inability to get at the asset value of their policies, and even in some instances, death benefit delays and reductions in annuity benefits.

Ward's Results Life & Health Edition is an annual publication that provides extensive financial information, as well as safety and performance information, on almost any company with which you might be doing business. It is available to you at many public libraries across the county. The phone number is 513-791-0303, and the web site is www.wardinc.com. *Ward's Results*, 1991, reported on 1658 life insurance companies. *Ward's Results*, 2000, reported on 1079 life insurance companies. In the 9-year period, 579 insurance companies disappeared from the Ward's database due to failures, mergers, and acquisitions—approximately 65 companies per year. The implosion of the insurance industry continues. The insurance company you buy from may well not be the insurance company you die with, not only as a result of failure but also as a result of mergers and acquisitions.

How do you protect yourself against potential insurance company failures? You deal with only the biggest and the best, those that have been in business for many years. You avoid those with portfolios that are obviously taking exceptional risk to earn higher yields. You avoid the general accounts of insurance companies as much as possible by using products that provide access to separate accounts. You will want to deal with variable products that are sold with a prospectus, and that allow you to make use of the subaccounts within the separate account so that you may diversify your investments. When you own a general account– only life insurance product, you are accepting what investment people refer to as *unsystematic risk*, a type of risk that can be mitigated by diversification. Prudence recommends diversification. General–account only products do not provide for diversification. Make sure the company you deal with has multiple-pocket policies (separate accounts) available and use them.

A number of sources of assistance and information are available to you in your effort to deal with high quality insurance companies. Sources to check include your state's insurance department, some of the rating services, and pertinent publications.

STATE REGULATION

Insurance companies are regulated primarily by the individual states. Assuming that the insurance company that you have chosen is licensed to do business within your resident state, you have that first level of protection. You may assume that your state insurance department has examined the company and its products and found them in compliance with state regulations. Unfortunately, this first level of protection isn't always totally reliable. In spite of state regulations, insurance companies have failed and caused economic harm to their customers. As William H. Smythe said while executive director of the NAIC securities valuation office in New York, "We regulators don't have the authority to tell guys how to run their businesses. We almost have to wait for a disaster to happen, when it comes down to it."

The state does, however, collect information about companies doing business within the state that can be of value. Documents such as the company's annual convention statements and Schedule M should be available upon request. These documents will give you the information the company is providing to the regulators regarding its financial condition and the assumptions used in its illustrations. If you have a concern about a company, call your state insurance commissioner's office and ask questions. Your call may trigger action that saves you and possibly others from economic harm.

The states vary in the quality and quantity of their regulation. New York State is noted for being one of the toughest within the industry. Many people say that New York is too conservative and difficult, but a restrictive approach can be an advantage to you as you try to pick a company that will be a survivor in these volatile times. Ask if the company is licensed to do business in New York. If it is and it has agreed to follow New York State rules wherever it does business, you have another level of assurance from New York regulators.

RISK-BASED CAPITAL RATIO

The NAIC has written model legislation for the states to adopt. This legislation created *risk-based capital* regulations to help regulators identify how much capital (surplus) is *enough* for various companies, depending upon the *riskiness* of their assets and business. Risk-based capital is an important consideration in evaluating insurance companies

Four components go into creating a risk-based capital ratio for a company: (1) the company's asset risk, which is the most highly weighted component at 67 percent, (2) insurance risk, which is weighted 13 percent, (3) interest rate risk, which receives a 17 percent weighting and (4) business risk with a 3 percent weighting in the formula. We will examine each one in detail:

1. *Asset risk: 67 percent.* Higher levels of capital are required to be set aside for assets held by the company which are deemed to be of lower quality or higher risk. Exhibit 15.1 shows the amount of capital that must be set aside in reserve for each category of asset. You can see that the regulators are sending a message to insurance companies. By requiring less capital for what are deemed "safe" investments and more for more risky investments, it shows the regulators favor safer, lower-yielding investments.

2. *Insurance risk: 13 percent.* The insurance company has to hold higher reserves when it gives you, the policy owner, stronger guarantees. When an insurance company

EXHIBIT 15.1

NAIC Capital Requirements for Life Insurance General Account Investments

Investment Bonds	Capital Requirement
Bonds	
AAA government	0.3%
Low quality credit	9%
Lower	20%
Mortgages	2%
Mortgages in foreclosure	20%
Common stock	30%
Real estate	10%

issues you a disability insurance policy and guarantees
that it can never change its cost to you, and that it can
never cancel the policy or reduce the benefits, it is
referred to as *non-can* for *noncancelable*. The reserves that
must be held are a percentage of the premium you pay
for the policy. For example, 35 percent must go to
reserves on the first $50 million in non-can disability
premiums the company receives, and 15 percent on
premiums in excess of that amount. Other premiums are
reserved at 25 percent of the first $25 million and 15
percent on the balance. For group accident and health,
20 percent must go to reserves on the first $50 million
and 10 percent on the balance plus 5 percent claim
reserve. For life insurance, 0.15 percent must go to
reserves on the first $500 million. You can see that life
insurance is perceived to be a less risky business than
the health-related types of insurance.

3. *Interest rate risk: 17 percent*. For life insurance, reserves
   must equal 0.5 percent; for annuities, reserves must be 1
   percent plus a cashflow testing factor that increases
   reserve requirements for companies with total assets
   under $100 million

4. *Business risk: 3 percent*. The reserve requirements are
   based upon the amount of premium subject to the state
   guarantee funds, for example, life and annuity 2 percent;
   accident and health 5 percent.

Based upon these individual company components, the regulators determine the total risk-based capital that they require for
the company. The calculated amount is equal to the square root
of [(asset risk + interest rate risk)^2 + (insurance risk)^2] + business risk.

The total adjusted actual capital of the company is then calculated. Total company-adjusted capital is equal to the company's
total capital, surplus, and asset valuation reserve plus one half of
its dividend liability.

The final step in calculating the company's risk-based capital
ratio is to compare what the regulators say a company should
have with what the company does have, with the obvious objec-

tive of making sure that the company has more than that which is required. In fact, today the industry objective seems to be about 2.5 times what is required, or a risk-based capital ratio of 250 percent.

If a company is found to be close to or below the regulator-determined minimum risk-based capital ratio, the state regulator and the insurance company are required to take the actions shown in Exhibit 15.2. The National Association of Insurance Commissioners, through its risk-based capital model legislation, is telling insurance companies that they must reduce risk (and thus return) in their general accounts.

The Financial Accounting Standards Board (FASB) also is causing insurance companies to reduce risk, and thus return, by requiring that financial institutions in their financial reporting to mark bonds to market if they are "for sale." On April 13, 1993, FASB voted 5 to 2 to adopt a new standard for reporting bonds on financial reports. It determined that bonds held by insurers and other financial institutions must be reported at market value unless they are classified as "investments held to maturity" and the companies or institutions have the intent to hold them until maturity. All other debt securities would be classified as either "trading securities" or "securities available for sale" and reported at market value.

Note that this changes how *assets* are valued but makes no change in how *liabilities* are valued. The result is that volatile asset

EXHIBIT 15.2

NAIC Actions Required at Certain RBC Levels

Ratio	Regulatory Action
125% or less and trend is negative	File RBC plan and projections for approval
Less than 100%	Company action level event—submit plan
Less than 75%	Regulatory action level event—corrective order
Less than 50%	Authorized control level event—regulatory receivership (optional)
Less than 35%	Mandatory control level event—receivership within 90 days

values cause volatile surplus values. One year a company may have a strong RBC ratio and the next year it may have trouble meeting NAIC RBC requirements.

Insurance companies have reacted to these regulatory and reporting requirements by:

- Shortening bond maturities to reduce volatility
- Investing less in equity because of the NAIC's reserve requirements of holding 30 percent in reserve for equities versus 0.3 percent in reserve for highest-quality bonds
- No longer being the traditional private source of capital for industry
- Having even more difficulty raising capital/surplus
- Moving away from general account–based products

In regard to the last point in the list, note that general account policies have become less attractive to the insurance-buying public and their advisors as the returns earned in the general account have decreased as a result of the general level of interest rates and the impact of these regulatory requirements. Fred McCombs, the owner of the Minnesota Vikings, was being interviewed on the radio on September 3, 2000, about something totally unrelated to life insurance, but his comment is applicable to general account life insurance today. Asking the general account of an insurance company to provide long-term returns in excess of 8 percent is, in McCombs's words, "Like asking a crippled bird to fly."

RATING SERVICES

A number of rating services provide information about the insurance industry. Be aware, however, that each service has its own rating standards and criteria (see Exhibits 15.3 and 15.4).

A. M. Best Company

A good source of public information is the A. M. Best Company of Oldwick, New Jersey, the oldest insurance industry rating service. A. M. Best provides information regarding a company's financial condition, a synopsis of its history and data on its man-

EXHIBIT 15.3

Rating Categories and Rank*

Rank	S&P†	Ratings			
		Moody's	Fitch	Weiss	Best
1	AAA	Aaa	AAA	A+	A++
2	AA+	Aa1	AA+	A	A+
3	AA	Aa2	AA	A−	A
4	AA−	Aa3	AA−	B+	A−
5	A+	A1	A+	B	B++
6	A	A2	A	B−	B+
7	A−	A3	A−	C+	B
8	BBB+	Baa1	BBB+	C	B−
9	BBB	Baa2	BBB	C−	C++
10	BBB−	Baa3	BBB−	D+	C+
11	BB+	Ba1	BB+	D	C
12	BB	Ba2	BB	D−	C−
13	BB−	Ba3	BB−	E+	D
14	B+	B1	B+	E	E
15	B	B2	B	E−	F
16	B−	B3	B−	F	
17	CCC	Caa1	CCC+		
18	CC	Caa2	CCC		
19	R	Caa3	CCC−		
20		Ca	CC/C		
21		C	DDD		
22			DD/D		

*The rating categories in a given rank are not equivalent to one another. See the descriptions of the rating categories from the rating companies.
†Standard and Poor's uses a "pi" subscript to indicate that a rating is only based on its analysis of information in the public domain.

agement, operating commitments, and the states in which it may write business. A. M. Best also provides its own company ratings, designed to evaluate strengths and weaknesses in four areas: underwriting, expense control, reserve adequacy, and investments. In most cases, you would be wise to place your trust in companies with A ratings by Best. A. M. Best Company may be contacted directly at Ambest Road, Oldwick, New Jersey, 08858, or at its web site at www.ambest.com.

EXHIBIT 15.4

Ratings—Secure or Vulnerable?

	A. M. Best	Moody's	S & P CPA	S & P Qualified	Fitch	Weiss
Secure	A++, A+ Superior A	Aaa, Aa1, Aa2, Aa3 A1, A2, A3	AAA, AA+, AA AA-, A+, A, A-	AAA, AA BBBq	AAA, AA+ AA	A+, A, A- B+,
	A- Excellent B++, B+ Very good	Baa1, Baa2, Baa3 Ba1, Ba2, Ba3	BBB+, BBB, BBB-	A BBB, BBq	AA-, A+, A, A-, BBB+, BBB, BBB--	B, B-, C+, C, C-
Vulnerable	B, B- Adequate C++, C+ Fair C, C- Marginal D Very vulnerable	B1, B2, B3	BB+, BB, BB- B+, B, B-	BB B CCC Bq	B+, B, B-	D+, D, D- E+
	E Under state supervision F In liquidation	Caa, Ca, C	CCC R		CCC E+ all DDD E+ all	E, E- F

You will find the Best reports in your local library. Use only the most current book. Many insurance companies and agents also can provide summaries of Best reports regarding the companies they are recommending.

Standard and Poor's

Standard and Poor's (www.standardandpoors.com) has a service that rates a number of companies on their *claims-paying ability*. Major employers, trying to find a source for guaranteed interest contracts (GICs) for their retirement plans, use this service to evaluate the financial strength of competing insurance companies. An insurance company pays to obtain a rating from Standard and Poor's Corporation. If the company is dissatisfied with the rating S&P has given it, it has the option of instructing S&P not to publish it. S&P modifies its ratings with the addition of a plus (+) or minus (−) sign. A company could have an A+ rating from S&P and be in at the third ratings level. You easily could be misled if you assumed that this A+ rating was equivalent to a Best's top rating. Know what these ratings mean if you are going to use them in your decision making.

Standard and Poor's also provides ratings on a broader number of companies for which it does not charge.

Moody's

Moody's (www.moodys.com) concentrates heavily on the quality of the company's investment portfolio. Moody's is located at 99 Church Street, New York, New York 10007. Moody's ratings, like S&P's, generally are not available unless the insurance company chooses to make them available to you.

Fitch IBCA

Fitch IBCA & Duff and Phelps Credit Rating Company merged to form Fitch International. As a result, Fitch has two web sites, www.fitchratings.com and www.dcrco.com. Fitch International (55 East Monroe Street, Chicago, Illinois 60603) provides an overall approach in its credit ratings and has a reputation for quality and integrity. The Fitch ratings apply to corporate debt, preferred stock, real estate, asset-backed financing, and the insurance company's claims-paying ability. When rating a company, Fitch includes in its evaluation a management interview, quantitative analysis, and a view of the company's future. The ratings are updated quarterly in an effort to make the material more timely. Fitch ratings are available from insurance companies that have contracted for Fitch's services and its ratings are included under DCR (Duff Credit Ratings) in Morningstar's *Principia Pro* along with those of A. M. Best.

Weiss Ratings, Inc.

The Weiss ratings are described as "safety ratings." Weiss issues financial safety ratings using publicly available information, and invites companies to provide additional information. Weiss ratings are independent of the companies. The insurance companies are not charged by Weiss, and the ratings are published whether the companies like it or not. Weiss derives its revenue from what it charges you when you request a company rating.

According to the September 2000 *Insurance Forum*, of 1221 life and health insurance companies rated by Weiss, the spread of Weiss's ratings were as shown in Exhibit 15.5. You can see from the exhibit that of all the companies Weiss rates, only 3.9 percent are in the "A" category. In contrast, of the 794 companies STP rates, 54.9 percent are rated A; of the 202 companies that Moody's

EXHIBIT 15.5

Number and Percent of Companies in Each Weiss Rating Category

Ratings	Companies	Percent
A+, A, A−	47	3.9
B+, B, B−	354	29.0
C+, C, C−	492	40.2
D+, D, D−	260	21.3
E+, E, E−	68	5.5

rates, the figure is 90.0 percent; out of 223 companies, Fitch puts
98.2 percent in the A category; and A. M. Best gives 56.3 percent
of 1345 companies it rates a grade of A. One reason for this dis-
parity in percentages in the A category is that if the insurance
company has to pay the rating service to get a rating, it won't ask
for a rating or allow it to be published unless it expects it to be a
good one. It is also obvious that many insurance companies that
get A's from the other rating services do not get A's from Weiss,
and thus may not be favorably disposed toward Weiss's ratings.

For more information about Weiss ratings contact its customer service hotline at 800-289–9222, check its web site at
www.weissratings.com, or write to Weiss Ratings, P.O. Box 109665,
Palm Beach Gardens, Florida 33410. Verbal ratings are available
for $15, a one page consumer safety update costs $25, and a 25
page personal safety report can be obtained for $45.

RATING SERVICES MISS
CONFEDERATION LIFE

Confederation Life was taken into receivership by the regulators
on August 12, 1994. The rating services generally did not see the
failure coming. A. M. Best first downgraded the company from
A+ to A on June 21, 1993, then to A − on April 14, 1994 and to
B ++ on August 4, 1994. Standard and Poor's lowered Confederation Life's rating to "A + on credit watch with negative implications" on April 14, 1994. Duff and Phelps rated the company
"AA− rating watch-down" on the same day. Weiss Ratings downgraded the company's U.S. affiliates from C to C− on June 2, 1994.
All these dates are too close to the failure date of August 12, 1994,
for policy owners to take action to protect themselves.

The message in this scenario is that when evaluating companies, you need to place more importance on the direction of the
ratings—are they going up or going down—rather than on the
ratings themselves. And don't rely on just the ratings—do more
extensive research on the insurance companies themselves.

COMPANY ANNUAL REPORTS

A review of the company's financial statements and annual report
also is in order. Annual reports are readily available from all in-

surance companies, and you definitely should ask for them. At least read the president's letter. It should help you to determine what is going well for the company and what is going poorly. Obviously, you want products and services that are doing well because they have a greater claim on the resources and attention of the company. Poorly performing products and services are likely to receive less enthusiastic attention and may even be eliminated. Skim the remainder of the report for information pertinent to the sector of the company in which you are interested. Don't skip the footnotes, which often contain the most important warnings. Also, since practically every company has its own web site, you will want to review it. Normally their financial rating will be given on their site.

Caution

The bottom line is that you can't know everything. The information you obtain will inevitably be dated. If an insurance company is trying to fool you and the regulators, you are likely to find out too late. For this reason, it is best to work with the biggest and the best. Work with companies whose primary business is insurance. Other companies will find it very easy to rid themselves of underperforming insurance subsidiaries. *Additional advice:* Use companies that offer multiple-pocket variable contracts.

STATE GUARANTEE FUNDS

There are state guarantee funds for insurance, and if your state has an adequate guarantee, you may benefit. When Baldwin-United failed in 1983 (its primary business was piano making), the life insurance industry and regulators worked diligently for 5 years to contain the damage. Those who owned Baldwin-United contracts endured 5 years of uncertainty about their investments. They finally did receive a settlement that generally covered the principal they had invested, but not the exorbitant interest rates they had been promised. You certainly couldn't say that they did not suffer a loss!

You, the consumer, must consider carefully the creditworthiness of the general accounts of the insurance companies to which you are entrusting your funds. In short, don't bet on state guarantee funds, mergers, acquisitions, and reorganizations in the insurance industry to bail you out of a failing company.

JOSEPH M. BELTH

Joseph M. Belth, Ph.D., as noted earlier, has been referred to as the Ralph Nader of the insurance industry. He exhibits a bulldoglike tenacity in his pursuit of financial information on insurance companies to keep consumers and financial professionals informed. He is not the least bit hesitant to point out the companies that he believes are involved in questionable practices. His monthly publication can be obtained by writing to *The Insurance Forum*, P.O. Box 245, Ellettsville, Indiana 47429–0245. The phone number is 812-876–6502, and the web site is www.theinsuranceforum.com. In the fall of each year, he publishes a special rating issue that is excellent.

Belth is a controversial source of information. He has the courage to express his opinions in no uncertain terms, and consequently, many take issue with him. However, he does give the background data that lead him to his conclusions. This helps you to understand the issues and risks involved so that you can make more informed purchase decisions.

PRODUCT IMPACT ON COMPANY SELECTION

Another important factor in company selection is the product line offered by the company you are considering. Some multiline companies will provide for both the property and casualty needs of individuals and companies, as well as the life, annuity, and health insurance needs. However, it is unusual for one insurance professional to have expertise in all these fields, although there are, of course, exceptions. There are many partnerships of property/casualty and life agents who combine their expertise to serve their clients. Most insurance companies are oriented toward property and casualty or toward life, annuity, and health. One rule of thumb to remember is that the company you choose should have a sufficiently diverse product line so that if one of its products is legislated out of existence, the company does not fail with it, leaving you *orphaned*. Diversification of product provides a degree of safety and flexibility for insurance companies, just as it does for individuals.

You want to avoid the risk that the insurance product you select may fail to perform as promised. This can happen not only if the insurance company becomes insolvent, but also if the product becomes unprofitable and the company decides to divest itself of the unprofitable unit.

COMPANY SELECTION INVOLVES INTERMEDIARY SELECTION

Intermediaries can greatly influence product selection and satisfaction. You should learn to distinguish the *client-oriented* salesperson from the *product* salesperson. The product salesperson develops an expertise and an efficient marketing plan for a specific *hot product*. Product specialists can be used to your advantage because of their focused knowledge in their area of expertise. However, it could be to your disadvantage if the product is sold to you as a solution to a problem you don't have. For example, single-premium life is a good product, but it is not appropriate for every client. In the 1986–1987 period, much of it was sold indiscriminately.

On the other hand, highly technical products such as pension plans, profit-sharing plans, 401(k) plans, and other qualified plans may be more efficiently handled and serviced by product specialists. Frequently, a client-oriented generalist works jointly with a product specialist to ensure that you get adequate service and technical assistance.

You need to understand the type of salesperson or intermediary with whom you are working so that you can determine that person's role in your risk-management process. The choice is yours. Hiring a qualified, empathetic salesperson or a qualified advisor for a fee is not an admission of naivete. Can you go through the selection process alone? If so, could you do it better than if you had the proper help? Exactly what would that help cost you?

Know what you are *paying* the salesperson in the same way that you would evaluate the fee and the qualifications of any other advisor you might hire. How much of the money transferred to the insurance company is allocated for that commission? In these days of products that have contingent-deferred sales loads, you often will find that the salesperson receives more commission dollars than are subtracted from your funds. This is because the insurance company advances the pay and plans on recouping this expense from profits on your product over the years you keep the product in force. If you keep the business there long enough, for example 15 years, the commission, along with other expenses, is all recouped and you are charged no contingent-deferred sales charge after that point. However, if you take your business away too soon and the company is unable to recoup these expenses, it will charge you a contingent-deferred sales charge, or back-end load. It really is a rather fair and economical way to pay for the services of good salespeople. If you choose to pay them simply because they are persistent rather than helpful, it is a waste and is nobody's fault but your own. In short, know whom you are buying from, what you are paying, and why.

Financial journalists like to debate the need for intermediaries. They contend, "Read our magazine or column and you will not have to pay salespeople." Some suggest that you are best served by dealing directly with a company like USAA that markets by direct mail and referral because you avoid the salesperson's commission. Alternatively, you have the choice of dealing with the low-load companies that market directly to the public, or in some cases to financial planners who then add an independent charge for acting as your intermediary. Don't be deceived—you pay marketing expenses whether they involve commissions to salespeople, overhead, costs of direct mail and advertising, or direct fees to those who find you a product.

PAYING FOR THE PRODUCT AND SERVICE

Understand that you will pay for the sales process. Even if a product is supposedly *no-load*, there is a cost of bringing that product to your attention, and you pay that cost. No-loads and low loads typically have substantial marketing costs and can be expected to make more use of advertising than companies that employ a sales force. Companies that market to independent agents can do so with good products and services or with high-commission promises and loss-leader interest rates that they do not intend to maintain. What is your independent agent recommending—superior products or higher-commission products?

Previously, common wisdom suggested that you would be better served by dealing with a *broker* or *independent agent* than with a *captive* agent. The former would have access to all products from all companies, while the latter would have access only to those products provided by the employing company. This theory never did work very well because all insurance salespeople, captive or independent, are limited in their capacity to know everything about every product available. Now, more than ever, every broker or agent must question the promises made by the product providers and limit their product search to companies they trust.

The distinction between the independent and captive insurance agent is irrelevant when you consider registered products, i.e., those that are related to the securities markets and sold with a prospectus. These stock and bond-based products are provided to a salesperson through a *broker-dealer* or parent organization that screens the products before they are sold. Most broker-dealers insist that their salespeople sell only the securities-based products that they have preapproved, which means that the salesperson's broker-dealer affiliation limits the products the salesperson can offer.

This book recommends that you make your first cut based on the financial strength and integrity of the insurance company and your second cut based on the products the companies offer, *making sure that the companies you have selected offer the products you want* currently, together with a diversified portfolio of products available for your use.

Interview Intermediaries

The third cut is the agent or intermediary. Interview a number of them. Find out what products they are licensed to sell. Ask them questions about their background, their approach to the business, their present educational credentials, and those they expect to attain in the future. If the agents you are interviewing are relatively new in the business, find out what backup services are available to them. Ask whom they go to for help in a difficult case; and if you think you'll need them, ask to meet those individuals also. Never before has an insurance expert's advice been more important to you.

You will find that financial planners like to have quality insurance professionals available to them. Certified financial planners (CFPs) and Chartered financial consultants (ChFCs) will look for insurance professionals with educational credentials comparable to their own in the insurance field. They will look for a chartered life underwriter (CLU) who has received that designation from the American College in Bryn Mawr, Pennsylvania.

CLUs must have completed 10 semester courses and 10 examinations over approximately a 5-year period to attain this designation. Certified financial planners and chartered financial consultants also have had education in the personal risk-management area. If the agent that you are interviewing has taken any of these advanced courses, it indicates two things that are advantageous to you. First, the individual is capable of passing such exams; and second, he or she is committed to learning more in order to serve you better. The agent has, in effect, worked to become qualified to serve as your insurance consultant.

When you find the person who meets your requirements, with who you can communicate, and who you know can obtain the insurance products that you want, the person will *earn* what you pay for services. The individual will either have integrity and a professional approach in serving your best interest or not. It will be up to you to sense the presence or absence of such integrity. That is why the interview is so important.

When dealing with professional insurance intermediaries, your most effective questions are, "What would you do to solve this problem if you were in my shoes? Why? How have you handled this need for yourself? Show me!" This puts a great deal of pressure on the professional, and it is likely that response will help you to judge if the two all-important qualities—-personal integrity and empathy—are present. If they are not, do not do business with that intermediary.

The bottom line is that most of us need help in selecting and managing insurance products. We will pay for this help one way or the other. Seek the best-qualified help you can find, because poorly designed insurance is detrimental to your economic health, whereas properly owned, designed, funded, and managed insurance products are productive and valuable in enhancing your family's financial security.

Once you have found the company, product line, and professional intermediary, you are in an excellent position to compare costs and benefits. The objective at the outset of this book was to give you the tools to manage the products you purchase from insurance companies profitably and efficiently. The hope is that by now you are able to do just that. With the tools that have been provided herein, you are the new sophisticated consumer. You know that when you are offered choices within the various insurance company products, your basic rules of thumb will be to:

1. Know the costs built into the product, especially in the yearly years.
2. Establish long-term relationships with quality insurance companies and quality intermediaries.
3. Choose multiple-pocket contracts.
4. Choose control over no control.
5. Choose flexibility over inflexibility.
6. Choose quality and alternatives over current or future interest rate promises.
7. Choose a survivor among insurance companies and intermediaries.
8. Accept the fact that assets within insurance contracts require your management, as does every other asset on your balance sheet. Vigilance pays.

Life insurance and annuity contracts that are carefully purchased and well managed are wealth-building and wealth-preserving vehicles. The basic truth is that you can do almost everything you can do with CDs, stocks, bonds, and mutual funds within life insurance and annuity products today and at the same time protect the return on those investments from being diminished by current income taxes.

CONCLUSION

As this book goes to press, the most important risk facing the life insurance industry and *you*, if you are an owner of a whole life or universal life policy, is the possibility of continuing low interest rates. The effect of low interest rates on the general accounts of insurance companies is being exacerbated by the regulators and raters of insurance companies. The National Association of Insurance Commissioners, through the *risk-based capital* model legislation being encouraged in every state at this time, is telling insurance companies that they must reduce risk (and thus return) in their investments. This overreaction by the regulators and raters, pushing toward lower-return investments, is happening at a time when it is conceivable that the yield on long-term bonds could decrease to 5 percent and that the lower-risk investments being forced upon insurance company general accounts could go to 4 percent, the minimum guaranteed interest rate in many of your whole life and universal life policies. If you are shaking your head and don't believe this can happen, keep in mind that we would be merely returning to historical norms. The average annual yield on long-term bonds over the past 199 years is 5.2 percent. If this condition prevails for an extended period of time, you can forget about your dividends or excess interest—there will not be *any!* You will then understand the constraints of a single-pocket contract (only one investment). You do not have choice and you do not have control in a single-pocket contract, and in today's world, that is a risky investment. You will then appreciate the importance of owning multiple-pocket contracts (multiple investments). Flexibility, control, and the opportunity to diversify your money within your life insurance policy produce a policy with less risk than a policy that accepts your money and lets the insurance company decide how to invest it.

You'll hear the handwringers say, "What will happen to variable universal policy owners when the market falls?" "What about guarantees?" And so on. Well, who said that all the money in your variable universal policy will be in the stock market? Won't you indeed diversify? Use a little guaranteed interest or conservative government bond fund and dollar-cost-average into your volatile stock accounts. The most important factors affecting performance will be the amount of your investment and asset allocation. *Invest enough!* Overfund your policies, or do not buy them. Do not ask a crippled bird to fly. Try to get VUL policies up to the maximum they will hold while still allowing you all the advantages of a life insurance policy, allowing you to borrow or withdraw from your policy without fear of income taxes or pre–

age 59½ penalties. Make sure they stay below the modified endowment contract status. That is when they work best for you and provide the best investment results, along with life insurance purchased with income tax–free earnings. As our grandchildren would say, "Fill it up to the top!"

GLOSSARY

Accidental death benefit This optional benefit provides an additional death benefit should the insured's death occur as a direct result of an accidental injury.

Account value The account value is the total of (1) any amounts in any variable investment option, (2) any amounts in the guaranteed interest option, and (3) any amounts that are being held to secure policy loans (including any interest on those amounts that has not yet been allocated to the variable investment options).

Accumulation-type policy In this type of policy, specific expense charges are taken out of the gross premium paid, resulting in the net premium. The accumulation of these net premiums with interest is referred to as the accumulation value. At the end of each specified period, cost of insurance charges are removed from the accumulation value just prior to adding the interest credits.

Accumulation value The value of the policy prior to deduction of any surrender charges. The accumulation value less surrender charge is often called the cash value or cash surrender value. The net cash value is the cash value less any policy loans.

Actuary A professional trained in evaluating insurance and other financial transactions based on relevant historical data.

Age basis In determining the age for which premiums are charged, the company may set the insuring age based on the age at the nearest birthday or the age at the last birthday basis.

Allocation date The date the funds are reallocated from a money-market type of account to those investments in accordance with your premium allocation instructions then in effect (typically about the twentieth day after the policy has been issued).

Alternative death benefit The alternative death benefit is computed by multiplying the policy's account value on the insured person's date of death by a percentage specified in the policy. The percentage depends on the insured person's age. This death benefit will be paid if it is *higher* than the basic Option A or Option B death benefit the insured has selected.

Amount of risk The amount at risk (also described in a policy as "net amount at risk") on any date is the difference between (1) the death benefit that would be payable if the insured person died on that date and (2) the then total account value under the policy.

Anniversary The year or years measured from the policy's register date.

Anti-selection The result of individuals applying for, or already covered by, insurance, taking advantage of knowledge about their own situation that results in a worse experience for the insurance company.

Assign/Assignment The rights in a policy may be assigned (transferred) to someone else as collateral for a loan, to effect a change of ownership, or for some other reason, if agreed to by the issuing insurance company. An **absolute assignment** is a change of ownership. Consult your tax advisor prior to making a transfer or other assignment.

Automatic premium loan An option under some fixed premium policies, whenever a premium is not received, to create automatically a policy loan for the amount necessary to pay the premium. When the remaining net cash value is no longer sufficient to cover a premium due, the policy will lapse with no (or minimal) net cash value unless premium payments are resumed in cash.

Automatic transfer service A dollar-cost-averaging service that enables the policy owner to make automatic monthly transfers from a money market option to the other variable investment options available.

Back-dating Applying for a life insurance policy with a coverage effective date prior to the date of application.

Basis Generally, basis will equal the premiums paid, less the amount of any previous distributions from the policy that were not taxable.

Beneficiary The person(s) or entity that receives the policy proceeds at the death of the insured. The policy's beneficiary is designated in the policy application but may be changed by the owner at any time during the insured person's life.

Best's ratings The service provides a standardized financial comparison and rating basis among insurance companies. It provides information as to the levels of a company's mortality, lapse, and expense results compared to industry norms. In addition, it ranks companies as to overall financial soundness. The highest ranking is A+, which is achieved by about the top 200 life insurance companies.

Business day Very often considered to be every day that the New York Stock Exchange is open for regular trading. It ends at the time regular trading on the exchange closes (or is suspended) for the day.

Cash surrender value The net cash surrender value equals the account value in the policy, minus any outstanding loans and unpaid loan interest, minus any amount of the account value that is "restricted" as a result of previously distributed "living benefits," and minus any surrender charge that then remains applicable.

Collateral This is the amount equal to the loan from a policy that will be taken from one or more of the investment options within the policy to secure the loan and to be held as collateral for the loan's repayment.

Commissioners' standard ordinary mortality   Mortality rates from tables promulgated by the National Association of Insurance Commissioners (NAIC) for use in calculating minimum reserves for individual life insurance.

Cost of insurance charge   This is the amount that the insurance company will charge the policy owner for the amount at risk. It is determined by multiplying the cost of the insurance rate that is then applicable to the policy by the amount *at risk* under the policy.

Cost of insurance rates   Rate per $1000 of the amount at risk.

Crediting rate   The interest rate credited to the accumulation values of accumulation-type policies.

Current charges   Accumulation-type policies have both current basis charges and guaranteed charges. Current basis charges are those being applied today and are based on the company's currently expected experience levels. Guaranteed or maximum charges are the highest levels that the company can apply if experience under the policy deteriorates.

Death benefit   The total amount payable to the beneficiary upon death of the insured.

Death benefit corridor   IRC 7702 defines the minimum amount of death benefit required in a policy in order for the policy to qualify as life insurance for federal tax purposes. (See Exhibit 2.1.)

Death benefit guarantee   The guarantee that the policy will not terminate until the insured reaches age 70 (for example), but in no case less than 10 years. Paying at least certain amounts of premiums, called "guarantee premiums," purchases this guarantee.

Declared interest rate   This is the interest rate that a company credits to an accumulation-type policy. It is based on the company's actual investment results. It is the same as the credited interest rate.

Definition of life insurance   Under IRC 7702, two alternative tests are set up to allow a policy to qualify as life insurance. Under the cash value accumulation test, there is no limit to the amount that is paid in premiums as long as there is enough death benefit relative to the accumulation value. The guideline premium and corridor test provides for (1) a maximum premium per thousand dollars of initial death benefit, and (2) a minimum "corridor" of death benefit which results in a death benefit that ultimately is less than the amount of death benefit required under the cash value accumulation test.

Direct recognition policies   Participating policies on which the dividend payable reflects the amount of, and interest rate payable on, outstanding loans. These policies preserve the equity among the dividends payable on policies with loans at various interest rates and those with no loans outstanding.

Dividend accumulations   A dividend option where the policy's total cash value is increased by the sum of the dividends paid each year with interest thereon. No extra death benefit, above the accumulated dividend value itself, is associated with this benefit. The dividends paid are a reduction of policy basis, and the interest credited each year is taxable income.

Dividend options The owner of a participating policy typically has the option of taking dividends in cash, applying them automatically to reduce current premiums due, letting them accumulate at interest, or purchasing additional insurance called paid-up additions.

Dividend scale The schedule of nonguaranteed dividends paid each year for a participating policy. The dividend scale reflects the difference between the company's actual level of mortality, expenses, and investment earnings since the policy was issued and the more conservative levels of those parameters on which the guaranteed values were based.

Dollar-cost-averaging service Also referred to as "automatic transfer service." This service automatically moves monthly (or at other regular intervals) a specific amount of money, or amount of interest earned from a money-market type of account, to other variable investment options available within the policy.

Endow A policy is said to "endow" when its cash value reaches its face amount.

Enhanced death benefit guarantee The enhanced death benefit guarantee rider guarantees the policy against termination for a monthly charge that is deducted from the account value. Very often all of the policy's account value must be allocated to variable investment options. While in effect, the policy will not lapse, even if the net cash surrender value is insufficient to pay a monthly deduction that has become due, as long as there is not an outstanding loan.

Exchange of insured provision A provision that allows the policy owner to exchange a new insured for the original insured without new policy expense loads, if satisfactory evidence of insurability is provided on the new life insurance.

Expense charges Charges made on accumulation-type policies to reimburse the company for a portion of its costs of issuing and maintaining the policy.

Extended term insurance A nonforfeiture option available when the policyholder stops paying premiums. The existing cash value is used to purchase term insurance for the entire face amount of the policy for as long as possible, according to *guaranteed* purchase rates specified in the policy.

Face amount The face amount is the amount of insurance coverage on the life of the insured person.

First-to-die insurance A life insurance policy covering two or more insureds, with the death benefit payable at the time the first death occurs. The surviving insured generally has the right to purchase a new policy at the time of the first death without new underwriting.

Fixed-premium policy   A policy that requires specified premium payments.

Flexible premium adjustable life policy   Another term for universal life policy.

General account   All the assets of a life insurance company other than those held in separate accounts.

Grace period   The policy owner has a certain period (usually 30 to 60 days) during which he/she will be able to pay at least an amount prescribed in the policy, which would be enough to keep the policy in force for approximately 3 months. No transfers or any requests for policy changes may be made during a grace period. If payment is not received by the end of the grace period, the policy (and all riders to the policy) will terminate without value and all coverage under the policy will cease.

Gross premium   The premium paid for the policy. On accumulation-type policies, this is the premium from which the loads are deducted to arrive at the net premium.

Guaranteed interest account   *See* guaranteed interest option.

Guaranteed interest option   If a policy contains a guaranteed interest option or guaranteed interest account, any assets allocated to this option in a policy will be invested as part of the general account of the insurance company and are subject to the outside creditors of the company.

Guaranteed interest rate   This is the minimum interest rate that can be credited to a policy. On whole life and universal life policies, the guaranteed minimum rate is usually from 3 to 4 percent.

Guaranteed investment contract   An insurance company product that guarantees a fixed interest rate for a fixed period of time, usually with a repayment of the entire principal at the end of that time. These contracts have been used as pension fund investments.

Guaranteed issue   Insurance that is placed in force without requiring any health or underwriting information about the insured.

Guaranteed premium   If a policy's net cash surrender value is not sufficient to pay a monthly deduction that has become due, the insurer checks to see if the cumulative amount of premiums that have been paid to date at least equals the cumulative guaranteed premiums due to date for either of the guaranteed options that are then available under that policy.

Guideline premiums, guideline premium tests   The maximum premium that can be paid per $1000 of insurance under the IRC 7702 guideline premium/ corridor definition of life insurance to still have the policy qualify as life insurance for federal tax purposes.

Index fund   A separate account or mutual fund having the goal of matching the total performance of a specified index such as the S&P 500.

Indexed interest rate   Some accumulation-type policies guarantee that the credited interest rate will not be less than some function of a published interest rate, such as a treasury note rate. If it is, the interest rate is said to be indexed.

Insurance guaranty association   A state-sponsored association that guarantees benefits to those insured by failed insurance companies.

Insured person   The insured person is the person on whose life the insurance has been purchased. If the insured person dies, a death benefit will be paid to the named beneficiary.

Interest adjusted premium   On nonlevel premium policies, this is the equivalent level premium that would have to be paid each year to accumulate the same amount as would the actual nonlevel stream of premiums paid, based on the stated interest rate, usually 5 percent.

Interest adjusted surrender cost index   This is a state insurance department promulgated measure used to compare similar types of policies. It is the level amount that is theoretically paid each year for the death benefit. It is calculated as (A) − (B) where:

> (A) is the gross annual premium, if level, or the interest-adjusted premium that is equivalent to the actual gross premiums at 5 percent interest, and
>
> (B) is the level annual amount that would accumulate at 5 percent to the cash value.

See pages 196–200.

Interest-sensitive policy   This is a form of accumulation-type policy that usually has a fixed premium and fixed death benefit. In other respects, it is very much like a universal life policy.

Interest spread   The difference between what the insurance company earns on its investments and what it credits to the policy.

Internal rate of return on surrender or death   The interest rate that, if credited to the annual premiums, would just yield the cash surrender value or death benefit at the measurement point.

Investment funds   The variable investment options available as subaccounts under the separate account option available in the policy. The investment results will depend on the investment performance of the corresponding portfolio that follows investment practices, policies, and objectives that are appropriate to the variable investment option the insured has chosen.

Investment management fee, advisory fee   A charge made as a percentage of a variable policy separate account fund value to pay the investment advisor for the selection and management of investments. These fees are set in advance and typically vary by fund. Although there is not a comparable explicit charge made with fixed-interest products, carriers deduct the expenses of investment management for these general account products before setting their declared interest or dividend rates.

Investment option   *See* Investment funds.

Investment year-based interest   A method of crediting interest whereby the company treats all policies issued in a given year as a distinct class for segregating investment results. In an increasing interest rate climate, this method allows a company to project higher interest rates for new policies, as the higher interest rate would not have to be averaged with the rate for older, lower yielding policies.

Issue date   The date that the policy is issued; the first day that the policy is in force.

Lapse   A policy will lapse (also referred to in a policy as "default") if it does not have enough "net cash surrender value" to pay the policy's monthly charges when due. Coverage under the policy will cease if a payment is not made within the grace period.

Lapse rate   The percentage of policies that terminate with no value or are voluntarily surrendered each year.

Lapse-supported product   A product for which the carrier will not achieve its desired profit margin if persistency is *better* than expected.

Leveraged policy   A life insurance policy on which loans have been taken.

Life expectancy   The actuarially projected period of time that a person is expected to live.

Liquidity   The ability to convert assets to cash. Short-term investments and cash are the most liquid assets, but they comprise a small portion of the typical insurance company's portfolio. Publicly traded investment-grade bonds may also be considered liquid because they can be readily marketed.

Loan, loan interest   The policy owner may borrow from the account value within the insurance policy. At such time, the insurance company removes an amount equal to the loan from one or more of the investment options and holds it as collateral for the loan's repayment. The interest charged by the insurance company on a policy loan is called the policy loan interest and usually accrues daily at an adjustable interest rate.

Loan spread   The difference between the interest rate credited to borrowed policy values and the interest rate charged on the loan balance. Because policy cash values that have been borrowed by the policy owner continue to earn interest, the cost of the loan to the policyholder is just the net difference between the interest earned and the interest charged.

Minimum premium   The lowest premium that can be paid on universal life-type policies during the first few years.

Modal premiums   This is the amount of premium that may be paid monthly, quarterly, or semiannually, instead of annually. The most financially efficient way to pay premiums on a fixed premium life insurance policy is annually. The next most efficient way is usually monthly automatic bank check withdrawal, since companies have better persistency under this payment method than with regular monthly billed, quarterly, or semiannual payments.

Modified endowment contract   A policy may be deemed to be a modified endowment contract (MEC) if it was issued after June 21, 1988, and if, at any time during the first seven years of the policy, a cumulative amount of premiums is paid that exceeds the seven-pay limit. Being characterized as an MEC may subject the policy owner to additional taxes and penalties on any distributions from the policy.

Monthly deduction   Charges deducted from the account value of the policy each month, which consist of an administrative charge, cost of insurance charges, optional rider charges, and a charge if an enhanced death benefit guarantee has been elected.

Mortality and expense risk charges   A separate charge made on variable products as a percentage of the account value to cover any potential deficiencies in the explicit cost of insurance and expense charges made by the carrier.

Mortality table   A table that shows expected death rates by individual age.

Mutual insurance company   An insurance company that is owned by its policy owners rather than by stockholders. Mutual companies typically sell participating policies, which return to the policyholders an equitable share of any profits earned on the business.

National Association of Insurance Commissioners   An organization of state insurance regulators that promotes uniformity of state regulations by adopting model laws and specifying the form and instructions for the annual statement (statutory statement).

Net amount at risk   The difference between the total death benefit and the policy's accumulation value, both measured at the same point in time. This is the base against which the cost of insurance charges are assessed.

Net cash surrender value   The net cash surrender value is the amount received by the policy owner if the policy is surrendered (given back) to the insurance company for its value at any time prior to the death of the insured. The net cash surrender value equals the account value, minus any outstanding loans and unpaid loan interest, minus any amount of account value that is "restricted" as a result of previously distributed "living benefits," and minus any surrender charge that then remains applicable.

Net cash value or net equity   These terms are often applied to a policy's cash value after reduction for any outstanding loans.

Net death benefit   This is the total death benefit less any policy loans, which have to be repaid at death.

No-lapse guarantee   The no-lapse guarantee is a guarantee that a policy will not terminate for a certain number of years, e.g., the first five years of the policy. Paying at least a certain amount of premiums can purchase this guarantee.

Net premium   The gross premium paid less loads for expenses.

New money rates   Interest rates earned on new investments or credited on new contributions.

Nonforfeiture option   A provision in fixed-premium life insurance policies that gives options for some continued coverage when required premiums are no longer paid. If the policy owner does not wish to surrender the policy for its cash value when premiums stop, extended term or reduced paid-up insurance may be elected. Normally, once a traditional nonforfeiture option has been chosen, the remaining benefits are provided on a guaranteed basis. The policy cannot be returned to premium-paying status unless the insured provides new evidence of insurability and pays missed premiums.

Nonguaranteed elements   An element of current policy performance that is subject to change by the insurer in future years. In the broadest sense of the term, nonguaranteed elements can include current interest rates above the guaranteed level, current premium rates, expense or cost of insurance charges below the guaranteed level, or dividends on participating policies.

Nonparticipating policies   Policies that do not pay dividends to policyholders. Before the late 1970s, nonparticipating policies usually operated with guaranteed premiums, cash values, and death benefits. All differences between actual and expected experience then resulted in additional profits or losses for the insurer. Today, however, many nonparticipating life insurance policies contain at least some nonguaranteed elements, such as current interest crediting rates in excess of the guaranteed rate. In theory, the nonguaranteed elements are set to reflect the carrier's anticipated future experience, as opposed to participating policy dividends that reflect a return of past earnings.

Option A   Option A is a death benefit option available in universal and variable universal life-types of insurance policies. Under Option A (or Option 1), the death benefit is equal to the face amount of the policy on the date of the insured person's death. The amount of this death benefit does not change over time, unless action is taken to change the policy's face amount.

Option B   Option B is a death benefit option available in universal and variable universal life-types of insurance policies. Under Option B (Option 2), the death benefit is equal to the face amount plus the policy's "account value" on the date of death. The amount of death benefit generally changes from day to day, because many factors (including investment performance, charges, premium payments, and withdrawals) affect the policy's account value.

Optional benefits   Benefits such as waiver of premium or accidental death benefit that may be added to a life insurance policy for an additional premium.

Paid up   Paid up means that no future premiums will be required.

Paid-up additions   A dividend option that use dividends on a participating policy to purchase small amounts of guaranteed single premium life insurance on which no further premiums will be necessary. This option does not reduce the policy owner's basis in the policy and results in no taxable income unless and until the policy is surrendered.

Paid-up death benefit guarantee   The paid-up death benefit guarantee ensures that, thereafter, a policy will not lapse and the death benefit will never be less than the face amount, so long as the guarantee remains in effect.

Paid-up policy   This is a policy on which no future premiums are due. The company has guaranteed that either (1) the current level of cash value is sufficient to provide a specified, fixed death benefit, or (2) the current death benefit will increase based on the rate of growth in future cash values.

Partial withdrawal   A universal life-type of policy allows the policy owner to withdraw (as well as to borrow) funds from the account value of the policy. In an Option A policy, a partial withdrawal results in a dollar-for-dollar automatic reduction in the policy's face amount. If the paid-up death benefit guarantee is in effect, a partial withdrawal will generally reduce the face amount by more than the amount of the withdrawal. In an Option B policy, a partial withdrawal reduces the death benefit on a dollar-for-dollar basis, but does not affect the face amount.

Participating policies   Policies that pay dividends to policy owners, representing an equitable share of past earnings on the block of business of which they are a part.

Payment option   Choice among several payment options for all or part of any death benefit proceeds that subsequently become payable. The beneficiary cannot change a payment option selected by the policy's owner after the insured person dies.

Permanent insurance   Life insurance that is guaranteed to provide death benefit protection for the insured's entire life upon payment of sufficient premiums.

Persistency   The percentage of policies that remain in force from one year to the next.

Persistency bonus   An added benefit payable at certain policy durations, usually structured as a nonguaranteed or partially guaranteed increment to cash values in year 10 or later.

Planned periodic premium   The amount that a policy owner requests an insurer to bill in a flexible premium policy. However, payment of these or any other specific amounts of premiums is not mandatory. One needs to pay only the amount of premiums necessary to keep your policy from lapsing and terminating.

Policy   The policy is the actual contract that determines benefits and obligations of the insurance company.

Portfolio   Amounts that insured people allocate under their policies to any of the variable investment options.

Portfolio-based interest crediting   A method of allocating investment results whereby a company treats all policies, regardless of when they were issued, as a single class for investment purposes and credits the same interest rate to all the policies, both old and new.

Preferred policy   Often another term for a nonsmoker class policy. It may also refer to nonsmokers who have additional favorable health factors.

Premium payments   *See* Planned periodic premium.

Present value   The present value of money; the equivalent amount in today's dollars of a single payment or a series of payments made in the future, taking into account the time value of money.

Pricing factors   Variables used in determining the premiums, charges, and values for a policy. Pricing factors include the rate of mortality, the company's expenses, the rate of commission paid, the lapse rate, the projected investment earnings, federal income tax, and the company's profit goals.

Prospectus   The prospectus contains important information that you should know before purchasing, or taking any other action with a variable contract.

Rebalancing   A policy owner may wish an insurer to redistribute periodically the amounts the owner has in variable investment options so that the relative amount of the account value in each variable option is restored to an asset allocation selected by the owner. This can be accomplished automatically through an insurer's asset rebalancing service. The rebalancing may be at quarterly, semi-annual, or annual intervals.

Reduced paid-up insurance   A nonforfeiture option where the policy cash value is used to purchase paid-up insurance for the greatest amount possible according to purchase rates guaranteed in the policy.

Reserve   The liability that the insurance company carries on its books for a policy.

Retention   The maximum amount that an insurer will generally pay from its own assets for any one death. This amount is typically limited to ½ to 1 percent of surplus. When carriers issue policies with a net amount at risk greater than their retention level, the excess is reinsured. The issuing company essentially buys term insurance from another insurer for the excess risk.

Rider   Optional benefits or riders that are available:

- Disability waiver benefits
- Ten-year term insurance on the insured person or an additional insured person
- Accidental death benefit
- Option to purchase additional insurance
- Children's term insurance
- Cost-of-living rider

Risk-adjusted capital ratio   A ratio of a company's adjusted surplus to a formula estimate of the amount of capital the company "should" have based on the risk characteristics of its assets and liabilities.

Risk-based capital   The name given to the formula amount introduced by the NAIC in 1993 as part of annual statement oversight of insurer solvency.

Risk charge or mortality charge   In accumulation-type policies, this is the periodic charge to the accumulation value to cover the cost of paying death benefits in excess of the accumulation value. (*See* net amount at risk.) The current or projected level of risk charge is the level based on current mortality experience, whereas the guaranteed charges are the maximum level that may be charged.

Risk class   The risk class determines the level of cost of insurance charges assessed against the policy or the gross premium rate. Based on the information submitted with the application, the policy may be categorized into a preferred (nonsmoker), standard (smoker), or substandard (impaired) risk class.

Second-to-die insurance   Life insurance that names two insureds and pays the death benefit only upon the *second* death of the two. Second-to-die is typically used in estate planning situations covering a husband and wife. It coordinates payment of the death benefit with the imposition of the estate tax under an unlimited (100 percent) marital deduction plan.

Select and ultimate rate scale   A mortality scale that allocates death benefit costs based on both the age of the insured when a policy was issued and how long ago the policy was issued. It is found on many term policies and sometimes used as a basis to determine risk charges on accumulation-type policies.

Separate Account   Each variable investment option is a part (or "subaccount") of a Separate Account. Provisions prevent creditors from any other business the insurance company conducts from reaching the assets held in variable investment options for owners of variable life insurance policies.

Seven pay test   Under IRC secs. 72(e) and (v) and 7702A, as amended by the Technical and Miscellaneous Revenue Act of 1988, those policies whose premium levels would allow them to become paid up in fewer than 7 years, based on a prescribed measurement basis, are termed modified endowment policies and are subject to adverse tax consequences in the event loans or withdrawals are made.

SPDA   Single premium deferred annuity.

State   State refers to any other local jurisdiction whose laws or regulations affect a policy.

Stock insurance company   An insurance company owned by its stockholders.

Subaccount   Investment alternatives of the separate account.

Surrender   One can surrender or give back a policy for its net cash surrender value at any time.

Surrender charge or surrender penalty   The difference between the accumulation value and the cash surrender value is called the "surrender charge." During the first 5 to 15 years, many accumulation-type policies have surrender charges so the insurance company's early loss will be repaid on lapsed policies.

Target premium   The amount of premium on flexible premium policies on which the full level of commission is paid. Policies that allow flexible premiums achieve their competitive posture in high premium scenarios by having the excess premium paid above the target premium perform more efficiently.

Transfers   One can transfer amounts from one investment option to another.

Terminal dividends   Dividends that are payable on participating policies only when a contract terminates rather than being credited each year. The rationale for terminal dividends is that earnings on participating business can only be partially paid out as they are earned; the carrier holds a portion of those earnings for protection against possible adverse future experience on the policies remaining in force.

Term insurance   Life insurance that provides coverage only for a stated "term," generally not guaranteed to be renewable for the entire life of the insured. Initial premiums are usually lower than for whole life insurance and increase with advancing age. Cash values are usually minimal or nonexistent. This type of coverage is most economical for a death benefit need of no more than 5 to 10 years.

Underwriting   The process by which applicants for insurance are classified into an appropriate risk category for determining the level of premiums or risk charges. This categorization is based on the applicant's health history and other factors that affect life expectancy. Evidence of insurability is often provided by medical exams, attending physicians' statements from doctors who have treated the applicant in the past, or statements signed by the applicant concerning his or her health record. The amount of information required increases as the amount of insurance applied for and the applicant's age increases.

Units   The number of units in any variable investment option does not change, absent an event or transaction under your policy that involves moving assets into or out of that option.

Unit values   The value of each unit will increase or decrease each day, as though one had invested in the corresponding portfolio's shares directly (and reinvested all dividends and distributions from the portfolio in additional portfolio shares). The units' values will be reduced, however, by the amount of the mortality and expense risk charge for that period.

Universal life insurance   Life insurance that gives policy owners the ability to set and vary their own premium levels, payment schedules, and death benefits, within certain limits. This increased flexibility makes it easier to adapt these policies to changing needs and financial conditions.

Variable investment option   *See* Investment option.

Variable life insurance   Life insurance (or annuities) for which cash values are invested in separate account subaccounts, much like mutual funds. The policy owner chooses among various subaccounts offered by the insurer, permitting investments concentrating in common stocks and other assets that are more volatile but may provide higher long-term returns than does an insurer's general account. There is no guaranteed interest rate. Rather, the company guarantees that the actual investment fund performance, both net investment income and capital gains and losses, will pass directly through to the cash values after reduction for investment expenses and operating costs.

Waiver of premium   Optional benefits that continue a life insurance policy during the total disability of the insured. When an insured with wavier of premium is totally disabled, as defined in the policy, premiums will not be charged, but the policy values will continue to accumulate as if those premiums had been paid. Normal risk charges and expense loads will continue to be deducted.

Waiver of charges   When an insured with this benefit is totally disabled, the cost of insurance and expense charges will not be deducted from the universal or variable universal life policy accumulation values, and policy values will continue to accumulate. Should the insured later recover, resumption of premiums at the original level may not be sufficient to provide the originally planned benefits. That is because, in many instances, the charges that have been waived during disability will not be as great as the net premiums that would have been added to the policy under a waiver of *premium* option.

Whole life insurance   Life insurance that guarantees a continued death benefit for the insured's entire life upon payment of fixed annual premiums. The premiums are usually level for life, based on the insured's age at issue.

BIBLIOGRAPHY

AIPCA. *Guide to Risk Management and Insurance*. American Institute of Certified Public Accountants, 1992.

American Bar Association. *The Life Insurance Products, Illustrations, and Due Diligence*. Chicago, IL: American Bar Association, 1989.

———. *Life Insurance Counselor Series American Bar Association's Federal Income Taxation of Life Insurance*. Chicago, IL: American Bar Association, 1989.

———. *Insurance Counselor Series American Bar Association's Split-Dollar Life Insurance*. American Bar Association, 1991.

American Council of Life Insurers. *Life Insurer's Fact Book 2000*. Washington, DC., 2000.

Amling, Frederick and William G. Droms. *Investment Fundamentals*. New York, NY: Dryden Press, 1994.

Armstrong, Alexandra, CFP and Mary R. Donahue, Ph.D. *On Your Own*. Chicago, IL: Dearborn Financial Publishing Inc., 1993.

Baldwin, Ben G. *The Complete Book of Insurance*. Chicago, IL: Irwin Professional Publishing, 1989, 1991, 1996.

———. *Risk Management and Insurance in Personal Financial Planning*. AICPA, 1992.

———. *The Lawyer's Guide to Insurance*. Chicago, IL: American Bar Association, 1999.

———. *The New Life Insurance Investment Advisor*. New York, NY: McGraw-Hill Publishing Co., 1994, 2001.

———. "Risk and Return Potential in Life Insurance Products." *Trust & Estates*, April 1998, Volume 137, No. 5, p. 42.

Baldwin, Ben G. and William G. Droms. *The Life Insurance Investment Advisor*. Chicago, IL: Probus Publishing Company, 1988, 1990.

Becker, Benjamin M. *Simplified Estate Planning*. Chicago, IL: Twentieth-Century Press Inc., 1965.

Belth, Joseph M., Editor. *The Insurance Forum Monthly Newsletter*.

Blazzard, Norse N. and Judith A. Hasenauer. "Prediction: Sales of VUL & VL Will Outstrip VAs." *National Underwriter*, April 18, 1994, p. 8.

———. "VUL Accelerated Benefits Can Pay for LTC." *National Underwriter*, May 19, 1999, p. 15.

Breitbard, Stanley H. and Donna Sammons Carpenter. *The Price Waterhouse Book of Personal Financial Planning*. New York, NY: Henry Holt and Company, 1987, 1988.

Browlie, William D. with Jeffrey L. Seglin. *The Life Insurance Buyer's Guide.* New York, NY: McGraw-Hill Publishing Company, 1989.

Burton, Jonathan. "The World According to Richard Hokenson." *Fee Advisor,* November/December 1995.

"Will Insurers Buy This Policy?" *Business Week,* March 28, 1994, p. 152.

Commerce Clearing House, Inc. *Life Insurance Tax Provisions—Tax Reform Act of 1984.* Chicago, IL: 1984.

Craig, Ernest E. *The Craig Commentary.* New York, NY: Farnsworth Publishing Company, 1979.

Crowe, Robert M. and Charles E. Hughes, Editors. *Fundamentals of Financial Planning.* Bryn Mawr, PA: The American College, 1993.

Dacey, Norman F. *What's Wrong With Your Life Insurance.* New York, NY: Macmillan Publishing Company, 1963, 1989.

Daily, Glen S. *Low Load Insurance Products.* Chicago, IL: International Publishing Corporation, 1991.

Davids, Lewis E. *Dictionary of Insurance.* Totowa, NJ: Littlefield Adams, Inc., 1977.

Dolan, Ken and Darla Dolan. *Smart Money.* New York, NY: Random House, 1988.

Donohue, Mark T. "Unexpected Liability Awaits Many Trustees of Life Insurance Trusts." *Trusts & Estates,* April 1994, volume 133, number 4, p. 43.

Dorf, Richard C. *The Mutual Fund Investment Advisor.* Chicago, IL: Probus Publishing Company, 1986.

Dorfman, Mark S. and Saul W. Adelman. *The Dow Jones Guide to Life Insurance.* Homewood, IL: Dow Jones-Irwin, 1988.

Droms, William G., B.A., C.F.A. and Frederick Amling, Ph.D. *The Dow Jones-Irwin Guide to Personal Financial Planning.* Homewood, IL: Dow Jones-Irwin, 1982, 1986.

Droms, William G. and Ben G. Baldwin. "Evaluating the Investment Merits of Life Insurance." *Journal of Accountancy,* May 1989, pp. 63–72.

Duff, Richard W., J.D., CLU. *Preserving Family Wealth Using Tax Magic.* Denver, CO: RDW Enterprises, 1993.

Dunton, Loren. *Financial Planning Can Make You Rich.* Englewood Cliffs, NJ: Prentice Hall, 1987.

———. *The Financial Planner: A New Professional.* Chicago, IL: Longman Group USA Inc., 1986.

———. *Your Book of Financial Planning.* Reston, VA: Reston Publishing Company Inc., 1983.

———. *About Your Future.* San Francisco, CA: Allen M. Associates, 1988.

Dunton, Loren and Kim Ciccarelli Banta. *Preserving Family Wealth and Peace of Mind.* Chicago, IL: Probus Publishing Company, 1994.

Evensky, Harold R. *Wealth Management.* Chicago, IL: Irwin Professional Publishing, 1997.

Financial Profiles, Inc. *Dynamic Insurance Solutions, Historic Variability Module.* Version 3.07.21, copyright 1999, (800)-237-6335. www.profiles.com

Fishman, Ted C. "The Bull Market in Fear—Stock Speculation Becomes the Rule of Prudence." *Harpers Magazine,* October 1995.

Genetski, Robert J. *Taking the Voodoo Out of Economics*. Lake Bluff, IL: Regency Gateway Inc., 1986.

Gibson, James H. *Winning the Investment Game*. New York, NY: McGraw-Hill Publishing Company, 1987.

Gourgues, Harold W., Jr. *Financial Planning Handbook*. New York, NY: New York Institute of Finance, 1983.

Hammond, Josh and James Morrison. *The Stuff Americans Are Made of: The Seven Cultural Forces That Define Americans—A New Framework for Quality, Productivity and Profitability*. New York, NY: Macmillan, 1996.

Head, Wallace L. "Active Portfolio Management: Beating the Tax Bogey." *Trusts & Estates*, November 1995.

Huebner, Solomon S. and Kenneth Black, Jr. *Life Insurance*. Englewood Cliffs, NJ: Prentice-Hall, Inc., 1915, 1923, 1935, 1950, 1958, 1964, 1969, 1972, 1976, 1982.

Ibbotson Associates. *Stocks, Bonds, Bills, and Inflation 2000 Yearbook*. Chicago, IL: Ibbotson Associates, 2000.

Jacob, Dr. Nancy. "Tax-Efficient Investing: Reduce Tax Drag, Improve Asset Growth." *Trusts & Estates*, June 1996.

Janeway, Elliott. *You and Your Money*. New York, NY: David McKay Company, Inc., 1972.

Journal of Financial Planning. Institute of Certified Financial Planners. Quarterly Issues, 1999, 2000.

Kahn, Virginia Munger. "Much Ado . . ." *Financial World*, April 8, 1996, pp. 60–63.

Katz, Deena. *On Practice Management*. Princeton, NJ: Bloomberg Press, 1999.

Kaye, Barry. *Save a Fortune on Your Life Insurance*. New York, NY: Simon & Schuster, Inc., 1991.

———. *Die Rich and Tax Free*. Santa Monica, CA: Forman Publishing Inc., 1994.

Kimelman, John. "Magic Number." *Financial World*, April 12, 1994, p. 60.

Kuhn, Susan E. "Be a TAX-Savvy Investor." *Fortune*, March 18, 1996.

Lavine, Alan. *Your Life Insurance Options*. New York, NY: John Wiley & Sons, Inc., 1993.

Leimberg, Steven R. *The Tools and Techniques of Estate Planning 1999*. National Underwriter.

———. *The Tools and Techniques of Estate Planning 1993*. National Underwriter.

Levin, Ross. *The Wealth Management Index*. Chicago, IL: Irwin Professional Publishing, 1997.

Loeb, Gerald M. *The Battle for Investment Survival*. New York, NY: Simon & Schuster, Inc., 1935, 1965.

Lynch, Peter with John Rothchild. *Beating the Street*. New York, NY: Simon & Schuster, Inc., 1993.

Mackim, Robert E. *Insurance Legislative Fact Book and Almanac*. The National Conference of Insurance Legislatures, 1988.

McFadden, John J., Editor. *The Financial Service Professional's Guide to the State of the Art*, Third Edition. Bryn Mawr, PA: The American College, 1994.

Mehr, Robert I. *Fundamentals of Insurance*. Chicago, IL: Richard D. Irwin, Inc., 1983.

Munch, James C., Jr. *Financial and Estate Planning with Life Insurance Products.* Little Brown and Company, 1990, 1991, 1992, 1993.

Murray, Nick. *Serious Money.* New Jersey: Robert A. Stanger and Company, 1991.

———. *The Craft of Advice, Essays 1995–1998.* Mattituck, NY: The Nick Murray Company Inc., 1999.

National Association of Insurance & Financial Advisors. *Advisor Today,* monthly, 1999, 2000.

National Underwriter Life and Health/Financial Services Edition (newspaper/ weekly).

O'Donnell, Jeff. *Insurance Smart.* New York, NY: John Wiley & Sons, Inc., 1991.

O'Neill, Terry R. *The Life Insurance Kit.* Chicago, IL: Dearborn Financial Publishing Inc., 1993.

Plotnick, Charles K., L.L.B., and Stephan R. Leimberg, J.D. *How to Settle an Estate.* New York, NY: A Plume Book, Penguin Putnam Inc., 1998.

Porter, Sylvia. *Sylvia Porter's Money Book.* Garden City, NY: Doubleday & Company, Inc., 1975.

Prince, Russ Alan, William J. McBride and Karen Maru File. *The Charitable Estate Planning Process: How to Find and Work With the Philanthropic Affluent.* Lexington, KY: Lexington House, 1994.

Reichard, Robert S. *The Figure Finaglers.* New York, NY: McGraw-Hill Publishing Company, 1974.

Robinson, Peter. "Paul Romer." *Forbes ASAP,* July 1995, pp. 67–72.

Rubin, Harvey W., Ph.D., CLU, CPCU. *Dictionary of Insurance Terms,* Fourth Edition. Hauppauge, NY: Barron's Educational Series, Inc., 2000.

Rybka, J.D., CFP, Lawrence J. "A Case for Variable Life." *Journal of the American Society of CLU & ChFC,* May 1997, Vol. LI, No. 3, pp. 40–46.

Sanford, Editor. Jennifer, *Investment Performance Digest,* 2000 Edition. Rockville, MD: Weisenberger, a Thomson Financial Company.

Savage, Terry. *Terry Savage Talks Money.* Chicago, IL: Dearborn Financial Publishing Inc., 1990.

Schifrin, Matthew and Riva Atlas. "Hocus-pocus." *Forbes,* March 14, 1994, pp. 81–83.

Schwed, Fred, Jr. *Where Are the Customers' Yachts?* Burlington, VT: Simon & Schuster, Frazier Publishing Company, 1985.

Siegel, Jeremy J. *Stocks for the Long Run.* New York, NY: McGraw-Hill Publishing Company, 1998.

Snouffer, Gary H., J.D., CLU. *Variable Life Essentials.* Cincinnati, OH: The National Underwriter Company, 1998.

Steinmetz, Greg. "New Yardstick on Life Insurers Is Hard to Find, Tough to Use." *The Wall Street Journal,* March 12, 1994, C1.

Temkin, Bruce J. *The Terrible Truth About Investing.* St. Petersburg, FL: Fairfield Press, 1999.

Trusts & Estates Magazine. Argus Inc., monthly Issues, 1993, 1994.

VanCaspel, Venita, CFP. *The Power of Money Dynamics.* Reston, VA: Reston Publishing Company, Inc., 1983.

Vaughn, Emmet J. *Fundamentals of Risk and Insurance.* New York, NY: John Wiley and Sons, 1986.

Ward, John L. *Ward's Results.* The National Underwriter Company, 1991 thru 2000.

Watts, John M. *The Financial Services Shock Wave.* Englewood Cliffs, NJ: Prentice-Hall Inc., 1987.

Whitelaw, C. Markham and David M. Culver. "Managing Trust-Owned Life Insurance." *Trusts & Estates,* April 1994, volume 133, number 4, p. 39.

Winninghoff, Ellie. "Smart Buyer, Dumb Seller." *Forbes,* March 14, 1994, pp. 71–76.

Zaritsky, Howard M. and Stephen R. Leimberg. *Tax Planning with Life Insurance,* Second Edition. Boston, MA: Warren, Gorham & Lamont, RIA Group, 1998.

INDEX

ABOUT THE AUTHOR

Ben G. Baldwin, CLU, ChFC, CFP, is president and owner of Baldwin Financial Systems, a registered advisory firm serving both individual and corporate clients. The winner of numerous sales awards throughout his career and a former member of the Board of Governors for the Certified Financial Planner Board of Standards, he has consulted for major insurance companies including New York Life, Transamerica, Prudential, CNA, AIG, ING, AXA, and Equitable. Along with the first edition of *The New Life Insurance Investment Advisor,* Baldwin also wrote *The Complete Book of Insurance* and *The Lawyer's Guide to Insurance.*